Edward Francis Baxter Orton

First annual Report of the Geological Survey of Ohio

Edward Francis Baxter Orton

First annual Report of the Geological Survey of Ohio

ISBN/EAN: 9783337177058

Printed in Europe, USA, Canada, Australia, Japan

Cover: Foto ©ninafisch / pixelio.de

More available books at **www.hansebooks.com**

FIRST ANNUAL REPORT

OF THE

Geological Survey of Ohio,

(THIRD ORGANIZATION,)

BY

EDWARD ORTON, STATE GEOLOGIST.

PUBLISHED BY AUTHORITY OF THE LEGISLATURE.

COLUMBUS, O.:
THE WESTBOTE CO., STATE PRINTERS.
1890.

EDWARD ORTON, - - - - - - - *State Geologist.*
  STATE UNIVERSITY, COLUMBUS, O.
  Residence: 100 Twentieth St.

PROF. N. W. LORD, - - - - - - *Che...*
  STATE UNIVERSITY, COLUMBUS, O.
  Residence: Corner Highland St. and Fourth Ave.

PROF. S. W. ROBINSON, - *Special Assistant in Mea...*
                         of Gas Wells and Pip...
  STATE UNIVERSITY, COLUMBUS, O.
  Residence: 1353 Highland St.

PREFACE.

This first annual report of the Geological Survey of Ohio under its new organization has, to some extent, fallen short of the purpose with which it was begun. It was intended that the report should furnish a review of the various mineral interests of the State, brought down to the date of publication. Under this plan, which is deferred rather than abandoned, the new facts pertaining to our coal resources and their practical development, to our quarries, to our clay deposits and the manufactures based on them, to our limes, cements, marls and plaster beds as well as to petroleum and gas would all find place in the annual report of the survey. The interest at present pertaining to the last subject named in the list given above has, however, been so deep and wide-spread and its economic importance has proved so large that the logic of events has rendered it necessary to devote this entire report to Natural Gas and Oil. It has thus become a monograph upon this subject, and its entire 300 pages are occupied with facts and discussions growing out of the marvellous discovery of Findlay gas and Lima oil in a Lower Silurian limestone six years ago.

The natural gas interests of the State, in particular, have demanded and received in this report a measure of attention that is out of proportion to their intrinsic value. These interests are in marked contrast with the oil interests of the new fields in this respect, viz., that while the latter are almost exclusively in the hands of those whose knowledge has been derived from a varied and costly experience in the business, the former have been in many instances turned over to persons who have never seen a gas field aside from the particular one of which they are called upon to take charge. It is not surprising, under such circumstances, that crude and erroneous views in regard to the nature of the gas supply should find place among these companies and municipal boards, or that a wasteful and extravagant policy in the use of the gas should be established or allowed by them. To convince such officials that gas is not being generated in the underlying rocks as fast as their wells are able to withdraw it, that it is strictly stored power, and that every foot taken from the reservoir leaves the amount remaining there so much the less, has been a difficult, and in some respects a thankless task. Nature has, however, become the teacher of all these communities that have broken into her storehouses of force, and falling pressure and supply-pipes half filled, have come even more speedily than was expected to convince all who are able to learn that high pressure gas fields are always exhausted by use, and that in fact they begin to die the moment they begin to live.

For the most efficient service of all the interests involved, it has been seen from the first that some simple means for determining the amount of gas consumed in the various uses to which it is applied is essential. A system of measuring the volumes of gas wells was published for the first time in Volume VI of the survey reports. This system has been universally adopted in the gas fields of the country, and is recognized as authoritative, alike in business transactions and in courts of law. It is a great pleasure to add that the present report contains a supplementary system devised by the same auther and equally easy of application, by which the amount of gas flowing through a pipe of any size and under any pressure can be determined by a simple and inexpensive gauge, with absolute accuracy. The value of these two contributions of Professor Robinson to the natural gas interests of the country can not well be overstated. The pipe line gauge is sure to find an equally important field in its applications to producer gas or other varieties of fuel gas. It is an honorable distinction of the Ohio Geological Survey that it furnishes to practical science the only known methods of solving the two important problems already named.

There are no gas meters made that are able to take account of the gas required by large works, or that is passing through main pipe lines; but to the new gauge, such measurements are as easy as the determination of the amount used by a cook stove or a grate. The largest meters that are in market are so expensive that this fact alone forbids their adoption for any thing like general use, but the new gauge takes away all excuse from gas companies or municipal gas boards for disposing of the precious fuel that has come into their hands, with the ignorance and reckless extravagance that have hitherto prevailed. They can at least know what they are doing. It must be added that several of the companies and boards of trustees having the largest amounts of gas at their disposal have already availed themselves of the new system. The new gas rates of Findlay for manufacturers are based on measurements made by the Robinson gauge, and which were executed in part by the officers of the Geological Survey.

With this volume, the almost exclusive privilege which oil and gas have maintained in the publications of the survey for the last four years will terminate. In the next annual report, reviews of the coal fields, the stone quarries, the clay deposits and clay manufactures of the State will be made special features. Chapters on these subjects, indeed, are promised for the present volume in the introduction, page 8, but though a good deal of material has been gathered under these heads, both time and space are wanting for their proper presentation. The same line of remark will apply to the chapter promised on the Adams county fault, a careful study and survey of which have been already carried on.

Acknowledgments are due to so many persons throughout the State for assistance in gathering the data of the present volume, that it is almost invidious to select the names of any for special mention. Many of those indeed that have contributed information of the greatest value would prefer to be left unnamed. It is from the representatives of the leading gas companies and oil companies, that the most important facts relating to the several fields have been obtained. These companies can at least be credited with a kindly interest in science. Among those from whom the largest amount of information has been derived, may be named The City Gas Works of Findlay (municipal), E. B. Phillip, Sup't; The Lima Natural Gas Co., A. C. Reichelderfer, Sup't; The Northwestern Ohio Natural Gas Co., The Upper Sandusky Gas Trustees, (municipal), Dr. A. Billhardt, The Central Ohio Natural Gas Co., J. O. Johnston, Sup't; The Ohio Oil Co., The Shawnee Oil Co., The Geyser Oil Co., The Paragon Refining Co., The Eagle Refining Co., and the Bradner Refining Co., E. A. Edwards, Pres't. To this list the following names may be added viz: C. S. Wade, Esq., of Findlay, for special facts pertaining to Henry township; J. R. Ware, Esq., of Findlay, for special facts pertaining to the Stuartsville field, and John Raudabaugh, Esq., of Celina, for results of measurements of gas used in glass furnaces, made by the Robinson gauge.

TABLE OF CONTENTS.

		PAGE.
INTRODUCTION		1— 8
CHAPTER I.	Geological Scale and Geological Structure of Ohio	9— 54
CHAPTER II.	Origin and Accumulation of Petroleum and Natural Gas	55—104
CHAPTER III.	The Trenton Limestone as a Source of Oil and Gas	105—226
CHAPTER IV.	The Clinton Limestone as a Source of Oil and Gas	227—247
CHAPTER V.	Remaining Sources of Oil and Gas in Ohio	248—258
CHAPTER VI.	The Utilization of Natural Gas in Ohio	259—280
CHAPTER VII.	The Measurement of Natural Gas, by S. W. Robinson	281—305

LIST OF ILLUSTRATIONS AND MAPS.

PLATE   I.   Geological Scale of Ohio.. faces page   9
PLATE II.   Sections showing structure of Trenton Limestone............   "   "   105
PLATE III.   Sections showing rise of salt water in Findlay gas rock....   "   "   121
PLATE IV.   Illustrations of the Pitot Tube Gauge ....   "   "   281

MAPS IN POCKET.

Map of Hancock, Wood and other counties...... ....Scale, 2 ms. = 1 inch.
Map of Allen, Auglaize and Mercer counties.............. ....Scale, 2 ms. = 1 inch.
Map of the Trenton Limestone, Oil and Gas Fields in Ohio and Indiana.

GEOLOGICAL SURVEY OF OHIO.

Annual Report, 1890.

survey of the State was duly established. An appropriation of twelve thousand dollars was made for the survey and Dr. W. W. Mather, of New York, was placed at the head of it, with the title of Principal Geologist. Six assistants, comprising some of the best known of the scientists of the State, were appointed to work under his direction.

The period of financial distress which broke upon the country in 1837 proved disastrous to the newly organized survey. All possible retrenchment in public expenditures was demanded on every side, and the appropriation required for the prosecution of the survey was consequently withheld by the next succeeding legislature, and the work of the survey was thus abruptly terminated at the end of the second season. Other causes contributed in some degree to this result, a change in the political composition of the legislature being a factor.

Two annual reports remain to us from the first survey, the first one, covering the field work of 1837, sent to the legislature by Governor Joseph Vance, January 17, 1838, and the second one, covering the field work of 1838, sent to the legislature by Governor Wilson Shannon, December 16, 1838. These reports are respectively entitled, the First and Second Annual Reports " on the Geological Survey of the State of Ohio, by W. W. Mather, Principal Geologist, and the several assistants. Columbus, 1838."

These reports added much to our knowledge of the geology of Ohio, and the results attained by the first survey have been incorporated in all subsequent work. The volumes named above have never been reprinted, and although editions of five thousand copies were issued by the State, copies are now rare and when found in the book markets, they command a ready sale and a relatively large price.

SECOND GEOLOGICAL SURVEY.

The untimely suspension of the investigation of the mineral wealth of the State, which had been so well begun, was widely regretted by intelligent citizens and many unavailing attempts were made in subsequent sessions of the legislature to resuscitate the survey. The messages of the governors in particular, during the next thirty years, contain numerous urgent recommendations of the policy of continuing or renewing the geological examination of the State. Among those who invoked the favorable attention of the legislature to this subject may be especially named: Gov. Corwin, in 1841; Gov. Bartley, in 1844; Gov. Chase, in 1857; Gov. Dennison, in 1860; Gov. Cox, in 1868, and Gov. Hayes, in 1868. The survey was finally renewed under Gov. Hayes in 1869. An elaborate report on the desirability of resuming it on the part of the State, was made by Hon. Alfred E. Lee, then representing Delaware county in the lower House. The report was accompanied by a bill, also drawn up by

INTRODUCTION. 3

Mr. Lee, providing for the second geological survey of the State, and this bill became a law on April 3, 1869. J. S. Newberry was appointed Chief Geologist, and E. B. Andrews, Edward Orton and J. H. Klippart, were appointed assistants. Several changes were effected in the organization of the survey during its progress. Its duration was limited in the bill providing for it to three years, but the time of the corps was afterwards extended two years, and in fact the publications growing out of the work begun by it were continued to 1888. The last two volumes, viz., Volumes Five and Six, and the preliminary report that intervenes between them are the work of the present State Geologist, who was appointed to the specific task of preparing Volume V for publication in accordance with suitable legislation, by Governor Foster, in 1882, and to the preparation of Volume VI, by Governor Hoadly, in 1885.

It is unnecessary to review in this connection the character of the work accomplished by the Second Geological Survey. Its publications are numerous and they have been widely distributed throughout the State, and, indeed, throughout the scientific world. They have been unmistakably serviceable in the remarkable development of the mineral wealth of the State that has gone forward within the last twenty years, and, in fact, they are inseparably connected with this development. The investment of many millions of foreign capital in our mines and railways has been largely determined by the impartial and judicial testimony of our State reports. The publications of the Second Survey, with a single exception, viz., the Geological Atlas, have been printed by the State. They are as follows:

	Name.	Date.	No. pages.	No. copies.	Geologist in charge.
1	Report of Progress..................	1869	176	14,500	Newberry.
2	"	1870	568	14,500	"
3	"	1871	3	300	"
4	Geology of Ohio, Vol. 1. Part I, Geology	1872	680	20,000	"
5	Geology of Ohio, Vol. 1, Part II, Paleontology	1873	401 / 49 plates.	20,000	"
6	Geology of Ohio, Vol. 2, Part I, Geology	1874	701	20,000	"
7	Geology of Ohio, Vol. 2, Part II, Paleontology	1875	431 / 59 plates.	20,000	"
8	Geology of Ohio, Vol. 3, Geology	1878	958	20,000	"
9	Geological Atlas of Ohio..........	1879		5,000	"
10	Geology of Ohio, Vol. 4............ Zoology and Botany................	1882	1,070	20,000	"
11	Geology of Ohio, Vol. 5............ Economic Geology...................	1884	1,124	10,000	Orton.
12	Preliminary Report on Petroleum and Gas................................	1886	76	2,500	"
13	Geology of Ohio, Vol. 6........... Economic Geology..................	1888	831	15,000	"

Pockets containing maps, sections and charts have accompanied the reports marked as the second, fourth, sixth, eleventh and thirteenth. The large number of copies in the editions of volumes one to four, inclusive, necessitated large expenditures for publication alone for the years in which these several volumes appeared. Particularly was this true for volumes one and two, which were published in two distinct parts of different size, the second part of each volume being devoted to paleontology and being illustrated by fifty to sixty engraved plates of fossils. These latter volumes were highly creditable to the State and the survey on scientific grounds, and they have been eagerly sought for by the students of geology throughout the world. It was the purpose of the Chief Geologist, Dr. Newberry, to make each volume of the final report a double one, on the same plan that was carried out in the first two volumes. Suitable material was accordingly prepared for the second or paleontological part of Volume Three, but this material has never been published. Considerable expenditure has been already incurred by the State in the preparation of this second part of the volume. A large number of plates and the necessary descriptive text have been for years in Dr. Newberry's hands, awaiting the order of the legislature. The materials are undoubtedly of very interesting character, and it is much to be regretted that they should be so long lost to science.

It was not at the instance of the geologists of the State that so large editions of the reports as those already noted were issued. Dr. Newberry recommended an edition of five thousand copies of the final report, viz., Volumes I, II, etc. It was the judgment of the legislature, however, that four times this number was demanded, and, as already shown, four times this number were issued of each of the first four volumes of the final report. Something can be said in favor of this liberal policy. The reports were educational to a large extent, and in many cases they had a direct bearing on economic interests. They were consequently sought for by various classes of our people, and expenditures even as large as those needed for this purpose could be justified, or at least defended, on the grounds here indicated. When, however, we come to the distribution of these large and consequently costly editions, we find a state of things that is almost beyond belief. No two of the several volumes that constitute the series have been published and distributed by the same legislature. In other words, the several volumes have been ordered and distributed by distinct legislatures. The plan of distributing the editions has thus far been essentially as follows: One hundred copies or less have been assigned to the State Library for its exchanges; three to four hundred copies have been assigned to the State Geological Corps for the personal exchange of its members, and occasionally single copies have been assigned to the several State officers and also to the public institutions of the State. The balance of the entire editions has been divided *pro rata* among the members of the General Assembly. Provision has not been at any time made in case of the first four volumes, for those who would gladly purchase the volumes in open market. Of the distribution, no lists whatever have been kept, so far as State action is concerned. The legislature that distributed Volume II, for example, had no official knowledge of the disposition of the copies of Volume I; and, while intelligent and painstaking members have seen to it in some instances that the sets already begun in their respective counties were maintained by the volumes at their own disposal, in the large majority of cases no attention whatever has been given to such considerations, but the volumes have been handed out to personal or political friends of the members or to the first applicants, as the case may be. Many thousands of copies of the several volumes are thus scattered in broken sets throughout the State. Of the 20,000 copies issued of each of the earlier volumes, it is almost certain that there are not 5,000 complete sets in the State. As was suggested above, it is almost beyond belief that after making such liberal appropriations for publication, the legislators should have allowed the resulting volumes to have been scattered over the State in such a reckless and wasteful fashion.

The great revival of geological interest that has followed the search for gas and oil throughout the State, during the last five years, has led to a new demand for the earlier geological volumes, and many of the widely scattered copies of the several reports have been gathered into at least larger aggregates, if not into complete sets. Book dealers have taken advantage of the new demand and second hand copies are now to be bought at many points in the State at prices ranging from $1.50 to $3.50 per volume; complete sets are sold from $15.00 to $25.00. Volumes V and VI were not only published in smaller editions than those of the previous volumes, but provision was made for the sale by the Secretary of State of a certain number of copies at cost of publication. This arrangement has made it possible for all persons possessing the previous volumes to complete their sets by purchase, and also for persons living outside the State to procure copies of volumes that treat of subjects in which they may be directly interested.

PRESENT ORGANIZATION OF THE SURVEY.

By an act of the 68th General Assembly, passed April 12, 1889, the Geological Survey of the State has been put upon a somewhat different basis from any that it has hitherto occupied. Its work is now counted continuous. The State Geologist is appointed for a term of three years, and is required to present annual reports to the legislature. There are certain advantages incident to the new system which will not escape notice. In the first place, it is now possible to present to the public the important facts of the year, before they have lost their novelty and interest. Under the system previously followed, several years would necessarily elapse after a volume was begun before it could be completed, and consequently much of the information gathered during the first or second years might partially lose its importance before it could be made available to the public. In the second place, the new system allows methodical and continuous work. Plans can be formed covering several years for their accomplishment, and the task begun in one season can be carried forward in the next. Under the old system, questions would often arise to which, after more or less investigation, only incomplete answers could be given from a want of time to apply to them, and consequently the labor already spent on them would be in part forfeited. In the third place, it is obvious that a greater economy can be realized on this plan of procedure than under the former system and an inexpensive organization may be maintained by which the records of progress can be kept up, and by which a steady, though slow advance can be made. The expenses of publication can also be kept within the lowest limits by the present system.

In most of the States in which mineral wealth makes an important element, the system now adopted in Ohio has been found advantageous. Continuous work and annual reports are in force, among other States, in New York, New Jersey, Pennsylvania, Michigan, Indiana, Illinois, Kentucky, Minnesota, Missouri, Arkansas, Georgia and Alabama. It is especially desirable that while the remarkable and unexpected discoveries of the bituminous forms of mineral wealth in Ohio are going forward, opportunity should be afforded for geological examination and record of the facts as fast as they are brought to light. The developments of the present decade are scarcely likely to be repeated, and the geological information to be derived from them is of the highest interest and value.

The range of work to be included under the survey on its present basis can be learned from an examination of the law under which it is established. It is made the duty of the State Geologist "to study and determine, as nearly as possible, the number and extent of the various formations of the State, to represent the same, from time to time, upon properly constructed maps and diagrams; to study the modes of occurrence and the distribution of the useful minerals and products of these formations; to determine the chemical composition and structure of the same; to investigate the soils and the water supply of the State, and to give attention to the discoveries of coal, building stone, natural cement,

INTRODUCTION 7

petroleum, gas and other natural substances of use and value to the citizens of the State. He may also collect and describe the fossils of the various geological formations of the State, but no expenditure shall be incurred under this head, that is not expressly ordered and provided for by the General Assembly."

It is here seen that the objects of the Survey are essentially practical. The economic phases of geological science are those to which the work of the Survey must be principally devoted. In addition to the subjects ordinarily embraced under the head of economic geology, as the study of coals, clays, ores, building stones, oil and gas, there are two other subjects that unquestionably should be included here, viz.: the study of the soils and of the water supply of the State from a geological point of view.

The soil is strictly a geological formation, and by far the most important and valuable formation of the entire geological series of the State. The connection between the geology and the agriculture of Ohio has never yet been studied with proper care. It is confessedly a complicated and difficult subject, but it may be that the time has now come when some advance in our knowledge can be made. The fact that a thoroughly equipped and efficient Experiment Station is now in operation in the State, may render it possible to attack the problems involved with better prospects of success than have ever yet been offered. The only possibilities of success must obviously lie in the harmonious co-operation of the Survey and the Experiment Station.

Attention has been called, on a preceding page, to the cordial and earnest recommendations of the several governors of the State between 1840 and 1868, to the effect that the geological survey of 1838 should be resumed and completed. It is worthy of note that the arguments which seemed to weigh most with them were based on the belief that an adequate geological survey would be able to render valuable service to the agricultural interests of the State. While these anticipations may have been somewhat more sanguine than the facts would warrant, it would certainly be premature to conclude that geology can render no definite or valuable service to this great interest.

The water supply of the State, including as it does all the natural storage of the geological formations, is a subject of large and growing interest.

SCOPE OF THE PRESENT REPORT.

It is to be presumed that the present report will fall into the hands of many who have not had access to the volumes of the Second Survey. It is, therefore, necessary that it should contain a brief review of the geological scale and structure of the State, in order that the discussions of the topics to be treated in it can be intelligently followed. And, furthermore, since the production of gas and oil are to-day the leading features in the economic geology of the State, so far as the popular interest is concerned, the principal theories as to the origin and accumulation of these substances will be briefly reviewed, and the laws that govern their distribution, so far as they are now understood, will be briefly pointed out. The materials for these two reviews will be mainly drawn from the discussions of the same subjects in the sixth volume of the Geology of Ohio.

The largest section of the present report will naturally be devoted to a record of the surprising and important facts connected with the recent discovery and utilization of natural gas and petroleum, one or both, in various portions of the State. The two new horizons of oil and gas which have been brought to light in Ohio, viz.: the Trenton and Clinton limestones, will be specially considered in this connection.

Brief accounts will also be added of new facts pertaining to the coals, clays, ores and building stones of the State.

A description of the celebrated "fault" of Adams county will also be included here. This fault is the most marked feature of its kind in the geology of the State. It has been recognized since the time of the First Survey, but no detailed account of it, and especially no map of its location and extent, have been made public hitherto.

PLATE I.

SYSTEM		SERIES.		FEET
	18	GLACIAL DRIFT 0–550		100
CARBONIFEROUS.	17	UPPER BARREN COAL MEASURES		300
	16	UPPER PRODUCTIVE COAL MEASURES		200
	15	LOWER BARREN COAL MEASURES		500
	14	LOWER PRODUCTIVE COAL MEASURES		250
	13	CONGLOMERATE SERIES		250
	12	SUBCARBONIFEROUS LIMESTONE		25
	11	WAVERLY 500–800	11E LOGAN GROUP {SHALE, SANDSTONE, CONGLOMERATE}	150
			11D CUYAHOGA SHALE	200
			11C BEREA SHALE	25
			11B BEREA GRIT	75
			11A BEDFORD SHALE	50
DEVONIAN.	10	OHIO SHALE 300–2600	10C CLEVELAND SHALE	300
			10B ERIE SHALE	
			10A HURON SHALE	
	9	HAMILTON SHALE		25
	8	DEVONIAN LIMESTONES 25–75		75
UPPER SILURIAN.	7	LOWER HELDERBERG LIMESTONE 50–600		300
	6	NIAGARA SERIES	6D HILLSBORO SANDSTONE	200
			6C GUELPH LIMESTONE	50
			6B NIAGARA LIMESTONE	100
	5	CLINTON SERIES	6A NIAGARA SHALE. DAYTON LIME.	50
	4	MEDINA SHALES		25
LOWER SILURIAN.	3	HUDSON RIVER SERIES 500–1050		600
	2	UTICA SHALES 0–300		300
		TRENTON LIMESTONE		

CHAPTER I.

GEOLOGICAL SCALE AND GEOLOGICAL STRUCTURE OF OHIO.

In order to render intelligible the statements that are to follow, a brief account will here be given of the geological series of the State, and also of its geological structure. A somewhat elementary character will be given to this review, in order that it may meet as fully as possible the new demands for geological information that come from every section of the State. A few fundamental facts pertaining to the subject will be stated in the way of an introduction to this review.

1. So far as its exposed rock series is concerned, Ohio is built throughout its whole extent of stratified deposits; or, in other words, of beds of sand, clay and limestone, in all their various gradations, that were deposited or that grew in water. There are in the Ohio series no igneous nor metamorphic rocks whatever; that is, there are no rocks that have assumed their present form and condition from a molten state or that subsequent to their original formation have been transformed by heat. The only qualification which this statement needs pertains to the beds of drift by which a large part of the State is covered. These drift beds contain bowlders in large amount that were derived from the igneous and metamorphic rocks that are found around the shores of Lakes Superior and Huron. But these bowlders are recognized by all, even by the least observant, as foreign to the Ohio scale. They are familiarly known as "lost rocks," or "erratics."

If we should descend deep enough below the surface we should reach the limit of these stratified deposits and come to the great foundations of the continent which constitute the surface rocks in parts of Canada, New England and the West. The granite of Plymouth Rock underlies the continent. But the drill has never yet hewed its way down to these firm and massive beds within our boundaries.

The rocks that constitute the present surface of Ohio were formed in water, and none of them have been modified or masked by the action of high temperatures. They remain in substantially the same condition in which they were formed.

2. With the exception of the coal seams, and a few beds associated with them, and of the drift deposits, all the formations of Ohio grew in the sea. There are no lake or river deposits among them; but by countless and infallible signs they testify to a marine origin. The remnants of life which they contain, often in the greatest abundance, are decisive as to this point.

3. The sea in which or around which they grew was the former extension of the Gulf of Mexico. When the rocks of Ohio were in process of formation, the warm waters and genial climate of the Gulf extended without interruption to the borders of the Great Lakes. All of these rocks had their origin under such conditions.

4. The rocks of Ohio constitute an orderly series. They occur in wide spread sheets, the lowermost of which are co-extensive with the limits of the State. As we ascend in the scale, the strata constantly occupy smaller areas, but the last series of deposits, viz., those of the Carboniferous period, are still found to cover at least one-fourth of the entire area of the State. Some of these formations can be followed into and across adjacent States in apparently unbroken continuity.

The edges of the successive deposits in the Ohio series are exposed in innumerable natural sections, so that their true order can generally be determined with certainty and ease.

5. For the accumulation and growth of this great series of deposits, vast periods of time are required. Many millions of years must be used in any rational explanation of their origin and history. All of the stages of this history have practically unlimited amounts of past time upon which to draw. They have all gone forward on so large a scale, so far as time is concerned, that the few thousand years of human history would not make an appreciable factor in any of them. In other words, five thousand years, or ten thousand years, make too small a period to be counted in the formation of coal, for example, or in the accumulation of petroleum, or in the shaping of the surface of the State through the agencies of erosion. The time that has passed since man has been in the world has been computed by some geologists as less than half of one per cent. of the entire time occupied by geological history.

I. THE GEOLOGICAL SCALE OF OHIO.

The geological scale of Ohio comprises strata of Lower Silurian, Upper Silurian, Devonian, Sub-carboniferous and Carboniferous age, and also a series of glacial deposits. The principal divisions are shown in the following table. The thickness that is assigned to each of the elements is not necessarily the average thickness of the various exposures. In some cases, the general measure is given; in others, it is counted better

GEOLOGICAL SCALE AND STRUCTURE.

to indicate the thickness of some of the more characteristic exposures. In the text, the limits of each formation will be more definitely given:

18. Glacial drift...	0 to 550 feet.			
17. Upper Barren Coal Measures.....................	500 "			Carboniferous.
16. Upper Productive Coal Measures	200 "			
15. Lower Barren Coal Measures	500 "			
14. Lower Productive Coal Measures............................	250 "			
13. Conglomerate Group..	250 "			
12. Sub-carboniferous limestone, Maxville, Newtonville, etc.	25 "			Sub-carboniferous.
11. Waverly Group { 11e Logan Group, 0–350...... 11d Cuyahoga Shale,150–450. 11c Berea Shale, 20– 50...... 11b Berea Grit, 3 to 160...... 11a Bedford Shale, 50–150...	500′ to 800′ }	500 "		
10. Ohio Shale { 10c Cleveland Shale.. 10b Erie Shale......... 10a Huron Shale...... } 250 to 3,000 feet......	300 "			Devonian.
9. Hamilton Shale (Olentangy Shale?).............................	25 "			
8. Devonian Limestone, Upper Helderberg or Corniferous, including West Jefferson sandstone.	75 "			
7. Lower Helderberg limestone or Waterlime, including Sylvania sandstone, 50 to 600 feet......	500 "			Upper Silurian.
6. Niagara Group { 6d Hillsboro' sandstone............... ...... 6c Guelph or Cedarville limestone, 50–200.......... 6b Niagara limestone......................... 6a Niagara Shale, including Dayton limestone, 5 to 100.................	30 " 150 " 50 " 100 "			
5. Clinton Group, in outcrop, 20 to 75 feet; under cover, 75 to 150..	50 "			
4. Medina Shale, in outcrop, 25′; under cover, 50 to 150.....	75 "			
3. Hudson River Group, 300′ to 750′...............................	750 "			Lower Silurian.
2. Utica Shale, not seen in outcrop, but 300 feet thick under cover in Northern Ohio..	300 "			
1. Trenton limestone, seen only in Pt. Pleasant quarries.....	50 "			

The geological order above described is further represented in the accompanying diagram, figure I. A brief review of each of these divisions will next be made.

1. THE TRENTON LIMESTONE.

The Trenton limestone is one of the most important of the older formations of the continent. It is the most widespread limestone of the general scale. It extends from New England to the Rocky Mountains, and from the islands north of Hudson's Bay to the southern extremity of the Allegheny Mountains in Alabama and Georgia. Throughout this vast region, it is found exposed in innumerable outcrops. It gives rise, as it decays, to limestone soils, which are sometimes of remarkable fertility, as for example, those of the famous Blue Grass region of central Kentucky, which are derived from it. It is worked for building stone in hundreds of quarries, and it is also burned into lime and broken into road metal on a large scale throughout the regions where it occurs. But widespread as are its exposures in outcrop, it has a still wider extension under cover. It is known to make the floor of entire States in which it does not reach the surface at a single point.

It takes its name from a picturesque and well known locality in Trenton township, Oneida county, New York. The West Canada Creek makes a rapid descent in this township, from the Adirondack uplands to the Mohawk Valley, falling three hundred feet in two miles by a series of cascades. These cascades have long been known as the Trenton Falls, and the limestone which forms them was appropriately named, by the New York geologists, the Trenton limestone. The formation as seen at the original locality is found to be a dark blue, almost black, limestone, lying in quite massive and even beds, which are sometimes separated by layers of black shale. But it is to be noted that a few feet of its uppermost beds consist of crinoidal limestone of great purity of composition. Both limestone and shale contain excellently preserved fossils of Lower Silurian age. By means of these fossils, and also by its stratigraphical order, the limestone is followed with perfect distinctness from Trenton Falls to every point of the compass. It is changed to some extent in color and composition, as it is traced in different directions, but there is seldom a question possible as to its identity. The Trenton limestone forms several of the largest islands, in whole or in part, in the northern portion of Lake Huron, as the Manitoulin Islands and Drummond's Island. It dips from this region to the southward, but it is found rising again in outcrop in the valley of the Kentucky River, and probably also at a single point within the limits of Ohio, viz., in the quarries of Point Pleasant, which are located in the valley of the Ohio, in Clermont county, twenty miles above Cincinnati. The Point Pleasant beds have a thickness of about fifty feet.

The character of the rock found in the Point Pleasant quarries is briefly described in Vol. I, Geology of Ohio, page 370. The limestone is a light, or greyish-blue limestone, crystalline in structure, massive in its bedding and fossiliferous. The solid masses are interrupted to some extent by thinner beds of shale. It breaks under the drill into thin flakes, rather than into cubical grains. The analysis of a single sample of Point Pleasant limestone is as follows:

```
Carbonate of lime..................................................................... 79.30
Carbonate of magnesia................................................................. .91
Silicious matter.................................................................... 12.00
Alumina and iron..................................................................... 7.00
```

This composition represents the limestone fairly well in its Kentucky outcrops also. It is seen to be impure and of a character that, by its decay, would leave a large residue for the forming soil. In some parts of northwestern Ohio and adjacent regions, the uppermost beds of the Trenton limestone for five feet to one hundred feet are found to be magnesian limestone of a good degree of purity. Its composition as seen in the gas rock and oil rock of the new fields is given below:

1. Trenton limestone at Findley,   1,096 feet below surface.
2.   "   Lima,   1,247 "   "   "
3.   "   Bowling Green, 1,091 "   "   "
4.   "   Kokomo, Ind.,   950 "   "   "

	(1.)	(2.)	(3.)	(4.)
Carbonate of lime,	53.50	52.66	51.78	52.80
Carbonate of magnesia,	43.05	37.53	36.80	37.00
Alumina, iron and silicious residue,	2.95	4.16	4.89	......

The beds immediately underlying this magnesian portion of the stratum are found by analysis to have a composition similar to that noted in the outcrops of the rock in the Ohio Valley. They generally contain 75 to 85 per cent. of carbonate of lime, and ten to twenty per cent. of impurities. The thickness of the Trenton limestone proper, as it appears in outcrop in the rocks of central Kentucky, is given by the geologists of that State as 175 feet. It is immediately underlaid, in this region, by two other limestones, viz., the Birdseye and the Chazy, which have a thickness respectively of 130 and 300 feet; the entire set of unbroken limestones, including the Trenton, being thus about six hundred feet in thickness.

It is altogether probable that these three limestones constitute the solid mass which the drill has so often penetrated in Ohio within the last few years to a depth of five or six hundred feet. The formations which the geologist separates when they rise to the surface, are counted by the driller as a single limestone, for which he needs no other name than Trenton. The several divisions, however, are found to vary somewhat in grain, in color and in chemical composition. Below this great limestone, a sandstone more or less calcareous is reported in many of our deep wells. This is probably on the horizon of the St. Peter's sandstone of the northwest and very likely deserves to be called by this name. It is forty to sixty feet thick as generally found, and is charged with the rank salt and sulphur water, which is known as Blue Lick water, though water of the same grade is sometimes found in or between the limestones above named. Still deeper, impure magnesian limestones again occur for the next one thousand feet, as shown in the deep wells of Springfield and Dayton. These beds must be referred to the Calciferous period of the general scale. To the question so often asked, "How thick is the Trenton limestone?" it is thus seen that it is not easy to give a positive answer on account of the ambiguity of the term as it is popularly used. The interest of the question centers in those portions of the limestone that yield gas and oil, and in regard to this it can be stated, that no portions of the stratum more than a hundred feet below the top have thus far proved productive.

2. THE UTICA SHALE

The immediate cover of the Trenton limestone, from which it derives its name, is a well known stratum of black shale, three hundred to seven hundred feet in thickness, which, from its many outcrops in the vicinity of Utica, New York, received from the New York geologists the name of Utica shale.

This stratum has proved to be very persistent and wide-spread. It is sparingly fossiliferous, but several of the forms that it contains are characteristic, that is, they have thus far been found in no other stratum. The first of the deep wells that was drilled in 1884 in Findlay revealed at a depth of 800 feet, a stratum of black shale containing the most characteristic fossil of the Utica shale, and it was thus positively identified with the last named formation. This bed of shale has the normal thickness of the Utica shale in New York, viz., 300 feet, and with the other elements involved, it extended and continued the New York series into northern Ohio in a most unexpected, and at the same time, in a most satisfactory way.

The Utica shale, thus discovered and defined, is a constant element in the deep wells of north-western Ohio. Its upper boundary is not always distinct, as the Hudson River shale that overlies it sometimes graduates into it in color and appearance; but as a rule, the driller, without any geological prepossessions whatever, will divide the well section in his record so as to show about 300 feet of black shale at the bottom of the column or immediately overlying the Trenton limestone. This stratum holds its own as far as the southern central counties. In the wells of Springfield, Urbana and Piqua, it is found in undiminished thickness, but apparently somewhat more calareous in composition. From these points southward, the black shale thins rapidly. It is apparently replaced by dark colored limestone bands known as 'pepper and salt rock by the driller. No great falling off in black shale appears in the Dayton well, but at Middletown the driller reported a sharp boundary between ᶠgray shale 310 feet thick, and black shale 100 feet thick—the latter directly overlying the Trenton limestone. At Hamilton the same driller reported the boundary still distinct, but the black shale was here reduced to 37 feet, according to his record.

From these and similar facts it appears that the Utica shale is much reduced and altered as it approaches the Ohio Valley, and is finally lost by overlap of the Hudson River shale in this portion of the State and to the southward.

3. THE HUDSON RIVER GROUP.

The very important and interesting series now to be described appears in all the previous reports of the Geological Survey under another name, viz., the Cincinnati group. It is unnecessary to review here the long discussions pertaining to the age of this series, or the grounds on which the changes in the name by which it is known have been based. The return to the older name here proposed, is necessitated by the discoveries recently made in our underground geology, to which reference has already been made. So long as the Utica shale was held to be included in the section at Cincinnati but without distinct or recognizable boundary, so long could the maintainance of the name Cincinnati group be justified. It was held to cover two divisions of geological history which were practically inseparable, and therefore the name of either would be inapplicable to the compound series; but since it has been demonstrated or at least made highly probable, that the Utica shale forms either no part, or but a very small part, of the section at or near Cincinnati, there is no longer any reason for continuing the name Cincinnati group. It becomes a synonym and must be rejected as unnecessary and indefensible

The Hudson River group in southwestern Ohio consists of alternating beds of limestone and shale, the latter of which is commonly known as blue clay. The proportion of lime and shale vary greatly in different parts of the series. The largest percentage of shale occurs in the 250 feet of the series that begin 50 or 75 feet above low water at Cincinnati. The entire thickness of the series in south-western Ohio is about 750 feet. The division of the series into lower and upper is natural and serviceable. The lower is known as the Cincinnati division and the upper as the Lebanon division. The Cincinnati division has a thickness of 425 to 450 feet, and the Lebanon division a thickness of about 300 feet. The divisions are separated on both paleontological and stratigraphical grounds. Both divisions abound in exquisitely preserved fossils of Lower Silurian time; and in fact the hills of Cincinnati and its vicinity have become classical grounds to the geologist on this account.

As the series takes cover to the northward and eastward it retains for a time the same characteristics already described, but as it is followed further it rapidly becomes less calcareous. The limestone courses are thinner and fewer, and inasmuch as they resist or delay the drill but little in its descent, the entire series comes to be counted shale. One other fact needs to be mentioned. The shale at certain points, and especially on the western border, often grows dark in color so that the boundary between this and the underlying Utica division is somewhat obscure. The entire interval in such circumstances may pass with the driller as black shale. The shales of this series are thinnest in this part of the State, the entire measure running as low as 300 feet, or even less. To the eastward the greenish blue element already named, is always found and the shales also thicken considerably in this direction. The Hudson River shales are fossiliferous, as the fragments of corals and shells brought up in the drillings abundantly testify. A few of the fossils are identifiable.

The Hudson River group occupies in its outcrop about 4,000 square miles in southwestern Ohio, but it is doubtless coextensive with the limits of the State. The shales of the series contain in outcrop large quantities of phosphates and alkalies, and the soils to which they give rise are proverbial for their fertility.

The presence of these fine-grained and impervious shales in so many separate beds forbids the descent of water through the formation. In its outcrop the formation has no water supply, and, as found by the driller, it is generally dry. It gives rise to frequent "blowers" or short-lived accumulations of high-pressure gas when struck by the drill, as has been found in the experience in many towns of western Ohio within the last two years, and it also yields considerable amounts of low-pressure shale gas, which has proved fairly durable.

4. The Medina Shale.

A stratum of non-fossiliferous shale, often red or yellow in color and having a thickness of ten to forty feet, directly overlies the uppermost beds of the Hudson River group at many points of outcrops in southwestern Ohio. The occurrence of 50 to 150 feet of red shale in most of the recent deep borings in northwestern Ohio at exactly the place in the general column where the Medina should be, and so much nearer to the known outcrops of the formation that its continuity with these was hardly to be questioned, this fact, taken in connection with the occurrence of like beds of red shale holding the same relative position in all the deep borings in the central portions of the State, gives warrant for counting the Medina epoch duly represented in the outcropping strata of southwestern Ohio. It occurs here only in included sections, its thin and easily eroded beds never being found as surface formations for extensive areas. There is good reason to believe that the Medina formation is coextensive with the limits of the State, except in the regions from which it has already been removed.

The red color of the shales is quite persistent, but there are many well-records in which this color does not appear. This is especially true in Allen county, and to the westward and northwestward from Lima. Blue shales alternate with the red in the eastern sections. In the western they replace the latter. Thin beds of sandstone are found in the Medina, especially to the westward. Small pebbles occur in some of these beds.

5. THE CLINTON LIMESTONE.

The Clinton group of New York appears as a surface formation in Ohio only in the area already named. It forms a fringe or margin of the Cincinnati group through eight or ten counties, rising above the soft and easily eroded rocks of this series, and of the previously named Medina shale in a conspicuous terrace. It is every-where a well-characterized limestone stratum. It is highly crystalline in structure, and is susceptible of a good polish. In some localities it is known as a marble. A considerable part of it, and especially the upper beds, are almost wholly made up of crinoidal fragments. In thickness, it ranges between ten and fifty feet. Its prevailing colors are white, pink, red, yellow, gray and blue. At a few points it is replaced by the hematite ore that is elsewhere so characteristic of the formation. The ore is generally too lean and uncertain to possess economic value, but it was once worked for a short time and in a very small way in a furnace near Wilmington, Clinton county.

The limestone contains a notable quantity of indigenous petroleum throughout most of its outcrop, but the only valuable accumulations of oil or gas that have been found in it thus far have been brought to our knowledge since 1885. It is the source of the low-pressure gas of Fremont (upper vein), and also of the gas at Lancaster, Newark and Hadley Junction. In a few instances it has proved itself an oil rock. A well near Trombley, Wood county, drilled to this horizon, yielded twenty to thirty barrels of oil for a number of months, the oil being referable to this formation.

Under heavy cover and particularly in the new gas fields named above, beds of sharp sandstone are interstratified with the limestones. The main reservoir of the Lancaster gas is in fact a sandstone.

In outcrop the stratum is quite porous as a rule, and the water that falls upon its uncovered portions sinks rapidly through them to the underlying shale (Medina), by which it is turned out in a well-marked line of springs.

GEOLOGY OF OHIO.

In composition the limestone, in its outcrops in southern Ohio, is fairly constant. All of its most characteristic portions contain eighty to eighty-five per cent. of carbonate of lime, and ten to fifteen per cent. of carbonate of magnesia. At a few points, however, it is found as the purest carbonate of lime in the State. Under cover, to the northward, it is much more magnesian in composition, being indistinguishable from the Niagara. It also becomes shaly and changeable in character at many points. As it becomes shaly the thickness is much increased.

It is every-where uneven in its bedding, being in striking contrast in this respect to the formations below it and also above it. The beds are all lenticular in shape, and they extend but a few feet in any direction. They seldom rise to one foot in thickness.

The uneven bedding, the crystalline and crinoidal characters, the high colors, and particularly the red bands and the chemical composition, combine to make the Clinton limestone an exceedingly well-marked stratum throughout southwestern Ohio, and from the hints yielded by the drill in northwestern Ohio, it seems to have something of the same character there, especially so far as color is concerned. It becomes more shaly and much thicker to the eastward. It carries bands of red shale almost universally throughout the northern central and central parts of the State.

The limestone is directly followed at a number of points in the territory occupied by it, by a stratum of very fine-grained, bluish-white clay, containing many fossils distributed through it, the fossils being crystalline and apparently pure carbonate of lime. Some of them are characteristic of the formation elsewhere, while others are known only in this bed. A similar bed of white clay is reported at the same horizon, by the drillers in northern Ohio, and the drillings show the presence of fossils of the same characters. This clay seam can be designated the Clinton clay, but it merges in and is indistinguishable from the lowest element in the next group. The Clinton, in its outcrops, is entirely confined to southern Ohio.

6. THE NIAGARA GROUP.

The Clinton limestone is followed in ascending order by the Niagara group, a series of shales and limestones that has considerable thickness in its outcrops, and that occupies about 3,000 square miles of territory in Ohio as a surface rock. The lowest member is the Niagara shale, a mass of light-colored clays, with many thin calcareous bands. It has a thickness of 100 feet in Adams county, but it is reduced rapidly as it is followed northward, and in Clarke and Montgomery counties it is not more than ten or fifteen feet thick. Still further to the northward, as appears from the records of recent drillings, the shale sometimes disappears entirely, but in the great majority of wells, especially in Hancock and Wood counties, it is a constant element, ranging from five to thirty feet. Wells are often cased in this shale, but a risk is always taken in doing so, as water is liable to be found in the underlying Clintou rocks.

In Montgomery, Miami and Greene counties the shale contains in places a very valuable building stone, which is widely known as the Dayton stone. It is a highly-crystalline, compact and strong stone, lying in even beds of various thickness, and is in every way adapted to the highest architectural uses. It carries about ninety-two per cent. of carbonate of lime. The Niagara shale is, as a rule, quite poor in fossils. It is apparently destitute of them in many of its exposures.

The limestone that succeeds the shale is an even-bedded, blue or drab, magnesian stone, well adapted at many points to quarrying purposes. It contains many characteristic fossils of Niagara age. It is known in Ohio by various local names, derived from the points where it is worked. There are several subdivisions of it that are unequally developed in different portions of the State. Like the shale below it, this member is thickest in southern Ohio. It can not be recognized as a distinct element in the northern part of the State either in outcrop or in drillings. It may be that its horizon is not reached in any natural exposures of the formation in this part of the State.

The uppermost division of the formation is the Guelph limestone, which differs very noticeably in several points from the Niagara limestone proper. It obtains its name from a locality in Canada, where it was first studied and described. It has a maximum thickness in southern Ohio of 200 feet. It differs from the underlying limestone in structure, composition and fossils. It is either massive or very thin-bedded, rarely furnishing a building stone. It is porous to an unusual extent. It is generally very light in color, and is every-where in the State nearly a typical dolomite in composition. It yields lime of great excellence for the mason's use.

It is exceedingly rich in fossils, containing a large number that are thoroughly characteristic of the formation.

Unlike the previously named divisions of the Niagara, the Guelph limestone is as well developed in northern as in southern Ohio in all respects. Not more than forty feet are found in its outcrops here, but the drill has shown several times this amount of Niagara limestone without giving us all of the data needed for referring the beds traversed to their proper subdivisions. What facts there are seem to point to the Guelph as the main element in this underground development of the formation in this portion of the State.

GEOLOGY OF OHIO.

The Hillsboro sandstone is the last element in the Niagara group. It is found in but few localities, and its reference to the Niagara series in its entirety is not beyond question. In Highland county it has a thickness of thirty feet in several sections. It is composed of very pure, even-grained, sharp silicious sand. Other deposits of precisely the same character are found in the two next higher limestones of the scale at several points in the State. One of these deposits is interstratified with the Waterlime in Scioto, Wood and Lucas counties, and others are imbedded in the Corniferous limestone in central Ohio. The latter have been referred to the Oriskany period, but, strictly speaking, this reference is inadmissible, inasmuch as normal Corniferous limestone with its most characteristic fossils is found below as well as above the sandstone. The subject will be further considered on a succeeding page.

The Hillsboro sandstone is sometimes built up above all the beds of the upper Niagara limestone, but again, it is, at times, interstratified with the beds of the Guelph division. In the latter case it is itself fossiliferous, but when found alone it seems destitute of all traces of life. These sandstones in the limestone formations suggest in their peculiarities a common origin. They all consist of unworn and nearly perfect crystals, in considerable part. Their occurrence in outcrops becomes a matter of interest to us, now that we are called to interpret the varied records of deep drillings throughout the State. What would otherwise be altogether anomalous sections may be rendered intelligible by the known presence of such elements in our series.

The Salina Group.

This group has appeared in all the recent sections of the rocks of the State, but in the light of facts recently obtained, it can no longer be counted a distinct or recognizable element in the Ohio scale. Newberry gave it the place it has lately held in the column, and assigned to it a thickness of forty feet. To it he referred the plaster beds of the Ottawa county peninsula and certain impure limestones of Put-in-Bay Island. He also recorded the disappearance of what he counted the same stratum a few miles south of the lake shore in a shaly bed that rests immediately upon the Niagara limestone.

These identifications are, however, incompatible. The limestones of Put-in-Bay and the plaster beds of the peninsula do not directly overlie the Niagara limestone, but on the contrary are separated from it by several hundred feet of the brown, even-bedded, sparingly fossiliferous magnesian limestone that we call the Lower Helderberg limestone or Waterlime. In other words, the plaster beds of Gypsum are buried in the middle, or above the middle, of this great sheet of limestones, instead of being planted at its base. The reference of this formation to the Salina was rendered probable at the time from the fact that all the gypsiferous formations of New York were then counted of Salina age. It has since been proved by Prof. S. G. Williams, of Ithaca, that gypsum is also contained in the Waterlime of central New York, and it is in like situations that the Ohio quarries are found.

The Salina period is an important one in the New York scale, a thousand feet of deposits being credited to it, and there are probably some deposits in Ohio that are contemporaneous with it; but it can not be the gypsum bearing beds of Ottawa county, unless it is made to take in at least one-half of the entire formation that we now call Waterlime. This gypsiferous series proves to be of considerable thickness and to be wide-spread. It is struck in scores of the wells that are being drilled in northern and central Ohio. In Sandusky, gypsum was found in quite pure and thick beds, through several hundred feet of the strata through which the drill passed, and in the deep well at Cleveland both rock-salt and gypsum (anhydrite) were found in considerable deposits. Salt-beds of considerable thickness have also been recently discovered at a depth of 2,650 feet at Wadsworth, Medina county. Small deposits of gypsum, also, have been found in the deep wells of Columbus, Newark, and many other towns. Salt and gypsum are geological accidents, and can not well be used in determining the geological order of regions that are separated by intervals of hundreds of miles.

The reference of distinct portions of our geological scale to the Salina period must accordingly be discarded for the present, at least.

7. THE LOWER HELDERBERG OR WATERLIME FORMATION.

The interval that exists between the Niagara and the Devonian limestones is occupied in Ohio by a very important formation. This formation was first separated from the previously undivided mass of the Cliff limestone by Newberry in 1869. He found and identified its fossils, and showed by means of them, and by the position of the stratum in our series, that the rocks of this interval are the equivalents, in part at least, of the Waterlime of the New York scale. The Waterlime of New York is classed by most geologists with the Lower Helderberg series; but Hall counts it the upper member of the Salina Group, a reference that seems likely to be ultimately considered the true and proper one.

The name is unhappily chosen. Strictly applicable to only an insignificant fraction of the beds of this series in New York, we are still obliged to apply the designation Waterlime, with its misleading suggestions, to all deposits of the same age throughout the country.

Though the last to be recognized of our several limestone formations, the Waterlime occupies a larger area in Ohio than any other, its principal developments being found in the drift covered plains of the northwestern quarter of the State. It has also a much greater thickness than any other limestone, its full measure being at least 600 feet, or twice the greatest thickness of the Niagara limestone.

It can be described as, in the main, a strong, compact, magnesian limestone, poor in fossils, and often altogether destitute of them for considerable areas, microscopic forms being excepted. It is, for the most part, drab or brown in color; but occasionally it becomes very light-colored, and again it is often dark blue. It is brecciated throughout much of its extent, the beds seeming to have been broken into sometimes small and sometimes large angular fragments after their hardening, and then to have been recemented without further disturbance. In addition to this, it contains an immense amount of true conglomerate, the pebbles, many of which are bowlders rather than pebbles, being all derived from the rocks of the same general age. The surface of many successive layers at numerous points are covered with suncracks, thus furnishing proof of having been formed in shallow water near the edge of the sea. In such localities, the beds are usually quite thin, and are also impure in composition. In these respects, it suggests the conditions of the Onondaga Salt Group of New York. These features are very characteristic ones. A rude concretional structure is also quite distinctive of the beds of this age. The Waterlime in Ohio every-where contains petroleum in small quantity which is shown by the odor of freshly broken surfaces. No noteworthy accumulations of oil or gas have thus far been found within it. At some points, it carries considerable asphalt, distributed through the rock in shot-like grains, or in sheets and films. Thin streaks of carbonaceous matter traversing the rock parallel to its bed planes are one of the constant marks of the stratum in Ohio. It is generally thin and even in its bedding; but in some localities it contains massive beds. At some points, it is remarkable for its evenness, and great value is given to the formation on this account, when combined with other qualities already named. It is frequently a nearly pure dolomite in composition, and accordingly, it yields magnesian lime of high quality and is extensively burned in the State,·rivaling in this respect the Guelph beds of the Niagara.

In southern Ohio, it has a maximum thickness of 100 feet, and here it reaches its highest quality in all respects; but in central and northern Ohio it attains the great thickness previously reported. There also, it contains several distinct types of limestone rock. A considerable part of it is very tough, strong, dark blue limestone, while other portions are white, porous and soft.

GEOLOGICAL SCALE AND STRUCTURE.

The line of junction between the Niagara and Waterlime is sometimes obscure, and no means are at hand for drawing sharp lines of division.

All that has been thus far said applies mainly to the formation as found in outcrop; but well-reamings brought up from considerable depths at various points in the State render it certain that the principal features now given mark the formation below ground, as well as above. There is no reason to doubt that the Waterlime has as wide a distribution in the subterranean geology of Ohio as the formations already described. It is to be found in every part of the State in which it is due.

This formation has come into new prominence through the revelations of the drill within the last few years. In regard to no other element in the series have the geologists been so wide of the mark as in regard to the Lower Helderberg formation. What belongs to it was taken from it and given to a stratum that has no existence in the State; and it was credited with but one-sixth of its real thickness. Its outcrops ought to have shown that it has a greater thickness than was assigned to it, since it covers several scores of miles in an east and west line. It demands a large amount of additional investigation to put it in order; and to secure such a mastery of it as to be able to determine from an inspection of any outcrop what place it holds in the general series will be a valuable service to the geology of the State. Winchell established approximately one horizon in it which promises to be of some service, namely, the horizon of the Tymochtee Slate, a bed of dark blue shaly limestone that is found in outcrop in the Tymochtee Creek near Carey, Wyandot county. It is below the middle of the formation and probably within 100 to 200 feet of the Niagara limestone. A few other facts can be added that bear upon the same point. The excessively hard and strong dark blue impure limestone of Allen, Hardin and Hancock counties and some adjoining regions, which often has its surface conspicuously marked with suncracks, belongs to the middle portion of the formation, but probably rather above than below the middle. A single other element remains to be inserted in the Lower Helderberg column, the interpolation of which at this point will occasion surprise to all who are conversant with the older statements in regard to our geological scale.

The Sylvania Sandstone.

A remarkable deposit, or rather series of deposits, of extremely pure glass sand has long been known in Lucas and Wood counties of northern Ohio and in adjacent territory. The two best known deposits are those of Sylvania and Montclova, which respectively lie ten miles northwest and west of Toledo. Other similar deposits are known in Wood c and it is probable that the sand deposits of Monroe county, Michigan, belong to the same horizon.

The sandstone, twenty or more feet in thickness, seen in the Sylvania quarries, rests upon beds of normal Waterlime, which are exposed a few rods to the eastward. The rocks are sharply inclined here, descending in an almost due west direction, at the rate of one foot in seven. The rocks overlying the sandstone, as seen in extensive quarries, are unmistakable Waterlime, containing all the characteristic marks of the formation, its chemical composition, its bedding, its bituminous character and its fossils. Further on, the conglomerate phase of the Waterlime appears. There is nothing in the whole formation more characteristic than this. At the end of the series, 80 rods to the westward from the sandstone quarry, a few feet of undoubted Corniferous limestone occur, rich in the fossils of the formation and true to its chemical composition. All this is absolutely decisive as to the age of the sandstone. It lies nearly, or quite two hundred feet below the Corniferous limestone.

The Monclova or Holland sandstone occupies the same position in the series as the Sylvania sandstone does. The Grand Rapids sandstone, of Wood county, probably belongs to the same horizon. It is probably the Sylvania sandstone that appears in the thirty-foot bed of sharp and pure sand that has been reached in the deep wells of Cleveland within the last four years, at a depth of about two thousand feet from the surface and under the cover of three hundred feet of limestone. At least the sandstone found at this level is of very much the same character as that found in the Sylvania quarries.

That there is another sandstone of character similar to that of the Sylvania sand, included in the Corniferous limestone, is beyond question. This formation will be treated in the next section. The Sylvania sand can henceforth be counted an Upper Silurian sandstone and a part of the Lower Helderberg series. Whether the sandstone beds of Champaign and Logan counties are all to be referred to one horizon remains to be determined by further study.

8. THE UPPER HELDERBERG LIMESTONE

All of the limestone of Devonian age in Ohio has been referred by Newberry to the Corniferous limestone, and this term is in general use at the present time. It may be questioned whether it is wise to break in upon this use, but inasmuch as several geologists hold that the Devonian limestone of Ohio covers more than the simple epoch known as the Corniferous in New York, a more comprehensive term, viz., the Upper

Helderberg limestone, is on the whole counted preferable. A twofold division of the series is possible and proper in Ohio, the division being based on lithology and fossils. The divisions are known as Lower and Upper Corniferous, or as Columbus and Delaware limestones. For the upper division, the term Sandusky limestone is sometimes used. In central Ohio, at a few points, there is a marked contrast between the lower and the upper beds, the latter being thin and shaly, non-fossiliferous in the main, and interrupted with frequent courses of black flint. This phase is seen at the State quarries near Columbus. Generally, however, both divisions are calcareous and fossiliferous, and the differences consist in changes of color and composition, in thickness of the several beds and in the distribution, and also in the kinds of fossils present.

The maximum thickness of the Upper Helderberg series in Ohio, so far as present records show, is 75 to 100 feet.

Included in the lower beds of the limestone there are, at many points, deposits of sharp sand of the same character as the deposits already described under the names of Hillsborough sandstone and Sylvania sandstone These beds may be known as the West Jefferson sandstone, one of the localities at which the sand is found being near this village. This Upper Helderberg sandstone is not Oriskany in age. It nowhere underlies the Corniferous limestone, but is always underlain by it and interstratified with it, at least where its place in the series can be determined. It attains a thickness of but few feet at most, and is nowhere worked for economic uses except upon the smallest scale.

In chemical composition, the Corniferous limestone is easily distinguished from all that underlie it. It is much less magnesian than the other members of the Cliff limestone of Ohio, already described. It is never a true dolomite in composition, as the Waterlime and Niagara limestones almost always are. The carbonate of magnesia ranges in it from two to thirty-five per cent., reaching the latter figure in but few cases. The composition of the typical, heavy-bedded lower Corniferous may be taken as seventy-per cent. carbonate of lime and twenty-five per cent. carbonate of magnesia. The higher beds of the Columbus stone regularly yield ninety-one to ninety-five per cent. carbonate of lime. The upper division, or the Delaware stone, is much less pure in central Ohio than the lower, a notable percentage of iron and alumina, as well as silica, generally being contained in it. It is, therefore, seldom or never burned into lime. In northern Ohio, on the contrary, it is often found a fairly pure limestone.

Both divisions, but particularly the lower one, carry occasional courses of chert, that detract from the value of the beds in which they occur. The chert is found in nodules which are easily detached from the limestone for the most part. In some conditions in which the chert occurs, fossils are found in it in a remarkably good state of preservation. The percentage of chert and flint in any section would be considerable, and this fact must be borne in mind in the analysis of drillings from bore holes that penetrate the formation.

The beds of the lower division are prevailingly light-colored, ranging from whitish to gray, drab and brown. The upper beds are oftener blue than otherwise.

The beds of the lower division are, as a rule, much thicker than those of the upper. The lowermost courses are sometimes quite massive. In the State quarries they are not less than five feet thick. In the upper division the separate courses seldom reach a thickness of one foot.

Throughout the entire formation Devonian fossils abound in great variety and in great numbers. They are often found in an excellent state of preservation. The oldest vertebrate remains of the Ohio rocks are found in the Corniferous limestone, a fact which gives special interest to it. The uppermost bed of the lower or Columbus division is, in many places, a genuine "bone bed"; the teeth and plates and spines of ancient fishes, largely of the nearly extinct family of ganoids, constituting a considerable portion of the substance of the rock. Corals of various types are also especially abundant and interesting in this limestone. In fact, the formation is the most prolific in life of any in the Ohio scale. At a few points in central Ohio, the upper division has been found in a shaly state and carrying characteristic fossils of the Marcellus slate. This fact was first noticed in its true significance by Whitfield.

9. THE HAMILTON OR OLENTANGY SHALE.

Under this head Newberry has recognized fifteen to twenty feet of highly fossiliferous blue shale, intervening between the Corniferous limestone and the black shale. He finds it at only one or two points in northern Ohio, and notably at Prout's Station, seven miles south of Sandusky. The fossils found here are all of Hamilton age, unmingled with those of the underlying Corniferous limestone.

On stratigraphical grounds it seems probable that the Olentangy shale of Professor N. H. Winchell is the extension and equivalent of Newberry's Hamilton shale. The Olentangy shale is a bed of blue calcareous shale, twenty or thirty feet in thickness, holding exactly the position of the northern Ohio stratum, but it is almost destitute of fossils. It is found in a few sections of three or four counties in central Ohio. In the well-driller's record it would seem likely to be classed with the limestone below rather than with the black shale above, and, as already suggested, the incorporation of this element might easily serve to expand the measurement of the limestone by a small amount.

With this formation the great limestones of Ohio were completed. While they are built into the foundations of almost the entire State, they constitute the surface rocks only in its western half. The Upper Silurian and Devonian limestones of our scale, which were formerly known as the Cliff limestone, have an aggregate thickness of 750 to 1,150 feet where found under cover, and though differences exist among them by which, as has already been shown, they can be divided into four or more main divisions, there is still no reason to believe that any marked change occurred in the character of the seas during the protracted periods in which they were growing. The life which these seas contained was slowly changing from age to age, so that we can recognize three or more distinct faunas or assemblages of animal life in them. Differences are also indicated in the several strata as to the depth of the water in which they were formed, and as to the conditions under which the sedimentary matter that enters into them was supplied, but no marked physical break occurs in the long history. No part of the entire series indicates more genial conditions of growth than those which the Devonian limestone, the latest in order of them all, shows. It is the purest limestone of Ohio. Foot after foot of the formation consists almost exclusively of the beautifully preserved fragments of the life of these ancient seas. In particular the corals and crinoids that make a large element in many of its beds could only have grown in shallow but clear water of tropical warmth.

The change from the calcareous beds of this age to the next succeeding formation is very abrupt and well marked, as much so, indeed, as any change in the Ohio scale.

10. THE OHIO SHALE.

(Cleveland Shale, Erie Shale, Huron Shale, of Newberry.)

A stratum of shale, several hundred feet in thickness, mainly black or dark brown in color, containing, especially in its lower portions, a great number of large and remarkably symmetrical calcareous and ferruginous concretions, and stretching entirely across the State from the Ohio Valley to the shores of Lake Erie, with an outcrop ranging in breadth between ten and twenty miles, has been one of the most conspicuous and well-known features of Ohio geology since this subject first began to be studied. It separates the great limestone series already described, which constitutes the floor of all of western Ohio, from the Berea grit, which is the first sandstone reached in ascending the geological column of the State, and which, in like manner, may be counted the floor of all of eastern Ohio. By the geologists of the first survey it was designated as the *Shale Stratum* or the *Black Slate*. It will be treated in this report under the designation *Ohio shale*. Newberry divided it into three divisions, which he named respectively the Cleveland, the Erie and the Huron shale. He based the separation of the hitherto undivided mass in part upon the colors of the proposed divisions, the Cleveland and the Huron being counted black shales, and the Erie greenish-blue. The names Huron and Erie were unfortunately chosen, for both are liable to be confounded with current names of other geological formations. The name *Huron* was adopted from Winchell, but a very different range was assigned to it from that which its author originally claimed. Winchell's "Huron group" extends, in his own words, from the top of the Devonian limestones, "to the conglomerate above the gritstones of Huron county." It is thus seen to include Newberry's Huron, Erie, Cleveland and Bedford shales, together with the Berea grit and the Cuyahoga shale. It would have served the interests of geological classification much better to have replaced the term altogether than to have thus restricted it to a small fraction of what it was originally made to cover. The name is also likely to be confused with the *Huronian slates*, an older and well-established division of the Canadian system of rocks.

The Erie shale, in like manner, is sure to be confounded with the Erie clay, the older name of an important deposit of the Glacial epoch. Both shale and clay have their typical exposures in the same localities, and their outcrops are not dissimilar in appearance. It is not therefore surprising that the names should be confused in popular use.

But aside from these grounds of objection to the particular names employed, the classification referred to is itself inconsistent with our present knowledge of the shale formation. We have records by the score of wells drilled through the shale at many points in northern Ohio during the last few years, and we have also the results of continued study of the formation in its outcrops. The facts gathered from both of these lines of investigation, not only fail to confirm the three-fold division above announced, but they demonstrate the impossibility of applying to the shale formation any system of classification based upon the color of the shales, and as for the fossils they are so sparingly distributed that they can not well be used to mark horizons in the formation, aside from a few that will be mentioned later.

10a. *The Lower Beds—Huron Shale.*

The Huron shale was defined by Newberry as a homogeneous mass of black, bituminous shale, 200 to 350 feet in thickness, directly overlying the limestone series already described. The objection to this definition is that there is no such mass of shale in Ohio. The mass on which the main statements pertaining to the Huron rests, and which furnishes nearly all of the examples instanced, is the shale stratum of central and southern Ohio, but this is not merely the bottom portion of the shale series of northern Ohio. It comprises all of the elements of the northern section. In other words, the so-called Huron shale of central Ohio is the Cleveland, Erie, Huron shale of northern Ohio. It is not a homogeneous mass of black shale, as it is commonly counted, but beds of blue or greenish-blue shale are frequently interstratified with the prevailing black beds, especially in the middle portion of the series. The top and bottom of the column are generally black shale, and the same thing is true in northern Ohio. These facts show the grounds on which the classification now referred to is based, but the objection to it is that no line of division can be drawn between the Huron and Erie, or the Erie and Cleveland shales. The records of many drilled wells in northern Ohio show that alternations of black and blue shale recur not once only, but many times, in the formation.

10c. The Upper Beds—Cleveland Shale.

The Cleveland shale has, it is true, a somewhat better chance for survival as a distinct division than the Erie or Huron. There is a tolerably distinct upper boundary for it, inasmuch as a belt of back shale generally underlies by 50 to 100 feet the Berea grit, by far the best landmark in this part of the scale, the interval being occupied by the Bedford shale, itself a well characterized formation. In some sections, however, there is no black shale at the point where the Cleveland shale belongs, and in all sections the lower boundary of the formation is likely to be uncertain, unless the bottom of the first bed of black shale found below the Berea grit is in every case taken for the bottom of the Cleveland division. If this is done, the Cleveland shale must stand for very unequal periods of geological time, as the uppermost black bed has a great range in thickness. It often falls to thirty feet and sometimes exceeds two hundred feet. It is probably the larger half of the great black shale of southern Ohio. It is this element that proves most persistent in the southerly extension of the black shale. The shale that covers the Lower Silurian limestone in central Kentucky is the upper or Cleveland division, as its most characteristic fossils, presently to be named, prove.

The mineral basis of all these shales, whether black, brown, blue, grey or red, is essentially one and the same thing, viz., a fine-grained clay, derived from the waste of distant land. As supplied to the sea basin, it was originally blue or gray, but a small percentage of peroxide of iron goes a great way in coloring such deposits red, and in like manner, organic matter in comparatively small amount gives them a dark or black color. The organic matter that colors these shales was probably derived in large part, as Newberry has suggested, from the products of growth and decay of sea-weeds by which these seas were covered like the Sargasso seas of our own days.

These organic matters seem to have accumulated along the shores and is shallow water in greater quantity than in the deeper seas. Hence, if the section of these shale deposits is taken near the old shore-lines, or where shallow water occurred, a larger proportion is black, than if the more central areas are examined. The only land of Ohio at this time was to be found in and along the Cincinnati axis, a low fold that had entered the State from the southward at the close of Lower Silurian time, and that had been slowly extending itself northwards through the succeeding ages. Southwestern Ohio was already above water, a low island in the ancient gulf. But the shales on their western outcrop, where they are largely black, are exactly equivalent in age to the alternating beds of black and blue shale, the latter being in large excess, that were forming at this time in the central parts of the basin, viz., in eastern Ohio. The color of the shales is, in this view, an accident, and can not be safely used as a ground of division. The entire shale formation that we are considering seems to have been laid down without physical break or interruption. It must have required an immensely long period for its accumulation. This is shown not only by the fineness and uniformity of the materials which compose it, and which could not have been rapidly supplied, and by the great thickness of the formation in eastern Ohio, but also by the geological equivalents of the shale in the general column which furnish even more convincing proof as to its long continued growth. The Ohio shale, as Newberry has shown, is certainly the equivalent in the general scale of the Genessee slate, the Portage group and the Chemung group, the last named being itself a formation of great thickness and extent. In other words, the shales of our column bridge the interval between the Hamilton proper and the Catskill group, and in the judgment of some geologists a wider interval even than that named above. As Newberry was the first to show, the oil sands of Pennsylvania are banks of pebble rock that are buried in the eastward extension of the Ohio shale, but which make no sign within our own limits.

But while definite boundaries for the division proposed can not be laid down or applied within the shale formation, the facts that the top and the bottom of the column, on their western outcrops, are prevailingly black, and that the middle of the series is oftener interrupted with light-colored beds are important ones in the history of the formation and

GEOLOGICAL SCALE AND STRUCTURE.   31

deserve to be held in mind. From what has been already stated, it is seen that the composition and thickness of the shale series depend on where it is measured, whether on the border of the formation or in the interior of the old sea-basin in which it was formed. On the western border of the shales in southern Ohio, in Highland county, for example, the interval between the Upper Silurian limestone, on which the shales here rest by overlap, and the Berea grit is 300 feet. In Ross county, the same interval is nearly 400 feet. From both of the measurements, fifty feet must be deducted for the thickness of the Bedford shale in order to give the real thickness of the series now under consideration. In the sections named the shales are mainly black, although blue beds are still recognizable in the series. Passing northwards to Crawford county, the series is found about 450 feet thick. In Lorain county, at Elyria, it is about 950 feet, and at Cleveland about 1,350 feet, while in Tuscarawas county the drill has descended through 1,860 feet of alternating beds of blue and black shale without reaching the bottom of the series, and in the Ohio Valley, at Wellsville, through 2,600 feet of shales without reaching bottom. In the last two sections, the blue shales decidedly preponderate, though the separate black beds can be counted by the score.

Fossils of the Shales.

The shales are for the most part poor in fossils, except in those of microscopic size. Banks representing scores of feet in the vertical column often fail to reward the most careful search with a single specimen of vertebrate, molluscan or articulate life, and so far as the unaided eye is concerned, they are almost equally barren of vegetable remains. Occasionally, however, fossiliferous bands are found, the contents of which serve to determine the geological age and equivalence of the portion of the series in which they occur.

A calcareous band near the bottom of the series at Bainbridge, Ross county, has yielded a few Hamilton fossils. A band of similar character near Defiance, and in the same part of the column, yields a few forms in abundance, but not in a very good state of preservation. Newberry reports from northern Ohio a number of forms that are counted characteristic of the Portgage group of New York.

The Erie shale of Newberry, embracing the central and most of the upper portion of the shale column, has yielded a somewhat larger list of fossils at a few points in northern Ohio, from which the age of the beds is shown to be Chemung, a determination of great importance in Ohio geology. In higher beds of the same blue shale there are found, at a few points, forms that are referred to as the Sub-carboniferous. Counting this the boundary line between the Devonian and Sub-carboniferous, Newberry took what he deemed the first identifiable horizon above as the base of the last-named division, and accordingly drew the line at the base of the so-called Cleveland shale. This boundary is not a definite one, as subsequent investigations have shown, but the *top* of the upper black, or Cleveland shale would answer fairly well for this purpose. It is the first stratigraphical mark that has any claims to persistency above the beds that hold the fossils already named. The fossils of the black shale proper offer no serious difficulty in the way of extending Devonian time to the upper limit of the stratum, and this boundary is consequently assumed as the only one that can be made practically serviceable.

The Cleveland shale, limiting the term to the highest bed of black shale in the series, and which is about fifty feet thick at various points near Cleveland, contains a few fossils, most of which are quite small, but the most striking and remarkable fossils, at once of the shale formation and of the entire scale of Ohio, remain to be named. They are the great fishes, which have been described under several genera and species, by Newberry. Some of them belong to the basal beds of the black shale (Huron), and others, including the largest, near the summit (Cleveland). The first of the series were found at the centers of the great concretions that have been already named as characteristic of the formation. The latter are also found in the uppermost beds of the formation in central Ohio, proving the age of the latter to be the same as that of the upper beds of northern Ohio.

Brief mention must be made of the vegetable fossils of the shales.

Fossil wood, derived from ancient pine trees, is quite common in the lower beds (Huron). The wood is silicified and the original structure is admirably preserved. This wood is sometimes found, like the fish remains already noted, at the hearts of the concretions, but occasionally large sized blocks are found free in the shale. On account of its enduring nature it is often found in those beds of glacial drift that have been derived largely from the destruction of the shales.

Strap-shaped leaves, presumably of sea-weeds, are occasionally found upon the surfaces of the shale layers. Sometimes they form thin layers of bright coal which deceive the ignorant. Fossil rushes, of the genus Calamites, are also occasionally met with.

But the forms already named are of small account, so far as quantity is concerned, when compared with certain microscopic fossils that are, with little doubt, of vegetable origin, and which are accumulated in large amount throughout the black beds of the entire shale formation, composing, sometimes a notable percentage of the substance of the rock, and apparently giving origin, to an important extent, to the bituminous character of the beds.

The leading forms of these microscopic fossils are translucent, resinous discs, ranging in long diameter from $\frac{1}{30}$ to $\frac{1}{250}$ of an inch. Several varieties have already been noted, depending on the size, particular shape and surface markings of these bodies.

They were first discovered by Mr. B. W. Thomas, an expert microscopist, in the water-supply of Chicago, which is derived from Lake Michigan, and Mr. Thomas afterwards learned that they were washed by the water from the bowlder clays that compose the banks and bottom of the lake. He found the discs present in fragments of black shale, and also free in the clay which was derived from the comminution of the shale.

They were afterwards rediscovered in the black shale of Kettle Point, Lake Huron, by Professor, now Sir William Dawson, who published a description of the form here found under the name *Sporangites Huronenis*. Sir William counted them at this time the spore-cases of some lycopodiaceous tree.

The facts pertaining to them have of late been more widely published, and the attention of geologists in various parts of the world has been called to these and similar forms, and thus there is the promise of a speedy enlargement of our knowledge in regard to them. Sir William Dawson now considers the common forms to be the spore-cases of rhizocarps allied to *Salvinia* of the present day. This identification would refer these bodies to floating vegetation on the surface of the seas in which the shales were formed, and is thus directly in line with the sagacious interpretation of Newberry, who many years ago attributed the origin of these black shales to Sargasso seas.

11. THE WAVERLY GROUP.

The important mass of sediments of Sub-carboniferous age, which is known in Ohio and in some adjoining States as the Waverly group, comes next in the column. The name Waverly was given to these strata by the geologists of the first survey, from the fact that at Waverly, in the Scioto Valley, excellent sandstone quarries were opened in them, the products of which were quite widely distributed throughout central and southern Ohio, as far back as fifty years ago. Associated with the sandstone at this locality, and every-where throughout the district, were several other strata that were always counted as members of the group by the geologists who gave the name. In fact, the boundaries were made definite and easily applicable. The Waverly group extended, by its definition and by unbroken usage in our early geology, from the top of the great black shale

(Cleveland shale), to the Coal Measure conglomerate. This latter element was, in a part of the field, confused with the Waverly conglomerate, afterwards recognized and defined by Andrews, until a recent date, it is true, but the intent of the geologists is apparent, and many of their sections were complete and accurate. If the term Waverly is to be retained in our classification, and it bids fair to be, every interest will be served by recognizing and retaining the original boundaries. The departure from them that has been proposed has led already to great confusion. To make the Cleveland shale the base of the Waverly is, as has been already shown, to turn the entire shale stratum into a no-man's land. Aside from a few sections in northern Ohio, where an arbitrary limit was fixed for this upper division, there is no place in the State where a line can be drawn with any approach to certainty between Cleveland and Erie or between Erie and Huron. The plan was proposed before the true equivalence of the northern and southern ends of the column had been established. If the fact that the Cleveland shale of northern Ohio forms the top of the great shale of central and southern Ohio had been known, certainly no proposal would have been made to break into this undivided and indivisible series which had been held to underlie the Waverly group ever since the name was first applied.

11a. *The Bedford Shale.*

At Waverly and in its vicinity, numerous sections are afforded reaching from the black shale to the Waverly sandstone courses. This interval ranges from fifty to ninety feet in thickness, and its boundaries are generally very clear and distinct. It is occupied with shales, for the most part light-blue or gray, but sometimes reddened with peroxide of iron in the lower portion. The latter phase is seen in the excellent section found at Piketon. These shales are thin-bedded, occasionally interrupted with fine-grained sandstone courses, and sometimes carrying very ungainly nodular masses of the same material, apparently shaped by a rough concretionary force. The beds are almost entirely destitute of fossils, aside from the burrows of sea-worms, which are found on the surfaces of most of the layers, and often with great sharpness of outline. At a few points, however, fossiliferous bands containing a considerable number of species are found. These have recently been pointed out by Prof. C. L. Herrick of Cincinnati. All the layers, and especially the upper ones, are likely to be ripple-marked. In many instances, every sheet, for many successive feet, is marked with most symmetrical sculpturings of this sort.

This stratum, thus definitely characterized and bounded, received the name of the Waverly shale in the reports of the second Geological

Survey, but in northern Ohio it was named by Newberry the Bedford shale, the equivalence of the strata not being at that time recognized. The latter name deserves to be universally accepted, being applied to a perfectly distinct and homogeneous formation. The stratum has precisely the same boundaries in northern that it has in southern Ohio, viz., the top of the great black shale (Cleveland) and the Berea Grit, and, in the main, precisely the same characteristics throughout its whole extent. The description of the stratum at Waverly applies to it at every other point, except that in northern Ohio at a few localities, and especially about Cleveland, there are fifteen to twenty feet of valuable stone included in it. This stone is even-bedded, very strong and durable, and it supplies a large quantity of flaggings, caps and sills, of the best grade. It is known as the East Cleveland, Euclid and Independence blue stone. In northern Ohio, more of the formation is red-colored than in southern, and here it is the top of the formation rather than the bottom that is thus marked. In the lower beds of the Bedford shale, fossils are, in northern Ohio, at a few points, abundant. They are of pronounced Sub-carboniferous character according to Newberry's determinations, but Professor Herrick inclines to place them lower in the scale. None of these fossils have been reported south of the lake shore, but the stratigraphical relations of the shale are so clear and its lithological characteristics so pronounced, that there is not a stratum in our geological column that can be followed across the State in more easily demonstrated identity than this.

11b. *The Berea Grit.*

We have reached in our review the Berea grit, the second element of the Waverly series, and not only the most important member of the series, but by far the most important single stratum in the entire geological column of Ohio. Its economic value above ground is great, but it is greater below. In its outcrops it is a source of the finest building stone and the best grindstone grit of the country, and when it dips beneath the surface it becomes the repository of invaluable supplies of petroleum, gas and salt-water. Its persistence as a stratum is phenomenal. Seldom reaching a thickness of fifty feet, its proved area in Ohio above ground and below, is scarcely less than 15,000 square miles, and beyond the boundaries of Ohio it extends with continuity and strength unbroken into at least four other adjacent States. In the opinion of our best stratigraphical geologists the Berea grit becomes the famous Murraysville gas sand and also the Gantz oil sand of Washington county, Pennsylvania. As a guide to the interpretation of our series, and especially as a guide in our subterranean geology, it is invaluable.

The stratum was named by Newberry from the village of Berea, Cuyahoga county, where the largest and most important quarries of the formation are located. The name is the most appropriate that could have been selected for this stratum, and inasmuch as it has priority in all fields, it ought to be made to supersede all others.

From what has already been stated, it will be seen that the Berea grit and the Waverly quarry-stone of southern Ohio are one and the same sheet of sandstone. This identity was missed for a long while in the study of our geology, and a wrong order of arrangement found temporary acceptance. The resulting dislocation of our Sub-carboniferous series brought into all our work upon it an element of confusion that is scarcely yet eliminated.

The Berea grit, as seen in outcrop, is a sandstone of medium grain in northern Ohio and of fine grain, from the center of the State southward. In northern Ohio, it contains one pebbly horizon over a considerable area, but the seam is thin and the pebbles are small. The stratum is sometimes false-bedded and sometimes remarkably even in its bedding-planes. Its main beds, or sheets, have a maximum thickness of six feet, but this is an unusual measure and is seldom reached. It ranges in thickness from 5 to 170 feet, and it very rarely fails altogether from the sections in which it is due.

Like the Bedford shale below it, it stands for an old shore-line, many of its surfaces being ripple-marked and worm-burrows abounding in its substance.

It is poor in fossils, but not entirely destitute of them. Fish remains are the most conspicuous, but by far the rarest of the forms that it contains. Plant impressions are also unusual through most of the formation, but in northeastern Ohio there is a certain part of the stratum in which they are quite abundant. Throughout the great quarry district the material of which the stratum is composed is as clean sand as can be found on any sea beach. It grows more impure as its sand grows finer in grain in central and especially in southern Ohio. A small percentage of clay is held in it at most points.

Under cover it retains the same characteristics as to composition that it possesses above ground, ranging from fine to middling grain and very seldom showing pebbles. It has been proved by many hundred borings in southeastern Ohio during the last few years, and its composition there is almost as well known as in its outcrops.

11c. *The Berea Shale—Waverly Black Shale of Andrews.*

A bed of dark, often black shale, fifteen to fifty feet in thickness, makes the constant and immediate cover of the Berea grit throughout its entire extent in Ohio. The shale is highly fossiliferous. The bottom layer, which is especially rich in fossils, is very hard and stubborn, being composed of sand bound together with pyrites. It is often referred to the sandstone below rather than to the shale above, but its fossils and its bituminous character favor the reference here given, inasmuch as it marks new conditions in the history of these beds.

The stratum was first described by Andrews under the name of the Waverly black shale, the typical outcrop being found at Rockport, on the Ohio River, but about the same time Meek, who was studying its fossils in northern Ohio, introduced the designation Berea shale. (Pal., Ohio, Vol. II, Plate XIV.) The latter name is clearly preferable and ought to obtain currency.

In southern and central Ohio, and indeed in almost all of its outcrops, the boundaries of the Berea shale are sharp and perfectly distinct. The Berea grit is its base, and the blue beds of the Cuyahoga shale overlie it. In Cuyahoga county, however, and eastward, the upper limit cannot always be fixed with precision, neither the dark color nor the fossils of the shale disappearing abruptly, but both gradually diminishing. There are, however, twenty to forty feet that always deserve to be counted here.

When struck by the drill under cover, the formation uniformly yields a line of facts similar to that already reported. Of the records of the many hundred wells that have been carried down to and below this horizon in southern Ohio and in adjacent territory during the last few years, there has not a single one been found that has failed to give a place to this little band of black shale. Its services in setting in order our Sub-carboniferous geology have been simply invaluable. It is apparently wanting at a few points in northern central Ohio. At least some of the drillers who have sunk deep wells here declare that they have found no trace of this stratum.

The Berea shale contains a larger percentage of bituminous matter than the Ohio shale, the amount sometimes reaching 24 per cent. It is a source of petroleum on a small scale, as is shown by the fact that in southern Ohio an important ledge of sandstone that belongs just above it is often saturated with a tar-like oil, derived from this source.

11d. *The Cuyahoga Shale.*

It is impossible to retain for this great division of the Waverly the limits assigned to it by Newberry when he gave it its name. He made it fill the entire interval between the Berea grit and the Coal Measure conglomerate, and according to present knowledge, at least three distinct elements are to be found in every normal section of this interval. One of them has already been described, viz., the Berea shale, cut off from the foot of the column. Another, and a much more conspicuous element must be taken off from the top of the column, viz., the Logan group. But there still remain 150 to 400 feet of a perfectly distinct, homogeneous and most persistent formation that deserves a name as much as the Berea grit itself, or any other stratum in the Ohio scale, and for which no more suitable name could be found than that which it already bears, viz., Cuyahoga shale.

It consists of light-colored, argillaceous shales, which are often replaced with single courses of fine-grained sandstone, blue in color, and in southern Ohio weathering to a brownish-yellow. As a constant characteristic, there are found through the shales, flattened nodules of impure iron ore, concretionary in origin, and often having white calcareous centers.

By good rights the shale should suffer one more reduction at its lower extremity. Every-where through the State there is found directly above the Berea shale or at a short remove from it, a number of courses of fine-grained stone. These courses are sometimes separated from each other by beds of shale, or they may be compacted into a single stratum. The individual courses also vary greatly in thickness, and in color and general characters. Throughout southern Ohio, and particularly in Ross, Pike and Scioto counties, the stratum yields freestone. It is best known from its outcrops on the Ohio river at Buena Vista, where it has long been very extensively worked for Cincinnati and other river markets. The Buena Vista stone, at its best, is one of the finest building stones of the country. The same horizon yields excellent stone near Portsmouth, Lucasville and Waverly. It is known as the Waverly brown stone at the latter point.

Northward, through the State, stone of more or less value is found in the bottom courses of the Cuyahoga, but in Trumbull county, near Warren, the horizon acquires extreme importance as the source of the finest natural flagging that is found in our markets.

It would have been well if the thirty or forty feet containing these courses had been cut off from the Cuyahoga shale, in which case the division thus formed would have been well named the Buena Vista stone, but inasmuch as the series does not absolutely require the change, it is left unmodified. The Sharpsville sandstone of White (Second Penna. Survey, Q. 4), belongs to this horizon, and is the proper equivalent of the Buena Vista stone.

There are a few sections in which the Cuyahoga shale is more largely

GEOLOGICAL SCALE AND STRUCTURE.   39

replaced by these freestone layers than in the general account above given. In the cuts of the Marietta and Cincinnati Railroad, east from Chillicothe, the freestone appears to constitute a notable proportion, perhaps. fifteen or twenty per cent. of the whole material. There are other points at which the stone has no value.

Under cover the Cuyahoga shale retains with great distinctness and persistency the same characteristics that are found in its outcrops. From the deep drillings of eastern Ohio, wherever its horizon has been reached, there are uniformly reported 300 to 400 feet of white shales with occasional sandstone layers, through which the drill descends rapidly and easily. The Buena Vista courses are also frequently reported directly above, or at least near to, the Berea shale.

The fossils with which the Cuyahoga shale has been credited have been largely derived from the division next to be described, while this was counted a part of the shale. As here limited, it is, for most part, poor in fossils. The surfaces of many of its beds are marked with the impressions of the cock-tail fucoid, and in its upper portions occasional courses are found in which the animal fossils of this age are abundant and well-preserved. Its most interesting fossils are preserved in concretions, as has recently been shown by Prof. C. L. Herrick of Cincinnati University.

11e. *The Logan Group.*

(The Olive Shales of Read. The Logan Sandstone of Andrews. The Waverly , Conglomerate of Andrews.)

The divisions of the Waverly series in northern Ohio happened to be made at a point where the section is abnormal and incomplete. By atrophy or by overlap, the upper member of the series is wanting in the Cuyahoga Valley, or is at least very inadequately represented there. The missing member is in volume second only to the Cuyahoga shale, among the divisions of the Waverly. It is much richer in the fossils of the Sub-carboniferous than any of the other members. In composition it is varied and striking, one of its elements being a massive conglomerate or series of conglomerates, not less than 200 feet in its largest sections, which extends in unbroken outcrop through at least a half dozen counties of Ohio. No good reason can be found for dividing the Waverly series at all, if a member like this is to be left without a name, or is to be merged with an unlike and incongruous division from which it is as sharply differentiated as any one stratum of Ohio is from any other.

The real, though not the formal, separation of this group from the underlying shale, is due to the late Professor E. B. Andrews, and constitutes one of his most important contributions to our knowledge of Ohio geology. He was the first to show that the great conglomerate of Hocking, Fairfield and Licking counties is Sub-carboniferous in age, and he further called attention to a highly fossiliferous, fine-grained sandstone overlying the conglomerate, to which he gave the name of Logan sandstone, from its occurrence at Logan, Hocking county. Up to this time this conglomerate had been universally counted as the Coal Measure conglomerate. Read made known the existence of a heavy body of shale, which he called Olive shales, overlying the conglomerate and replacing the Logan sandstone in Knox, Holmes and Richland counties.

As both conglomerate and sandstone have their typical outcrops at Logan, no better name can be found for the formation which must include conglomerate, sandstone, and shale, than that here adopted, viz., Logan group.

The maximum thickness of the Logan group is not less than 400 feet. Its average thickness is perhaps 200 feet. It has received less study than the rest of the series, and much work is needed in the correlation of its several elements.

A typical or representative section of this group is scarcely possible, but the most characteristic and persistent part of the series is the conglomerate that is found at the bottom. At all events, coarse rock, if not always technically conglomerate, is generally found here. Pebbles do not make a conspicuous part of the rock when it takes a conglomeritic phase, in all cases. The most characteristic feature of the pebbles is their small and uniform size. The larger pebbles are generally flat. There is, however, a good deal of variation in all these respects.

Much of the conglomerate is fairly even in its bedding, and otherwise adapted to quarry purposes. The formation yields in central and southern Ohio quite a large amount of valuable building and bridge stone.

The conglomerate is peculiar in this respect, viz., it is fossiliferous, containing both animal and vegetable fossils. The usual Sub-carboniferous types of both divisions are found in it.

It is interrupted by layers of fine or medium-grained sandstone, and sometimes by shale deposits. In central Ohio; there are two fairly persistent beds of conglomerate as recently shown by Herrick, that can be used in stratigraphical determinations.

The prevailing colors are yellowish, red or brown. Much of it is handsomely variegated.

Its best developments are in Hocking, Fairfield, Ross, Vinton, Licking, Knox and Wayne counties, which constitute the northwestern arc of the sea-boundary of Ohio in Sub-carboniferous time. South of Ross county it loses most of its pebbles, and south of the Ohio it becomes the knobstone of Kentucky. It is also the knobstone of Indiana, at least in part. In northeastern Ohio the Logan group is also destitute of pebbles, and perhaps the conglomerate element proper does not appear here at all.

White gives a generalized section of the rocks of Erie and Crawford counties, Pennsylvania, in Report Q. 4, page 66, of the second Pennsylvania Survey. He shows the presence of six sandstones in the scale, and three of these are common to the Ohio scale as well. The Shenango sandstone of his column is, without doubt, the representative of our Logan sandstone and Waverly conglomerate. His Sharpsville sandstone is our Buena Vista stone, and his Corry sandstone is none other than our persistent and important stratum, the Berea grit. The sandstones of the Pennsylvania column that underlie the Berea grit do not appear as such in the Ohio scale, as has been already shown. By the same token, White's Orangeville shale is the equivalent of our Berea shale, his Meadville shales are our Cuyahoga shale in part, and his Shenango shales are a part of our Logan series.

Interstratified with the conglomerate courses in southern Ohio, are two or more fairly persistent layers of impure limestone. No fossils have been found in them. Similar layers occur in the Logan series of northeastern Ohio, except that in this case the limestones are fossiliferous. They are the Upper and Lower Meadville limetones of White, and can be followed into Ohio from Crawford county, Pennsylvania, where they were first described.

The Logan sandstone that succeeds the Waverly conglomerate in the full section is an uncertain and inconstant element, for the reason that it plays fast and loose with the stratum last described. Much could be said in favor of counting it the upper portion of the conglomerate. In its typical exposures, it is a fawn-colored, fine-grained, even-bedded sandstone. In this phase of the formation, the most favorable conditions for the marine life of the period seem to have been attained, the sandstone being prolific in fossils. The characters above given are quite widely held through the State. The Logan sandstone often rises to the base of the coal series.

The Olive shales of Read are probably the exact equivalent of the Logan sandstone in age. They seem to take its place in the central counties in part. Overlying the coarse rock in Knox and Coshocton counties, Read reports more than 300 feet of sparingly fossiliferous shales to which he gives the name here used.

Diverse as these elements are, they are blended and interlocked in the Logan group, leaving it in stratigraphy and fossils a well-defined and easily followed series throughout all parts of the territory in which it is due, except in possibly a small area in northern Ohio, as already noted, and even here, there is no difficulty in recognizing the pressure of this series. The several elements are, however, of smaller volume than elsewhere.

Under cover, throughout southeastern Ohio, the series is in the highest degree persistent and regular, much more uniform, indeed, than in its outcrops. It consists of 200 feet or more of prevailingly coarse rock almost every-where pebbly in spots, but interrupted with sheets of shale, yellowish and reddish colors being the characteristic ones. It has considerable interest in connection with gas, oil and salt-water in Ohio, being the reservoir of the brines of the Hocking and Muskingum Valleys, and furnishing in the latter large supplies of gas in the early days of salt manufacture in the State. It is also the "Big Indian" sandstone of the oil well drillers of western Pennsylvania.

As stated above, this extensive series of deposits needs much more study, especially in the line of paleontology, before its relations and equivalences can be counted settled. Very valuable and promising contributions to our knowledge of the group have lately been made by Prof. C. L. Herrick of the University of Cincinnati. They are published in the bulletins of the Scientific Laboratories of Dennison University for 1888. In view of Professor Herrick's studies, it seems probable that the Waverly group will admit of distinct divisions on paleontological grounds and that these divisions can be correlated with the leading members of the Sub-carboniferous system in Indiana, Kentucky and the West.*

The Sub-carboniferous series of Ohio has now, with the exception of a single element presently to be named, been passed in review. It is seen to be a very sharply characterized series, a most persistent sandstone, though not a thick one, lying near its base, bedded in shale and covered also by shale, the lower shale being often red in color and the roof shale being always black, and another sandstone or conglomerate stratum, 200 feet or more in thickness, forming the upper member of the series, these two persistent sandstones being separated from each other by 300 or more feet of light-colored, soft, argillaceous shales. No conditions could be more favorable for tracing such a group under ground than the conditions here found, and consequently the records of deep drillings in southern Ohio become almost as clear and legible as if the rocks, through which the drill has passed, lay exposed to the light of day.

12. THE SUB-CARBONIFEROUS LIMESTONE.

This element is of comparatively small account as a surface formation in Ohio, but it gathers strength to the southeastward of its outcrops, and

---

*Professor Herrick's most recent work may be counted as settling the questions raised in these paragraphs on paleontological grounds. He finds the best of reasons for believing that the entire series here named the Logan group overlies the Cuyahoga shale of northern Ohio. His results are extremely interesting and valuable.

GEOLOGICAL SCALE AND STRUCTURE. 43

shown in many well records as a stratum fifty or more feet in thickness. It was recognized as a member of our geological column by the geologists of the first survey, but Andrews was the first to assign it to its proper place and to show its true equivalence. He named it the Maxville limestone, from a locality in southwestern Perry county, where it is well exposed in beds that aggregate fifteen feet in thickness. Still heavier deposits of it he found in the valley of Jonathan's Creek, in Muskingum county, near Newtonville. He collected fossils by which its age was shown to be about that of the Chester limestone of the Missouri and Illinois sections.

The limestone, in its best development, is a fairly ·pure, very fine-grained, sparingly fossiliferous rock. It breaks with a conchoidal fracture. In fineness and homogenity of grain it approaches lithographic stone and has been tested in the small way for this special use. It is seldom even and regular in its bedding. Its color is light drab or brown, and often it is a beautiful building stone, though somewhat expensive to work. The fire-clay found at this horizon in southern Ohio is one of the most valuable deposits of this sort in our entire scale. The limestone is found in outcrop in Scioto, Jackson, Hocking, Perry and Muskingum counties. It is reported in the well records of Steubenville, Brilliant, Macksburg, and at several other points in the Ohio Valley.

There remains to be briefly described, with reference to its gas and oil-producing properties, the great Carboniferous system of Ohio. An extended and careful review of its composition, as understood at the present time, is given in Geology of Ohio, Volume V, and consequently it will be enough at this point to call to mind its more salient features. In the review in Volume V, the Conglomerate series of Pennsylvania was included with the Lower Coal Measures, though the boundaries of each were shown to be clearly recognizable here. There are, however, less imperative grounds for the separation in Ohio than in Pennsylvania and the Virginias, and if only the Ohio series were to be classified, it is not probable that the divisions would have been made. But they stand for great and conspicuous facts elsewhere, and it probably would have been better to have maintained them in our territory also. The separation will be recognized in this review.

13. THE CONGLOMERATE GROUP.

This group consists of three great sandstones, between which and in which, are distributed two thin but persistent limestones and four coal seams of considerable value. The order is shown in the table below. A fifth coal seam is occasionally found.

Conglomerate group.
{
HOMEWOOD SANDSTONE.
(Tionesta coal.)
Upper Mercer Group. { Ore. Limestone. Coal.
Lower Mercer Group. { Ore. Limestone. Coal, No. 3, Newberry.
MASSILLON SANDSTONE, UPPER.
(Quakertown Coal.)
MASSILLON SANDSTONE, LOWER.
Sharon coal—Coal No. 1, Newberry.
SHARON COMGLOMERATE.
}

This group has an average aggregate thickness of 250 feet. At least, this figure need not mislead the student of our geology, though the range is great. It has some importance as a source of gas and oil in a few localities, as will hereafter appear.

14. THE LOWER COAL MEASURES.

This division includes for Ohio the most important section of the Coal Measures. In it are found six seams of coal, four horizons of limestone, including the most important of the Coal Measure limestones, viz., the Ferriferous, and several valuable iron ores and fire-clays. Its interest in the present connection is, however, chiefly confined to its sandstone ledges, four of which attain to fair development and extension. They are, in ascending order, the Hecla sandstone, immediately underlying the Ferriferous limestone, and mainly confined to the southwestern boundary of the coal field; the Kittanning sandstone, also mainly confined to the southwestern part of the coal field, and lying betwen the two Kittanning coals; the Lower Freeport sandstone, quite massive, and in a number of counties distinctly conglomeritic; the Upper Freeport sandstone, less massive and important in Ohio, but still a persistent deposit. Some of these sandstones probably take a small part in gas or oil production in a few fields.

15. THE LOWER BARREN MEASURES.

No detailed account of this section, nor of Nos. 16 and 17, need be given here. There is but one sandstone in all of these divisions that is known to be important in connection with the subjects of the present chapter. This is the Mahoning sandstone, a massive and conglomerate ledge at the base of the Lower Barren Measures. It produces quite an amount of petroleum in several fields of Ohio, particularly from its upper division which is also known as the Buffalo sandstone.

GEOLOGICAL SCALE AND STRUCTURE. 45

18. THE GLACIAL DRIFT.

Over the various bedded rocks of at least two-thirds of Ohio are spread in varying thickness the deposits of the Drift, the most characteristic and important of which is the Bowlder clay. This frequently contains in its lower portions large accumulations of vegetable matter, the remains of coniferous forests that occupied the country before the advent of the Drift, or at some interglacial stage of its duration. Peat bogs are sometimes found buried in like manner in or under the bowlder clay. Thus the latest of our geological formations, as well as the earliest, contains materials that can give rise to supplies of inflammable gas.

II. THE GEOLOGICAL STRUCTURE OF OHIO.

The geological structure of Ohio is as simple as that of almost any other 40,000 square miles of the earth's surface. As already shown all of its strata except a small portion of the Coal Measures, were deposited in the waters of an ancient arm of the sea, of which the present Gulf of Mexico is the dwarfed and diminished remnant and representative. Its most fossiliferous limestones, as the Corniferous, for example, stand for clear waters of tropical warmth. Its conglomerates and sandstones required strong currents for their transportation from distant shores. Its shales must have been deposited in seas of at least moderate depth, large areas of which, as well as all of the shores were covered with sargasso-like masses of sea-weed.

These strata seem to have been deposited on a fairly regular and level floor, and they have never been subjected to very great disturbance, that is, they have nowhere been raised into mountains nor depressed into deep valleys, but still they have been warped and distorted to some extent in the course of their long history.

In the southeastern quarter of the State are a few anticlinal arches, all of which, however, are very gentle and low, and none of which can be traced for many miles in the direction in which they extend. They involve all of the strata that belong in the district in which they are found. A modification of the arch resulting in a terrace-like arrangement of the strata, is one of the most important phases of the structure in this portion of the State. In southwestern Ohio, the structure is exceedingly simple and easily read, so far as now appears. The movements to which this section of the State have been subjected, are as small as is consistent with their ready recognition and measurement.

Less is known of the structure of northeastern Ohio, and especially of the lake counties from Cuyahoga county eastward, than of any other quarter of the State. This fact is due in part, possibly, to the want of recognizable horizons in those counties from which dip can be readily calculated. In the shale formation that prevails here, and which attains a thickness of a thousand feet or more, there are but few marks known by which we can follow particular horizons from point to point without the aid of directly connected outcrops, such for example, as are found in the walls of a gorge. The upper and lower boundaries of the shale wherever they can be reached, give every needed opportunity for such measurements. The lower boundary is the Upper Helderberg limestone, and this has been used in all the sections in which it is available. It is known to have been reached at Elyria, Cleveland, Massillon, Akron, Wadsworth and at other points on the lake shore. Further back from the lake we obtain in the Berea grit an excellent horizon to follow in tracing the disposition of the strata. By means of it an important flexure has been brought to light.

The surface of northwestern Ohio is much more nearly level than that of either of the sections already reviewed. It constitutes a great plain, which is covered, and often heavily covered with drift, deposits that entirely obscure the underlying rock for scores and hundreds of square miles. Up to a recent date it was not known that the underlying rock failed to share the monotony of the surface, but the explorations of the last four years have revealed the surprising fact that the rocky floor of the "black swamp" of old time is characterized by far greater irregularity of structure and by far greater suddenness and steepness of dip than the strata of any other portion of Ohio. The entire floor of northwestern Ohio, including the lake counties, as far east as Lorain county, is seen to lie in a disturbed and uneasy condition. It is not uncommon to find the rocks descending at an angle of two to ten degrees, but the descent is not, as a rule, long continued, and all of these irregularities are subordinate to, and included in the main dip of the strata.

The structure of the State can best be studied by taking one-half of it at a time. The western, or older half, will be first considered. The dominant feature in the structure and physical history of Western Ohio, is the so-called Cincinnati anticlinal. A number of facts pertaining to this will now be given.

1. THE CINCINNATI ANTICLINAL.

As soon as the geology of the Mississippi Valley began to be studied, it became apparent that there had been in early time an extensive uplift of the older rocks in the central parts of Tennessee and Kentucky and

GEOLOGICAL SCALE AND STRUCTURE. 47

n southwestern Ohio which had exerted a profound influence on all the subsequent growth of the regions traversed by and adjacent thereto. This uplift has received several designations, but the name given to it by Newberry, viz., *The Cincinnati anticlinal* or uplift, will here be adopted, inasmuch as this geologist has furnished by far the most careful and connected account that has yet been given of it.

It is to be recognized, however, that this structural feature has in it little or nothing of the character of an anticlinal or arch, as these terms are commonly understood. There is no roof-shaped arrangement of the strata whatever, but they are spread out in a nearly level tract, 100 miles or more in breadth. The slopes within the tract are very light and are quite uniform in direction, and the boundaries of the tract are well defined, as a rule.

This Trenton limestone, as has already been shown, makes the floor of western Ohio. By means of the deep drilling that has been carried on throughout this part of the State, we have obtained soundings to this limestone floor so extensive that we are already able to restore approximately its topography.

The underground disposition of the Trenton limestone becomes very significant in connection with the Cincinnati uplift. In fact, it *is* the Cincinnati uplift; and the study of the facts pertaining to it will be found to throw more light on this earliest and most important structural feature of the State than can be obtained from any and from all other sources. Some of the results of these recent explorations are unexpected. A few of the principal points that are now established will be stated here.

1. Instead of bearing uniformly to the northeast, as the facts available to us before the deep drilling of the last few years was undertaken seemed to show, the Cincinnati uplift bears to the northwest, so far as the highest lying regions of the Trenton limestone are concerned. The lines of level bearing in this formation are approximately northwest lines. Starting from Point Pleasant, where the sole outcrop of the Trenton limestone in Ohio is found at an elevation of about 450 feet above tide, the line of slowest descent passes through Clermont, Hamilton and Butler counties to the Indiana boundary, and thence through Union, Fayette, Wayne, Henry, Delaware, Madison and Grant counties, of the last named State. The Trenton limestone descends but about 500 feet in this entire line, but at its termination it descends with some abruptness to the southwestward and also to the northward. If a similar line were to be followed from Point Pleasant an equal distance due northward its descent would be nearly 2,000 feet, or four times as much as in a northwesterly direction. If the line should be drawn northeastward from Point Pleasant, in the direction in which the Cincinnati axis has hereto-

fore been held to extend, the descent would again be found to be 2,00 feet.

The apparent easterly trend of the Cincinnati uplift which appears in the surface limestones of northern and central Ohio, is found not to be due to a flexure of the rocks as was naturally supposed at first, but to a considerable thickening of the great shale series that underlies the Upper Silurian limestone. The Medina, Hudson River and Utica shales which are generally counted together in their underground sections, reach twice as great a measure in the counties due south of Toledo, for example, as they have in the counties on the western boundary of the State.

2. In the second place, it is to be noted, that a northeasterly offshoot from the main uplift is found in the Trenton limestone of western central Ohio. It enters the State from Indiana in Darke county, and holds a northeast course from the point of beginning through Lima to Findlay. At this point the uplift bends abruptly and bears due north or a little west of north to the Michigan boundary, which it reaches near Sylvania. The northeasterly portion of this tract may be named the Lima axis. It is twenty to thirty miles wide at its narrowest portion, and the deep floor of the Trenton limestone lies very nearly level throughout this entire area. The descent in any direction is often found to be less than five feet to the mile.

The structure at Findlay is that of a well-marked monocline, descending to the westward, and often at the rate of one foot in eight, for 1,000 to 1,200 feet of horizontal distance. The break can be traced with perfect distinctness to the north of Findlay, passing a little westward of Van Buren, North Baltimore, Bowling Green, Monclova and Sylvania.

3. In Sandusky and Ottawa counties there is a two-forked axis of no great force, that extends from the vicinity of Fremont northward to the lake shore. This axis is plainly shown on the geological map of the State, the surface formations revealing distinctly the conditions of the underlying Trenton limestone. The map was made in 1871–2, and the existence of the two-pronged axis was noted at that time, but of course no suspicion existed as to the facts of recent development. One fork of the axis gives rise to the Gibsonburg oil and gas field, and the other supplies the gas that has been struck at Oak Harbor and elsewhere in the vicinity. The last of these arches has been found to lie 700 feet below tide. It is of small extent, so that the gas wells that are found in it are rather speedily overrun by salt water. The Gibsonburg oil and gas rock lies about 600 feet below tide. At Tiffin also several flexures have been found by the driller, but none of them have any large extent. They have proved effective in the differentiation of oil, gas and salt water, but the reservoirs have been found to be very small.

4. A local elevation of the Trenton limestone of small force has been found by the drill in Williams county, in the vicinity of Bryan and Edgerton. The relief of the rock is but slight and the quantity of gas or oil contained in it is accordingly small. This so-called elevation may be in fact only the normal extension of the limestone from the southward, while the relief may have been caused by a trough of depression that passes through Fulton county to the eastward, as shown by the drilling at Wauseon. On the western edge of the trough, there is possibly the effect of an uplift. The facts from this part of the State are too few to allow any large or confident generalizations.

In the preceding statements the structure of the western half of the State has been considered, the disposition of the Trenton limestone being taken as the determining factor. The opportunities for using this stratum in such a study are of recent date and are not likely to be soon repeated. It is probable that the larger features of the arrangement of this universally extended sheet have been already brought to light, but wherever exploration by the drill goes forward minor phases of structure of more or less interest will always be disclosed. The geological work that has been carried on in the northwestern counties of the State during the last four years has revealed an amount of disturbance of this minor sort for which we were not prepared. The southwestern quarter of Ohio is characterized by exceptionally regular structure, but there are very few rock outcrops of any considerable extent in the northern counties that do not betray flexures and disturbances on the small scale already noted. The rocks everywhere lie in an uneasy condition, in striking contrast with the monotonous features of the central and southern portions of the State adjacent to them.

STRUCTURE OF EASTERN OHIO.

The structure of Eastern Ohio can not be referred to the same base as that used in the western half of the State. The Trenton limestone sinks out of practicable reach before the middle line of the State is passed.

An easterly or southeasterly dip of the rocks begins at the margin of the tract that has been described as the Cincinnati axis and continues through the subsequent history of the State, constituting the most important physical feature of its geology. All of the Sub-carboniferous and Coal Measure strata, in particular, are affected by it. The southerly element of it gradually increases as we pass to northeastern Ohio, and it is probable that the dip becomes due south at some points in this portion of the State. Beyond the limits of Ohio, in Pennsylvania and West Virginia, the corresponding strata descend sharply toward the westward.

4   G.

These facts considered together mark out the limits of the arm of the sea in which, and around which, the northern extension of the Appalachian coal-field was built up, the Cincinnati axis forming its western boundary. These uniform and continuous southeasterly dips can be explained by the steady growth of the westward-lying land, after the fashion already described. The dip is at right angles to the constantly advancing border of the sea. It seldom exceeds thirty feet to the mile, or but little more than half a degree in the large way, but it is alternately sharpened and reduced, so that for short distances a much greater fall, or much less, may be found.

The facts of our present topography seem to point to an original equality of elevation of those portions of the State that were successively brought under this uplifting force. The western outliers of all of the formations are at the present time at least at approximately the same elevation above the sea.

The general regularity of structure that has been repeatedly affirmed for the State is not inconsistent with the existence of a few minor folds and arches distributed through the eastern half of its area.

Beginning at Columbiana county on our eastern border, a low axis is found entering the State from western Pennsylvania. It crosses the Little Beaver River a few miles above its mouth near Fredericktown and has been named from this town by Prof. I. C. White of the Pennsylvania Survey, who was the first to indicate and describe it. It is probably this axis that enters the valley of the Ohio near East Liverpool and that makes the conspicuous arch between that place and Wellsville.

Another light fold is found along the line of the Cleveland and Pittsburgh Railroad. Its elevation is small and its extent has not been traced. The highest point of this arch on the line named is near Salisbury, and it may be named from this fact the Salisbury anticlinal.

Below Steubenville for a few miles there is an arrest of normal dip which has the effect and is probably the result of a low fold. The now extinct Wellsburg gas field is located in this region and probably depended on the structure already indicated.

A gentle anticline of considerable longitudinal extent passes through Harrison county. It may be designated the Cadiz anticline from the fact that it was first recognized and tested near this town. Stevenson called attention to it in his report on Harrison county in the third volume of the Second Geological Survey, but within the last three years, considerable money has been invested in developing the arch as a possible gas or oil field. Details of this practical exploration will be found on a subsequent page. This arch probably crosses the line of the Baltimore and Ohio Railway near Quaker City, but it is of very small force at this point or indeed any where through its extent as far as followed. To the northeastward, the Cadiz anticline may become the low Salisbury anticline already named. Possibly also it gives rise further to the southwest to the Macksburg oil field.

In Belmont county some weak uplifts of the same general sort as those already described have been located in the work of searching for gas and oil. The Cadiz anticline possibly shows itself near Barnesville. But in a general way, the structure is exceedingly monotonous, the strata descending to the southeastward with a slow and very regular dip.

A somewhat more conspicuous uplift crosses the line of the Baltimore and Ohio Railway in Guernsey county. It has long been known as the Cambridge arch or anticline, being first pointed out by Professor Stevenson in the reports of the Second Survey. A large amount of practical exploration has been carried forward on this line, the results of which will be described on a later page.

In Washington county, the Cow Run anticline is a distinct and more effective arch than any which have thus far been described. The strongest development of it, however, is found south of the Ohio River.

The Macksburg anticline has been by far the most effective thus far found in southeastern Ohio in the way of oil and gas accumulation. It has already been suggested that it may be the prolongation of the same slight fold that crosses Harrison county, viz., the Cadiz anticline. The structural feature here named the Macksburg anticline can be so called only by a considerable extension of the term. It is a terrace rather than an arch. The strata that are descending regularly to the southeastward are interrupted in their descent for a tract that is a mile or more in breadth and this tract is almost a dead level. On its higher edge dry gas was found in good volume. On the terrace itself a valuable oil field has been already worked out, while on the lower border, an ocean of salt water holds possession of the rock. The credit for the recognition of this very important feature in the structure of oil and gas fields belongs to Mr. F. W. Minshall, of Marietta. He discovered it in the particular field now under consideration. The terrace structure prevails in the great oil fields of northwestern Ohio. It would, no doubt, be found in some at least of the Pennsylvania fields if data for the determination were] at hand. The famous Bradford field would probably exhibit this feature. In fact, it seems probable that the terrace rather than the arch is the essential feature in all large oil fields.

NORTHEASTERN OHIO.

There is a district of the State bordering Lake Erie and extending at furthest one or two counties back from the lake that deserves to be treated

GEOLOGY OF OHIO.

by itself in this connection. The predominant element in the geological section is the Ohio shale, a thousand feet thick in at least a part of this territory.

The difficulty of determining the dip in the shale series of northeastern Ohio has been already pointed out. It arises from the absence of easily recognized horizons in this formation. In the ravines and gorges by which the shales are traversed, opportunities are often afforded to follow particular beds or bands for a mile or two, thus rendering it possible to note their flexures, but it is only when the Berea grit above the shales is reached or when the drill strikes the Devonian limestones underneath them that we acquire horizons clear and trustworthy enough to be used in large and connected calculations of the dip in which all the strata share. The Berea grit is used in all cases where it occurs. In Lorain, Erie and Huron counties particularly, the local disturbances involving this formation are numerous and considerable. There are but few of the sandstone quarries in which steep dips are not found, the direction of which sometimes change in a single quarry. It is easy, however, to confuse a true inclination of the series which is attested by the shale sharing the pitch of the Berea sandstone, with the false bedding by which the last-named formation is often marked. The floor on which the sandstone was deposited was in many places irregular, having been made so doubtless by erosion, and the sand was laid down in sharply pitching beds. There is a great display of this mode of origin in the region already named.

There is, however, a ridge of high-lying Berea sandstone that runs parallel to the shore of Lake Erie, though distant from it thirty or more miles, that demands a brief consideration. The sections that have been obtained from the lake southward, which involve the continuity of the Berea grit, bring to view a low arch along this line. At Mecca the stratum (base) is about 925 feet above tide. At Akron it has nearly the same elevation, 910 to 930 feet. At Shelby it is 945 feet, and Plymouth, Huron county, about 996 feet above tide.

The uplift has been noticed before, and an attempt has been made to explain it by an assumed thickening of the underlying shale series. Where the sandstone lies highest, viz.: at Plymouth, the shales are thinner by 150 feet than they are at Elyria on the lake shore, where the Berea grit is 300 feet lower than at Plymouth. The only explanation of the facts that appear adequate, is the obvious one that a low anticlinal extends from Shelby through Akron to Mecca, in a line about N. 70° E.

It is this Akron arch that constitutes the watershed of northern Ohio for at least a part of its extent. It also seems to provide a natural

GEOLOGICAL SCALE AND STRUCTURE. 53

southern boundary for Lake Erie. The lake basin would, according to this view, be a syncline.

It must be acknowledged, however, that we have not yet facts enough to fully establish the continuity of the fold that is here suggested. The points from which measurements are reported are so far apart that there is room between them for depressions in the stratum on which we rely.

To sum up the statements now made, we know but comparatively few arches in Ohio, and these few are moderate in slope and small in height. Fuller knowledge of our geology will doubtless give us a larger number of these low folds, but there is little probability that any sharp and well defined anticlinals have altogether escaped notice. Those that remain to be discovered will agree with those already known, in breaking up the monotony of our series by the suspension or occasional reversal of the prevailing dip and in requiring close and accurate measurements for their detection.

By untrained observers, the watersheds of our drainage channels are often mistaken for anticlinals. If anticlinals traverse the series where these identifications are made, they may well serve to divide the drainage systems from each other, but such "divides" do not by any means require these structural accidents as the conditions on which they depend. Anticlinals must be demonstrated, not inferred.

The problems of our geology in this field are dependent on the use of the level. Accurate and connected series of elevations of well-settled horizons are indispensable to their solution. In the First Geological Survey of the State, Whittlesey recognized the need of physical determinations of the various elements of our coal fields in particular, and he began at that time a valuable series of measurements, but his work was of necessity hampered by a want of well-determined geological horizons. The essential facts of identification of strata, without which the most careful measurements are futile, could only be secured by the prolonged study and the economical development of the field, the latter by means of the introduction of railway lines and the utilization of its minerals on a large scale.

This work of development has now been carried forward on both the scientific and the economic sides to such a point that definite solutions of many of the questions of our structural geology are easily attainable.

There are but few districts known in Ohio in which disturbances are to be found that fairly deserve the name of faults. In the northeast corner of Adams county and in adjacent territory, there are a number of square miles throughout which the strata are really dislocated. The

Berea grit is found in contact with the Niagara shale in some instances. The throw of such faults must be at least 400 feet. Faults of this character in Ohio geology are as unusual and unexpected as trap dykes in northern Kentucky, the latter of which have been recently reported by Crandall (Ky. Geol. Survey). An account of the Adams county fault will be found in a succeeding chapter.

. In Geology of Ohio, Vol. V, page 262, mention was made of a small area of disturbance in the vicinity of Mineral Point, Tuscarawas county. The Findlay monocline has been referred to already, and will be further described in a subsequent chapter.

The account of our structural geology, here given, seems called for in this connection by reason of the prominence that is given to anticlinals in the discussion and discovery of the recent natural gas supply of western Pennsylvania. The great wells upon which Pittsburgh depends are unquestionably located on the summits of pronounced folds. This fact has lead to an eager inquiry in regard to similar folds in Ohio. The answer to such inquiries is that folds similar and equal to the great anticlinals of western Pennsylvania and West Virginia were never formed and consequently will never be found in Ohio. Our supply of this much-prized and eagerly-sought fuel, whatever it shall prove to be, must be independent of any conspicuous and easily-traced folds in our surface rocks.

CHAPTER II.

ORIGIN AND ACCUMULATION OF PETROLEUM AND NATURAL GAS.

If one were asked what subject of Ohio geology commands the largest amount of popular consideration and interest at the present time, the answer would not be hard to find. The subjects of natural gas and petroleum hold decidedly the leading place. The discovery and the development of seams of coal, or of beds of iron-ore, have occasionally aroused great interest in particular districts or neighborhoods of the State, especially when the discoveries have been unexpected; but never before has there been found any line of geological questions that has awakened one-hundredth part of the general interest and inquiry which has been bestowed upon the subjects of gas and oil within the last ten years in Ohio. The interest, in fact, has grown to be universal. There is scarcely a township of the State that it has not invaded. In entire sections, as northwestern Ohio, embracing several thousand square miles of continuous territory, there is not a township in which schemes for drilling wells to test the territory have not been agitated; and in a number of counties every township has been actually tested by the drilling of one or more deep wells. There is no population so stolid or unprogressive as to resist the introductions of these questions; and the discussions arising from their introduction have contributed in a wonderful degree to the general diffusion of geological information. Since this excitement began to spread, the most intelligent and wakeful-minded citizens of many of our communities have acquired a great deal of sound knowledge as to the order and character of the strata directly underlying the several districts of the State, and in many instances they have developed a good degree of sagacity in the interpretation of the strata and structure of their own sections. On the part of all such persons there has been a great demand for all available geological literature. The earlier publications of the State Geological Survey have been taken down from the shelves where they long have gathered dust, and the scattered volumes of the series have been made into numerous complete sets. The more recent publications of the Survey, as the Preliminary Report of 1886, and Vol. VI, which was published in 1888, both of which are entirely devoted to these subjects, have been eagerly taken up and studied in all sections of the State. To meet this growing demand for information, the newspapers and journals have also devoted a good deal of space to facts and theories pertaining to these subjects.] ¡These latter sources of information are, however, compiled without discrimination, as a rule, and consequently, exaggerated and erroneous ‚statements abound in the facts that they present, while the theories which find the largest currency are apt to be crude and ill-grounded. But the interest in the subjects is undoubtedly kept alive by these agencies. The search for oil and gas is not going on as widely or as enthusiastically at the present time as in some recently preceding years; but the interest awakened by the discoveries of the last decade has not as yet ebbed to any great extent. It, therefore, seems proper and necessary to recognize and provide for this interest in the present report. This second chapter will accordingly be devoted to considerations pertaining to the nature and origin of petroleum and gas and to the modes of their accumulation that are found in operation in the rocks of the earth's crust.

1. CHEMICAL COMPOSITION OF THE BITUMENS.

Natural gas and petroleum belong in a line of products in the crust of the earth, to which we give the name of bitumens. Other bodies in the same list are the extremely volatile naptha, and the semi-fluid maltha, or mineral tar, and the solid asphalt. Still other gradations are sometimes recognized as mineral pitch and mineral wax. It is impossible to draw a definite line of demarkation between the last-named bodies of this list. All unquestionably have a similar general history, though some qualification may be made for natural gas, which has possibly distinct sources in nature. These substances are found under the same general conditions, and all the steps of the transformation of one to the other, as from petroleum to asphalt, can be often noted. They are technically known as hydro-carbons, and they belong principally to the methane series. Carbon constitutes about eighty-five per cent., and hydrogen about thirteen per cent. of their general composition. A small percentage of oxygen appears in all and occasionally a minute amount of nitrogen is found and varying, but small percentages of sulphur also occur in all or at least in most petroleums. When sulphur occurs in the form of sulphureted hydrogen, it gives to the oils or gas that contain it a pronounced and offensive odor.

2. EARLY HISTORY OF THE BITUMINOUS SERIES.

These bituminous substances, especially in the form of asphalt, have been known to mankind very widely and from the earliest times. The Egyptians made considerable use of asphalt, particularly in the embalming of their dead. They derived their supply, according to the old notices, from the Dead Sea.

Another ancient use of asphalt and mineral pitch that we can definitely trace is to be found in the ancient cities of Mesopotamia. Asphalt is shown to have been generally used as a mortar in both the sacred and profane structures of Babylon. All the earliest histories refer to this use of asphaltic material, and even the fountains from which the supplies were derived have been definitely pointed out. Herodotus gives many particulars in regard to this production. References to asphalt, under the name of pitch and slime, occur also in the earliest Hebrew literature. Noah is said to have covered the ark within and without with pitch, and the reed cradle in which the child Moses was exposed in the Valley of the Nile was protected from the invasion of water by the pitch with which it was coated. In the building of the Tower of Babel also, slime or pitch is said to have been largely used for mortar; and, again, the slime pits of the Vale of Siddim are mentioned in a single passage. The bituminous series was also used in very early times as a medicinal remedy or application, as many references testify.

The gaseous form of the series also attracted attention at an early date. The Apsheron Peninsula, which is so famous in later time as the source of the Baku oil, gives rise to many escapes of gas that can be ignited and which will continue to burn, in some cases, for a long time. As early as the sixth century, the fire worshipers of Persia are known to have had a temple established over one of these gas vents, in which a perpetual fire from these natural sources was maintained. It is even believed by some that Zoroaster himself established the worship of sacred fire at this very point.

India, China and Japan are also known to have developed sources of these substances in very early times, and to have continued their use even to the present day. Gas is said to have been discovered in China more than 2,000 years ago in the drilling of salt wells in the interior, and the gas was turned to economic account in the evaporation of the brine at this early time. Petroleum has been well known in Japan for more than one thousand years. In European countries also, there are numerous centers from which small production has been maintained for long periods of time. Italy and Galicia may be named as representatives. In both of these countries petroleum derived from natural springs has been turned to some small account as a source of light and heat from a time to which the memory of man does not go back.

In the United States also, the occurrence of petroleum and gas have been noted for a very long time. The earliest authentic reference is found in the letter of a Franciscan monk, who briefly described the since famous oil spring of Cuba, Allegany county, New York. His letter bears date 1629. The Aborigines valued these products of the natural oil springs very highly for medicinal application.

The petroleum springs of Oil Creek, Pennsylvania, also attracted early attention. Mention was made of them in letters and reports directed to the old world more than a hundred years ago. In other parts of the North American Continent similar observations have been made, and especially around the shores of the Gulf of Mexico and in the islands pertaining thereto. This last named source is a conspicuous one. Asphalt, tar and crude oil, one or all, have long been known as occurring in Cuba, Barbadoes and Trinidad, and in fact in many other localities.

These references to the early and long-continued use of the several substances belonging to the bituminous series have been made to show how erroneous is the popular opinion which counts the utilization of petroleum and its derivaties as a modern discovery. It has been shown that crude oil has been employed for light and fuel for many hundred years in Europe and Asia, and that inflammable gas derived from and associated with the oil has been burned for perhaps two thousand years in China and in the Caspian Basin; while various applications and uses of mineral pitch and asphalt are co-eval with the oldest records of civilization, and which very likely antedate these records. The other continents doubtless possess like accumulations of these substances, but they have not to so large an extent fallen under the observations of civilized man.

3. Distribution of the Bitumens.

It has been shown incidentally, at least, that very many and widely separated regions give rise to these several bituminous products. Each of the northern continents has in turn been shown to contain one or other of the series in quantity, and the geological range of these substances has been found to be as wide as is their geographical distribution. They occur in rocks of all but one of the great divisions of geological time. From the oldest division, viz., the crystalline schists, the quartzites, slates and granites that make the foundations of all the continents, they are mainly or wholly wanting, and they are also wanting, as a rule, in formations of later age that have been metamorphosed in the process of mountain making. But in all unaltered strata, from the Paleozoic age to the present time, in shales, sandstones and limestones, petroleum is found in greater or less amount. Distributed in minute proportions through the substances of the rocks, it may easily escape notice; but when intelligently looked for, and with proper means for its detection, its presence is revealed, and though the percentage is small, the aggregate is often vast. If, for example, a stratum carries but one-tenth of one per cent. of petroleum, the presence of this substance may be very easily overlooked; but if such stratum is a few hundred feet in thickness, every square mile of its surface, even with this proportion, will be found to contain more oil than has ever been taken out from a like area of the most productive field. Disseminated petroleum is well-nigh universal; it is only the accumulations that are rare.

4. LATER HISTORY OF PETROLEUM AND ITS DERIVATIVES.

After all has been said as to the wide use that has been made of the bitumens from the earliest times, it still remains true that the important history of oil and gas all belongs to our own day. The modern development of these substances began in this country with the present century. Oil and gas were first found here in large quantity in connection with the search for brine to be used in salt manufacture, derived from wells drilled deep into the rocks. The art of drilling salt wells was originated in the valley of the great Kanawha River, and gas and oil, one or both, were invariably found associated with the brine. For both of these substances a small use was soon found; but the large production that was sometimes afforded interfered with the main purpose of the wells and was therefore counted a nuisance to be abated, or if this were impossible, it might even become a serious misfortune to the well driller.

It is not necessary to trace the slow stages by which the real value of petroleum came at last to be recognized. This took place at about the middle of the century; but it was not until 1858 that a well was drilled, the sole object of which was to develop as large a production of oil as possible. This well was located in the valley of Oil Creek, Pennsylvania, in the immediate vicinity of the springs that had yielded oil from time immemorial. The exploration was carried on under the personal direction of Col. E. F. Drake. The search was successful, and the production of petroleum on the large scale dates from this time. The Drake Well marks the beginning of one of the most important economic movements of the century. From this new supply of light and power, very large additions have been made to the comfort and service of the civilized world. Some of the great fortunes of our day, also, which are greater than any ever gathered in any previous age, have been derived directly or indirectly from the new production, and the largest and most successful of the business combinations which make so important a feature of our time is founded on this same interest.

The introduction of natural gas on a large scale, as a source of domestic and manufacturing fuel, constitutes the latest, and perhaps on the whole, the most important chapter in this remarkable history. Natural gas is not so important in itself, however, as in the relations which it bears to the replacement of solid by gaseous fuel. It is educating many of our most progressive communities to the unspeakable advantages of the gaseous form of heat and power. It is to be hoped and expected that when the sources of natural gas fail, the cities that have enjoyed the wonderful advantages which it always brings will be led to devise practicable methods for maintaining the use of gaseous fuel in some other form. It will be a long step backward if the systems of distribution and use of the natural product that have been laid at such great expense, shall be abandoned the moment the necessarily short-lived reservoirs run dry. But these unfavorable results do not seem probable at the present time. There is great interest in all questions pertaining to the manufacture of gas for fuel purposes, and expensive experiments are going forward on the large scale, out of which we are certain to learn what are the most available substances and processes for the replacement of the gas wells of the several fields as they reach exhaustion.

5. Origin of Petroleum and Gas.

What is the mode of origin of petroleum and gas? From what substances and by what agencies in nature are they formed? To these questions it is not possible at the present time to give answers which will command any thing like universal acceptance in the scientific world. In other words, we have not yet attained full, accurate and final knowledge upon these subjects. While the same thing can be said of most of the questions which geology raises, it is still true that at present there is more discrepancy in the views of those who have a right, by reason of their knowledge, to form opinions upon these questions than in most other fields of inquiry. Widely divergent theories have more or less currency in the scientific world, but after all the case is not as discouraging as might at first sight appear. An examination of the leading theories that have been broached during the last twenty-five years, shows that they are divisible into two main classes: those, viz., (1) that have been originated by chemists and that are based on assumed chemical possibilities, with but little knowledge of or reference to the facts of their geological occurrence; and (2) those that have been deducted by geologists from a study of the facts of their occurrence and association. These classes of theories can be conveniently distinguished as chemical and geological theories, though as a matter of course, chemical laws are in every way as directly concerned in the process to which the second group of theories appeals as in the process of the first group. Each of these classes of theories, will be briefly discussed.

1. *Chemical Theories.*

Under this head the theories of two celebrated chemists which have obtained wide circulation in our day will be presented. One of them was originated by Berthelot, a distinguished French chemist, and the other by an equally distinguished Russian chemist, viz., Dr. Mendeljeff, of St. Petersburg.

(a) Berthelot published in 1866 a theory which, in his view, was adequate to account for all natural hydrocarbons by the action of chemical force on inorganic matter. He apparently adopted a suggestion of Sir Humphry Davy, which never found currency in the scientific world, viz., that the alkali metals, potassium and sodium, may exist in the interior of the earth in a free or uncombined state. If at considerable depths, they would necessarily have a high temperature; and further, if surface water carrying carbonic acid in solution, as all natural waters do, should find access to them, it is easy to show the chemical reactions by which some of the hydrocarbon series would be generated.

The only solid ground in all this theory is the last point. It is entirely true that various compounds of the bituminous series can be formed artificially. This discovery and others of like character associated with it constitute one of the most marked advances of chemistry. But the remaining elements of the theory, and particularly its main postulate that the alkali metals exist uncombined in the interior of the earth, have never commanded any large acceptance from those whose judgment on such points is best entitled to consideration. In any case, it is altogether unverifiable, and can never advance in the minds of most men beyond the rank of a highly improbable hypothesis.

(b) The second theory to be named in this class was proposed by Dr. Mendeljeff in 1877. It has attracted a much larger share of attention from the scientific world than the theory above described, probably because it seems less inherently improbable in its main features. Moreover, its author is still urging it in various forms on the attention of the world. Particularly he claims that it is in harmony with all the present facts of experience in the great Russian oil field.

Dr. Mendeljeff holds that petroleum is never of organic origin, but is as purely a product of chemical affinity, acting on inorganic substances, as a vein-stone or an ore. A re-statement of his theory was made at considerable length in the presidential address of the Mechanical Science section of the British Association in September, 1889, by Mr. William Anderson. From this re-statement a good synopsis of the theory as apparently now held by the author can be obtained. Correspondence with him in regard to the subject was published in the same connection, in which the special features of his theory were again repeated. Inasmuch as this is by far the most prominent theory of the class to which it belongs, a full account of it will here be given, mainly in the words of Mr. Anderson. If it fails to bear examination there is certainly no hope for any other theory that falls under this head.

"Dr. Mendeljeff commences his essay by the statement that most persons assume, without any special reason, excepting, perhaps, its chemical composition, that naphtha, like coal, has a vegetable origin. He combats this hypothesis, and points out in the first place that naphtha must have been formed in the depths of the earth. It could not have been produced on the surface, because it would have evaporated; nor over a sea-bottom, because it would have floated up and been dissipated by the same means. In the next place he shows that naphtha must have been formed beneath the very site on which it is found; that it could not have come from a distance, like so many other geological deposits, and for the reasons given above, namely, that it could not be water-borne, and could not have flowed along the surface; while in the superficial sands in which it is generally found no one has ever discovered the presence of organized matter in sufficiently large masses to have served as a source for the enormous quantity of oil and gas yielded in some districts; and hence it is most probable that it has risen from much greater depths under the influence of its own gaseous pressure, or floated up upon the surface of water with which it is so frequently associated.

"The oil-bearing strata in Europe belong chiefly to the tertiary or later geological epochs; so that it is conceivable that in these strata, or in those immediately below them, carboniferous deposits may exist, and may be the sources of the oil. But in America and in Canada the oil-bearing sands are found in the Devonian and Silurian formations, which are either destitute of organic remains or contain them in insignificant quantities. Yet, if the immense masses of hydrocarbons have been produced by chemical changes in carboniferous beds equally large masses of solid carboniferous remains must still exist; but of this there is absolutely no evidence, while cases occur in Pennsylvania where oil is obtained from the Devonian rocks underlying compact clay beds on which rest coal-bearing strata. Had the oil been derived from the coal it certainly would not have made its way downwards; much less would it have penetrated an impermeable stratum of clay. The conclusion arrived at is, that it is impossible to ascribe the formation of naphtha to chemical changes produced by heat and pressure in ancient organized remains.

"One of the first indices to the solution of the question lies in the situation of the oil-bearing regions. They always occur in the neighborhood of, and run parallel to, mountain ranges: as, for example, in Pennsylvania, along the Alleghanies; in Russia, along the Caucasus. The crests of the ranges, formed originally of horizontal strata which had been forced up by internal pressure, must have been cracked and dislocated, the fissures widening outwards, while similar cracks must have been formed at the bases of the ranges; but the fissures would widen downwards, and would form channels and cavities, into which naphtha, formed in the depths to which the fissures descended, would rise and manifest itself, especially in localities where the surface had been sufficiently lowered by denudation or otherwise.

"It is in the lowest depths of these fissures that we must seek the laboratories in which the oil is formed; and, once produced, it must inevitably rise to the surface, whether forced up by its own pent-up gases or vapors, or floated up by associated water. In some instances the oil penetrating or soaking through the surface-layers loses its most volatile constituents by evaporation, and in consequence deposits of pitch, of carboniferous shales, and asphalt, take place; in other cases, the oil, impregnating sands at a lower level, is often found under great pressure, and associated with forms of itself in a permanently gaseous state. This oil may be distributed widely, according to the nature of the formations or the disturbances to which they have been subjected; but the presence of petroleum is not in any way connected with the geological age of the oil-bearing strata, it is simply the result of physical condition and of surface structure.

"According to the views of Laplace, the planetary system has been formed from incandescent matter torn from the solar equatorial regions. In the first instance, this matter formed a ring analogous to those which we now see surrounding Saturn, and consisted of all kinds of substances at a high temperature; and from this mass a sphere of vapors, of larger diameter than the earth now has, was gradually separated. The various vapors and gases which, diffused through each other, formed at first an atmosphere round an imaginary centre, gradually assumed the form of a liquid globe, and exerted pressures incomparably higher than those which we experience now at the base of our present atmosphere. According to Dalton's laws, gases, when diffused through each other, behave as if they were separate; hence the lighter gases would preponderate in the outer regions of the vaporous globe, while the heavier ones would accumulate to a larger extent at the central portion; and at the same time the gases circulating from the centre to the circumference would expand, perform work, would cool in consequence, and at some period would assume the liquid or even the solid state, just as we find the vapor of water diffused through our present atmosphere does now. That which is true of changes of physical condition, Henri St. Claire Deville, in his brilliant theory of dissociation, has shown to be equally true with respect to chemical changes; and the cooling of the vapors forming the earth while in its gaseous condition was necessarily accompanied by chemical combinations, which took place chiefly on the outer surface, where oxides of the metals were formed; and, as these are generally less volatile than the metals themselves, they were precipitated on to what there then was of liquid or solid of the earth, in the form of metallic rain or snow, and were again probably decomposed, in part at least, to their vaporous condition. The necessary consequence of this action is that the inner regions of the earth must consist of substances the vapors of which have high specific densities and high molecular weights—that is to say, composed of elements having high atomic weights—and that the heavier elementary substances would collect near the centre, while the lighter ones would be found nearer the surface. Our knowledge of the earth's crust extends but to an insignificant distance; yet, as far as we do know it, we find that the arrangement above indicated prevails. Hydrogen, carbon, nitrogen, oxygen, sodium, magnesium, aluminium, silicon, phosphorus, sulphur, clorine, potassium, calcium—substances whose atomic weights range from one to forty—became condensed, entered into every conceivable combination with each other, and produced substances the specific gravity of which averages about two and one-half, never exceeds four, and are found near the immediate surface of the globe.

" But the mean specific gravity of the earth as determined by Maskelyne, Cavendish, and others, certainly exceeds five, and consequently the inner portion of our globe must be composed of substances heavier than those existing on the surface; and such substances are only to be found among the elements with high atomic weights. The question arises, ' What elements of this character are we likely to find in the depth of the earth?' In the first place, since gases diffuse through each other, a certain proportion of the elements of hight atomic weight will also be found on the surface of the earth. Second, the elements forming the bulk of the earth must be found in the atmosphere of the sun—if, indeed, the earth once formed part of its atmosphere. Of all the elements, iron, with a specific gravity exceeding seven, and with an atomic weight of fifty-six, corresponds best with these requirements, for it is found in abundance on the surface of the earth; and the spectroscope has revealed the very marked presence of iron in the sun, where it must be partly in the fluid and partly in the gaseous state, and consequently iron in large masses must exist in the earth; so that the mean specific gravity of our planet may well be five, the value of which has been determined by independent means.

"It is not easy, however, to define in what condition the mass of iron which exists in the heart of the earth is likely to be. Iron is capable of forming a vast number of combinations, depending on the relative proportion of the various elements present. Thus, in the blast furnace, oxygen, carbon, nitrogen, calcium, silicon and iron are associated, and produced under the action of heat, besides various gases, a carburet of iron and slag, the latter containing chiefly silicon, calcium and oxygen; that is to say, substances similar to those which form the bulk of the earth. But these same elements, if there be an excess of oxygen, will not yield any carburet of iron; and the same result will follow if there be a deficiency of silicon and calcium, because of the large proportion of oxygen which they appropriate. In the same way, during the cooling of the earth, if oxygen, carbon and iron were associated, and if the carbon were in excess of the oxygen, the greater part of the carbon would escape in the gaseous state, while the remaining part would unite with the iron. It is certain that in the heart of the earth there must have been a deficiency of oxygen, because of its low specific gravity; and the argument is supported by the fact that free oxygen and its compounds, with the lighter elements, abound on the surface. Further, it must be presumed that much of the iron existing at great depths must be covered over and protected from oxygen by a coating of slag; so that, taking all these considerations into account, it is reasonable to conclude that deep down in the earth there exists large masses of iron, in part at least in the metallic state, or combined with carbon.

"The above views receive considerable confirmation from the composition of meteoric matter; for it also forms a portion of the solar system, and originated, like the earth, from out of the solar atmosphere. Meteorites are most probably fragments of planets, and a large proportion of them include iron in their composition, often as carbides, in the same form as ordinary cast iron; that is to say, a part of the carbon is free, and a part is in chemical union with the iron. It has been shown, besides, that all basalts contain iron, and basalts are nothing more than lavas forced by volcanic eruptions from the heart of the earth to its surface. The same causes may have led to the existence of combinations of carbon with other metals.

"The process of the formation of petroleum seems to be the following: It is generally admitted that the crust of the earth is very thin in comparison with the diameter of the latter, and that this crust encloses soft or fluid substances, among which the carbides of iron and of other metals find a place. When, in consequence of cooling or some other cause, a fissure takes place through which a mountain-range is protruded, the crust of the earth is bent, and at the foot of the hills fissures are formed; or, at any rate, the continuity of the rocky layers is disturbed, and they are rendered more or less porous, so that surface waters are able to make their way deep into the bowels of the earth, and to reach occasionally the heated deposits of metallic carbides, which may exist either in a separated condition, or blended with other matter. Under such circumstances, it is easy to see what must take place. Iron, or whatever other metal may be present, forms an oxide with the oxygen of the water. Hydrogen is either set free or combined with the carbon which was associated with the metal, and becomes a volatile substance; that is, naphtha. The water which had penetrated down to the incandescent mass was changed into steam, a portion of which found its way to the porous substances with which the fissures were filled, and carried with it the vapors of the newly formed hydrocarbons; and this mixture of vapors was condensed wholly or in part as soon as it reached the cooler strata. The chemical composition of the hydrocarbons produced will depend upon the conditions of temperature and pressure under which they are formed. It is obvious that these may vary between very wide limits; and hence it is that mineral oils, mineral pitch, ozokerite, and similar products differ so greatly from each other in the relative proportions of hydrogen and carbon. I may mention that artificial petroleum has been frequently prepared by a process analogous to that described above.

"Such is the theory of the distinguished philosopher, who has framed it not alone upon his wide chemical knowledge, but also upon the practical experience derived from visiting officially the principal oil-producing districts of Europe and America, from discussing the subject with able men deeply interested in the oil industry, and from collecting all the available literature on the subject. It is needless to remark that Dr. Mendeljeff's views are not shared by every competent authority; nevertheless the remarkable permanence of oil wells, the apparently inexhaustible evolution of hydrocarbon gases in certain regions, almost forces one to believe that hydrocarbon products must be forming as fast as they are consumed, that there is little danger of the demand ever exceeding the supply, and that there is every prospect of oil being found in almost every portion of the surface of the earth, especially in the vicinity of great geological disturbances. The extraordinary pressures, amounting to three hundred pounds per square inch, which have been measured in some wells, seem to me to yield conclusive evidence of the impermeability of the strata from under which the oil has been forced up, and tend to confirm the view that it must have been formed in regions far below any which could have contained organic remains"

Many interesting facts and speculations of science are stated in the paragraphs quoted above, but most of their applications to the production of oil and gas are wide of the mark, so far, at least, as American experience is concerned and particularly as far as they relate to the production of these substances in Ohio. Indeed, we should be obliged to oppose and deny almost every individual statement that is applied to the substances under consideration which these paragraphs contain. "One of the first indices to the solution of the question," Dr. Mendeljeff says, "lies in the situation of the oil-bearing regions. They always occur in the neighborhood of and run parallel to mountain ranges." He then goes on to show that only where the rocks are deeply broken and where fissures penetrate them to great depth, can petroleum find access to the surface.

So far is this from being true, that not a barrel of oil nor a foot of gas is found where the rocks show any trace of such fractures as are here described. There are wide areas in Pennsylvania, for example, adjoining the productive oil fields, in which the rocks have just the structure that is here pointed out; but all of these areas without exception are entirely destitute of gas and oil, so far as present experience goes. It is true that the oil and gas of the Pennsylvania field is found in low arches or folds, and that these arches are approximately parallel to the main folds of the Allegheny Mountains; but the sides of these arches slope, as a rule, less than one degree, and they are found productive only where the movements which have originated them are of the lowest order that could be called movements at all.

When we come to the present productive fields of Ohio, we find neither mountains nor the semblance of mountains within five hundred miles of them. But, instead, the oil and gas flow forth from as nearly level a portion of the earth's surface as is to be found in this entire portion of the Mississippi Valley. The range of elevation for areas of a thousand square miles will not exceed one hundred feet. A single well characterized but deeply buried monocline of less than two hundred feet downthrow, accomplished in one-third of a mile, it is true, traverses the Findlay field, as the drill has shown, and it is found to be connected in a very important way with the accumulation of gas and oil in this district. But in other portions of the new oil territory, as Lima, no such structure is found, and the dip of the oil rock is reduced for many square miles nearly to zero, and in fact, as will afterwards be shown, the horizontal or terrace structure of the reservoir rocks is one of the chief factors in the large accumulation of oil. The slopes, moreover, by which the terraces are bounded are, as a rule, very gentle and regular, never reaching the amount of one degree.

So far as this part of the theory is concerned, it not only fails to conform to American experience, but on the other hand the facts of our experience are diametrically opposed to its postulate.

Again, Dr. Mendeljeff declares that petroleum could not have been produced on the surface of the earth because it would have evaporated; nor on the sea-floor, because it would have floated to the surface and been dissipated there. In these speculations, he ignores the absorbing power of clay which is found on every shore and in every stream that runs into the sea. Dr. Joseph Leidy, the distinguished naturalist, noted a few years ago that the bed of the Schuylkill River within the city limits of Philadelphia was covered by a deposit of dark and oily clay. Upon due investigation, the oil was found to have been derived from the waste of the city gas works. But, as Mendeljeff asserts, we should naturally expect this oil to float upon the surface of the waters to which it found access and there be evaporated. How, then, did it find its way to the bottom of the river and become accumulated there? The answer is that the clay floating in the stream absorbed the oil and sank with it to the river bed, especially in the eddies and slack portions of the current. This observation of Dr. Leidy proves to be of great significance and value in the explanation of petroleum accumulation. It cuts away the ground from under Dr. Mendeljeff's objection and leaves no force to it whatever. Petroleum, whether formed above or beneath the surface of the sea would in every case certainly be absorbed by the floating particles of clay and would thus find its way to a permanent deposit on the sea-floor. The Ohio shale, for example, is the largest clay deposit of our geological column, and it is charged with this disseminated petroleum from top to bottom. We can recover from portions of it at least one-fifth of one percent. of crude oil. In point of fact, petroleum is so widely distributed in nature that we may say that it is absent only from the crystalline rocks and from the broken and fissured strata which the theory now under consideration makes its chief repository. In all other rocks, and especially in all shales and limestones, it is invariably present and can always be detected in them by appropriate means of investigation.

Again, the present theory demands that the storage should be provided for in fissures and rents formed in the rocks. The entire range of the facts of American experience demonstrates the contrary. All accumulation has been abundantly proved to be dependent upon and strictly conditioned by the natural porosity of the rocks that constitute the reservoir. In the earlier and cruder stages of our experience the same notion, that is expressed above, found entrance to the minds of those who were engaged in either the practical or scientific study of the subject, and "fissures" figured largely in the literature of this early time, more especially among the practical men engaged in oil production; but advancing knowledge has swept all this away as entirely destitute of foundation. In every field the fact is demonstrable that the productiveness of the oil rock is gauged by its porosity. This porosity is secured either by the natural character of the material, as in sandstones and conglomerates or crinoidal limestones, or by the acquired characteristics of a formation, as where a bed of true limestone has been converted into a dolomitic limestone. In this last named change small cavities in great numbers are left between the interlocking points of the re-placing crystals, equaling or even greatly exceeding the spaces between grains of sand or pebbles. If caverns and fissures were the store houses, according to the theory now discussed, there would be no need of porous rocks, and the relation already described between them and the productive oil fields would be altogether inexplicable.

When the theory is examined with reference to its remaining relations to dynamic geology, it is found to be equally out of harmony with all modern views. The author seems to have adopted bodily the cruder speculations of an earlier time, many of which have been shown to be entirely untenable and which therefore have no standing in geological science to-day. His discussion, based upon a thin crust of the earth, ignores all the multiplied proofs of the last twenty-five years, that this crust can not be less than 500 to 1,000 miles in thickness, and that it is highly probable that the globe solidified from the center outwards. To speak, as the author does, of a fissure taking place through which a mountain range is protruded, is to adopt ideas as obsolete as the phlogiston theory in chemistry, or the instantaneous and miraculous creation of species in the living world. Such views are entirely irreconcilable with the best knowledge of our day.

The only semblance of foundation that it can borrow from modern geological theories is that part of it which supposes iron to exist uncombined in large quantities at considerable depths beneath the surface of the earth. A few geologists hold some such view, and a measure of support can accordingly be brought forward in favor of it as a theoretical opinion. But as to the existence of carburet of iron in this situation there are no known facts outside of meteorites that point to such a combination. All that part of the theory which, indeed, is the vital part, is pure assumption, and assumption of the sort that can never enter into any explanation which is to obtain acceptance in the modern scientific world. There is a vast preponderance of probability against it, even upon the side from which it draws all its support.

The further statements of Mr. Anderson, in defense of the theory, that "the remarkable permanency of oil fields, and the apparently inexhaustible evolution of hydrocarbon gases in certain regions, almost force one to believe that the hydrocarbon products must be formed as fast as they are consumed, and that there is little danger of the demand ever exceeding the supply," is almost ludicrously at variance with the whole history of this double production of oil and gas in this country, where by far the greatest experience of the world has been accumulated. Every producer of petroleum knows that a field begins to die the moment it begins to live. A promising sand rock is often entirely drained of its contents, which may amount to several millions barrels of oil in a single year, and the longest life of the best American field has never yet attained to a score of years.

The views above presented and discussed are not only crude and unscientific, but they are often very mischievous, so far as they gain acceptance in the popular mind. They are responsible for much of the reckless waste that has characterized our use of these hydrocarbons thus far. It is this promise of perennially renewed supplies, in fact, that gives them the currency that they now enjoy. Some phase of this theory is always found full-fledged in a neighborhood that has discovered oil or gas within this year or the last. Two years, or three years at most, of successful development, serve to convert all judicious observers from the error of this way of thinking; but the masses often persist in holding to the perpetuity of the reservoirs until they are completely exhausted, and even then there are explanations in plenty by which the unwelcome conclusion can be avoided.

Much more could be said in contravention of the theory which has now been examined. In the subsequent discussion of explanations of origin that have a better scientific basis than the one now examined, many things will be brought to view that bear also upon this theory, in the way of answering objections which it raises to other explanations. In particular, the true understanding of the cause of rock pressure in gas and oil-wells, which is innocently stated by the author as amounting to the extreme figure of 300 pounds to the square inch, bears with fatal force against the chemical hypothesis. The 300 pounds here named as extraordinary are commonplace or even low figures in this connection. Pressures of 600, 700 and 800 pounds to the square inch are not unusual. The limit of present experience is set at 1,000 pounds.

The best accessible statement in its most expanded and authentic form of the theory that finds the origin of petroleum and gas in the operation of chemical force on inorganic matter, has now been presented and its weakness and inconsistency have been in part pointed out. When

PETROLEUM AND NATURAL GAS.   71

confronted with the geological facts which it essays to explain, it is found entirely inadequate and inadmissible. It is safe to say that petroleum and gas have not been originated in the way which this theory suggests.

2. *Geological Theories.*

Under the present heading, the leading theories that are based on the origin of petroleum and gas from organic sources will be briefly considered. They are termed geological theories as opposed to chemical theories, because they have been originated and are held by geologists, or at least by those that look at the facts from the geological point of view. In this list many chemists are included, and as before observed, chemical force is by no means dispensed with in the processes to which these theories make appeal. In this country no geologist of standing has adopted either of the theories of the preceding group, so far as known. Without exception, those who have studied and discussed the subject have found themselves obliged to adopt in some form the organic origin of the substances under consideration. In Europe there is occasionally a geologist of note who has fallen in with one or other of the theories of origin from inorganic substances above given. Professor Abich, for example, a German geologist of some distinction, adopted the last theory viz., that of Dr. Mendeljeff, and undertook to apply it in the interest of German capitalists to the great Baku oil field in which the latter were interested. It is not a matter of surprise to learn that all the forecasts which he made for the field on this basis proved erroneous. In no single case, it is said, were his predictions as to the behavior of the oil territory verified.

Prof. Hans Höfer, of the Royal School of Mines, Leoben, Austria, published in 1888 a treatise on petroleum and the substances associated with it, in which he made a thorough and judicious review, the best in fact that has ever been made, of all the prominent theories that have been advanced in regard to the origin of petroleum. He shows that by far the greater number of the geologists who have interested themselves in the question have reached the conclusion that it must have been derived from organic substances. To this conclusion he himself gives hearty support; and the fact that he has acquainted himself by personal investigation with the great oil-fields of the United States, renders his judgment all the more valuable. Discussions carried on by those who are ignorant of this, the most important section of our experience, lack authority and weight.

But while there is practical unanimity of opinion among geologists on this point, viz., that petroleum has deen derived from organic sources, their agreement ceases here. Organic substances are in the first place divided into two great classes—vegetable and animal. To which class is etroleum to be referred? The larger number of geologists, especially in

America, are disposed to refer it to a vegetable origin; but in Europe there is apparently a growing disposition to find its source in animal remains. There are also many to be found who would not hesitate to accept both sources as possible and probable.

Again, among those who count a vegetable origin probable, there is considerable room for difference of opinion. One refers petroleum to algal vegetation, or sea-weeds; another to the mosses from which peat is derived, and still others to land plants and to coal. So, also, various tribes of the animal world are counted by different authors the main source of petroleum.

Furthermore, when we begin to theorize on the mode of transformation of vegetable or animal substances into oil, still greater divergencies of view are brought to light. Some insist that the transformation is accomplished by a peculiar process of chemical decomposition, while others refer the entire formation of petroleum to destructive distillation. There are also some who advocate a mode of origin to which they give a new name, viz., spontaneous distillation, but this term has not been precisely defined, and its exact meaning can not therefore be determined. In the language which is used in regard to it, chemical decomposition and destructive distillation seem to be blended in an illegitimate way.

The differences of opinion on these several points are seen to be such as to justify the statement with which the present chapter was opened, viz., that no explanation of the origin of petroleum can be furnished that will command any thing like general acceptance among those who are interested in the study and discussion of these questions. A few of these theories that have secured the most attention will be briefly stated and discussed.

Newberry's Theory.—One of the most lucid and widely accepted theories as to the origin of petroleum and gas is that of Dr. J. S. Newberry, formerly State Geologist of Ohio, and now Professor of Geology in Columbia College, New York. For the first statement of it, we must go back to a paper published in the State Agricultural Report of 1859, entitled *Rock Oils of Ohio.* The theory is restated and emphasized in Volume I, Geology of Ohio, and also in later publications.

Dr. Newberry refers the origin of the oil and gas of the great Allegheny field to the extensive deposit of Devonian and Sub-carboniferous shales, and especially black shales that underlie the productive districts of Pennsylvania and New York. In the first paper he speaks as follows:

"The precise process by which petroleum is evolved from the carbonaceous matter contained in the rocks which furnish it is not yet fully known, because we cannot in ordinary circumstances inspect it. We may fairly infer, however, that it is a distillation, though generally performed at a low temperature."

PETROLEUM AND NATURAL GAS. 73

Again he says (Geology of Ohio, Vol. I, p. 192):

"The origin of the two hydrocarbons (petroleum and gas) is the same, and they are evolved simultaneously by the spontaneous distillation of carbonaceous rocks."

In Vol. I, Geology of Ohio, p. 158, he says:

"I have already referred to the Huron shale as a probable source of the greater part of the petroleum obtained in this country. . . . . . The considerations which have led me to adopt this view are briefly these:

"First. We have in the Huron shale a vast repository of solid hydro-carbonaceous matter which may be made to yield ten to twenty gallons of oil to the ton by artificial distillation. Like all other organic matter this is constantly undergoing spontaneous distillation, except where hermetically sealed deep under rock and water. This results in the formation of oil and gas, closely resembling those which we make artificially from the same substance, the manufactured differing from the natural products only because we can not imitate accurately the process of nature.

"Second. A line of oil and gas springs marks the outcrop of the Huron shale from New York to Tennessee. The rock itself is frequently found saturated with petroleum, and the overlying strata, if porous, are sure to be more or less impregnated with it.

"Third. The wells on Oil Creek penetrate the strata immediately overlying the Huron shale, and the oil is obtained from the fissured and porous sheets of sandstone of the Portage and Chemung groups, which lie just above the Huron, and offer convenient reservoirs for the oil it furnishes."

Particular attention is called to the first of the paragraphs above quoted. In it an adequate source for the petroleum of the great producing districts is clearly pointed out, and the objection urged by Dr. Mendeljeff to the effect that no source could be found for the great accumulations in the rocks, is shown to be entirely without foundation. In support of this general view of origin, it is to be noted that distillation is resorted to in the large way at the present time to manufacture from carbonaceous shales just such a series of products as oil and gas would supply. There is nothing questionable or doubtful in the process.

The obscure point in Dr. Newberry's theory is his use of the term "spontaneous distillation," which he repeatedly asserts, is carried on at "low temperatures." There are several ways in which vegetable and animal substances can be resolved into compounds of a simpler order than those that are formed in the living world. One of these methods is known as *decay*. When the vital force is withdrawn from the organic substance, chemical affinity asserts itself and a rearrangement of the elements composing the bodies is effected. The oxygen of the air has an important part in this process when the decaying body is exposed to it. A modification of this process is effected when the presence of oxygen is excluded from the decomposing body, as, for example, when it is covered with water. The results of decay in the open air are carbonic acid, water and ammonia; decomposition under water results in the formation of carbonic acid and light carbureted hydrogen. Another method is that of *combustion*. When organic substances are burned in the open air, their elements are forced rapidly into the same general line of products that result from decay; the latter is, in fact, slow combustion. Still another method of producing the same line of change is known as *distillation*, or more accurately as *destructive distillation*. It is effected by applying heat to organic substances in enclosed spaces from which the air is excluded. It can be defined as the decomposition of an organic substance in a close vessel, in such a manner as to obtain liquid products. By a product is meant a body not originally present in the substance distilled. If the body is merely extracted without change, it is called by some authors an educt. Distillation is a very ancient process. The chemistry of the sixteenth and seventeenth centuries consisted of little beside it. All sorts of bodies were subjected to it, but the chemists of that time lacked the ability to classify the products obtained except in a crude and general way that possessed but very little significance. Destructive distillation is at the present time a process of immense practical value. Illuminating gas, for example, is one of its main products. So far as we can learn by observation, the temperature at which destructive distillation can be effected artificially is never less than 180° F. The ordinary forms of vegetable matter are entirely unaltered at 150° F., and but little change is accomplished below 300° F. Most of the transformations are accomplished from 400° F. upwards. The process always and necessarily leaves a charcoal residue or coke.

It is possible that like changes in organic matter are accomplished where time is exchanged for temperature; or, in other words, it may be that distillation is effected, as Newberry asserts, at low temperatures continued through long periods, but there are no facts known that establish this view. Thus far we have nothing but the bare and unsupported suggestion, and this certainly can not furnish solid grounds of belief. It will not answer to say that the presence of petroleum in the rocks proves this view correct, because there are other ways possible of accounting for this fact Neither is the suggestion strengthened in any way by frequent reiteration.

If it could be proved probable and actual, it would simplify the question under discussion to a great extent, but until some advance is made in this direction, we are obliged to consider destructive distillation as necessarily involving temperatures of at least 200° F., and in either case a carbonaceous residue must also be found as a result of distillation.

It militates against Dr. Newberry's theory that the rocks show no trace of even the lowest degree of the heat necessary to effect distillation. Chemical geologists have shown that silica is rendered freely soluble in rocks at a temperature of 212° F., especially where alkaline carbonates are present. The rocks of the Ohio shale that are now under consideration contain alkaline chlorides, and these would, without doubt, take part in the reactions by which silica would be set free at the temperature named. But siliceous sheets are nowhere found in the deep drilling by which oil and gas are reached The rock cuttings brought up even from depths of four thousand and five thousand feet below the surface show the strata to be entirely unaltered. This fact renders it certain that temperatures of even two hundred degrees have never been reached even at the great depths named.

Neither has there been in any case pointed out the carbonaceous residue in the shales, which the process of destructive distillation would render strictly necessary. There is carbonaceous matter in the shales in considerable amount as has been already shown, but it exists in the form of hydrocarbons and not as coke.

Dr. Newberry occasionally speaks of the process which he evokes as if it were one with the ordinary chemical decomposition of decay. He says in a passage already quoted, " like all other organic matter, this is constantly undergoing spontaneous distillation except where hermetically sealed deep under rock and water." This description applies to decay rather than to distillation in the proper sense of the word.

Dr. Newberry holds that the vegetable matter of the shale derived from floating marine vegetation, presumably of the algal type, is the proper source of the production of the great fields. This theory, as above stated, is one of the most lucid and attractive of all that have been proposed, and while exceptions must be taken to some portions of it, it is certain that it contains many elements of great value.

Peckham's Theory.—In the United States Census Reports for 1880, Prof· S. F. Peckham, Special Agent for the collection of the statistics of petroleum, has given an extended and very valuable review f the various theories which have been proposed as to the origin and m le of accumulation of this substance. The bibliographical list which he has compiled of the literature of the subject is probably the best that has ever been made in the English language. He states the leading theories of the origin of bitumens anda dopts Newberry's theory in the main with hearty approval, counting destructive distillation as the process involved in it. He recognizes, however, the two elements of weakness in it that have been already pointed out, and aims to supply the deficiency by showing first, how an adequate source of heat can be supplied and, secondly, by explaining why no carbonaceous residue is met within the rocks that are open to our inspection.

The heat necessary to the destructive distillation of organic matter, he considers to have resulted from the elevation of the Appalachian border of the continent. The metamorphic action due to heat, which is so well seen in the strata that compose the eastern and central slopes of the Alleghenies, he says, could not have died out abruptly, and must have extended as far to the westward as the oil fields lie..

But the heat action to which petroleum is due, he holds must have taken place at immense depths, and the scene of the transformation must accordingly be sought far below the unaltered rocks in which petroleum is now found. We are also led to infer that if we could descend deep enough into the strata, we should find the carbonaceous residue required by all forms of the distillation theory.

To these claims, we are obliged to answer, as under the previous head, that the rocks, for at least a mile in depth, show no signs of the metamorphic action required by the theory; they have not suffered the mineral transformation that would have been inevitable if they had passed through this history. In his anxiety to get deep enough to account for the heat and also to escape the necessity of showing a carbon residue, Professor Peckham drops far below the available sources of oil and gas even according to his own views. He accepts unreservedly Newberry's reference of these substances to the great shale system, but he is obliged to go to great depths below it in order to find heat enough to work the necessary transformation. He says of the Pennsylvania oils, " they are undoubtedly distillates and of vegetable origin," but the last stratum that we know that contains vegetable materials on the large scale is the great Ohio shale —(Huron shale of Newberry). There are still other considerations that oppose this view. The close-grained shales that make the cover of the several oil and gas reservoirs prevent the passage of petroleum from lower depths to higher ones; otherwise, they would not themselves be reservoirs. And again, the petroleum of different horizons differs considerably in character and composition. Such differences would not be explicable if all of them had a common source.

This theory is thus found on examination to show the same weakness as the theory first examined, and in fact it gives no advantage whatever over it. It is defective on the geological side, since it fails to make account of the established facts with reference to geological order and certain geological conditions of petroleum productions.

Professor Peckham's theory is seen to differ from Newberry's as to the date at which petroleum was formed. Newberry considers the process a constant one; Peckham refers it to the date of the Apalachian revolution, or shortly subsequent thereto.

Hunt's Theory.—The two theories already given furnish the best presentation of the general view which refers petroleum and gas to the destructive distillation of organic matter originally buried in the rocks of the earth's crust. The process is considered a secondary transformation of this organic matter. It was buried as organic matter; it is raised again in a new form, and the change is referred to the process already named and defined, viz., destructive distillation.

There is, however, one other view of great promise and importance in this connection which refers oil and gas to the primary and not to the secondary decomposition of organic matter. It holds that the remains of living bodies, animal and vegetable, pass, under appropriate circumstances, directly into petroleum. In other words, the *bituminous decomposition* must be added to the ordinary decay of organic bodies. The facts to which this theory appeals are comparatively few, and, as at present stated, they lack the full authority necessary to establish so novel a doctrine, but some of them seem to carry great weight. If careful investigation shall hereafter show them to be thoroughly founded, the problem of petroleum production can be considered solved. The most elaborate and effective exposition of this theory is that of Dr. T. Sterry Hunt. He urges, with great force and vigor, the view that petroleum mainly originates in and is derived from limestones. When found in limestones he counts the oil indigenous, but when found elsewhere, as in sandstones and conglomerates, he counts it adventitious, and he then refers it to underlying limestones. In regard to this latter point, however, he makes concessions, as will be seen on a later page.

The following extracts from various articles that he has published contain a clear statement of his views upon this subject.

In speaking of the oil fields of Canada, he says:

"The facts observed in this locality appear to show that the petroleum, or the substance which has given rise to it, was deposited in the bed in which it is now found at the formation of the rock. We may suppose in these oil-bearing beds an accumulation of organic matters, whose decomposition in the midst of a marine calcareous deposit, has resulted in their complete transformation into petroleum, which has found a lodgment in the cavities of the shells and corals immediately near. Its absence from the unfilled cells of corals in the adjacent and interstratified beds, forbids the idea of the introduction of the oil into these strata either by distillation or by infiltration. The same observations apply to the Trenton limestone, and if it shall be hereafter shown that the source of petroleum (as distinguished from asphalt) in other regions is to be found in marine fossiliferous limestones, a step will have been made toward a knowledge of the chemical conditions necessary to its formation."[1]

Again, he says:

"In opposition to the generally received view, which supposes the oil to originate from a slow destructive distillation of the black pyroschists, belonging to the middle and upper Devonian, I have maintained that it exists, ready formed, in the limestones below."[2]

This statement seems to recognize the possibility of the transfer of petroleum from its sources to reservoirs in associated strata.

78   GEOLOGY OF OHIO.

Again, after describing the occurrence of petroleum in certain fossils and certain layers of the Corniferous limestone, he says :[3]

"The facts observed in this locality appear to show that the petroleum, or the substance that has given rise to it, was deposited in the bed in which it is now found at the formation of the rock."

Finally, in referring to bitumen-bearing dolomite in the Niagara series near Chicago, he says:

"With such sources ready formed in the earth's crust, it seems to me, to say the least, unphilosophical to search elsewhere for the origin of petroleum, and to suppose it to be derived by some unexplained process from rocks which are destitute of the substance." (Essays, p. 174.)

In this passage, also, a possible transfer of petroleum seems to be recognized.

These statements leave nothing to be desired as to clearness and explicitness. The author's view could not well be put into more concise terms than he has used. It must be added, however, that he has sometimes described the oil of Pennsylvania and Ohio as indigenous to the Devonian and Carboniferous sandstones which contain it. (Essays, p. 171.)

There is something to be said in favor of this theory, that petroleum originates in the primary decomposition of organic substances, but the author's restriction of oil production to limestones must, of course, be discarded, and just why the process should be made to terminate with the formation of the rock is not apparent. We know that vegetable substances may remain unchanged when buried in the earth for long periods, and so long as they are present in unchanged state, they would seem to be available for the process here appealed to.

Hunt denies that the so-called bituminous shales, "except in rare instances, contain any petroleum or other form of bitumen." (Essays, 169.)

This statement is wide of the mark so far as the Ohio shale is concerned. Either gas or oil, or both, are unmistakably present throughout our great shale series, and especially in the black bands that traverse it. Whether taken from the natural outcrops or from the deepest drillings, every fresh sample of the black shale attests by the characteristic odor the presence of these substances. In drilling through the shale along the shore of Lake Erie, in particular, the gas is generally found in some harder portion of the light-colored bands that compose so large a portion of the series, each harder cap or "shell" giving a new though short-lived supply, but the real source of the gas becomes apparent if the drill descends a little lower than the gas-producing "shell," when a darker band is almost invariably reported. Quantitative examinations show that the shale often carries at least one-fifth of one per cent. of petroleum, existing in it as petroleum and not merely there potentially.

Newberry states the facts bearing upon this supply in the passage already quoted, and Shaler sets the same line of facts in strong light in his discussion of the Ohio shale in Kentucky. (Vol. III, page 109, Geology of Kentucky.)

But the limestone series of Ohio is in very much the same case as the shale, so far as oil and gas are concerned. These substances are present in nearly all the limestone formations of the State, and apparently indigenous to them.

The Corniferous limestone, the first to be reached below the Ohio shale, in some of its fields and in certain courses, contains representatives of this class of substances. The Marblehead limestone, of Ottawa county, gives out a bituminous odor when struck with a hammer, and other portions of this limestone stratum are even more bituminous than the Marblehead stone.

The Waterlime or Lower Helderberg formation that comes next below, is decidedly bituminous. It contains grains of asphalt in cavities in the rock and carbonaceous films that have had the same origin, distributed through its substance. When struck with a hammer, it gives out the fetid odor of "limestone oil." Bowlders of it in the drift can be distinguished by this means from all associated limestones, except a part of the Corniferous. In Auglaize county, this stone becomes an asphaltic limestone, the bituminous element rising to a notable percentage. In other parts of the State, also, the amount of asphalt is so great that it is counted a decided advantage in the calcination of the stone for quicklime.

The Niagara limestone, as a whole, is less bituminous than the Helderberg, but there are parts of it, as in portions of Highland county, that contains a considerable amount of these products, mostly in the shape of asphaltic films and grains. Fossil corals are often partially occupied by this asphalt, and petroleum is sometimes found in small amounts.

The Clinton limestone is decidedly petroliferous in almost all of its outcrops. It yields oil in small amount at many points where quarries are opened in it, and springs that issue from it carry out small quantities of oil. These facts led, in the oil excitement of 1860, to the drilling of several deep wells along its line of outcrop. By the time the drill was buried in the rock, this source of oil was passed, and the remainder of the descent was relieved by but little encouragement.

Small deposits of asphalt have been found under convex surfaces of the Dayton limestone, just above the Clinton stratum, the asphalt being obviously derived from an inspissation of the oil of the latter formation.

The limestones of the Hudson River (Cincinnati) group always contain bituminous matter in their outcrops, but when penetrated by the drill, they have seldom yielded at any point large supplies of oil or gas. Short-lived flows, especially of gas, have been occasionally found in this series, both in northern and central Ohio.

The Trenton limestone has been proved by the drill to be a prolific source of oil and gas in a few localities, but aside from this great production, it almost everywhere carries diffused petroleum in appreciable amount.

The limestones and shales of our geological series are thus seen to agree in these respects. Both of them carry petroleum through all of their substance, and the product of each class has its own characteristics. In other words, these supplies appear to be indigenous to both groups.

Hunt's theory as to the petroleum in the limestones is that it was formed in them at the time the beds themselves were formed "by a peculiar transformation of vegetable matters or in some cases of animal tissues analogous to them in composition." But why shall not this view of the origin of petroleum be extended for what it is worth to other rocks that also contain this substance? If there is good reason for believing in the contemporaneous origin of oil and limestones, there would seem to be as good reason for holding to a like contemporaneity of petroleum and shale.

In referring the origin of petroleum to the primary and not the secondary decomposition of organic matter, the process is made to be one that ought to be found in present operation in the world. Is this true? Can it be shown that the formation of petroleum is now going on in nature? The answers to these questions are not as positive and definite as we should desire; nevertheless, there are some facts that seem to point to this conclusion. It is very desirable that more observations should be made.

One of the most important papers on the subject is Mr. G. P. Wall's report on the Trinidad asphalt. A remarkable passage in it bears directly on the question before us. It is as follows, two sentences being italicized:

"When *in situ*, it (the asphalt) is confined to particular strata which were originally shales containing a certain proportion of vegetable *debris*. *The organic matter has undergone a special mineralization, producing bituminous in place of ordinary anthraciferous substances. This operation is not attributable to heat, nor to the nature of distillation, but is due to chemical reaction at the ordinary temperature and under the normal conditions of the climate.* The proofs that this is the true mode of the generation of the asphalt repose not only on the partial manner in which it is distributed in the strata, but also on numerous specimens of the vegetable matter in process of transformation and with the organic structure more or less obliterated. After the removal by solution of the bituminous material under the microscope, a remarkable alteration and corrosion of the vegetable cells becomes apparent, which is not presented in any other form of the mineralization of wood.

Sometimes the emission is in the form of a dense, oily liquid from which the volatile elements gradually evaporate, leaving a solid residue." (Quart. Journ. Geol. Soc., XVI, 467.)

Wall's testimony is confirmed by other authorities. (See Hunt's Essays, 177.)

Petroleum, rapidly hardening into asphalt, is also recorded as occurring in some of the small tributaries of the Coaxocoalcas River in Central America. The petroleum seems to arise from the decomposition of vegetable remains with which certain beds of shale are stored.

If Wall's statements are to be trusted—and they bear the marks of intelligent and discriminating observation—the facts are as follows:

Beds of shale, formed in comparatively recent times beneath the sea, but now raised above its level, containing in abundance vegetable remains brought down by the Orinoco River, near the mouth of which Trinidad is situated, are yielding petroleum in large amount, by a direct decomposition of vegetable tissues and the petroleum rapidly passes into asphalt, inasmuch as it is exposed directly to the atmosphere.

At how great a depth in the rocks these changes are going on we have no observations to show, but no reason is apparent why these phenomena should be superficial. In subsiding areas, and almost all river deltas are such, the beds containing vegetable remains may be buried to a considerable depth before the decomposition can be fully effected, especially if the buried substances consist of the more durable vegetable products. In such a case we might expect the resulting petroleum to remain stored in the shale where it originated.

Why the phenomena of oil-production have been generally reported from shales, and not from sandstones, has not been explained. The difference between the two formations in this respect may be, in part, due to the fact that the shale seals up the vegetable matter more perfectly than the sandstone. In the latter ordinary decomposition would seem to have a better chance to go on.

From the fact that all of the chief bituminous accumulations of recent age belong to the torrid zone, it seems necessary to conclude that a tropical climate, or a climate of at least 80° F. average temperature, is most favorable to a large production of this class of bodies. The main asphalt bodies of commerce are found about the southern and western shores of the Gulf of Mexico.

The asphalt of Trinidad which seems to be in constant process of formation is derived from shales that belong to the later Tertiaries, and though derived from the most recent of all rocks that precede the present geological age, must still be separated from our time by a considerable interval. If then the formation of petroleum is made contemporaneous with the rock that contains it, it must be a geological contemporaneity that is meant, in which a thousand years will be counted as a single day. But according to this theory, what is there to hinder the process of petroleum formation from going forward as long as vegetable matter remains undecomposed in the rocks. Why should it be restricted to the particular time in which the materials of the strata are being deposited?

It would seem, however, that in the vast periods that have elapsed since the Paleozoic era, there would have been time enough and to spare for all of these changes to be accomplished, and that the process would be necessarily arrested, either for want of material or for lack of proper conditions.

The essential point in Hunt's theory of the origin of petroleum is, not that it was produced contemporaneously with the rock, nor that it is especially a product of limestones, but that it results from the primary decomposition of organic substances. Discarding these incidental elements of the theory, and applying its central postulate to the explanation of the origin of the petroleum of eastern Ohio and Pennsylvania, we can see what some of the steps in the history must have been.

The shales which constitute its chief source were accumulated in a tropical sea. The Devonian limestone which immediately preceded them in time bears witness to most genial conditions of climate. Its massive corals required at least as high an annual temperature as is found in any part of the Gulf of Mexico to-day.

The sedimentary deposits that were laid down on the floor of this Devonian sea consisted of clay and sand with occasional gravel bars, the sources of which must be sought in the rising Atlantic border or in the Canadian highlands, as is proved by all the deposits thickening and growing coarser in those directions. To the western limit of this sea, along the shores of the emerging Cincinnati axis, only fine clay was borne, and this fine and homogeneous material accumulated very slowly, one foot requiring as much time as ten or twelve feet of the coarser and more varied series to the eastward.

In these seas, as we know, there was a vast development of marine vegetation. Some plants of rhizocarpean affinities were especially abundant and their resinous spores and spore cases, which constituted by far the most durable portions of the plants, were set free in enormous quantities. Even now, in some parts of the series, these spores constitute a notable percentage of the shale. In structure and composition, they are but little changed from their original condition. Other portions of this and like vegetation may have been carried to the sea-floor in a macerated condition and have there passed through the coaly transformation, resulting in the structureless, carbonaceous matter that constantly characterizes the black shales. This carbonaceous substance can still be made to yield the members of the bitumen series through the agency of destructive distillation, and, doubtless, so also can the spores that remain unaltered in the shales, both leaving a carbon residue thereafter.

The shales that were slowly accumulating on the floor of this tropical gulf, thus charged with vegetable remains, must have behaved as similar shales do around the border of the present gulf. The vegetable matter was turned into petroleum as it is in Trinidad and the West Indies now. The petroleum would have been absorbed by the particles of clay in contact with which it was originated, or if liberated in the water it would there have been laid hold of by like floating particles of clay, to be carried with them in due time to the sea floor, and the work would have gone on until the material was exhausted or the requisite conditions were lost.

The resulting stratum of bituminous shale would have been much more highly charged with petroleum than any portion of these shales is at the present time. Over it at last a bed of sandstone is deposited which in turn is roofed in by another bed of fine-grained shale. The pores of the sandstone are occupied by sea-water, but a slow system of exchanges would be established between the rocks by which at last the petroleum would be gathered into its final reservoir. The presence of petroleum in considerable amount in a shale might give it a measure of permeability.

Such would appear to be some of the steps in the production of petroleum, if Hunt's view of its origin by the primary decomposition of organic tissue is adopted. The result would correspond fairly well with those of the "spontaneous distillation" theory already discussed. Both would find petroleum distributed through the substance of the shales, and both would expect its constant escape from outcrops of shale or sandstone. Continuous origination is by no means a necessary conclusion from continuous outflow.

The advantage that the present theory has over others is that it seems to find more support in the processes of nature at the present time. We find the bitumen series in actual process of formation in many parts of the world to-day, and as some good observers hold, resulting from the primary decomposition of organic matter under normal conditions. On the other hand, we do *not* find this series in any cases which are open to observation and subject to measurement, resulting from the secondary decomposition of carbonaceous matter contained in the rocks, unless the comparatively high temperatures of destructive distillation are reached.

The several views of the origin of petroleum that seem best to deserve attention have now been stated as fairly as possible. Some liberty has been taken with the last in the way of removing limitations, but no new theory has been broached, and no real contribution to our knowledge of these very interesting questions is claimed. In subjects which tempt speculation as much as those which are now under discussion, it is well to know the opinions that are most entitled to respect, even where grounds of positive knowledge are wanting. How little real knowledge we have of this subject has been made to appear in this brief review, and it is safe to conclude that until the boundaries of our knowledge are considerably extended, every theory in regard to the origin of petroleum should be held as provisional only.

The theoretical views that we hold as to the origin of petroleum will influence our judgment also as to the duration of its supplies. The question is often asked, whether there is any provision in nature by which the supplies that are now drawn upon or exhausted, can be renewed. It is to be observed that of the several theories passed in review, only the discarded chemical hypotheses hold out any promise of a perennial supply. Of the three views from which most will feel obliged to make their choice, two answer the questions raised above emphatically in the negative, and the remaining theory gives in reality no more encouragement. Newberry's theory makes the process of oil formation a continuous one, it is true, but it extends it through such vast cycles of time that 1,000 years or 10,000 years would not constitute an important factor. In other words, the reservoirs that we are now piercing with the drill, and that are yielding such vast and valuable stores of light and power, would in all probability have yielded about the same supply 1,000 or 10,000 years ago.

Practically the stock is now complete, as much so as the contents of coal mines and mineral veins. As a result of our interference with natural conditions, small local movements of oil or gas may go on in the rocks, but these would be but insignificant exceptions to a general rule that the reservoirs hold all the oil and gas that they will ever hold, and that when once exhausted they will never be replenished.

Gas and oil have been considered together in all the preceding discussions, as if the history of one would cover the history of the other also. There are, however, speculations which dissociate them in origin. By some, gas is counted the first and original product, and it is supposed to be converted into petroleum in the sandstone reservoirs by some unknown process of condensation.

This question, like those that have preceded it, does not admit of a final and definite answer at the present time, but the chemical probabilities do not seem to favor this view. Petroleum is more composite and unstable than gas, and in those respects it seems to stand at less remove from the organic world than the latter. A large percentage of natural gas is light carbureted hydrogen, one of the simplest and most stable products of decomposition. Petroleum readily gives rise to marsh gas when subjected to destructive agencies, but we have no known experience in which the higher compound results from synthesis of the lower. It seems, therefore, safe to consider petroleum first in the order of nature.

While, therefore, we can confidently assert that petroleum is derived from organic matter, we are obliged to confess that we do not *know* the exact steps of the transformation. There is, however, one mode of derivation that seems highly probable.

The discussion of this class of theories can be concluded with the following summary:

1. Most geologists hold that petroleum is derived from organic substances that were incorporated with the strata when the latter were formed. There is substantial harmony among the entire class of geologists as to this point.

2. The majority incline to the opinion that vegetable substances have supplied the chief sources, but some count animal remains as also an important source. There are a few authorities upon the subject, chiefly foreign, who consider animal remains the chief, or, perhaps, the sole source of petroleum.

3. Many hold that it is the result of *destructive distillation* of the organic matter of the rocks. They rely upon such facts as have been already adduced, that certain shales, for example, contain a considerable percentage of hydrocarbonaceous material that is easily transformed by heat into the several products of the bituminous theory.

4. In accounting for the origin of oil and gas by destructive distillation of the shale, the advocates of the theory seem bound to furnish an adequate source of the heat required, and also to show what has become of the carbon residue that is inseparably connected with the process of destructive distillation. Real difficulties beset this theory in these regards. The view that destructive distillation is accomplished at ordinary temperatures would relieve the first difficulty, if a such process could be substantiated, but at present it only stands as an entirely unsupported suggestion.

5. According to one phase of this theory, petroleum is constantly forming in the rocks; though, of course, as the world is old, the great stocks were formed thousands and millions of years ago. According to a second phase of the theory, the oil of the Allegheny field was formed at the time when the Appalachian mountains were elevated.

6. A small number of geologists hold the view that petroleum results from the *primary decomposition of organic matter;* that the produc-

tion is not a lost art of nature, but is in actual, though perhaps feeble operation at the present time, its chief seats being in tropical or subtropical regions. According to this view, the disseminated petroleum that the rocks contain was formed when the rocks themselves were formed. Organic matter which is notoriously unstable reaches in the bituminous series its stage of rest, and we may, therefore, truly speak of Silurian oil, Devonian oil, Tertiary oil and the like, the several stocks really having the age of the beds that hold them. The process of oil formation, according to this theory, ceased long ago in the older rocks.

7. The facts upon which the last theory must rest are not well enough substantiated to allow as to build upon them with full confidence, but we are justified in looking upon it with great interest us it furnishes on the whole the best explanation of the facts for which we are obliged to account.

6. MODES OF ACCUMULATION.

In the preceding pages, petroleum has been shown to be widely distributed in the rocks of Ohio. The limestones and shales of the series, in particular, every-where contain it. Hunt has made a calculation, showing the amount of petroleum which the oil-bearing dolomite of Chicago holds to the square mile for every foot in thickness of the stratum. If we apply a like calculation to the rocks of the Ohio scale, we shall find the total amount of oil enormously large. We may take, for example, the Waterlime stratum, which is notably and almost universally petroliferous. Estimating its petroleum content at one-tenth of one per cent., and the thickness of the stratum at 500 feet, both of which figures are probably within the limits, we find the petroleum contained in it to be more than 2,500,000 barrels to the square mile. The total production of the great oil field of Pennsylvania and New York, to January, 1885, is 261,000,000 barrels. It would require only three ordinary townships, or a little more than 100 square miles, to duplicate this enormous stock from the Waterlime alone. But if the rate of one-tenth of 1 per cent. should be maintained through a descent of 1,500 feet at any point in the State, each square mile would, in that case, yield 7,500,000 barrels, or nearly one-thirtieth of the total product of the entire oil field. These figures pass at once beyond clear comprehension, but they serve to give us some idea of the vast stock of petroleum contained in the earth's crust. If petroleum is generally distributed through a considerable series of rocks in *any* appreciable percentage, it is easy to see that the aggregate amount must be immense. Even $\frac{1}{1000}$ of 1 per cent. would yield 75,000 barrels to the square mile in a series of rocks 1,500 feet deep, but this amount is nearly one-tenth of the greatest actual production per square mile of any of the leading Pennsylvania fields.

It is obvious that the total amount of petroleum in the rocks underlying the surface of Ohio is large beyond computation, but in its diffused and distributed state, it is entirely without value. It must be accumulated in rocks that serve as reservoirs before it becomes of economic interest. In respect to the need of concentration it agrees with most other forms of mineral wealth.

The conditions of the accumulation of oil and gas have come into clearer view in the late experience of Ohio in the production of these substances than ever before in the entire history of their exploitation. There are several interesting and important points connected with the subject that can now be considered settled. The sources of oil and gas do not need to be further discussed. Their well nigh universal distribution in the unaltered strata of all geological ages has been already pointed out. As has been shown, their origin is to be found in some form of organic matter acted on by some form of chemical force. There remain to be considered the mechanical arrangements and the order of the strata by which concentration and large accumulation are rendered possible. The subjects pertaining to this division will be treated under the following heads, viz., *Reservoir, Cover, Structure, Rock Pressure.*

a. Reservoir.

The rocks of every stratified series can be divided into two general divisions with reference to their porosity, viz., the permeable and the impermeable strata. We do not find, however, hard and fast boundaries in this particular any more than elsewhere in nature. Some rocks are freely permeable, others are less so and still others resist the passage of water so effectually that we call them impermeable. Sandstones and conglomerates, the coarser the grain the better, are types of the porous group. Shales, on the other hand, the finer the grain the better, represent the impervious series, but shales of the slaty order are often fairly permeable. Dolomitic limestones that have originated in fossiliferous strata and, in some instances, crinoidal limestones are also found to furnish excellent examples of the first division, while certain other forms of limestone are fairly impervious. Shaly sandstones come near the dividing line, though, as a rule, a small percentage of diffused shale in a sandy formation detracts greatly from its porosity, or even renders it altogether impermeable.

Practically it comes to this, that sharp and clean and especially coarse sandstones, with conglomerates and dolomitic limestones, when the latter have been derived from originally fossiliferous beds, constitute the main reservoir rocks in most series. *These porous rocks are never found empty.* They generally contain water, since this substance is almost universally diffused through the outermost layers of the globe. If found within four or five hundred feet of the surface, the water is mainly fresh; but if the porous rocks are struck at a greater depth, they are generally found to contain saline, sulphur or brackish water.

These porous rocks are also the oil and gas rocks of our series. It has already been shown that neither cavities nor fissures are required for the storage of these substances; they take their chances in the water rocks and can go wherever water goes. Not all porous rocks contain accumulations of gas or oil, but the majority of them do at least in small quantity and in portions of their extent. But the large accumulations of these substances are of insignificant amount when compared with the whole area of the stratum in which they are found.

It often happens, and in fact it may be said that it generally happens that there is more than one porous rock traversed by the drill in a deep well. All of them contain water in parts of their extent, as above described, and sometimes all may contain petroleum or gas in the same well. When this occurs, the oils from the different levels often vary noticeably in character. The uppermost porous rock often contains fresh water, while the deeper beds generally hold salt-water of varying composition and strength.

The porosity of the reservoir rocks often extends to great distances. When it comes to gas and oil territory, this porosity has been so abundantly proved and has been found so full of practical importance that important legislation has been based upon it. In productive territory, for example, the laws of several States provide that wells must not be abandoned when they have proved destitute of oil or gas, until steps have been taken by plugging them to prevent the surface water from flooding the deep-lying rock. Striking proofs of this porosity are also supplied in the practical development of many gas-fields. In the new district of northwestern Ohio, wells separated by intervals of a half or three-quarters of a mile are found to affect each other's flow and pressure to an important degree, and it is also found that areas of several consecutive square miles can sometimes be drained of their gas by a single well.

The deductions from this observation are of the highest moment in relation to the life of the fields.

b. Cover.

It goes without saying that the porous rock which has become the reservoir of water, oil or gas has done so by virtue of the fact that its contents, acquired from some sufficient source, are confined within it by an impervious cover which generally consists of shale. This element is obviously a vital one in all accumulation. It is evident that of the three conditions already named, source, reservoir and cover, the source must come first in order of nature, the porous rock or reservoir next and last of all, the cover. But in point of fact, the sources of oil are so wide-spread that they may almost be taken for granted. Petroleum belongs in every rock series that we penetrate; there are also but few sections of a thousand feet in extent that do not contain one or more water-bearing or porous rocks, and thus it comes about that practically the close-grained cover is the condition hardest to find. This is shown in the fact that wherever an impervious shale is met with in the descent of the drill, covering a porous rock, we are warranted in expecting the presence of oil or gas under favorable conditions of structure. The accumulations are, of course, mainly small, but their presence testifies to the influence of this element in the oil and gas series.

The facts on which this order is based came clearly to view in the first experience in the modern search for petroleum in Western Pennsylvania. Similar facts have been repeated in the discovery of every succeeding field. That these covers do their work thoroughly is seen in the fact that the boundaries of the several substances under discussion are in many cases sharp and well-defined. A descent of a few inches will often unlock a great fountain of water, oil or gas. These substances are wanting altogether in the shales until the last inch of this formation has been passed.

Almost every important mass of shale in the Ohio series has been proved to be somewhere the cover of accumulated petroleum; as, for example, the Cuyahoga and Berea shales, covering the Berea grit; the Ohio shale, covering the Corniferous limestone; the Niagara shale, covering the Clinton group, and finally the Utica shale, covering the Trenton limestone. Minor deposits of shale also scattered through the Coal Measures are found to have a like effect.

c. Structure.

A third vital factor in all petroliferous accumulation is found in the *structure* or arrangement of the porous rock that contains the oil, gas and water. But the porous rock is never affected alone; in most instances the entire series with which it is associated, exclusive of the drift deposits, have been uplifted or flexed by the same movement to which it has been subjected.

The facts brought to light in the drilling of the first oil wells of the country, forty years ago, suggested to the geologists, who studied them, the influence of structure. The existence of arches and troughs, or in geological language, of anticlines and synclines, was recognized more or less clearly, and an obvious and rational use was made of the facts. It requires no argument to show that if gas and oil are associated in any porous rock that has been bent into an arch, the force of gravitation will necessarily affect a separation of these substances in the order of their specific gravities. An anticlinal theory was, therefore, evolved at an early day; but, beyond the simple statement of it, little progress was made for thirty years. The geological work done in connection with the remarkable petroleum production of Western Pennsylvania, though of great value in many respects, failed to bring out the structural facts of the productive territory, and, indeed, attention was rather diverted from these facts by the suggestion of other elements thought to be concerned in oil accumulation.

It was only when the new value began to be placed on natural gas in connection with its utilization on the large scale, which occurred about ten years since, that the prominent influence of structure came distinctly into view. For the most effective statement, and the most successful use of this theory, we are indebted to Professor I. C. White, of Morgantown, West Virginia. He came to see, with perfect distinctness, that the gas-producing territory of Western Pennsylvania and West Virginia was strictly confined to anticlinal lines. If a gas well seemed to occur in a syncline, the presence of the gas was really due to the interruption of the syncline by a low fold at the deepest portion of the basin—a fact of structure which is very frequently met throughout the entire Appalachian region. Other limitations and qualifications he soon came to recognize, but the theory was only strengthened and confirmed by the apparent exceptions to it. For a time Professor White's statements were called in question by other geologists, but in his replies to their criticism he proved himself to have so decided an advantage that interruptions of this sort soon ceased. He commended the theory, moreover, to the practical men engaged in the exploration, by his prompt application of it to prospective territory, approving or condemning localities on this basis; and, in addition to this fact, he located a considerable number of excellent gas wells far in advance of previous development by the drill.

The oil and gas production of Ohio, and especially the newer phases of this production, have brought the strongest confirmation to the view that structure is vitally connected with all the important supplies of either. The facts brought to light in the development of the Macksburg field proved to be very important in this connection. Under the skillful interpretation of Mr. F. W. Minshall, of Marietta, it was shown that the productive territory of this field consisted of a well defined terrace of the oil rock, bounded by gas on the rise and by salt water on the descent. The oil terrace, which occupies almost a geographical level, was traced by the surface rocks and checked by the well records, the event proving that the entire series, from top to bottom of the wells, had been affected equally by the same forces which made a terrace of the gas rock. In other words, the terrace shows through to the surface, so far as the level of any particular stratum is concerned; but to the eye the effect is lost on account of the excessive action of recent erosion, the present surface being very irregular. These facts were all demonstrated by careful instrumental measurements after the general structure had been made known.

The terrace which was thus found proves to be the result of what may be called a suppressed anticline. The force which, if great enough, would have resulted in a well-marked arch, has proved able only to arrest the previous dip of the strata for a short space. In other words, nature began to build an arch which she was not able to complete.

It now seems as if the terrace is a form of structure particularly effective in petroliferous accumulation. It gives to the reservoir relief or variation of level as distinct as the arch, though in many cases less pronounced in its influence.

The recent experience of northwestern Ohio has, however, furnished a greater number and even a more striking series of facts pertaining to the influence of structure on accumulation than the older fields. This district affords many advantages for the determination of the structural laws which govern it. Its surface is almost a plain, and, furthermore, is thoroughly intersected by railroad lines, the levels of which afford convenient points of departure in establishing the elevations of well heads. No other American field has equaled this in simplicity of structure, but on this very account the effect of the structure becomes all the more easily recognizable and traceable. Moreover, there are several easily identifiable horizons passed through in the drilling of every well, which attest and prophesy the facts that the oil rock is finally found to show as to its structural relations.

It is not necessary to give details in this connection at this point. A single illustration will be taken from the famous Findlay field. The drilling of the first dozen wells in Findlay showed the following facts of structure. The bedded rocks are bent at this point into a very low arch, the axis of which bears approximately north and south. On the west side the arch is found to have a well defined boundary, the strata descending from a terrace, or an approximately horizontal position, 150 feet, in the course of one-third of a mile, to another flat-lying or gently-sloping area. In other words, a slope of 150 feet in a third of a mile, rising to the east, connects two terraces of the same stratum, the surface of the country meanwhile lying at the same absolute geographical level. The structure can well be called a monocline, so far as these features are concerned, though when all is considered, it is seen to be as previously named, a very low arch.

The distribution of gas, oil and salt water in the Trenton limestone follows the lines of geographical level in a very interesting way. When the field was first opened, each element had a definite boundary. The dry gas occupied all of the stratum from about three hundred feet below tide water to about four hundred feet below; to the oil a vertical measurement of fifteen to twenty feet was assigned directly below the gas, while underneath the oil, in turn, the salt water found its place. Sometimes, however, the latter element occurred at the levels where the oil would properly be expected. But with the development of the field and the exhaustion of the gas, all of these levels have been gradually changed until the salt water has now intruded upon, if it has not entirely overrun the whole of the slope and the terrace as well.

In the oil fields, in like manner, the elevations of different portions of the reservoir are always found connected in the most important and significant way with the production. Every foot is counted by nature in increase or loss of efficiency. If a well in the Lima field, for example, shows an elevation of the top of the oil rock of even five or six feet in excess of the wells around it, it becomes thereby a gas rock for a few days, instead of an oil rock.

The Upper Sandusky field furnishes excellent illustrations of the same law, as will be clearly shown on a subsequent page.

In short, the rational deductions as to the distribution of gas and oil in a reservoir, common to themselves and to water, are abundantly supported by testimony derived from the Ohio oil fields, both old and new. There is but little obscurity and but few, if any, anomalies in the facts so far as known. Certainly there is nothing to raise even a question as to the validity of the explanations already proposed.

Closely connected with the same line of facts is the very important element in gas and oil production that remains to be briefly discussed in a few succeeding paragraphs.

d. Rock pressure.

What is known as rock pressure in gas wells is the maximum pressure reached when the gas is shut within the well. It is supposed to be the pressure of the gas in the rock reservoir, this pressure equalizing itself throughout the new space. It is also known as closed pressure. The open pressure of the gas, on the other hand, is the pressure registered on

PETROLEUM AND NATURAL GAS.   93

a gauge held in the current while the gas is escaping freely from a pipe of any size. When the gas escapes from the casing, a pipe of five and five-eighths inches in diameter, it requires a vigorous well to produce any effect on an ordinary high-pressure steam-gauge. The highest pressure noted in the casing (five and five-eighths inches) of any Ohio wells up to 1889 was six or six and one-half pounds, but during the last year three wells have been drilled, the first flows of which have registered from eighteen to thirty-five pounds. The open pressure increases rapidly when the opening of the well is reduced in size. A well that showed six pounds in the casing registered $20\frac{1}{2}$ pounds when the gas was made to escape through a four-inch pipe. The rock pressure, or closed pressure of Trenton limestone gas varies in different fields, but is generally the same in all the wells of one immediate neighborhood, in case the production of the wells is large. The present usual range is between two hundred and three hundred pounds to the square inch. Higher figures than these are sometimes obtained, especially from the deeper wells. At the opening of the Findlay field, 450 pounds was shown in most of the wells. The rock pressure in the Bowling Green field was about the same. The Carey wells attained a pressure of 435 pounds. In a Tiffin well a pressure of 600 pounds was registered, the graduation of the gauge stopping at this figure. A considerable excess was indicated. The wells of Lancaster have shown a maximum pressure of 700 pounds to the inch, but they have not held these extreme figures long. The present pressures in the several fields will be given in the subsequent chapters of this report.

In the Saint Mary's and Saint Henry's gas wells the original range was between 350 and 400 pounds. In the Indiana field it varied between 300 and 335 pounds to the square inch in the instances where reliable observations were obtained.

The closed pressure in the great gas wells of Pennsylvania is more than twice the highest pressure found in Trenton rock gas. Pressures of 750 pounds are reported on good authority, and many facts are on record indicating a pressure of nearly or quite 200 pounds beyond this figure. The rock pressure of the Ohio shale gas of the northern part of the State rarely exceeds 100 pounds to the square inch.

With some remarkable exceptions the rock pressure, as already stated, is generally the same for all the wells of a particular field, whatever their production may be. In other words, pressure gives in itself no indication or clew to the amount of gas a well yields. By joining to it, however, the element of time, an empirical but uncertain calculation of the volume of gas produced may be made. If a well gains a certain number of pounds pressure in a certain number of seconds or minutes, for example, the volume may be measured by one of the methods presently to be given and

GEOLOGY OF OHIO.

then used as a check on other like increase of pressure in wells of the same depth. The well that produces the largest amount of gas in the Findlay field shows the same closed pressure that the smallest well of the field shows; but in the case of the large well the entire pressure is reached in one or two minutes; in the other, hours are required for it to creep slowly up to its maximum.

The phenomena connected with high rock-pressure of gas and oil wells are among the most astonishing and impressive in the entire range of mining enterprise. When a reservoir of the character above named is penetrated, the gas, suddenly released from a pressure of 300 to 950 pounds to the square inch, rushes forth with amazing velocity and indescribable force. It drowns like a tornado all ordinary sounds in the vicinity of the well. Unless great care be used by one engaged about the well his sense of hearing is very likely to be permanently impaired. When the gas is lighted the roar is greatly increased and can be heard for miles. The light from a great well can be seen, under favorable circumstances, forty miles away.

The cause of the rock pressure of gas and oil wells, is a subject upon which our best authorities have not been in haste to commit themselves, by offering definite and comprehensive theories to account for the facts. Three causes have been suggested as adequate to explain the results:

(1) The gas produces its own pressure. Solid or liquid matters are converted into the gaseous form in the deeply buried porous rocks and the gas thus formed requires larger space than the solid bodies from which it was derived. In seeking this larger space, it exerts the pressure noted.

(2) The weight of the overlying rock produces the pressure of the gas. According to this view, the gas is in the rock and the weight of the earth above it exerts a constant pressure upon it, and forces it out with the velocity observed whenever an exit is made for it.

(3) The pressure is due to a water column that is behind the gas and oil. The porous stratum that makes the reservoir of gas and oil and salt water, and which always has an impervious roof, somewhere rises to the surface. Water entering at its outcrops will exert its pressure through all the flexures of the stratum upon the salt water that it contains, and thus upon the accumulations of oil or gas that are held within the arches and terraces of the stratum. This explanation makes the flow of gas and oil depend upon precisely the same cause that occasions the flow of water from artesian wells, viz., a water head of greater or less elevation, at a greater or less remove.

The first theory doubtless has in it elements of truth. The beginning of gas pressure in any rock and all the pressure ever found in some formations may very well be referred to this source. For the pressure of shale gas, for example, no other cause need be sought. But all the elements pertaining to this theory are vague and unverifiable. It is an explanation in name more than in reality. Moreover, the facts in regard to the great oil and gas rocks seem to require a cause at once more energetic and more variable than the expansive power of gas would furnish. If gas originates its own pressure, it would be difficult to account for the extreme range of pressure that we find in the same stratum, all the gas of which has essentially the same composition. The theory certainly is inadequate on this side, and we must look to either the second or third theory for a satisfactory explanation of the remarkable facts observed.

The second explanation, viz., that which refers the pressure of reservoir gas to the weight of the superincumbent rock, appears to have found the largest measure of popular favor, but the theory is certainly unsound. It gives way when subjected to the slightest examination. Professor Lesley furnishes an excellent discussion of this theory in the Annual Report of the Pennsylvania Survey for 1885, and he demonstrates its invalidity. The rock can exert no pressure on the gas, as he clearly shows, unless its particles are free to move upon one another, or, in other words, unless the rock is in a crushed state. The pebbles and grains among which the particles of gas are distributed, unless themselves actually moved, can exert no pressure on the gas, as Lesley well observes, any more than the walls of a cave can exert pressure on the river that flows through it. There is nothing whatever to support the belief that the rock exists in the state which this theory demands. There are many facts that demonstrate the opposite view. No force can be found adequate to crush the rock at the depths at which the gas occurs. The slightest examination shows that the weight of the overlying rocks is altogether insufficient. The Trenton limestone, for example, in its nearest outcrops, is a firm, strong stone; and all the information we obtain as to its structure in the gas wells points to the same sort of rock there. But at its lowest measure of strength, it can bear, without giving way, 720 tons to a square foot, and much of it can bear four or five times this weight. On the other hand, the weight of the superincumbent rock that is to do the work of crushing the Trenton reservoir, is approximately one ton to the square foot for every fourteen feet in height, and there would thus be but eighty tons pressure on a foot of Trenton limestone in a Findlay well at a depth of 1,100 feet. This is but one-ninth of the lowest resistance of the rock, and but an insignificant fraction of its highest resistance to crushing weight. Besides this the driller finds the rock firm and compact to a high degree. The driller can not be deceived in this respect. It is unnecessary to follow this subject further. There is no standing ground whatever for the theory.

When we come to the third theory we see at once that it rests on a different basis from the theories previously discussed. It depends upon principles and facts of familiar experience and every-day use. Every one is acquainted with the flow of artesian wells. The present theory relegates gas wells to the same category. In fact, it makes the flow of gas from the rock reservoirs which the drill has penetrated due to the same cause that propels artificial gas through the mains of a city, viz., a water column behind and above it. This theory has been held more or less distinctly by numerous geologists. Professor I. C. White was one of the first to openly adopt it. In an article in the American Manufacturer early in 1887 he urged that artesian pressure would be found necessary to account for the compression of gas in the great reservoirs.

Before entering more fully upon the discussion of the question to what the rock pressure of gas wells is due, let us ask another question, the answer to which may advance us in our inquiries. The driller in the Ohio field, as well as in all other oil fields, finds gas in the higher levels of the productive rock, and, at a somewhat lower range, he finds the stocks of oil, if any, with which the reservoir is charged. If he goes below the horizon of the oil or gas, or if he goes beyond its productive limits, he reaches at once salt water, which rises in the well to a greater or less height, sometimes filling it entirely, and sometimes even flowing out of the top of the well. This experience is universal in the great fields of the United States, at least. Every oil or gas field has a margin of water, generally more or less saline, surrounding its productive portion in whole or in part. The influx of this salt water is one of the most common evidences of total failure in wells drilled for oil or gas. The moment this fatal flood is reached all hope departs.

The question which should first be considered is this: "Why does salt water rise in wells drilled to the productive rock, but outside of the productive portion of the rock?"

Whatever explains the rise of the salt water from one portion of the oil rock will explain the flow of the gas or oil from another portion. The explanation that should reverse this order and make the rise of the salt water depend on the pressure of gas somewhere held in the rock would be ludicrously inadequate. There is an ocean of salt water; there is but a thimbleful of gas. The gas is confined to narrow streaks, it may be, on the crests of anticlines, and it occupies but a few feet at most in the upper portion of the rock, while the salt water stretches out for scores of miles on every side and through great depths in the rock. Salt water makes the normal and well-nigh universal contents of the oil sands. The rare exceptions, in locations favored by the accidents of structure, are the stocks of gas and oil, which in reality are very scanty, but which by comparison with each other we sometimes call great. Their total volume is insignificant when compared with the other elements with which they are associated. We have no reason to believe that all the accumulations of petroleum contained in the crust of the globe would exceed a few cubic miles in volume, but the salt water contained there would make a sea.

What makes salt water rise when its porous reservoirs are tapped by the drill? Let us ask one question more: What makes fresh water rise under similar circumstances? The mystery is dispelled with regard to artesian water supply. Every school-boy knows the explanation of the facts involved. If in its underground course water has dissolved from the rock more or less mineral matter, the laws which governed it before such solution took place are not thereby affected. It has grown a little heavier by its mineral contents and consequently will not rise in quite as high a column as fresh water will, but this is all the difference. Salt water rises in the rocks in which it has been sealed from precisely the same cause as fresh water. It is an artesian flow or an artesian ascent, as the case may be. No other explanation of the facts involved is possible. From what source is the water head derived? The answer is the same as for all artesian flow. It is derived from water entering porous strata at their outcrops. The conditions for an artesian flow must all be found united in every oil or gas field.

But whatever causes the salt water to rise in wells drilled on the edge of an oil field or a gas field is beyond question the cause of the flow of oil or gas contained within the field. This is demonstrated by the close connection that exists between the salt water and the oil or gas. Working from the edge of the field towards the center, we find a progressive diminution of salt water and an increase of oil or gas in the common reservoir. With the exhaustion of a field the oil and gas are followed up and finally replaced by salt water. This is the common fate of gas and oil wells; the death to which they seem to be appointed.

The height to which salt water rises in wells drilled on the margin of a gas field gives a measure of the force of the gas within the field. This is true, at least, within the several divisions of the Trenton limestone. The height to which the gas rock rises in its nearest outcrop will, in like manner, determine the height to which the salt water will rise in the wells, and this factor is seen to control the rock pressure of the gas. The outcrops of porous rock; it is evident, must be followed. A stratum, though continuous in geological name, may be so changed in character that it will cease to be a factor in problems of this sort. The porous character of the Trenton limestone appears to be maintained in a northerly and northwesterly direction from the new gas fields and it is, perhaps, in the outcrops of Michigan, Illinois and Wisconsin that the water head originates which gives its spring and energy to the gas of Findlay, Bloomdale and St. Mary's, and also to that of Kokomo and Marion, Indiana. While many questions pertaining to the subject can be raised that can not be fully answered from lack of knowledge at the present time, it still appears that the only rational explanation of the rock pressure of gas is to be found in the artesian pressure of the water that accompanies it.

It is also apparent that if this is the cause the fact must be susceptible of demonstration. If we know the height to which the salt water rises in any division of the field, and if we know the specific gravity of the salt water, by taking account of the depth of a well, the effective force of the water in compressing the gas can be calculated, and its relation to the observed pressures can be noted. Agreement between the calculated and observed pressures in a sufficient number of instances and through a sufficient range of figures would furnish a demonstration of this hydrostatic theory.

The facts that we need to know, in order to complete the demonstration, have been suggested in the preceding paragraph. They are as follows: (a) the height to which the water rises in wet wells; (b) the density of the water; (c) the depth at which the water is found; (d) the initial rock pressure of the gas when found.

Can these several elements be obtained? All of them, it can be answered, are matters of observation, and if an intelligent interest in the questions could be assured on the part of the well-driller no difficulty would be experienced in supplying all the information necessary. Part of the facts are always easily determinable in any case. The questions have not been urged upon the driller, however, until recently, and in regard to one of them, viz., the normal rock pressure of the fields, the only time for noting it has long gone by. The facts can be obtained only from testimony as to figures observed several years ago.

(a) As to the height to which the salt water rises in wet wells there is not as much *exact* information as could be desired. The general facts of its occurrence are thoroughly understood, but when the driller has once become certain that his well is a salt water well, as a rule, " the subsequent proceedings interest him no more." He is seldom likely to spend more time or trouble upon a venture that has already proved a dead loss. He can tell you that the water rose in the well at the rate of fifty or one hundred feet in an hour, or that it came up even into the casing for 100 or 200 feet, but the exact figures he has no curiosity to obtain. Some of these statements can be made, however, to give us a clue to the height of the rise. The level at which the bottom of the casing stands is one of the important points in the record of every well. In the salt water portions of both the Findlay and the Lima fields, this level ranges from 300 to 400 feet above tide. If, therefore, we know that the salt water rises .100 or 200 feet above the bottom of the casing, we know that it stands from 400 to 600 feet above tide. When the surface of the ground in which the well is begun is lower, however, than in the fields already named, more definite figures can be obtained. Along the shore of Lake Erie, and in the Wabash Valley of Indiana, we find the most reliable data. The salt water in these districts rises so nearly to the surface that its height can be definitely determined, or it may, as in the last named district, flow from the well in a true artesian fashion.

In a well drilled at Lindsey, Sandusky county, Ohio, for example, the elevation of the well head was about that of the railway station, viz., 622 feet above tide. The salt water rose within twenty-five feet of the top of the well, or in round numbers to a height of 600 feet above tide.

In the Wabash Valley the elevation of the bottom lands falls below 600 feet above tide. Wells drilled to the Trenton limestone in such stations unlocked a flood of bitter and sulphurous salt water that flowed from the well head, but if the wells were drilled in the adjacent uplands the water would rise to apparently the same height as in the other cases but would not overflow. In a few instances figures were given which would show an ascent of the water above the 600 feet level already named. At Huntington, for example, the water was reported to rise to a height of 900 feet in the well. This would make its actual elevation 617 feet above tide, but the figure given was undoubtedly a round number and not the result of careful actual measurement. The wells that were found most useful in this connection were those of Wabash City, Peru and Logansport, and of the districts contiguous to these towns.

As a result of all these observations it can be stated that the strong and free flow of salt water from the Trenton limestone, when struck in the Ohio and Indiana fields, rises to approximately the same height in all the wells, viz., to about 600 feet above tide. There are a few exceptions to this statement in which the water rises higher than 600 feet.

In various sections of the field, however, the salt water, when found, does not rise to this elevation. Whenever a shorter column is found, the gas that occurs nearest lacks the full pressure of the main fields. Both facts are associated with a harder and more compact condition of the petroliferous limestone than that found in productive wells, which the driller promptly notices and from which he draws valid conclusions.

This 600 feet rise of the salt water represents the height of some outcrop of the porous condition of the Trenton limestone. We find such outcrops on the shores of Lakes Superior and Huron at approximately the same elevation as that which the salt water reaches. Fresh water finds access to the limestone in these outcrops, but its influence while available for pressure would not go far towards changing the character of the peculiar bitterns or brines that occupy this great sheet in its subterranean expansion.

(b) The specific gravity of the salt water that occupies the Trenton limestone is high. Several determinations made by the Survey show a gravity of 1.1, and some samples were even heavier. A column of fresh water, one foot in height and having one square inch for the section, weighs .43285 pound avoirdupois. The average weight of such a column of sea water is .445 pound, but the Trenton brine when counted at 1.1 is found to weigh .476 pounds for twelve cubic inches. The heaviest samples would even reach a weight of .5 pounds to twelve cubic inches.

The gravity undoubtedly differs in different samples of the brine and this element accordingly introduces to this extent a variable factor into the calculations. Its influence could not, however, in any case affect the result beyond a few feet in a thousand.

(c) The depth at which the gas or water is obtained is the one element in the calculation that can, as a rule, be definitely ascertained. The depth at which the Trenton limestone is struck is one of the principal facts in the history of every well. The gas generally lies not lower than thirty or forty feet below the top of the limestone.

(d) The remaining inquiry, that, namely, pertaining to the original rock pressure of the wells, does not generally admit of present determination and we are obliged to go back to the records of the earliest wells in each main section of the field. There is but one date in the history of a gas field when its rock pressure can be properly obtained and that date is at the drilling of the first wells. As wells are multiplied, and especially as the gas is utilized, the pressure is soon reduced. If time enough could be given, and if the wells could be completely closed, the field would undoubtedly regain its normal pressure, but this restoration of the compressing force would in most cases be gradual and not immediate.

There would be a slight reduction in this force in any case from the fact that by the exhaustion of a portion of the gas the salt water would reach a slightly higher final level in the reservoir than it previously occupied.

When we inquire as to the first records of rock pressure, we find several elements of uncertainty as to the facts. Gauges were not applied in some instances until the wells had been open for weeks or months. The gauges themselves are not always trustworthy in the record of the high figures that the wells require. The natural tendency to make as good a showing of the field as possible often leads to the reporting of the pressure in round numbers and these are never *below* the actual figures. In the list of early pressures noted, the following are counted fairly trustworthy and also fairly representative of the several fields. All are based on observations of the author except those for which other authority is given. The highest pressure noted in any gas well derived from the Trenton limestone was found in the Loomis and Nyman well of Tiffin. The gauge used read only to 600 pounds. This figure was reached and passed, the well indicating a considerable surplus beyond 600 pounds. The Upper Sandusky well No. 1, as reported by Dr. A. Billhardt, of the Board of Gas Trustees, showed a pressure of 515 pounds. The Kelly well No. 1, known as the Godsend well, Bloom township, Wood county, showed a pressure of 465 pounds, as reported by Mr. J. Stock, of the Northwestern Ohio Natural Gas Company. This measurement was not taken until some time after the well was drilled. The Bairdstown well, as reported by Mr. M. C. Briggs and many others, showed a pressure of 460 pounds. Higher figures are recalled as having been observed in it originally, but no authentic record was made of them at the time, and they can not therefore be counted any thing more than tradition. There is nothing improbable in them, however, as will presently be shown. These figures are given as 515 pounds. The Pioneer well at Findlay, and other wells drilled in the town during the first year showed, according to Mr. W. M. Martin, the contractor who finished most of them, a pressure of 450 pounds. The original pressure for part of the field was undoubtedly much more than this. The Axe well of St. Mary's, according to the observations of Mr. A. C. Reichelderfer, and many others, after blowing into the air for three months, showed a pressure of 390 pounds. The first well at St. Henry's, according to the testimony of Judge Dennis Dwyer, of Dayton, for whom it was drilled, after treatment similar to that named in the last instance, showed a pressure of 375 pounds. Passing into Indiana, the Kokomo well No. 4, showed a pressure of 320 pounds, six months after the field was opened. Col. J. T. Stringer, Secretary of the Natural Gas Company, informed me that the first wells registered, to his knowledge, 328 pounds. In Marion, well No. 3, showed at the opening of the field 323 pounds pressure. The wells at Muncie, according to common report, has a pressure of less than 300 pounds. The testimony of some good observers was to the effect that it was between 280 and 290 pounds. The figures for Tiffin, Upper Sandusky, Findlay and Marion, Indiana, were all obtained when these fields were freshly opened.

These figures will now be combined with other data from the respective wells, and to them will be added for comparison a column containing calculations of the pressure that should result from the following factors, viz., an assumed height of the salt water head to 600 feet above tide, and an assumed specific gravity of the salt water of 1 1, which gives .476 pounds to the square inch for every foot in height. To the depth of the gas rock below tide must be added the 600 feet to which the salt water rises above tide. This sum will be the effective water column. The pressure will be the product of this sum and the weight of a column of the water one foot in height, which is .476 pounds.

Locations.	Depth to gas.	Relation of gas rock to sea level.	Original pressure.	Calculated pressure.
Tiffin, Loomis & Wyman well	1,500 feet.	747 ft. below tide.	600 lbs.+	1,347 × .476=641 lbs.
Upper Sandusky well, No. 1	1,280 "	478 " "	515 "	1,078 × .476=513 "
Bloom Township Kelly well, No. 1	1,145 "	395 " "	465 "	995 × .476=474 "
Bairdstown well, No. 1	1,112 "	365 " "	460 "	965 × .476=459 "
Findlay Pioneer well	1,120 "	336 " "	450 "	936 × .476=445 "
St. Mary's, Axe well	1,159 "	238 " "	390 "	838 × .476=399 "
St. Henry's, Dwyer well	1,156 "	200 " "	375 "	800 × .476=385 "
Kokomo well, No. 4	936 "	98 " "	328 "	698 × .476=332 "
Marion well, No. 3	870 "	78 " "	323 "	678 × .476=323 "
Muncie City wells	900 "	* 0 " "	280-290 "	600 × .476=286 "

* At tide level.

The agreement between the last two columns of the tables affords nothing less than a demonstration of the principal cause of the rock pressure of natural gas. It is due to the weight of the salt water that occupies the porous rock jointly with itself, though by a very unequal partnership, and the water pressure in turn is unmistakably of artesian origin. A better knowledge of the facts may modify to some small extent the assumed data, but it is certain that the general relations expressed above indicate a law of nature bearing upon the question with which this section was begun, viz., what is the cause of the rock pressure of natural gas? The close correspondences of the table may be accidental to a small extent. The general relation is all that need be insisted on. Strictly, we ought to reckon each field from the salt water level, whereas the figures given are those that show the depth at which gas was found. In several instances, however, and particularly in those which show the closest agreements, the salt water level is but little lower than that of the gas. An increase of pressure beyond the figures reported could however be accounted for on this basis in some of the fields. For example, the great Simons well of Bloom township is reported to have shown an original pressure of 520 pounds. The Bairdstown well is also reported to have shown 515 pounds. These figures stand for a depth of the salt water of 400 to 490 feet below tide, which is more than 100 feet below the original level of the gas. There is nothing improbable in such a relation, however.

The results of this discussion can be summed up in the following statement, viz., *the rock pressure of Trenton limestone gas is due to a salt water column, measured from about 600 feet above tide, to the level of the stratum which holds the gas.* The law is here limited to the Trenton limestone, for the reason that the data were derived from the wells of this horizon, but it is exceedingly improbable that the gas production of this stratum differs in any important way from that of any other great gas rock.

The importance of this deduction will not escape observation. A few obvious inferences from it will close this discussion.

1. There is no danger that the great gas reservoirs of to day will "cave in" or "blow up" after the gas is withdrawn from them. The gas will never leave the porous rock in which it has been stored until it is obliged to leave by the pressure of the water that is behind it. The last end of a gas rock is a water rock or an oil rock. Considerable uneasiness has been caused in the minds of even reasonably well-informed persons by the sensational articles that have appeared from time to time in the newspapers, predicting the subsidence of extensive areas from under which the gas has been withdrawn, or explosions resulting from admixture of air and gas as the latter is diminished in the reservoirs. The so-called science on which these predictions are based is of the spurious sort, and the authors of these predictions have been speculating in regard to subjects of which they had no adequate knowledge. There is not the shadow of a shade of danger in sight in these directions.

2. This doctrine lays the ax at the root of all the optimistic theories that blossom out in every district where natural gas is discovered, and especially among the real estate speculators of each new field, to the effect that nature will not fail to perpetually maintain or perpetually renew the supplies which we find so delightfully adapted to our comfort and service. Profound opinions of this sort, coming from such sources, have constituted a large part of our newspaper literature on these subjects hitherto, but the logic of events is rendering these claims more and more untenable each day, and they are blind, indeed, who now pretend to see any promise of an unfailing supply.

3. Unwelcome though it may be, this doctrine ought to be kept clearly and constantly before the communities that have begun to enjoy the inestimable advantages of the new fuel. If they believe that the supply is indefinitely great or that it is being constantly renewed, they can scarcely be brought to employ any proper economy in its use, but just as far as they accept the demonstrated limitation of the supply, they will be ready to adopt all proper measures for husbanding the stock to which they have obtained access. The doctrine has also an important bearing on the question as to what uses natural gas should be put. Manufacturing establishments of any sort that consume a million or more feet in a day can not be greatly multiplied in any Ohio field without rendering a tolerably speedy exhaustion of the supply a certainty.

4. When the salt water takes possession of a former gas rock it comes to stay. A permanent equilibrium is established by its advent in the

GEOLOGY OF OHIO.

place of the unstable equilibrium which prevailed so long as the gas remained imprisoned in the arches of the rock. The "rest" which it is sometimes proposed to grant to an overworked and prematurely exhausted gas field will be a long one. Nothing but small and short-lived accumulations can ever be found in it again.

5. Of the original rock pressure of any field not all can be counted available for the supply of the pipes that are to carry the gas away. There is a large fraction that must always be left upon the well, if the best results of production are expected. This is called "back pressure." The amounts and the proportions required vary in different fields, but in northern Ohio it is seldom safe to reduce the pressure below one-third of its original figure. If, for example, the gas showed 450 pounds pressure at first, it should never be allowed to flow with less than 150 pounds on the well. In other words, only the surplus of gas above 150 pounds belongs to the line. As the energy of the field decreases, which is shown in the diminution of the r ck pressure, the amount of back pressure to maintain the protection of the gas must be increased, which is the same as saying that the available amount of gas is constantly decreasing. Nothing is so destructive of a gas field as to allow the wells to run "wide open" or without back pressure. Such a course is always an invitation and a persuasion to the oil and water by which the gas is surrounded to come up higher and the invitation is always accepted. In the case of rival corporations occupying the same field, it sometimes happens that it seems to the interest of one to exhaust the field as rapidly as possible. To accomplish this result but two things are necessary, first, to drill a good many wells, and secondly to allow them to flow with the gates opened full.

PLATE II.

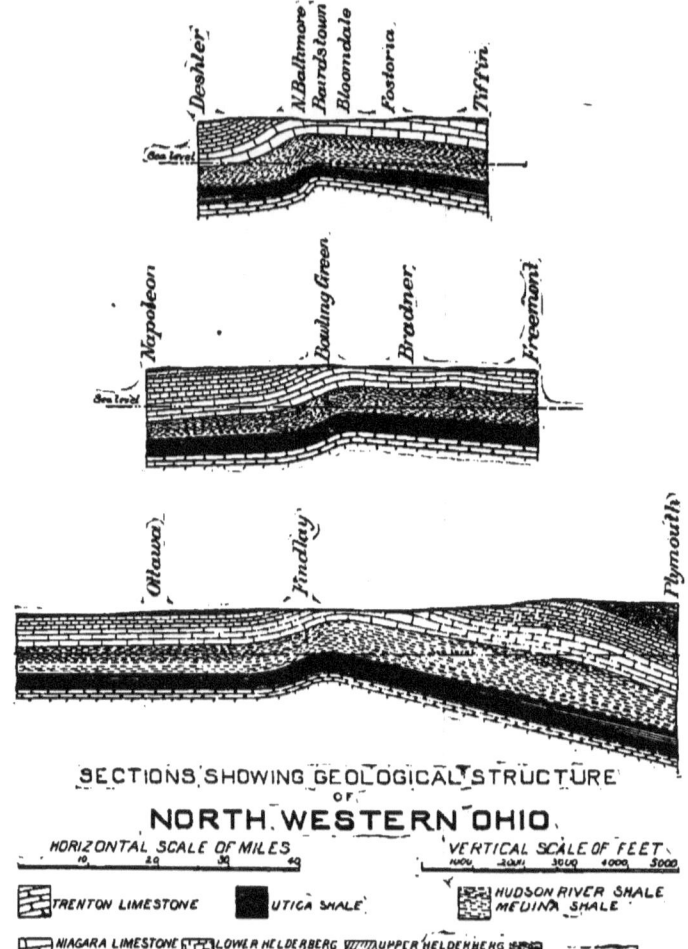

CHAPTER III.

THE TRENTON LIMESTONE AS A SOURCE OF OIL AND GAS

In the present chapter the development of the Trenton limestone as a source of oil and gas will be continued from the date at which it was closed in the last preceding volume of the State Geological Survey, viz., Vol. VI, Economic Geology of Ohio. In this last named work a fairly complete account of the facts which make up this surprising history to the fall of 1887 was given, and in a supplementary chapter a few facts gathered from the first two or three months of 1888 were published. It will therefore be necessary in the present review to take up the history from the spring of 1888 and continue it to the present time, covering a period of about two years. For the benefit of those readers who are not acquainted with and can not obtain access to the above named volume, a brief resumé of the leading facts that were established in it, pertaining to the new and important source of petroleum will here be given.

Discovery of Gas at Findlay.

(1) The discovery of high pressure gas in the Trenton limestone was made in Findlay in November, 1884. During 1885 a dozen wells were drilled here, the best of which reached a production of three and a half million cubic feet per day. The first great well at Findlay, viz., the Karg well, was struck on January 20, 1886. It gave new character to the entire field. Its production from the casing was about fourteen million cubic feet per day, and from the four-inch tubing about twelve million cubic feet per day. Since that time the development and the utilization of Findlay gas have been pushed forward very rapidly.

The first oil obtained from the new source was found in a well drilled in Lima in May, 1885. Oil was also found during the same year and at but little later date at Findlay. The first large production of oil from any well is to be credited to the Hume well of Lima, which was completed in the Spring of 1886. It produced 250 barrels for the first day. The full development of the Trenton limestone as a source of oil production was not accomplished before the middle of 1887.

(2) These large productions of gas and oil from a Lower Silurian limestone were entirely unexpected. It would be hard to say whether the geologist or the oil producer was most surprised by these results. That the Trenton limestone is petroliferous to a small extent was long ago known at least to the geologist. The fact was distinctly pointed out by Dr. T. Sterry Hunt in his Geological Essays. He showed that the outcrop of this great stratum on the Manitoulin Island is charged with oil, and further that a well drilled into the stratum, thirty or forty years ago, produced a number of barrels of oil. Dr. Hunt also argued very earnestly in favor of the view that limestones are the true sources of oil. But neither he nor any one else, so far as known, ever ventured to suggest or even to hint that this widespread stratum would become one of the great oil rocks of the continent and the world. Least of all, did the sagacious men who have been for the last forty years engaged in oil production have any suspicion of such a result. The Ohio experience constitutes an entirely new chapter in the geological as well as in the practical history of petroleum production. No one, as has been said, suspected it, or at least no one had prophesied it.

(3) By the study of the facts of the new fields, the conditions of its oil and gas production soon came to view with great distinctness. In the first place, it was learned that the common reservoir of both of these substances was not a true limestone, as the name of the stratum might lead us to suppose, but that it consisted of one or more sheets of magnesian limestone or dolomite, these sheets being situated either at the very summit of the series, or distributed at one or more levels in the uppermost fifty to one hundred feet of the formation. The composition of the Trenton beds generally is that of an ordinary impure limestone. It contains from eighty to ninety per cent. of carbonate of lime and from five to fifteen per cent. of silicious impurities. Occasionally, however, thin beds of exceptionally pure limestone are brought to light by the drill, carrying ninety-five to ninety-nine per cent. of carbonate of lime. This form of the rock frequently occurs at the very summit of the series, directly overlying the gas rock proper.

The oil and gas rock, on the other hand, as has been said, is generally a fairly pure dolomite of about fifty-four per cent. of carbonate of lime, and forty-four per cent. or less of carbonate of magnesia. The silicious impurities are commonly included within a small figure and their absence in this connection deserves to be noted, for it shows that the limestone from which the dolomite was derived by metamorphosis was of a very pure character, resembling, in fact, the last phase of the calcareous rock that was described above. If silicious impurities to a large extent had ever been present in the limestone, they would be there to-day, as there are no means known by which they can be removed from a stratum with which they have once been incorporated.

The precise steps by which a true carbonate of lime is converted into a magnesian carbonate or dolomite, we not do know, but the process is one that has been carried on in nature on an extremly large scale. Half of the limestones of the Ohio series are dolomites, many of them of exceptional purity. As deduced from a somewhat limited series of facts and observations, the following steps in the history of the dolomitization of the Trenton limestone are suggested as probable. In the first place, the original cap or uppermost beds of the great formation consisted of very pure carbonate of lime, derived from the remains of crinoids or stone lilies. The uppermost beds at Trenton Falls, N. Y., have this constitution to-day. They consist of very pure crinoidal limestone. Secondly, the purest beds and those only admitted the magnesian replacement in which the dolomitization consists; one-half of the atoms of carbonate of lime being removed and their places being supplied with atoms of carbonate of magnesia derived from the sea water. By means of this replacement, the rock became porous, the new crystals never entirely filling the spaces from which the lime crystals had been removed. The impure portions of the rock would have resisted this change in all its phases.

Be the origin what it may, it soon became evident in the development of the new horizon of oil that all its value was associated with this dolomitic composition. Whenever the normal composition of the limestone above described was found, the stratum was dry and unproductive, so far as gas and oil were concerned.

In the second place, it was soon learned that each productive field was surrounded by salt water, or at least that salt water made a part of its boundary, while another part of the boundary was often found to be determined by the non-porous condition of the Trenton limestone. The level at which salt water was reached in each field proved to be fairly constant, and this level could be counted a dead line as to oil or gas. Wherever the drill descended to this or to any lower level, the rock was found occupied with the heavy brine peculiar to this horizon. The dead line for the Findlay field was found to be five hundred feet below tide water; for the Lima field, four hundred feet below tide; for the Saint Mary's district, about 350 feet below; while west of the State line, in the great Indiana gas field, the salt water was reached at a hundred feet below tide. The inference was soon drawn that for the entire productive territory, the line of 500 feet below tide could be taken as a dead line. Subsequent exploration has brought several exceptions to this deduction, but only one of them is thus far important, that, viz., of the Gibsonburg oil field. The exceptions, as a matter of course, depend on the discovery of other arches or terraces in the series at a lower level than those of the Findlay field. Aside from the Gibsonburg field, none of these arches have proved large enough to contain any considerable amount of oil or gas, and most of them have cost in their development a good deal more than has been got out of them. Bryan, Tiffin and Oak Harbor can be named as centers of these out-lying fields, the last being the most favorable of the list. As the work of exploration proceeds, other exceptions will probably be found, but there does not seem to be room for very large or very important additions to present territory between the various points that have been already proved.

The results of the drilling done in 1886-7 are thus seen to have disclosed two important conditions of production, one pertaining to the chemical composition of the Trenton limestone and the other pertaining to its relative depth in each field This knowledge did very much to rationalize the work of exploration on the part of all who possessed intelligence enough to make use of it.

(4) Another clew to gas and oil production was brought to light in 1887. It was observed that all of the gas production in Ohio and Indiana as well, was derived from territory in which the Niagara limestone constitutes the surface rock; while the oil, on the other hand, was obtained from territory in which the Lower Helderberg limestone constitutes the surface rock. The explanation of this interesting line of facts speedily became apparent. In the order of deposition the Niagara limestone belongs below the Lower Helderberg. It has a total thickness of three hundred to four hundred feet against a thickness of four hundred to six hundred feet of the latter formation. In both States the surface of the country is approximately level for large consecutive areas, and hence it resulted that wherever the lower-lying Niagara limestone made the surface, the Trenton limestone must lie at a higher elevation than where the Lower Helderberg comes to the surface. The topography of the Trenton limestone, in other words, was found to be clearly indicated by the surface geology. The later facts have brought in a few exceptions to this generalization. The Gibsonburg field, for example is occupied by the Niagara limestone as a surface rock, but it produces mainly oil. The explanation is that a considerable thickening of the shale takes place in this direction, as is shown in the records of the wells. The Upper Sandusky field also began as a gas field, though its surface rocks are Lower Helderberg, but the gas was soon superseded by oil. In Indiana there are some notable departures from the lines here indicated, but it is still true that the heart of the gas field there agrees exactly with the generalization above given.

(5) Still another character of the new fields was made manifest

during these early explorations, but it is one which the driller and prospector found it hard to accept and recognize. It is this, viz., the new gas and oil fields are not confined to definite axes of elevation, but they rather expand after the continental type of uplift, in flat lying areas of scores, hundreds, or, as is the case in Indiana, of thousands of square miles in extent. These areas have in some cases sharp boundaries, on one side at least, and in all of them there is a prevailing direction for the very slight descent of one to ten feet to the mile by which they are characterized. In Ohio, this prevailing dip is to the northward, or in some cases to the northeastward; in Indiana, it is to the northwest.

The sharpest of the definite boundaries referred to in the preceding paragraph is found in connection with the Findlay, North Baltimore and Bowling Green gas fields. The Findlay Break, as this boundary has been designated, passes through Findlay a little to the west of north and holds this general direction as far, at least, as the State line. It is by all means the most important structural line in the oil and gas fields of the new horizon. On the east side of it dry gas belongs, often in extremely large volume; on the slopes to the westward the great oil production of the district is found, while at the foot of the slope lies the salt water which gives to both oil and gas its head of pressure. These facts are represented in the accompanying diagram, figure 2. Three east and west sections taken ten to twelve miles apart, reveal with perfect distinctness this monocline. It can be traced still farther northward.

The structural lines of the Gibsonburg and Oak Harbor fields, in like manner, bear to the northward; the Upper Sandusky and Tiffin production is derived from a line of elevation that bears a few degrees to the east of north; the St. Mary's and Lima uplift has a distinct northeasterly direction as its main feature. The Indiana gas field, as represented by a recent map prepared by Dr. A. J. Phinney and published in the American Manufacturer in February, 1890, is almost a miniature of North America in form and proportions. Dr. Phinney estimates the area of this gas field to be 2,500 square miles. Subtracting a large body from the southward extension of it, that possesses comparatively little force at the best and that is also uncertain in production, we should still find eighteen hundred or two thousand square miles in a fairly continuous territory. Its principal structural lines bear to the west of north.

The early history of petroleum production in this country, as is well known, was confined to Western Pennsylvania, a region which is traversed by a number of low, parallel folds that represent the dying out to the westward of the great anticlinal series into which the whole eastern border of the continent was bent during the progress of the Appalachian revolution. In the oil regions these folds were characterized by the same southwesterly direction that marks the mountains themselves. They were, however, so feeble and low that they were easily masked by the accidents of erosion, and they became apparent only as extensions of the productive oil fields. If the absolute levels of the oil rock had been determined by referring all of them to the height of mean tide, for example, the law of accumulation would certainly have come out to view with perfect distinctness at the very beginning of the recent remarkable history of petroleum. In default of this, we got nothing but "belt lines," "north, forty-five degrees east," or "north, twenty-two and one-half degrees east," according to the fancy of the explorer. We all believe at bottom in order in nature and in the presence of law, and the modern mind does not rest easy until it obtains some clew to the laws that affect the special division of nature with which it is individually concerned. These northeast and southwest lines, standing as they do for real facts in nature and admitting of a thoroughly rational explanation, which was, however, altogether missed in the earlier construction of the facts, furnished to the driller his only clew and guide. New fields were discovered by what are called "wildcat" wells; that is, wells drilled outside of known or probable territory. But as soon as a successful well was obtained, the northeast lines came at once into play and territory was thereafter taken up altogether on this basis. While the deduction had in reality an entirely rational foundation, as has already been pointed out, as it was held and used, it was purely empirical and was marked by all the disadvantages of such an origin. So long as the driller was confined to Western Pennsylvania, and the territory adjacent thereto, he did very well with his northeast lines. In following them, he was following the great structural lines of the country on which petroleum accumulation would entirely depend. He could have found, in fact, no better guide, though even then there were numerous qualifications that deserved to be recognized. But the Appalachian Mountain system does not after all cover the entire country, and as soon as this was left behind he had no longer a right to expect the old lines to be equally serviceable in guiding his explorations. But he was not prepared to make the necessary changes. The English coal miner, when asked what was the direction of the face of his coal answered that the coal faced "two o'clock sun, as all the coal in the world does." So, the Pennsylvania driller, if transported to the Caucasus or Rocky Mountains would still be trying to apply his northeast lines—he knows no other guide.

Working directly across Ohio from Pennsylvania, as he did, it is of course natural that he should have brought this line with him. In southeastern Ohio, indeed, he had already found it as distinctly applicable as in Pennsylvania, but when he struck in northwestern Ohio an oil and gas rock in a lower Silurian limestone, he ought to have been prepared to find all things becoming new. It cost him a great struggle to give up sandstone as the sole and necessary reservoir of oil, and even to this day he persists in calling the purest dolomite, which will promptly and wholly dissolve in acid, the "oil sand." The old law of direction for oil and gas accumulation has failed as thoroughly as the character of the reservoir rock. By far the most important single line of structure in the new fields is found in Hancock and Wood counties, and this line bears north, or a few points west of north. The production of the Findlay gas and oil field, the Van Buren gas field, the North Baltimore gas and oil field, the Bowling Green gas and oil field, are all conditioned and controlled by this factor.

In the Lima field, and a part of the St. Mary's field, it is true that a northeast line comes into play for a few miles, but the area affected by this northeast structure will not, at the outside, exceed one hundred square miles, while the new fields, taken together, comprise in Ohio and Indiana, at the very lowest calculation, 2,500 square miles, and the only portion of the entire area that can, by any lawful use of the facts, be counted as embodying a northeast line have been already named. The facts are represented to the eye in the accompanying sketch map, on which all of the principal areas of the gas and oil production, derived from the Trenton limestone, are represented in proper relations to each other. If any northeast lines are found in these tracts, except in the single district already named, they will be creations of the imagination, and rather poor ones at that. They are likely to prove in the future, as they have already done in the past, in many hundreds of instances, a delusion and a snare to those who attempt to find fortune along the belts that they indicate. But it is likely that the northeast line will continue to dominate the mind of the untrained driller and prospector for a good while to come. It meets the urgent demand that is after all so honorable and hopeful a characteristic of human nature, that we shall have a theory underlying our action. The more intelligent representatives of the oil interest in the new fields know that the old reliance has failed here, and that it can not be replaced by any other as simple and comprehensive as the "forty-five degree line" of Pennsylvania.

The points that can be used in intelligent direction of exploration are those already emphasized, viz., the facts pertaining to the *composition* of the Trenton limestone, and the facts pertaining to its *relative elevation*. The data for both must first be obtained from the point of the drill, it is true, but when obtained in any locality they often give some chance for forecast in advance of the drill. A prominent structural feature, like the Findlay break, can also be turned to the best of account in the location of gas and oil territory whenever it occurs; but of such factors there are but few.

In the review that is to follow the several gas fields will be described in the general order of their discovery and development. The oil fields will be considered in a separate section. The present review, therefore, must include the last two to three years.

SECTION I.

GAS PRODUCTION OF THE TRENTON LIMESTONE, 1888 TO 1890.

(A) HANCOCK COUNTY.

This county still occupies the most prominent place, all things considered, in the new gas production of northwestern Ohio. Of the eighteen townships of the county dry gas has been produced in the eight named herewith, viz., Findlay, Marion, Portage, Allen, Cass, Washington, Jackson and Eagle. Portage and Eagle townships both have small gas areas and scarcely deserve to be counted in this list, and though Jackson has furnished several large wells, none of them has proved to have staying quality, and it is hardly proper to count any longer this township as available for the supply of pipe lines or for any large and constant use. Weak production of dry gas has also been obtained in one or two other townships, while gas associated with oil has been found in the townships that constitute the important oil field of the county. There are but four or five of these eighteen townships that have failed to disclose one or other form of this bituminous wealth which has been so surprisingly added to the resources of this favored county during the last six years. Findlay township, which is now embraced entirely within the city limits of Findlay, no longer holds the first place in the gas production of the county. In this respect, indeed, it has lost most of its importance; but in the history of this production it will always be the center of interest. At the present time Allen township takes the first rank, and after it come in the order named, Cass, Washington and Marion. The principal developments, including the new features of the last two years, in each of these subdivisions, will be here noted.

(1) *Findlay.*—As will be remembered, gas was discovered in Findlay in November, 1884. The use of it was begun in 1885, but no great progress was made until 1886, beyond the furnishing of a domestic supply for the residences of the city. During this year glass factories, iron and steel mills, and various other manufacturing enterprises were established. In the winter of 1886 and the spring of 1887 a period of great speculative excitement prevailed. Foreign capital in large amount was brought in and invested in lands, buildings, manufacturing plants, street improve-

ments, water works and the like. Prices of real estate were, for a time, pushed to extravagant figures, but building sites and practically free gas continued to be offered to all manufacturers that were purposing location. As was to be expected, the attractions that were thus held out drew into Findlay several enterprises that were presently found to be financially weak. In order to establish themselves they needed something more than free land and free gas. Some of them were aided and reinforced by Findlay capitalists, but others collapsed after struggles variously protracted. A large majority of the establishments located here, however, have proved vigorous and successful from the start. The population of the town has increased to 25,000. Ten miles or more of street railroads are in successful operation. The city water-works on which a hundred thousand dollars has been expended, are already rendering invaluable service to the health and comfort of the town. Sewers are to be constructed and street paving on the large scale is already begun.

The great extension of the corporation limits of the city that took place in 1887, the location of factories far out from the old centers, and the building up of residences around the new factories, necessitated an equal extension of the city gas lines. The trustees pushed forward their work, connecting, from time to time, extensive manufacturing plants with their belt line, enforcing no economy in the use of the gas, and scarcely suggesting such economy to consumers. A monstrous waste was going on in almost every direction. The illumination of the city was provided for by street torches, consuming 50 to 200 feet per hour. Few of them were extinguished in the day time. It is speaking quite within the limits to charge upon this single source of waste the useless destruction of at least 15,000,000 feet of gas per month during at least a part of this year.

Few new wells were drilled and those that were drilled were located on city lots at a short remove from the older ones. None of them made very important additions to the gas supply. The trustees, in fact, proceeded on the assumption that a few square miles underneath the center of Findlay were an adequate source of fuel and power for all the uses that could possibly be accumulated on the surface, and that the Karg well, which had become the great reliance of the city line, could reasonably enough be expected to continue for an indefinite time to come its astonishing out-put.

Failure of Gas in Findlay.

The results of a policy based upon such expectation were, of course, bound to be disastrous. As the winter of 1888 and 1889 set in, and

8 G.

heavier drafts on the pipe line were made necessary, complaints began to be heard in many quarters of want of gas. The glass factories and iron mills were obliged to shut down for a part of each day. In the outskirts of the town the pressure was so much reduced that cooking stoves and heating stoves alike failed to do their work. One of the city schools was temporarily closed because the building could not be properly warmed. Occasionally the supply of gas was entirely cut off and the cause was found to be the filling of the pipes with salt water, and in some cases the stoppage proved to be due to the freezing of the water in the pipes. The magnitude of the failure was, however, for the first time made fully apparent when this flood of salt water was traced to the Karg well. This fact was not generally known at the time, but those that learned it saw at last that the Findlay field was like all other gas fields, a reservoir of stored power and that it not only could be but that it had already been practically exhausted. The Karg well was completed in January, 1886. For several months in its early history, it had poured out into the air its vast volume unrestrained. A calculation made in 1887 showed that this one well had been allowed to waste at the very lowest computation 1,500,000,-000 feet of gas, and after it was brought into the city line it was, especially for the last year, run wide open, or without any back pressure whatever. Its life under such treatment was unusually prolonged, reaching nearly three years. When first struck it had more than fifty feet in thickness of dry gas rock to draw upon, but the salt water flood that lay below, carrying a thin layer of oil upon its surface, was steadily rising in the reservoir as the highly compressed gas which resisted its advance was allowed to find egress through the well. Every step of its ascent was permanent; each foot of gas allowed to blow or burn left the volume within the reservoir so much less.

In this alarming juncture, the gas trustees turned at once to the nearest available sources of supply. The Jones well, which had been drilled in the summer of 1886, but which had never been drawn upon, was bought by the trustees. Its original volume was 1,100,000 feet per day, and it was confidently supposed that its gas was held securely in store for emergencies. When opened, however, it was at once seen that the well had shared the fortunes of the field and that its pressure and volume had been reduced as much as if it had been drawn upon directly. The Ballard well, of Jackson township, the measured volume of which had been found to be between five and six million feet daily, was also brought into use. The farm upon which the well was drilled was purchased by the trustees at a large figure, and connections were immediately made from the well to the city line. To meet the demand that at present existed, this well also was run wide open, and its term of service proved on this account very short. In the course of a few weeks, it began to fill the line with salt water, which renewed the trouble in the service pipes that had been already experienced and continued the disastrous interruptions that had begun.

The winter passed in this way, checking and sobering the growth of the city. At the time when the shortage began, there were many manufacturers at the doors, negotiating for some share in the wonderful advantages which Findlay had thus far been able to offer to all comers. They had been easily and naturally led to adopt the views which they found prevalent in Findlay, to the effect that the supply was a perennial one, that the gas wells, if not really growing more productive all the time, were certainly holding their own in all respects. But the disastrous experience of the winter changed all this. It is popularly said to have damaged Findlay to the extent of millions of dollars. This statement can be true only in the sense that many large establishments would have been added to Findlay during the next season if it had not been for this failure in the gas supply. But, in reality, instead of having been a source of damage, it has been a real service to the city. Enough manufacturing enterprises had already been brought in, and the true interests of the town would be best served by giving to those already on the ground a reasonable term of life in the way of gas supply. Nothing short of such an experience as has been recorded would have convinced the most of the citizens of the possibility of the exhaustion of their gas reservoir. It has been the fashion in Findlay to put the blame of the great failure upon the Board of Gas Trustees. They are held responsible for the fact that when the city wells were found to be practically exhausted they had no new territory leased and no outside wells drilled and ready to be connected with their lines of supply. But these charges are not altogether just. The most that can be said is that the trustees were not very much in advance of the most of the people whom they represented. There were a few citizens, it is true, that had foreseen the danger and had sought to guard against it. During the preceding year it had been suggested to the trustees by the city council that measures should be taken to secure more territory outside of the corporation lines. Good gas land could have been obtained at this time at very low rentals, but the trustees did not appreciate the necessity for action, and it is quite likely that if they had followed this advice their action would have brought down upon them the decided disapprobation of the citizens generally, who would have seen no necessity for using public money in this way. They were satisfied "to let well enough alone."

The city council, in this emergency, took the lead and placed at the service of the trustees an agent to represent them in leasing prospective gas lands in the adjoining townships. During the first half of 1889, nearly eight thousand acres of land in Allen, Cass and Marion townships were taken by the trustees for the ultimate service of the city line. But when Findlay appeared in this new capacity, there were other interests also represented in the field. The Northwestern Ohio Natural Gas Company and the Toledo gas trustees established a sharp competition with the Findlay interest for what were counted the most desirable lands, and such were readily taken up at six, eight and ten dollars per acre annual rental, and in some instances an annual rental of twenty dollars was paid. The present gas leases impose upon the city an annual burden of fifty to sixty thousand dollars. It is costing the city much more than this, however, to bring back from distant fields a fraction of the amount of gas which was so recklessly wasted in the first three years of its use. During 1889, many wells were drilled in the new territory. The pipe lines were connected with them and the city has since enjoyed a full supply as it did before the collapse of the home field. In speaking thus of the Findlay field, it is not to be understood that there is a complete exhaustion of its wells. Gas fields do not become extinct in this way. But so far as can be learned, there is not one of the wells drilled within two miles of the center of the corporation that has not been overrun to some extent with oil or water, or both. In short, the Findlay wells, when brought into service, no longer, with very few exceptions, produce dry gas. In the great majority of them, it requires all the rock pressure which they still possess to keep back the salt water. The gas is dry only when the wells are shut in.

Rock Pressure of Findlay Gas.

It has been somewhat difficult to ascertain the exact facts as to the rock pressure of the field from year to year, but so far as known, the figures are as follows: The original rock pressure of the Pioneer well was reported by W. M. Martin, Esq., at 450 pounds, but this extreme figure was soon lost. During 1886, the pressure rose but little, if any, above 400 pounds at any time. During 1887, the fall was very gradual, the gauges marking 370 and 380 pounds when the wells were closed. The figures for 1888 were not ascertained further than that they showed a steady decline. In May, 1889, the pressure had fallen to 250 pounds in independent wells, and in August of the same year it did not exceed 200 pounds. The wells in the city line fell as low as 170 pounds at this time. This amount, as has been already intimated, is not enough to keep back the salt water. To the northward a similar gradual reduction was extending. In May, 1889, when the wells within the city proper marked 250 pounds, the extreme northern wells of the township stood at about 350 pounds. The Heck well showed about 300 pounds, its position being intermediate. These facts can be best appreciated when they are arranged in tabular statement:

Rock pressure in Findlay, 1885, original, 450 lbs.
" " 1886, ——— 400 lbs.
" " 1887, August, 360–380 lbs.
" " 1889, May 1st, 250 lbs.
" " 1890, May 1st, 170–200 lbs.

The Tippecanoe Well.

During the last days of 1888, just while this alarming failure of the gas supply was becoming manifest, a larger well than any yet drilled in the field was struck two and a half miles north of the court-house. It was located on a town lot and when the ordinary depth for gas was reached by the drill, the well made a very poor showing. The well drilled for Bell Bros'. pottery, eighty rods north of the location now to be described, by Findlay parties who were interested in this company had found a light flow of gas at forty feet in the Trenton limestone. The contractor wished to stop at this point for fear of salt water, but he was obliged to go on until at a depth of sixty-five feet, a fine gas flow was struck and the well was considered fully equal to all demands. Drilling was accordingly continued in the new well to the same unusual depth, and at about seventy feet below the surface of the Trenton limestone the same large gas vein was struck; but to make the well as productive as possible, the effect of a torpedo was added. The result of the shot was the unlocking of the most monstrous volume of gas that had been seen up to this time in the State. The open pressure of the well for the first day after the explosion of the torpedo was thirty-eight pounds; on the second day, eighteen pounds; on the third day, eleven pounds. These figures stand respectively for 32,000,000, 24,000,000 and 19,000,000 cubic feet of gas per day. This remarkable result revived momentarily the courage of many, and great use was made of the fact that the greatest well in the field had been struck two years after the Karg well, and while the latter was collapsing from being overworked. The unwarranted conclusion that Findlay had just as much gas as ever was widely disseminated through the usual channels of information and misinformation on this subject. The owners of the well offered it to the gas trustees, who were in urgent need of gas for their lines; the price at which it was offered, as is understood, was ten thousand dollars. The trustees refused to purchase, but proceeded forthwith to avail themselves, if possible, of the new supply of gas. They purchased a lot adjoining the great well and proceeded with all possible dispatch to drill within sixty feet of it. The second well was a complete failure, even after being heavily torpedoed. The attempt to get possession of this great gas vein without paying for it attracted a good deal of attention and to many of the citizens themselves, much as they desired to see the gas supply replenished, the result was not unwelcome. The great well proved, however, short-lived and of no value.

The Tippecanoe well, as the great well was named, is thought to have struck a crevice in the rock. As has been said upon a preceding page, crevices do not play as important a part in modern theories of gas and oil production as they once did, but there is nothing to render improbable their occasional occurrence in this particular district. The Tippecanoe well is situated near the line of the Findlay monocline and notable fractures could occasion no surprise in strata that are bent downward 150 feet in one-fourth of a mile.

The Findlay city corporation is now co-extensive with the township, as will be remembered, embracing twenty-four square miles. The number of wells drilled within the township that deserve, or that have deserved at any time, to be called gas wells is not far from forty. Some of them were early overrun with oil and water. Some of them had but small volume at first and fell away very soon to such insignificant proportions that they were dropped out of use and account altogether. The rise of the level of oil and water in the Trenton limestone has brought it about that a great deal of land that was originally counted dry gas territory has now been invaded by oil in greater or less amount. This state of things is found near the margin of the Findlay break. Salt water has also gained upon the oil in all parts of the township where the Trenton limestone was found productive at a low elevation or near the line of 500 feet below tide. In the gas field proper, some wells are first invaded by oil and others by water as they are exhausted of gas. The former causes the most dangerous interruption of the pipes, being carried along in the system of distribution until the smaller lines are reached and in which it remains to clog the movements of the gas. In severe winter weather, however, the salt water is very dangerous. The same state of things prevails all along the boundary of the oil and gas territory, the former constantly gaining upon the latter. Some gas wells of old time are now producing oil on a considerable scale.

In the northern part of the township oil makes the great obstruction. The Heck well, for example, which originally produced eight million feet of dry gas per day has been overrun with oil to such a degree that the remnant of its gas can scarcely be utilized. It has never been subjected to a very heavy draught. For one year it carried the Hirsh & Ely Glass Works and the wire nail works. The glass factories in the northwestern part of the town were then attached, but it broke down under this duty in less than a year. Its gas is no longer suitable for use in glass works.

Utilization of Findlay Gas.

But little needs to be added to the account given in Vol. VI, as to the utilization of gas in Findlay. Glass making is still the ruling industry, and Findlay has become one of the important centers of this interest in the country. Several new works have been added to the list before published. The present enumeration is as follows:

WINDOW GLASS.

Findlay Window Glass Co.	18 pots.
Ohio Window Glass Co.	10 "
West Park Glass Co.	10 "
Buckeye Window Glass Co.	10 "
United Glass Co.	10 "
Total	58 "

TABLE WARE, GOBLETS, CHIMNEYS, ETC.

Dalzell Glass Co.	33 pots,
and two tanks of 12 and 5 pot capacity.	
Bellaire Goblet Works	30 "
Globe Chimney Works	16 "
Model Flint Glass Co.	14 "
Columbia Glass Co.	13 "
Lippincott Glass Co.	10 "
Findlay Bottle Works	8 "
Total	124 "

The system upon which the industry has been established in the new fields is essentially a vicious one. The towns that discovered or that got possession of natural gas entered into an eager competition with each other in securing for themselves the location among them of any glass manufacturers who stood ready to transfer their business to the new fuel supply. Practically free gas was at the manufacturer's command in any of these towns, and the selection generally turned on the question of how much besides could be secured from them. No question whatever, as a rule, was raised by the towns as to the amount of gas that would be required by the factory. Contracts to supply gas free, or at a nominal rate, were generally entered into on the part of the towns or the corporations controlling the gas, for three to five years. In rare exceptions the approximate amount to be used was specified. No necessity for an economical use was recognized on either side for some time. But when pressure began to fall in the lines, or when the constant demand for new wells became burdensome upon the gas companies, the question naturally arose as to whether proper economy was being observed on the part of the consumers. In many cases wells were drilled especially for the glass companies, the original production of which would many times exceed any possible

GEOLOGY OF OHIO.

use that they could make of it, and this state of things naturally tended in the same way to extravagant or, at least, careless use. Any question, or even any suggestion as to economy during the first year or two of this experience seemed like an impertinence; and many men, intelligent upon other subjects, could be found who would insist that their wells were growing stronger all the time.

But as sounder views slowly gained access to the minds of those specially interested, and as it at length became plain to even the dullest observers that the early condition of the gas supply could not possibly be maintained for a period of many years, efforts to reduce waste and establish economy began to be made on every side, and often the consumer joined with the gas companies or even took the initiative in the serious attempt to make this invaluable supply go as far as possible.

In the reckless and wanton waste of gas during the period that has thus far passed since its discovery, and in unsound and demoralizing business methods that have become general in connection with its introduction, in the giving of free gas and public and private contributions to intending manufactories, Findlay has had a bad pre-eminence, not from any worse counsels or conditions than its neighbors, but simply because the new fuel was discovered here in vastly larger quantity than any other town has found. It is a pleasure to record that at this late day, after having sustained an immense and irreparable loss, much of which was entirely unnecessary, Findlay is now doing something to establish an intelligent and economical administration of the remnant which still remains from its splendid original endowment. It is adopting a system of measuring the amounts of gas used by all of its leading consumers, and it is proceeding, so far as its contracts will allow, to base its charges upon the amount consumed. The recognition of this simple axiomatic business principle, which one might expect would be adopted without a question in all enterprises of this sort, is all that is needed to bring about the reformation so greatly to be desired throughout the entire natural gas field. At least there is but one other element that requires to be added and that is, the fixing of a proper price upon the gas. With a rate high enough to make economy an object, and with the knowledge that every foot consumed is to be paid for, a proper motive for economy will at least be brought to bear on all consumers. It is greatly to be regretted that the unmistakable teachings of science and common sense should have been ignored until incipient exhaustion had set its mark upon the field. These general remarks bear upon all the uses of natural gas and not solely upon that which is consumed in glass manufacture.

The principal iron working establishments of Findlay consist of the Briggs Iron Works, the Salem Wire Nail Works, the Findlay Iron and

PLATE III.

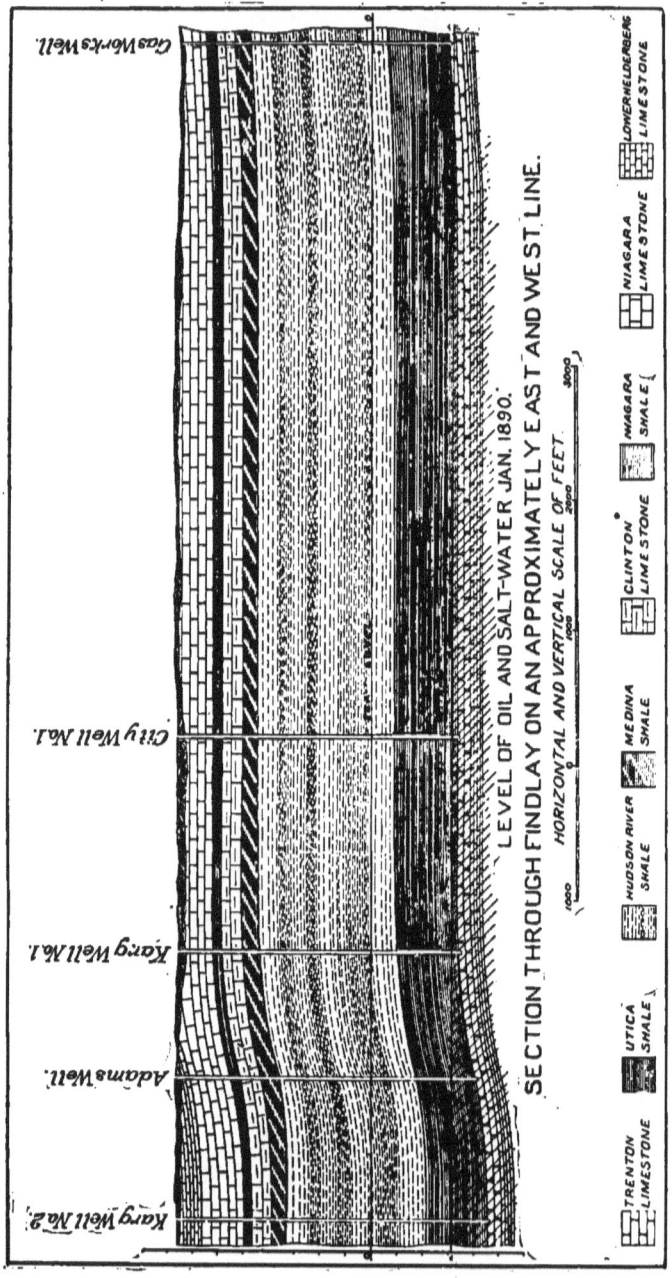

Steel Works, also known as the Wetherell Works, and the Chain Works of the west side.

The Briggs Iron Works are much the most extensive of this list. Originally consisting of the Briggs Tool Works alone, there have been added to the plant from time to time a ten-inch rolling-mill, a twenty-inch rolling-mill and a chain mill. The consumption of gas, measured on a day when the ten-inch mill was idle for repairs, was found to be 167,000 feet per hour. Making a proportional addition for the ten-inch mill, the consumption would be not less than 190,000 cubic feet per hour. The company is preparing to add an eight-inch mill to its present equipment. Such an addition would bring its total daily consumption to 5,000,000 feet.

Among the other establishments that are dependent on the Findlay gas plant for fuel and power there may be named the following:

The Findlay Water-Works, the Electric Light Works, eight machine-shops and foundries, seven boiler shops, fifteen planing-mills, three brick yards, four lime-kilns, seven stone quarries, one clay pot factory, one target works. In addition to these larger uses of gas in manufacturing, the city line supplies with fuel 7,600 stoves and maintains about 10,000 residence lights. Laundry stoves, bakeries, restaurant ranges, furnaces and the like, still further increase the consumption. The corporation owns thirty-three wells in the township, all of which are withdrawn from use at the present time. Its entire dependence is now on Allen, Cass and Marion townships, in which it owns twenty-six wells, twenty of which the corporation drilled and six of which it bought. It holds leases on 7,655 acres in these townships, the annual rentals on which exceed $50,000. It has expended in its gas plant nearly $500,000, and its present liabilities on this account are nearly $400,000.

The rates for domestic use from November 1, 1888, were as follows: Fifty cents per month for each stove, if paid before the 10th of the month. For lights a rate of five cents per jet was established, with numerous discounts as the number of lights in a residence was increased. From October 1, 1889, the rates were practically doubled, stoves now being charged $1 per month. A new schedule will soon be published, in which a further advance of rates is expected.

For the glass furnaces and other factories, various rates are charged, depending on the special contracts obtained by each at the time of its location. One glass factory, for example, pays $3.00 per annum for each pot, while another may pay as high as $10.00 per pot. In either case, and in all cases, however, the charges for gas are merely nominal. They have no relation whatever to the value of the fuel.

The Hydraulic Press Brick Works were offered free gas by an organization known as the Findlay Board of Trade at a time when speculation ran highest in the town. The Common Council in some way guaranteed this claim, and when the public supply fell short, two wells were drilled at the expense of the city in North Findlay, near the works, to provide the necessary fuel. The pressure of this part of the field had already gone down to 200 pounds and the rock was therefore overrun with salt water to a considerable degree, but the gas is still used successfully in burning the brick. A third well, too much overrun with salt water to be longer kept in the city lines, was sold to the brick works last year. The salt water drops from the pipes as the gas is burning in the kilns, but so long as the flow is not interrupted no disadvantage is recognized. These wells in reality furnish one of the most important of the later facts of the field. The rock pressure has been maintained in them at about 170 pounds for the last year and a considerable amount of wet gas has been turned to good account. Of course all the available back pressure is left upon them and the more there is of it the better the gas is. Their behavior warrants the expectation that a good deal of value may still be obtained from the overflowed territory. Wells behave differently, however, in different parts of the field. Sometimes they are drowned out abruptly and irrevocably like the blowing out of a lamp, and at other times they are slow in dying. In speaking thus of the possibilities of the utilization of the remnant of Findlay gas, it must be borne in mind that this can be continued only on a very small scale. If all the wells were opened the salt water would undoubtedly make a complete and permanent conquest of the gas rock in a very short time.

SUMMARY.

A brief summary of the facts pertaining to the gas supply of Findlay will be given here, embodying the principal results that have been already stated.

1. When Findlay gas was discovered in 1885, the slope of the Trenton limestone that underlies the town was occupied with dry gas for 100 feet in vertical range. At the present time, water or oil or both appear in every well. In other words, when a well is at the present time allowed to flow without obstruction, the presence of salt water or oil is always apparent in the gas in such quantities as to obstruct or arrest the flow. These facts are represented in the accompanying diagrams. (Figgure 3.)

2. The original rock pressure of the Findlay field was 450 pounds to the square inch. It nowhere now rises above 200 pounds, except in the extreme northern portion of the township. In parts of the central dis-

trict the maximum pressure at the present time does not exceed 170 pounds.

3. Of this original pressure of 450 pounds, not more than two-thirds could ever be properly counted available for gas supply. The last third and more should have been held in reserve to keep the gas rock free from water and oil. The life of the field would thus have been considerably lengthened if this course had been maintained.

4. The total consumption of gas in Findlay, at the present time, has not been absolutely determined. The following estimate is offered as an approximation to the quantity used each day:

Glass furnaces..	10,000,000	cubic feet.
Iron mills ....,...................................	10,000,000	"
Other factories	6,000,000	"
Household use..	4,000,000	"
Total..................:...	30,000,000	"

The last named element is estimated on the basis of winter use. In the summer this item would be reduced to 2,000,000 feet, or possibly less. The glass furnaces also are closed for several months in the summer and the consumption is correspondingly lessened thereby.

(2) *Allen Township.*—The great prospective value of Allen township as gas producing territory was recognized from the early days of the Findlay field. The Findlay break, which has been shown to be the structural feature that determines the value of Findlay proper as a source of gas and oil, was proved to continue without interruption to the northward and moreover a great well had been drilled on Section 12, in the immediate vicinity of Van Buren, in the fall of 1886. The Kagy well, which is the one referred to above, was described in Volume VI. Its production of gas was somewhat in excess of the Karg well of Findlay which, up to this time, had been by far the largest of the field.

At the present time, Allen township shares with Bloom township, Wood county, the honors of the gas producing territory of Ohio. In fact, the Trenton limestone reaches in it its highest mark in this line, and the recent great wells of the township leave even the Karg well so far behind that if the latter were discovered now it would be commonplace and would attract no particular attention.

Of the twenty-four sections of land in Allen township twenty belong to the gas belt, only the four following lying beyond its limits, viz., 14, 23, 26, 35. These sections occupy the western line of the township on its southern side and have recently been found to constitute an oil field of great value and promise.

Up to August last, forty-six wells had been drilled in the township. Since that time, Findlay City has drilled ten or twelve wells additional, and the other companies have each added a few. The number now, therefore, exceeds sixty. The distribution and ownership of the wells is partially shown in the following list, those of the southern sections being named first. The list is not complete at the present date.

GAS WELLS OF ALLEN TOWNSHIP.

Name of landowner.	Owner of well.	Section.	Quarter.	Position.
Miller	Findlay city	31	N. W.	Center of northern half.
Skinner	Kellogg Pipe Works	30	S. W.	N. E. corner.
Toledo city	Toledo city	30	N. E.	N. W. "
Toledo city	"	30	N. W.	N. E. "
Mellott	Northwestern	30	N. E.	Center of northern half.
Leiser	Toledo city	30	S. E.	" "
Leiser	"	30	"	" eastern half.
Leiser	"	30	"	" southern half.
Hart	"	30	S. W.	" northern half.
Crowell	Northwestern	29	N. W.	N. E. corner.
Harris	Findlay city	19	S. E.	Center of southern half.
Huntington, 1, 2 and 3	"	19	"	S. W. corner.
Ware	Toledo city	19	S. W.	N. E. corner.
Ware	"	19	"	S. E. corner.
Ware	"	19	"	"
Dewey Stave Co	Northwestern Ohio	19	"	"
Farmers Co. (village lot)	Farmers' Co.	19	S. E.	S. W. corner.
Findlay (village lot)	Findlay city	19	"	"
Luden, 1 and 2	"	19	"	S. E. corner.
Downs	"	13	"	N. E. corner.
Trout	Toledo city	13	N. E.	"
Frank		18	"	N. W. corner.
Kagy	Northwestern	18	N. W.	Central northern.
Kagy	"	18	S. W.	Central eastern.
Leiser	Toledo city	18	"	N. E. corner.
Leiser	"	18	"	Center.
Leiser	"	18	"	Central western.
Leiser	"	18	"	S. E. corner.
Hutson	Northwestern	17	"	S. W. corner.
Shelby	"	18	N. W.	N. E. corner.
Harris	Findlay city	24		
March	"	20	S. W.	Center of eastern half.
Carr	Findlay city	20	N. E.	S. E. corner.
Barnd	Northwestern	20	S. W.	N. W. corner.
George	"	20	"	Central western.
Weisel	"	12	N. W.	Central northern.
Eckerly		12	S. E.	Central southern.
Kagy	Northwestern	12	"	Central eastern.
Marks		12	"	Center of southern half.
Marks & Kelley		7	S. W.	S. W. corner.
Carnahan, 1	Findlay city	7	"	N. W. corner.
Carnahan, 2	"	7	"	Central northern.
Leiser	Toledo city	11	"	N. W. corner.
Baker, No. 1	Northwestern	6	N. E.	Central western.
Baker, No. 2	"	6	"	S. W. corner.
Slaughterbeck	"	6	"	S. E. corner.

To this list there may be added without special assignment of location the Stough, Routzen, Harry 1 and 2, Eceles, Biggs, Weinland, Mellott and Markle wells, all belonging to Findlay city.

The Great Wells.

Two of the wells of the township, viz., the Hutson on section 17, and the Mellott on section 30, have reached such astonishing figures that they stand by themselves among Ohio wells. The Tippecanoe well of Findlay township, if it had maintained its initial flow for more than a single day, would have deserved to be counted in the same list. The dynamic pressure of the Hutson well, as long as it remained open, reached the amazing figure of forty three pounds in the casing. This stands for a production of 32,000,000 feet in twenty-four hours. The facts pertaining to the well are as follows: The territory was not counted especially promising. A Findlay city well, located sixty rods south, had proved to be a small well. The Hutson well found the Trenton limestone at 1,135 feet below the surface, or at approximately 330 feet below tide. Before reaching the Trenton, a violent blower of gas was found, at a depth of 800 feet, the production of which was estimated to be at least 4,000,000 feet per day. It exhausted itself in the course of thirty-six hours. Gas was found as soon as the Trenton limestone was reached, and from ten feet below the surface of the stratum, the flow was counted large. Drilling was continued, however, for thirty-two feet in the rock, but when that depth was reached, a mighty torrent of gas was set free which was at once recognized by those acquainted with our greatest wells as outranking any thing yet found in the field. The gas was entirely dry. The well was tubed with four-inch pipe and the flow of the gas was able to just balance 400 feet of the tubing when the work was begun. It gained, however, some increase after this time. It was turned at once into the Northwestern Company's mains and makes a large factor in the present supply of one of its most important lines. This well was completed early in 1890.

The Mellott well, situated in section 30, was drilled in the summer of 1889. The Trenton was penetrated to a depth of about fifty feet. The gas showed an open pressure of twenty six pounds in the casing, which stands for a daily production of 27,000,000 feet. The well and the gas rights of the farm on which it is located were bought by the Northwestern Ohio Gas Company. The price paid for it was $25,000. This well was also promptly connected with the lines of the company, and is said to have been drawing with full force upon the territory from the first.

Among the other great wells of the township may be named the Dewey Stave Company's well at Stuartsville, the Findlay city well in the same neighborhood, and the Mays well, all of which are said to have shown eight pounds or more of open pressure in the casing. Their production began, therefore, with at leat 17,000,000 feet per day. The three Ware wells also, that belong to the Toledo city trustees were very large wells, yielding, one of them, in four-inch, and the other two in three inch tubing 11,860,000, 11,504,000 and 9,101,000 cubic feet in twenty-four hours respectively.

Characteristics of the Field.

The facts here given are enough to establish the wonderfully productive character of the Trenton limestone that underlies Allen township. The gas rock proper is very open in grain as a rule. It occurs in beds of varying thickness and at different depths. Sometimes the great flow is reached at fifteen or twenty feet in the Trenton, and sometimes at twice or even three times this depth. Sometimes it is found in the top of the stratum, and when this occurs drilling can be carried deeper than when the main flow is found at fifteen or twenty feet in the rock. The great flows often prevent any deeper descent of the drill. The current reports that the Stuartsville field has a thickness of seventy or eighty feet of gas rock are entirely without foundation. The gas rock is of as good quality and is found in as great a thickness as in any other portions of the entire field, but beyond this the facts do not warrant us to go. In explanation of the great production of the district, it is suggested that the best quality of rock is more continuous than in the other centers of production. In other words, it is the horizontal rather than the vertical extension of the gas rock to which the great wells are owing.

No section of the field shows on the whole greater permeability of the gas rock than this, but at the same time there are minor barriers established in it that give rise to surprising results. The Hutson well, which is beyond a question the largest gas well ever drilled in Ohio, is surrounded by moderate or even small wells on all sides, and separated from them by no great intervals. It may be suggested that the size of these great wells is in some way due to the disturbances of equilibrium and to the torpedo shocks that have preceded them in the field. Thus far none of the great wells has been struck until the field had undergone a good deal of development.

The Mellott well was no sooner brought in than a half dozen wells were located by different interests as near to it as they could find standing ground. One only of these proved large, and its volume was but little more than one-half of the volume of its great neighbor. Still more inexplicable is the history of a well drilled within sixty feet of the one last named. When the gas rock was reached less than one-half of the volume which the new well sought to rival was found in it. There are many such cases as these already on record, but they by no means invalidate the statements already made as to the general connection and interdependence of all portions of the township. These facts are abundantly substantiated on independent grounds.

Rock Pressure and Behavior of the Field.

Owing to the general permeability of the Trenton rock in Allen township all portions of the twenty square miles of the gas territory share a common fortune, so far as rock pressure is concerned. Strictly speaking, Allen township belongs to the Findlay field, and its rock pressure is really dependent on what goes on in that township. Passing northwards from the center of Findlay, during 1889, for example, the pressure was found gradually strengthening from the danger line of 250 pounds in the center of the town to 300 pounds in the Heck well, and 350 pounds in the northern tier of sections. Allen township started with this pressure at that time on its southern boundary, but it made important additions to the northward.

What the original rock pressure of the gas was in this special district we have no means of ascertaining. The great Kagy well at Van Buren had served as a relief to the highest tension of the gas before any observations of rock pressure were made. It flowed unrestrained for six weeks before it was tubed. A calculation of the pressure on grounds indicated in Chapter III would make it about 460 pounds. This estimate is confirmed by the fact that the first Stuartsville well showed in 1888 a pressure of 450 pounds. There was then no other well within two miles of it in any direction. From this it can be judged that a distance of two miles furnishes a measure of protection to an isolated well. In 1889 the great development began. The Northwestern Ohio Gas Company, the Findlay and the Toledo trustees competed eagerly with each other for territory, and wells were sunk in large numbers, as already shown. Several were located on village lots in Van Buren and Stuartsville, and the derricks of the rival interests confronted each other along all boundaries. Two series of gas mains were made to penetrate the new field forthwith, those, namely, of the Northwestern Ohio Company, and of the Findlay trustees. The Toledo pipe line was delayed, but fifteen or twenty wells were drilled in the township by the city trustees.

The experience that has been accumulated since this time is very important, and the deductions from it are certainly unexpected and startling. In August, 1889, the rock pressure of the Carnahan wells, on section 7, a mile north of Van Buren, was 395 pounds. The pressure at Stuartsville had fallen without any use whatever of the gas from 450 pounds in 1888 to 385 pounds in June, 1889. When the Ware wells were completed two or three months later, the pressure was 365 pounds; the Findlay Trustees' wells registered 325 pounds in October.

Since this date a rapid decline has set in, which has continued without arrest or abatement until the present time. The figures for May, in wells scattered through the township, range from 260 pounds to 285 pounds. In a single well, viz., the Trout well, section 13, separated from the main field, as has been proved, by a low ridge in the Trenton limestone, a pressure of 315 pounds is now reported. This is the highest pressure known in Allen township at the present time.

This reduction of pressure is not by any means restricted to wells that are being drawn upon for the supply of the pipe lines. It extends to all wells and nearly alike to all. A well that has been constantly locked in and that has never furnished a foot of gas for use reaches approximately the same pressure that the most heavily taxed wells show, if the latter are not more than one-quarter mile distant. The wells are so distributed that the reduction, as has been shown, covers practically the entire township. The figures are best appreciated when set in tabular statement, as they were for Findlay township:

Stuartsville (Section 19) 1888		450	pounds.
"	" June, 1889	385	"
"	" August, 1889	365	"
"	" October, 1889	325	"
"	" May, 1890	275	"
Van Buren (Section 7) August, 1889		395	"
"	" May, 1890	285	"

The last named wells have never been drawn upon, although connected with a pipe line.

The Stuartsville field is thus seen to have lost 28 per cent. of the pressure that it had nine months ago. A like reduction for the next nine months would carry the figures down to 200 pounds. But this last named figure stands practically for the death of the field so far as the support of pipe lines is concerned. The effective pressure at any time is the excess above 200 pounds. On this basis the field has lost 60 per cent. since one year ago.

Not only has the pressure decreased, but a corresponding loss has taken place in the volume of the wells. A large well of the Stuartsville field, which was drilled in the summer of 1889, was re-measured in May of this year and the loss in volume exceeded 40 per cent. It is not probable, however, that the same percentage of decrease would be observed in all wells of the district.

Still another feature of equally threatening import is the appearance of oil in many of the wells, and especially in the wells of the Northwestern Company. The rock pressure has been suffered to fall far below the danger line, and it is obvious that dry gas in time to come must be paid for by the sacrifice of a large part of the tension which the gas may still retain.

As to the future of the Allen township gas field we are not left in doubt. It is following directly in the track of the Findlay field to which indeed it truly belongs. Just how soon the remainder of the descent to 200 pounds will be accomplished can not, of course, be foretold. It is greatly to be hop d that when the Findlay glass furnaces are closed for the summr the decline will be arrested. It often happens that pressures are restored, to some extent, in gas fields between May and November. They are usually lowest in March and April.

We are obliged to conclude from the experience of Findlay that when the pressure falls to 200 pounds the field is practically dead. There will still be a large amount of gas left in the district, but it will be so encumb red with oil and water that it can no longer be safely distributed through the lines of the present systems.

The hope has been entertained by many that when the pressure of the fi ld has fallen to 250 or 300 pounds the further decline will be arrested or at least its rate of fall will be greatly reduced. The experience of some of the Pennsylvania fields is adduced as pointing in this direction. Unfortunately the experience which is, up to this time, available in northwestern O io, does not support this expectation. The decline of the Findlay field, for example, is arrested only when the consumption is stopped and the point at which the arrest is made is below that at which dry gas can be supplied to the pipes. Even without any large use the pressure of the Findlay field seems to be slowly falling at the present time, one of the best remaining wells in the city proper, showing a loss of twenty pounds between March and May of the present year, falling from 220 to 200 pounds. The gas in this case must be drawn away to portions of t e field somewhat remo e from the depleted district, as but little draught is made upon it here.

Allen township has been the great reliance of the Findlay and Toledo gas trustees, and the splendid industries of the f rmer city are leaning hard upon it now, but the record of the last year, as given in the preceding pag s, is undeniably alarming. The Findlay trustees are doing all that is in their power to maintain their supply and guard their wells, but the life of the field is not within their keeping

Of the twenty-four wells drilled, or purchased by the gas trustees of Toledo, about half are located in Allen township, and much more than half of their estimated production is credited to these wells. An account of the important action of this city in the matter of securing a supply of

9 G.

gas which shall be under municipal control, will be given on a succeeding page. The trustees made contracts with landowners to drill wells and sell them the gas when found, at specified amounts for each million feet produced by the completed wells. In one instance where ten acres were counted to a well, $1,000 per million feet of daily capacity were paid to the landowner on the completion of the wells. In another case, three wells were drilled for the trustees on fifteen acres of land, only five acres being thus allowed to each well. The price in this case was $750 per million feet. The territory proved productive to a high degree, and the three wells aggregated more than thirty million feet of daily capacity. There is good reason to believe that if fifteen wells had been drilled on the same territory, and under the same conditions, they would have averaged as well as the three that were drilled. In this case, the production of the tract could have been raised to 150 million feet per day, or even this amount might have been further multiplied by putting down a still greater number of wells. Of course such a multiplication would stand for nothing in the supply of a pipe line, the life and service of which should be expected to continue for a reasonable term of years. Just what acreage would have been best adapted to the character of the Allen township field, it is vain to inquire. The rival interests in the acquisition and use of the gas forbade from the first a wise and economical administration of this noble stock of power. But if at least eighty acres could have been left to each well, and if a back pressure of at least 200 pounds could have been assured to each, instead of running a meteoric race of one or two years, this sub-division of the field might have continued to pour out its store of light and heat and power for possibly a decade. A single well will undoubtedly drain a large acreage.

Owner of land.	Owner of well.	Section.	Quarter.	Position.
....	Northwestern Ohio Co	1	4 wells ...	E. half.
....	" "	2	N. E........	....
Border	" "	2	S. W........	N. E. corner.
Overholt.............	" "	10	N. E........	"
Frank	" "	10	N. E........	Center.
Beeson	Findlay City............	21	S. W........	"
Wills.................	"	21	S. E........	"
Weinland	"	21	S. E........	S. E. corner.
Baker	Toledo City	26	N. E........	Center.
Hammond	"	26	S. W........	Center, west.
Peebles..............	Northwestern Ohio	27	S. W........	"
Grubb................	Findlay City............	28	S. W........	"
Weinland	"	28	N. E........	N. E. corner.
Norris................	"	33	N. E........	Near center.
Gasman	Tiffin City	34	S. E........	"

(3) *Cass Township.*—Like Allen, Cass township consists of twenty-four sections. All of them have been counted good gas territory from the first and nothing has been found in the development hitherto to change this estimate. The southeastern sections give less promise than the rest. A partial list of the gas wells already drilled in the township is appended. Compared with the great wells of Allen township, the wells of Cass are moderate in volume. Their ordinary range is from one to four million feet per day. Those on the western boundary share all the conditions of the field last described. The rock pressure in wells located on section 21 was found to be 285 pounds in April, 1890, but the anomalous figure of 390 pounds is reported for a single well of small volume in the north central part of the township at the present time, May, 1890. This well is two miles or more distant from other wells, but it is probable that it is also protected by some structural features as yet undeveloped from the exhaustion that is now in progress in the entire region. The gas rock is known to be close and compact in this particular district.

(4) *Marion Township* —This township is strictly continuous with the Findlay gas field. It was proved to be productive in 1886 and has been an important source of supply since gas began to be piped away from the district. The Tiffin Natural Gas Company, which is now merged in or controlled by the Northwestern Ohio Company, has derived all the gas that it has carried to Tiffin from three wells located in this township, viz., the Thorntree well, located on the farm of Isaac Davis, and the Blair and Underwood wells. The company has drilled other wells in the township, but thus far has not utilized them. The well drilled in 1887 on the Adam Roth farm, in Section 14, was for one month, lacking one day, the greatest gas well that had at that time been drilled in the new field. The open pressure in the casing was fully six and one-half pounds, according to the testimony of the superintendent of the line. But at the end of the time named above, the well was overrun with a flood of salt water which it was hopeless to oppose. The gas was blown out like a lamp, and it gives no sign in the present heavy column of sulphurous brine that occupies its former place.

The Thorntree well was the main reliance of the line for a year or more, but its gas was never dry. Oil, in large quantity, appeared within a week after the well was finished, and for the last year it has gained so much that it has been found necessary to shut the well off from the line altogether. If it were allowed to flow freely, there is some ground for expecting that it would make a fair oil well. Though shut off from the line, its pressure has fallen nearly at the same rate as in the wells that have been most heavily taxed. It is reported as standing now at a little above 300 pounds ($311\frac{1}{2}$ pounds in May, 1890). When first drilled it showed

450 pounds, and it did not fall far below this figure for a long time. Its days as a gas well are already numbered.

Clustered around the Thorntree and the Roth wells, in Sections 10, 11, 14 and 15, are the four wells of the Carey Natural Gas Company, and the same number also of the Kenton Company. As pointed out on a previous page, these wells interlock in a way that is dangerous to the life of the field. Some of the wells are but one or two hundred feet apart and it is obvious that some have been run without any back pressure whatever. The gas rock has consequently been invaded by water and the pressure has declined at an alarmingly rapid rate. It is now below 300 pounds, having lost a full hundred pounds during the last eight months, and during the summer rest of the field it will scarcely reach 300 pounds.

A partial list of the wells drilled in the township is given below:

Owner of land.	Owner of well.	Section.	Quarter.
Isaac Davis	Northwestern Ohio Co.	11	N. W.
Adam Roth	" "	14	
Blair	" "	11	
Underwood	" "	11	
Mrs. Wolfe	Carey Natural Gas Co.	11	
Dr. Davis	" "	11	
Gick	" "	14	
Bond	" "	11	

Kenton Co.'s Nos. 1, 2, 3, 4 are located mainly in section 11. Several small wells have been drilled in other portions of the township.

As has been already shown, Marion township has lost 33⅓ per cent. of its original rock pressure, and counting 200 pounds as essential to the maintenance of the field in safe condition, it has lost 60 per cent. of the pressure which could properly be counted available at the opening of its wells.

(5) *Washington Township* —The northwestern corner of the township is to be counted as a part of the great Bloom township gas field. Section 6 has furnished four wells to the Northwestern Ohio Company, which are known as the Kelley wells. They are all of moderate volume, but have proved valuable sources of dry gas to the pipe line. They have received due care and protection through all their history and still show fair volume and pressure. No wells of the field exhibit more vitality than these.

In section 20, two or more wells of small production have been drilled for the supply of the village of Arcadia. The production of the wells is understood to be a few hundred thousand feet per day.

THE TRENTON LIMESTONE.

Tests in other portions of the township have not given encouragement to the driller, although, of course, oil and gas in small quantities are to be found every-where in this general district.

The same line of remarks applies to Big Lick township at the present time, but tests of the oil production of this township are in progress that will soon show the real character of the Trenton limestone underlying i

(B) GAS WELLS OF WOOD COUNTY.

This county takes the lead at present in the gas production of the State. In this production six townships have a part, but the gas wells of two at least are growing feeble, and of the remaining four one only is of great value. The townships named in the order of their importance are Bloom, Perry, Henry, Portage, Plain and Center. The production of these townships will be separately described.

(1) *Bloom Township.*—This township consists of thirty-six square miles. Its surface is approximately level, though there is a gradual fall to the northward. The elevations of a few wells are given to illustrate this uniformity of the surface. The entire range for the sections represented is less than 50 feet.

Smith, H............	Section 6........................	707 feet above tide.
Simon, G...........	" 9........................	750 "
Lefler...............	" 16........................	719 "
Bailey...............	" 16........................	723 "
Wyrick..............	" 17........................	721 "
Neihel...............	" 21........................	725 "
Richards............	" 25........................	751 "
Stove................	" 27........................	732 "
Fries.................	" 27........................	739 "
Painter..............	" 28........................	730 "
Fife, W. H.........	" 31........................	744 "
Welker..............	" 31........................	736 "
Stave Co., Bairdstown	" 33........................	743 "
Bloomdale Co......	" 35........................	755 "
Urie..................	" 35........................	752 "
Myers................	" 36........................	755 "

Sections 1, 2, 3, 4, 10, 11, 12, 13, 14, 24, can not in the light of present knowledge be counted gas territory. In part of them, the rock is occupied by oil and where oil is found in this part of the field, salt water is not far below. The most northeasterly sections seem to be verging toward barren territory. On the northwestern line of sections, viz., in 6, 7 and 18, the production is divided between oil and gas. The remainder of the township constitutes the largest and most valuable continuous portion of the original Findlay gas field. The upper surface of the Trenton limestone mainly lies between 300 and 360 feet below tide. It constitutes a low arch rising from 380 feet below tide at North Baltimore to 300 feet in the

Bloom Township Gas Wells.

Names of farms.	Names of owners.	Section.	Quarter.	Position.
Adams	Northwestern	28	S.E.	S. E. corner.
Bailey	"	16	S.E.	"
Barringer	"	35	S.W.	W. half, W. of ce'ter.
Beedle	"	17	S.E.	N. E. corner.
Brandeberry	"	27	N.E.	S. of Pike, in corner of road.
Brownheller	Tiffin	36	N.E.	N. W. corner.
Brubaker	Northwestern	15	N.E.	Near cen. of E. line.
Busby	"	22	N.E.	Near cen. of W. line.
Busby, T.	"	20	S.W.	N. E. corner.
Fife, W. H.	Toledo	31	N.E.	S. E. corner.
Fife, W. H.	"	31	S.E.	"
Fife, N	"	31	S E.	S. W. corner.
Fife, N	"	31	S.E.	N. W. corner.
Fries	Northwestern	27	N.E.	N. E. corn-r.
Fry	Toledo	16	N.E.	Near N. W. corner.
Gray, R.	"	30	N.E.	N. E. corner.
Handwick, J.	Northwestern	29	S.W.	"
Kunkler	"	22	S.E.	N. of cen. of S. half.
Lefler	"	16	S.W.	N. of center, near W. line.
Lenhart	Bloomdale Development Co.	35	S.E.	E. of cen. of N. half.
Leslie, D	Fostoria	25	N.E.	S E. corner.
Mincks	Northwestern	35	S.W.	N. E. corner.
Moore	"	14	N.E.	W. of center, near N. line.
Mock, M.	Toledo	30	N.E.	S. E. corner.
Myers	Bloomdale	36	S.W.	S. W. corner.
Painter	Northwestern	28	N.E.	N. E. corner.
Neibel, E.	"	21	S.E.	N. of cen. of E. half.
Pelton	"	24	S.E.	N. E. corner.
Rhodes, L	"	32	S.W.	Center of N. half.
Richards, Wm.	"	25	S E.	S. W. corner.
Rosendale	"	23	S.E.	Center of S. half.
Simon, E.	"	32	S.E.	N. E corner.
Simon, L	Tiffin	35	N.E.	Near cen. of W. half.
Simon, L.	"	36	N.W.	Near N. W. corner.
Simon, G.	Northwestern	35	N.W.	S. W. corner.
Simon, J. L.	Toledo	9	S.W.	S. E. corner.
Simon, L.	Northwestern	30	S.E.	N. E. corner.
Simon, L.	"	29	N.W.	"
Spacky	Toledo	9	S.W.	Center of N. half.
Smith, W. H.	Northwestern	36	S.E.	N. E. corner.
Smith, H.	Toledo	8	N.E	Near cen. of W. half.
Smith, S.	"	8	N.W	S. W. corner.
Swinehart	Northwestern	23	N.W.	Near cen. of E. half.
Stove	"	27	N.W.	N. W. corner.
Urie, Geo	"	35	N.E.	N. E. corner.
Toledo Co.	Toledo	17	N.W.	"
Wyric, D. H.	"	17	N.W.	"
Stave Co. of Bairdstown	Bairdstown	33	S.W.	N. W. corner.
Welker, Mrs. Cynthia	Welker	31	N.W.	Center.

vicinity of Bairdstown, and descending again to 380 feet on the eastern side of the township. There are, however, a few abrupt flexures of the

THE TRENTON LIMESTONE.   135

strata disclosed by the drill in the northern central sections and some disappointment as to the continuity of the gas territory has been occasioned by this discovery. Oil and salt water make an unwelcome appearance where all was thought to be highly productive gas land. The gas wells are not of the largest capacity, but they hold an excellent average. Few of them showed, while the field was fresh, less than 3,000,000 feet of daily flow from the casing. At the other extreme stood the great Simons well with its 12.000,000 feet of daily flow.

A list of the gas wells of the township, nearly complete to August, 1889, is here appended. The principal additions to the number since this date are the wells drilled by the Tiffin trustees on sections 26, 36 and 35 and a few others by the companies previously in the field, as Fostoria, the Northwestern Ohio, etc.

Rock Pressure and Behavior of the Field.

The original rock pressure of the Bloom township gas wells is commonly given as ranging from 440 to 465 pounds. A large number of the wells showed figures within these limits when the gas was first reached. The highest rock pressure of the township is recorded in the case of the great Simon's well, already referred to. When the well was new, by shutting off the flow, a pressure of 480 pounds would be almost instantly shown, and very soon thereafter 520 pounds would be registered, at which point the gauge was steady. These figures are anomalous. They have not been duplicated, so far as known, in the entire field. A pressure of 480 pounds would require a depth of the porous Trenton of 404 feet below tide, according to the calculations previously given, in which the salt water is assumed to rise 600 feet above tide. The Rocky Ford well, one mile to the northwest of the Simon's well, found the Trenton 424 feet below tide and buried in salt water. For the 480 pounds we could therefore well enough account, but not for the 520 pounds without the ascent of the water column to a height of more than 600 feet above tide. It would require a column 1090 feet in length to produce this pressure, or in other words, the salt water should have risen in the Rocky Ford well within 100 feet of the surface.

In July, 1889, the rock pressure ranged between 375 and 390 pounds in the wells of Bloom township. Wells situated three-quarters of a mile from any direct draught dropped to the same figure that wells of the pipe lines showed.

The present rock pressure of the most prolific portion of the township is 330 pounds. This figure was obtained on May 17, 1890, from the Bloomdale Improvement Company's well, located within the village limits, the original pressure of which is given as 460 pounds. The well has never been in use, and but little of its gas has been burned in vain display, but it has lost 130 pounds of pressure through the drainage of the territory effected by neighboring wells. The total reduction is seen to be twenty-eight per cent. of the original pressure, as in Allen township. Counting 200 pounds the danger line, as in the Findlay field, the original effective or available pressure was 260 pounds. Just one-half of this has been lost without any use of the well. A measurement of the volume showed also a considerable reduction from that recorded two years ago. Counting 445 pounds the average pressure of the township, the loss has already reached 26 per cent., and the available pressure has been reduced 47 per cent. These figures are appended in tabular statement.

Rock pressure, Bloomdale, 1887........ .... 440–465 pounds.
   "   "   1888 ....
   "   "   1889, July................................... 375–390 pounds.
   "   "   1890, May................................... 325–330 "

It is greatly to be hoped that the gas may be maintained in proper condition for piping in this most important center of the field when its pressure falls below 200 pounds, but such facts as have been obtained do not afford encouragement to this view. From all the light that is now available, we must conclude that gas can not be sent out to markets thirty or more miles distant after its initial pressure has fallen below the limit above named.

The presence of so many separate interests in Bloom township gas field is certain to lead to a comparatively rapid exhaustion of it, in the first place and principally because of the larger amounts required by the several pipe lines, and in the second place, because the conflicting interests whose respective lands interlock with each other can not be relied upon to maintain the back pressure that the preservation of the field demands. All turns, of course, upon the amounts required by the pipe lines. Most of the companies have a heavy responsibility on their hands in the supply of extensive factories, and so long as they can keep their pipes full to-day, they are sure to do it, even at the risk of damage to their field to-morrow or in a week, a month or six months. They put as far off as they can the evil day, even though they see it steadily coming nearer.

The volume of a well decreases with its loss of rock pressure, but the rate is not the same. If a well is heavily taxed its volume goes down faster than its pressure. One well has receded from a production of three and one-half million feet per day to one and one-half million feet during the two years of its flow.

THE TRENTON LIMESTONE. 137

The companies now drawing gas from Bloom township in the large way are the following, viz., The Northwestern Ohio Company, through two main lines, the Fostoria Corporation trustees and the Tiffin Corporation trustees. The Toledo trustees have also bought and leased lands in the township and have drilled a number of wells.

The Bowling Green Natural Gas Company has also acquired the gas rights of 500 acres in the southwestern portion of the township, namely, in Sections 28 and 33.

Some of the wells of the different companies have recently been drilled on small tracts, as on village lots. This policy, when adopted by any company, naturally leads to undue haste on the part of its neighbors to secure their share of the gas supply and the nearest wells are accordingly likely to be allowed to run into the lines without the proper back pressure. The gas in the rock does not respect surface boundaries, and a well drilled on a village lot has as good a hold upon the field as a well on a quarter section, provided other wells are not drilled near by. Around several centers of disturbance of this sort, the rock pressure has fallen considerably below that of the field at large and to a point that indicates danger in the near future if the fall is continued. It seems to be within the power of any party owning one or more wells to greatly reduce or even to destroy the value of the gas territory near its wells. The radius through which the evil effects of the abuse of a well can be felt varies, no doubt, in different parts of a gas field. It must, in this region, be as great as one quarter of a mile.

The Northwestern Ohio Company has secured the gas rights of almost the entire township. It did this at an early day, and most of its land is held at an annual rental of $1 per acre, with $100 for each well that is drilled paid to the landowner. Scattered farms, however, and small tracts, distributed here and there through the township, it failed to get, and these have become the points of attack on the part of the competing corporations. It has been especially easy to obtain ground on which a derrick might be planted in and around the small villages of the township. Wells have accordingly been drilled by the several boards of city trustees at or near Bloomdale, Bairdstown and Eagleville. The tracts that have been left over have been the objects of sharp competition. Annual rentals of $10 or $15 an acre are readily paid and farms, worth for agricultural purposes $50 to $75, are sold at $150 or $175 per acre. As old leases expire also, the farmers are quick to recognize their advantage, and each one expects to obtain a little more than his neighbor has been able to get.

The Fostoria trustees hold comparatively little land in Bloom township. They have recently drilled two wells, one forty rods east of Eagleville, and the other, in Section 35, a half mile to the southwest. The first is a well of small volume. The second produced a large volume of gas after being torpedoed, but salt water came with it. Its production is estimated by the trustees at four million feet per day. It remains to be seen how much of the gas can be rendered available for the pipe line. They have another well in Section 25, which was drilled last year.

The Tiffin trustees have drilled seven wells in Bloom township, and have others under contract. Two that are located on Section 26 are reported by the Superintendent as respectively yielding five and one-half and six million feet from the casing. Other wells are located in Sections 35 and 36. The Browneller well, on the north side of Section 36, is said to have shown a production of three million feet from the casing, with a rock pressure of 450 pounds as recently as November, 1888. If the observations of pressure are correct, the decline to 330 pounds within eighteen months, shows that the vitality of the field is giving way at an alarming rate. On the south side of Section 36, a weak well was drilled, which after being "shot," filled up with salt water and was abandoned.

The Toledo trustees' wells are located in Sections 8, 9, 16, 17, 30 and 31, all of which is justly counted excellent gas territory.

The Bowling Green Gas Company's territory consists of about 500 acres of well esteemed gas lands, mainly, located in Sections 28 and 35. No wells have been drilled as yet. The rock pressure of the nearest wells is, at the present writing (May, 1890), 325 pounds. For the gas rights of a part of its land, the company pays $10 an acre annual rental.

(2) *Perry township.* Sections 21, 22, 27, 28, 29, 30, 31, 32, 33 and 34, in whole or in part, deserve or have at one time deserved to be called gas territory. Section 31, in the extreme southwestern corner of the township, was the earliest to be proved, and it was found to have the same good character as the adjacent sections of Bloom, Cass and Washington. The Water Tanks or Godsend well was the pioneer well of this section, having been drilled in the summer of 1886. Twenty or more wells have since been finished in the township. The following is a list nearly complete to date.

It will be seen that the Fostoria and Tiffin trustees own the larger number of these wells. Fostoria was early in the field and acquired a fair acreage of the most desirable lands of the township at low annual rentals. On these lands the trustees have drilled eight wells, most of which are still on the line. The pressure is maintained better in No. 1 than in any of the others, obviously because of the greater interval, viz., one mile which separates it from other wells. It is, however, invaded to some extent by salt water and oil, producing probably four to five barrels per

THE TRENTON LIMESTONE.

LIST OF GAS WELLS IN PERRY TOWNSHIP, WOOD COUNTY.

Names of farms.	Company.	Section.	Quarter.	Position in quarter.	Elevation.
Brandeberry	Tiffin	22	N. E.	S. E. corner	
Brown	"	31	S. W.	Center of E. line	
Chilcote	"	29	S. W.	S. E. corner	746.28
"	Northwestern	21	S. W.	N. W. corner	
Cooper	Tiffin	15	N. W.	S. E. corner	
Graner	"	26	S. W.	N. side of N. half	
Hale	Fostoria	32	S. W.	Near N. E. corner	
Hatfield, A. (Oil)	Tiffin	29	S. W.	N. W. corner	748.18
"	"	33	N. W.	N. W. corner	748.57
Kelley	Northwestern	21	S. W.	N. W. corner	
Lambright	Tiffin	27	S. E.	S. W. corner, near road	752.38
Mason, S	"	32	S. W.	N. W. corner	
Peebles, No. 1	Fostoria	31	N. E.	Center of N. half	749.78
" No. 2	"	31	N. E.	150 ft. from cen. of E. line	
Pruyn	"	30	S. E.	S. E. corner	746.78
Stillwell, S	"	30	S. W.	S. E. corner	745.15
" (Dry)	"	30	S. W.	N. E. corner	
Wineland	"	32	S. W.	S. E. corner	

week Two wells of the corporation have been cut out of the line for the reason that they had turned into oil wells. The remainder require to be "blown off" two or three times a week to relieve them of the oil and water that constantly follow the gas. The rate of advance of these substances is not rapid, however, and the field shows fair vitality. The decline of pressure is the most serious feature in the case. The Fostoria wells, however, are so near the points of supply that they are taxed but little in delivering their gas, and they can maintain their supply when more distant stations will fall short. Some of the wells, according to the information at hand, have fallen as low as 275 pounds rock pressure, and none now exceed 325 pounds. The original pressure was 450 to 470 pounds. The loss of the last year has nowhere been less than fifty pounds and it has probably averaged seventy-five pounds.

The Tiffin trustees hold a large acreage of so-called gas territory in Perry township, for which they paid $20,000. On this territory they have drilled nine wells, and with their present knowledge they would scarcely drill one, and for the entire gas right they would be willing, with their present knowledge, to pay but a very small amount. The trustees have already expended on this township, at the lowest calculation, $30,000, from which no adequate return seems likely to be secured. By this costly experiment they have come to the same point which all who were properly intelligent in regard to the field had reached when the trustees started upon the development. They had no competition at any time from those who had followed the history of the gas production of the neighborhood. Of these wells—several are entirely unproductive—several others produce oil and water in such amount that they must be excluded from the lines, and the best of them is but very small in value.

(3) *Henry Township; North Baltimore.*—Henry township gets its distinction and value in the present connection from oil and not from gas; but in its southeastern corner, Sections 25 and 36 have proved fair gas territory. The gas field has been found by development to make an unusual excursion to the westward, through Sections 2, 3, 4, 10, 11, Portage township, and on its return to the general northward direction that it follows here, it includes the two sections of Henry named above.

The gas of these two sections has been turned to account by the village corporation of North Baltimore, and to some extent by the other companies whose lines traverse the field. It was first reached by a well drilled in 1886 by C. C. Conroy & Co. The well was located on the Peters farm, three-quarters of a mile east of the village The Trenton is found to have risen seventy one feet in the interval between this point and the center of the corporation. These wells now belong to the municipal corporation, and with two other wells furnish a full supply for the dwellings and the factories of the village. The original well is reported as continuing its production in fair volume still.

The corporation has secured the gas rights of 280 acres, mainly in the west half of Section 36, and has drilled the two wells named above. The second of these was drilled a little deeper than No. 1, and whenever the back pressure is allowed to fall it throws a little salt water. Well No. 3 shows, in like manner, a little oil. All the wells of the line need to be blown twice a week at least.

The line consists of 1,700 and 1 600 feet, respectively, of three inch and two-inch pipe, with a single line of four inch pipe to a glass factory.

The rates for gas in the corporation are as follows:

Cooking stoves, $1.00 per month.
Heating stoves, $1.37 per month, seven months of the year.
Lights, eight cents per jet, per month.

The lighting of the streets is thus far effected by torches and arches that make night hideous. It is surprising and discouraging, after all the experience that has been accumulated, to see the same wasteful policy that prevailed in the older centers blossom out on the smaller scale here. The trustees have no knowledge of the production of their wells, or of the amount of gas used from their lines. By reason of the manufactures recently established here upon free gas, and also by reason of the development of an important oil field included in and continuous with the village limits, the village is growing very rapidly at the present time. As in other towns, where gas is obtained, the first industry to find a foothold is glass manufacture. North Baltimore has secured three glass making establishments, viz.: The Enterprise Window Glass Works, with a capacity of ten pots; the Zihlman Flint Glass Works, with a capacity of eight pots, and the North Baltimore Bottle Works, with a capacity of ten posts. These establishments were brought in by the promise of gas at a total charge of five dollars each per annum for ten years, and by donations on the part of citizens of the town to the parties. Village lots were given, by the sale of which $8,000 were obtained for the building of the factory. The Bottle Works secured $15,000 in the same way, and the Zihlman Works, $1 500. None of these factories are under any restraint whatever as to the use of gas. If any of them chooses to double or treble its plant, there would be no power to interfere in the protection of the interests of the town. The only four-inch gas line in the town goes directly to the Window Glass Works. It is generally run wide open, and it is supposed by the trustees that this establishment consumes as much gas as both of the others combined.

There is also a large factory established here for the manufacture of a fine grade of pressed brick. This manufacture depends also on the gas supplied by the corporation line. The clay is an alluvial deposit, quite similar to that which is turned to such excellent account in Findlay. The North Baltimore Works turn out a very superior article, that meets with a ready sale in the best markets at $20 per thousand.

The corporation has bonded itself for eight thousand dollars, the proceeds of which have been used in securing gas territory, in drilling wells, and in piping the town. It is now proposed to increase this indebtedness by the issue of $25 000 of additional bonds. With even moderate returns from the factories that are consuming nearly all the gas, the village might begin at once to reduce its indebtedness. The rock pressure is practically the same as that of Bloom township at the present 'time, viz, about 325 pounds. It is reported as originally 480 pounds. This would show a loss of thirty-two per cent. of pressure to date, and of course a much larger per centage of loss of available pressure.

Pipe Lines of the Northwestern Ohio Natural Gas Company.

In the account of the gas fields of Hancock and Wood counties, mention has repeatedly been made of this great corporation, in which the Standard Oil Company holds the controlling interest. We find it occupying altogether the most prominent place in every important sub-division of the gas fields of the counties named above. It owns the gas rights of not less than thirty thousand acres, and its lands were selected from what was counted the best territory in the beginning of the development. Much of this territory it holds in large and continuous blocks. Bloom township, for example, when colored to show the areas of the different gas companies, strikes the eye as almost the solid possession of the Northwestern Ohio Company. The gas wells of the company are counted by the score. Its pipe lines in Ohio aggregate nearly two hundred miles, and are supplying fuel, and to some extent, light and power to a large population. Among the towns which they reach may be named Toledo, Fremont, Tiffin, Fostoria, Sandusky, Clyde, Bellevue, and a number of small villages that are situated upon or near their main lines. These systems probably reach 150,000 people. The Company has also constructed a line of large size to Detroit, Michigan.

All the outlays required by the best experience have been freely made in its entire plant, and its service throughout meets the highest demands. The relations of the great corporation to the landholders with which it deals are in the main amicable. Those who leased their lands before competition sprung up in regard to gas territory are somewhat discontented and unhappy because they are receiving so much smaller rentals than those of their neighbors who waited a year or two before leasing; and when any of the earlier contracts lapse, large advances are insisted upon and obtained for the extension of the leaseholds. In the opening of the field some of the contracts were based upon Pennsylvania experience and their terms would have proved very unjust to the landholders. As the real facts have appeared, the rentals have in many cases been voluntarily advanced by the company. Its disbursements in the region which it mainly occupies are very large, and the farmers are deriving great advantage from this new use of their lands.

The company has recognized from the first the value of the gas which it has acquired, and has carefully avoided all unnecessary consumption of it. While the city of Findlay, for example, was burning millions of feet in a day in vain display or in wanton waste, the Northwestern Company was locking in every well and reducing every standpipe along its lines to the smallest possible proportions. The difference lay in the fact that one company understood the work it was engaged in, while the other not only did not understand but proved very slow to learn.

The Northwestern Company has taken all needful care of its gas territory in every way. It has avoided alike the unnecessary multiplication of wells and the dangerous over-draft of any. In all ordinary cases, it maintains a back pressure of 200 pounds or more upon its wells.

To this statement there are, however, numerous important exceptions that have arisen within the last year or two, as the several municipal and other corporations that are engaged in piping gas have extended their lines into the main fields, and these exceptions are at the present time multiplying rapidly. The Northwestern Ohio Company gained possession at an early day of a very large acreage in such centers of gas production as Bloom township, but it was either unable to acquire or it did not count it necessary to acquire the whole of these gas lands. Occasional farms and many smaller tracts remained outside its holdings. Village corporations, with scores of owners of one or more lots, each of the lots embracing a few thousand square feet, were also left out of the account by the company. Its reasoning seems to have been that the lands which it did not acquire, being widely scattered and in small tracts for the most part, could not make a proper basis for any new company to enter upon the business of carrying the gas away on the large scale. The conclusion was a true one, whether taken by the company or not. There was no proper basis left in connected and sufficiently extended acreage for undertaking such line a of work, but in coming to the conclusion that on this account no one would undertake it the company was reckoning without its host. It did not make account of the boards of municipal gas trustees, and others who, following their example, presently appeared upon the scene with little or no knowledge of the business, as a rule, and with public money to expend, ready to lease or purchase any tract of land large enough to hold a derrick. A three acre or a five-acre tract, for example, was counted by such parties ample for a well. So, indeed, it would be, if let alone. A village lot would be just as advantageous a location for a well as a quarter section of land, provided other parties in interest would leave the well drilled upon the village lot the same acreage that the well of the quarter section could command. But it is certain that the other parties will not give the village well this unpurchased advantage. Where one such well appears, a second, a third and a fourth are likely to follow. Even then, although the drilling of four wells in the compass of an acre or two would be a useless waste of money, if each well were held locked back to a proper pressure so as to insure the safety of the immediate territory, no other evil effect would follow. The vitality of the field would be maintained for a proportionately short time, it is true, by the fourfold draught upon it, but this would only stand for rapid utilization of the gas. It is, however, certain that in such a case as is represented, every well will *not* be locked back to the point necessary to protect the field. One or another will be allowed to flow unobstructed, to make sure of its obtaining its proper share of the gas while it is going. As a consequence of this treatment, water and oil are invited into the gas rock, and presently the entire district is found to be overrun and perhaps destroyed. The advent of new companies owning only small tracts leads thus not only to the unnecessary multiplication of wells, but to the premature exhaustion of entire sections of the gas field. It is even conceivable that one company having large and undisturbed holdings elsewhere, will consent to, or even deliberately work to the destruction of some particular sub-division of the field in which it finds too many or too aggressive neighbors.

The most important section of the company's lines is the double system that reaches Toledo, which furnishes the domestic fuel of the city. Two glass furnaces and a large rolling-mill are also attached to its lines, and in addition they furnish power to a large number of manufacturing establishments of various grades. The company began the city supply under a contract running for three years, which terminates in July, 1890. A great deal of controversy has been carried on over the rates now in force and over the renewal of a contract for another term. An account of the gas question in the city is given at more length in the succeeding section. The glass furnaces are supplied with fuel and power at the rate of $30 per pot, per month. One of the establishments is a ten-pot window glass furnace. The other is a thirteen-pot furnace for the manufacture of the finest varieties of cut glass made in the United States. The rates to these two establishments are very unequal, as both pay the same price per pot, while a window glass furnace consumes two-fifths more fuel per pot than a table ware furnace. If $30 is a proper price for a window glass furnace, $18 would be the equivalent for a table ware factory.

It is almost a crime against a community to consume the natural gas that can be made tributary to it in rolling mills. The daily supply for such establishments can never be counted by less than millions of feet. It is greatly to be hoped that the Toledo lines will cut off this monstrous consumption forthwith. No gas field yet found in Ohio can bear the burden of iron working for any long term of years. It was a serious mistake for the gas companies to undertake this line of service. The gas that goes into a rolling mill every day would supply with the inexpressible convenience and comfort of gaseous fuel 1,000 to 5,000 families. When the interests of the people and the gas companies unite as they do in shutting off such vandal-like waste of natural gas, it is to be hoped that the exclusion of the iron mills from the lines will soon be effected.

The Toledo gas rates are given herewith.

For Cooking.

	From November 1 to May 1.				From May 1 to November 1.		
	Monthly charges.	If paid before the 10th.			Monthly charges.	If paid before the 10th.	
		Discount.	Charges.			Discount.	Charges.
No. 7 Mixer....	$2 78	.28	$2 50	No. 7 Mixer...	$1 66	.16	$1 50
No. 5 Mixer....	2 22	.22	2 00	No. 5 Mixer...	1 39	.14	1 25
No. 3 Mixer....	1 67	.17	1 50	No. 3 Mixer...	83	.08	75

THE TRENTON LIMESTONE. 145

FOR LARGE COOKING RANGE.

From November 1 to May 1.				From May 1 to November 1.			
Monthly charges.	If paid before the 10th.			Monthly charges.	If paid before the 10th.		
	Discount.	Charges.			Discount.	Charges.	
No. 9 Mixer....	$3 33	.33	$3 00	No. 9 Mixer...	$2 22	.22	$2 00

FOR LAUNDRY.

(When gas is furnished for cook stove also.)

Monthly charges.	Discount.	Charges.		Monthly charges.	Discount.	Charges.
No. 7 Mixer.... $1 11	.11	$1 00	No. 5 Mixer...	$ 83	.08	$ 75

Manufacturers' rates for fuel shall be 75 per cent. of the cost of coal, and no more.

FOR HEATING.

No. 7 Mixer.

Monthly charges.	If paid before the 10th.			Annual charges.	If paid before the 10th.	
	Discount.	Charges.			Discount.	Charges.
1st Mixer....... $5 00	.50	$4 50	1st Mixer......	$30 00	$3 00	$27 00
2d Mixer....... 4 44	.44	4 00	2d Mixer......	26 64	2 64	24 00
3d Mixer....... 3 89	.39	3 50	3d Mixer......	23 34	2 34	21 00
4th Mixer...... 3 33	.33	3 00	4th Mixer.....	19 98	1 98	18 00
5th Mixer...... 2 78	.28	2 50	5th Mixer.....	16 68	1 68	15 00
6th Mixer...... 2 22	.22	2 00	6th Mixer.....	13 32	1 32	12 00

No. 5 Mixer.

Monthly charges.	If paid before the 10th.			Annual charges.	If paid before the 10th.	
	Discount.	Charges.			Discount.	Charges.
1st Mixer...... $3 89	.39	$3 50	1st Mixer......	$23 34	$2 34	$21 00
2d Mixer...... 3 33	.33	3 00	2d Mixer......	19 98	1 98	18 00
3d Mixer...... 2 78	.28	2 50	3d Mixer......	16 68	1 58	15 00
4th Mixer...... 2 22	.22	2 00	4th Mixer.....	13 32	1 32	12 00
5th Mixer...... 1 66	.16	1 50	5th Mixer.....	9 96	96	9 00
6th Mixer...... 1 39	.14	1 25	6th Mixer.....	8 34	84	7 50

No. 3 Mixer.

(For heating small rooms, and for special purposes.)

	Monthly charges.	If paid before the 10th.	
		Discount.	Charges.
1st Mixer..	$2 22	.22	$2 00
2d Mixer...	1 66	.16	1 50

FURNACES.

	Monthly charges.	If paid before the 10th.		Annual contracts.		
		Discount.	Charges.	Annual charges.	Discount.	Charges.
"A" Mixer, 21-inch fire pot.......	$6 95	$ 70	$6 25	$41 70	$4 20	$37 50
"B" Mixer, 24-inch fire pot.......	8 66	86	7 80	51 96	5 16	46 80
"C" Mixer, 26-inch fire pot.......	9 44	94	8 50	56 64	5 64	51 00
"D" Mixer, 28-inch fire pot.......	10 00	1 00	9 01	60 00	6 00	54 00
"E" Mixer, 30-inch fire pot.......	11 66	1 16	10 50	69 96	6 96	63 00
"F" Mixer, 35-inch fire pot.......	13 89	1 39	12 50	83 34	8 34	75 00

The Toledo Pipe Line.

The city of Toledo has been engaged for the last two years in by far the largest undertaking in connection with natural gas of any municipal corporation in the State, and, although the work upon which it has entered, has not yet been completed, its importance demands that an account of the action already taken, shall be given in this chapter.

In 1887 natural gas from the Wood and Hancock county fields was introduced into Toledo by two companies, known respectively as the Northwestern Ohio Natural Gas Company, and the Toledo Natural Gas Company. In the former, leading representatives of the Standard Oil Company were known to hold a controlling interest. It was given out at first that the second company was independent of the great corporation, and that its presence in Toledo would insure competition in gas rates; but it soon became apparent that it was not likely to bring about such a result. The two companies evidently held the same views as to the business which they had in hand, and during the last year the second company has been formally merged in the first.

The maximum rate that the companies could charge for gas in the city was fixed by the common council, after considerable discussion, for a period of three years. The rates were not in excess of those prevailing in other towns of the country which obtain their supplies of gas from fields twenty or more miles distant. From a table published in the American Manufacturer, December 6, 1889, the following data are taken:

THE TRENTON LIMESTONE.

Annual Rates for Cook Stoves.

(1) Toledo, (5) Youngstown,
(2) Fremont, (6) Meadville, Pa.,
(3) Tiffin, (7) Jamestown, N. Y.,
(4) Titusville, Pa., (8) Erie, Pa.

(1)	(2)	(3)	(4)	(5)	(6)	(7)	(8)
$19.50	$19.00	$16.00	$24.00	$25.00	$32.00	$28.30	$31.50

Annual Rates for Heating Stoves—a single heater being employed.

(1)	(2)	(3)	(4)	(5)	(6)	(7)	(8)
$21.00	$16.00	$16.20	$24.00	$18.00	$21.00	$23.40	$26.45

The rate at Toledo on cook stoves was the result of a compromise, $18 being named by one company and $21 by the other. Considerable reductions were allowed when more than one heater was employed, and different rates were charged also for mixers of different sizes.

The years 1887 and 1888 marked great activity in the towns situated in or near to the gas fields. Such towns were, during this time, holding out potent inducements to manufacturers to locate in them, especially by the offer of free fuel, and many of these towns were securing the establishment of glass factories, iron mills and other like enterprises. Findlay, Bowling Green, Fostoria, and later Tiffin, all attracted large and important manufactures on the basis named. These towns were consequently making rapid gains in population and in volume of trade, and from some points of view they could be counted as gaining at the expense of Toledo. With these towns that were able to offer free fuel, Toledo could not compete. The companies above named had brought natural gas into the city, it is true; but they had brought it in to turn it into money, and they were not in any way directly interested in building up the town, and least of all in creating the state of speculative excitement, called a "boom," so dear to the heart of the real estate dealer. They had already learned that by far the largest returns for natural gas were to be derived from its use in domestic supply, and they were unwilling to appropriate any large part of the production of their lines to great factories that would not expect to pay more than a quarter or a tenth of what the former use would bring to them; if, indeed, such establishments did not expect the gas to be furnished without any charge, whatever. In other words, the companies preferred to make the money out of the gas themselves, rather than to turn it over with scanty advantage to themselves, to real estate dealers and manufacturers to make money out of. The inferior position of Toledo, as contrasted with the towns already named in these respects, became a source of annoyance and irritation to many of her active business men, and during the winter of 1887 and 1888, more than six thousand names were attached to a petition sent from Toledo to the State Legislature, to obtain authority for the city to construct a gas line from the southern fields to its limits. A vigorous opposition to this project was, however, made at this time by many citizens.

The dissatisfaction with the situation grew rapidly, however, during the subsequent year, and it had gathered such force that early in the session of 1889, the legislature was easily prevailed upon to pass an enabling act, authorizing the city to provide for a pipe line to the gas fields.

The bill was passed by the House of Representatives almost unanimously, and by the Senate by a vote of twenty-three to eleven, the vote of the last body being taken after a committee of its members had visited Toledo and had studied the situation on the ground. It became a law on January 22, 1889. This action of the legislature is said to have been vigorously opposed by the gas companies. A provision was inserted in the bill requiring ratification of the action by a three-fourths vote of the citizens. At the election in April, 1889, after an energetic and spirited canvass, the vote in favor of the city line was 7,002, and the vote in opposition 4,199. These figures show more than 62 per cent. in favor of the bill, and less than 38 per cent. opposed to it.

The governor forthwith appointed a board of five gas trustees, who entered upon their duties in April, 1889, the common council unanimously authorizing the sale of $75,000 of the bonds to enable them to begin their active work. The advertisement of the sale of these bonds was the signal for the beginning of open resistance on the part of the Northwestern Ohio Natural Gas Company. Application was at once made in the United States Circuit Court of the northern district of Ohio, for an injunction against the sale of the bonds. The case was heard in chambers at Nashville, Tennessee, Judge Howell E. Jackson presiding. A strong and sweeping decision was given by Judge Jackson in favor of the city, affirming the full right of municipalities to undertake work of the character proposed.

The first issue of bonds to the amount of $75,000, was sold in June, 1889, and the trustees at once proceeded to procure gas territory in the Hancock and Wood county gas fields. The Allen township district was at this time the most promising subdivision of the field, and here the chief investments of the Toledo trustees were made, though tracts were leased along their proposed pipe line, for a distance of nine miles from north to south. The acreage that they secured was comparatively small, aggregating not more than five or six hundred acres; but the separate tracts were located at the very centers of the best production.

In Allen township contracts of a peculiar kind in this line of business were entered into with certain parties owning gas lands. One company, organized under the designation of The Stuartsville Land Association, entered into a contract to furnish fifty million feet of gas per day from completed wells, the wells to be so located that each should have ten acres tributary to it. For every million feet of gas produced, the company was to receive one thousand dollars. The company owned or controlled about 150 acres. On one tract of fifty-three acres six wells were drilled. The contract was fulfilled and the aggregate specified amount was turned over to the trustees in completed wells. Three other wells which were drilled by J. R. Ware, Esq., on a fifteen-acre tract, near Stuartsville, proved the largest of the whole number secured by the city. Their aggregate daily volume was 32,465,560 feet, but because of the smaller acreage going with each well, only $750 per 1,000,000 feet was paid. Mr. Ware received for the combined production over $24,000. Still other wells were drilled on village lots. In their first annual report, dated December 31, 1889, the gas trustees gave a list of twenty-four wells that the city now owns, including those already named, the daily capacity of which is given as 154,880,054 cubic feet. When it became evident that the city of Toledo was to enter the gas fields as a competitor of the companies already established there, the price of gas territory was rapidly advanced. The Findlay gas trustees had been driven out of their own township by the exhaustion of the home supply and began leasing lands in the nearest available territory, viz., in Allen, Cass and Marion townships. For single farms they are now paying as high an annual rental as $20 per acre. The Northwestern Ohio Company, in like manner, sought to increase and consolidate its gas lands, and it did not hesitate to advance rentals to many times what they had previously been. The Toledo trustees were obliged to make all their leases and purchases under these conditions.

During the year the balance of the gas bonds, viz., $675,000, was placed upon the market. Of this amount a hundred thousand dollars was taken by citizens of Toledo, but no bids were obtained from the moneyed centers, by which it was expected that the bonds would all be promptly absorbed. The sales up to the present date are all reported in the two items already given. The balance of the bonds, $575,000, remain unsold. The friends of the pipe line project attribute the lack of bids to the efforts of the Northwestern Ohio Gas Company and its natural friends and allies, the Standard Ohio Company, by whom the money markets were prejudiced against the bonds. There seems no reason to doubt that this charge is founded in fact. Through the agency of the Northwestern Ohio Company, suit was afterward brought in the United States Courts, although the injunction had been denied, and a hearing was given to the case upon its merits. A decision was rendered in January, 1890, again in favor of the validity of the action entered upon by the city. The case is still, however, in court, and is probably destined to reach the highest tribunal of the United States for adjudication. The delay has, however, worked against the city and has served the opposing interests, almost as well as success in court would have done, as will be hereafter shown.

The gas trustees have come into possession, as will be seen, of somewhat more than $175,000, by the sale of the bonds and by accumulation of premiums. For gas territory and wells they have expended about $120,000, and for other purposes somewhat more than $30,000, leaving about $45,000, which has recently been applied to the construction of a pipe line from the gas fields, as far as the money would go. The line as laid begins in the northwest quarter of section 30, Allen township. As projected, it is to consist of twenty-nine miles of ten-inch, wrought iron, screw-joint pipe, opening into about eight miles of twelve-inch wrought iron pipe. Two eight-inch wrought iron pipes of extra strength are to be laid across and underneath the Maumee River. The field connections are to be made by three, four and six-inch wrought iron pipes. All of the materials it is designed shall be of the best. A few miles of the main line have been already laid, but the work is at present arrested for the want of available funds with which to continue it. There seems to be no present probability that the line can be completed during the current year.

Meanwhile, the portions of the field in which the best production of the Toledo wells is to be found, are being rapidly depleted of their gas. The Findlay trustees are obliged to draw hard upon the same region in order to meet the large demand which their factories make. The Northwestern Ohio Company sees to it that a well of its own is drilled close to every well of the Toledo Company. If the latter locates a well on a village lot, another lot near by is made to give standing ground for a new derrick, and pipe line connections are extended to every well as soon as it is completed. In this respect, the Northwestern Company has an overwhelming advantage. It can fill its lines from the new wells and shut back the protected portions of the field. The rock pressure in the Allen township field has fallen fully 100 pounds during the last ten months; and all the wells, whether worked, or locked in, have fallen alike. The gas rock is also being rapidly overrun with oil to a dangerous extent. Shrinkage in volume accompanies the fall of rock pressure. One of the large wells of the Findlay trustees, in the Stuartsville field, was re-measured in June, 1890, and it was found to have lost, without use, fully 40 per cent. of the volume that it showed in August, 1889. The figures given above for the Toledo production probably need to be divided by two or by even a larger number to express the present volume. It is certain that the rock pressure has been lessened more than 25 per cent. within the year, and all this without any use of the wells owned by the city trustees. If the line should reach the field this fall, it would find it in a state of incipient exhaustion, and if it does not reach the field until 1891, in case the decline that has been in steady progress for the last year shall be kept up during the coming winter, it will find no dry gas to take away. At least, it does not now seem possible that dry gas in large enough quantity for manufacturing supplies can be found in the Stuartsville field for more than one, or at most two winters, especially if severe weather occurs. Even if no delay had been experienced in the construction of the pipe line, the production reported in these figures of the trustees would have furnished but a short-lived supply, by reason of the crowding of the wells. More than one-fifth of the entire amount reported is derived from the three Ware wells, to which, as will be remembered, but fifteen acres of land are tributary. In a gas rock of the character shown in the Allen township field, fifty acres would be a small enough assignment of territory for a single well.

The controversy has engendered bitter feeling, and has led to more or less acrimonious discussion throughout the city and adjacent communities. There is probably a considerable number of the citizens, though a decided minority, that distrust the policy on which the city has entered. But some of this class appear to have laid aside their opposition through resentment at the depreciation of the credit of the city, which has been brought about by the Northwestern Gas Company in the course of the struggle.

The Gas Company takes the ground that, after being encouraged, and authorized by the people of Toledo through their regularly constituted representatives to bring the much-coveted fuel into the city, and after having done this by an outlay of more than a million dollars on its part, its business ought not to be destroyed by the action of the city itself.

It further holds that after having taken the only proper way to provide a basis for large pipe lines, by securing at heavy outlay large and continuous tracts of gas lands, it is not right for another company to come in and establish a line on the mere odds and ends of land that are left over from such occupation. It demonstrates that the second company has no proper basis when it empties the wells that this company has drilled without going off of its own ground.

(4) *Portage and Liberty Townships.*—The petroliferous production of these two townships takes the form of oil rather than gas at the present time. In fact, neither of these areas really deserves the name of gas territory. In the earlier stages of the development, when gas alone was valued and the discovery of oil was counted ill-fortune, a few sections along the borders of these two townships were considered available for the supply of the pipe lines that were being extended across them. But

these sections never produced dry gas constantly for any great length o time. Oil and water were almost the invariable accompaniments of the gas at an early stage in these wells. The best of the territory was the extreme northwesterly sections of Portage township. The tract of Waterlime or Lower Helderberg rocks, in which the valley of the Portage is now established, indicates a low level of the underlying Trenton, and all the facts of the development correspond to these indications of the surface geology. The most productive and best protected territory of the township is found as the rock rises from the swamp toward the northward. The gas wells of this territory have seldom ranged above one million feet in daily capacity. Several of them have showed fair vitality, responding to a heavy and steady drain for two years or more. They were not adequate, however, to the service asked of them, and both volume and pressure have fallen to such a point that they are no longer greatly valued.

(5) *Center and Plain Townships.*—Along the boundaries of these two townships, as in the case last described, a light production of gas was found in the early history of the field. The wells showed an original pressure of about 450 pounds, but their volumes were never large. A history of this district is found in Volume VI. Nearly all the gas it has produced has been utilized by the village of Bowling Green, and the further account of this part of the field can best be given in connection with the history of the gas supply of this town.

Bowling Green.—There are two companies bringing gas into Bowling Green, one a public, and the other a private corporation. The municipal corporation, through a board of gas trustees, has leased lands, drilled wells, laid pipe lines, and undertaken to supply the glass factories and other manufacturing enterprises of the town with fuel. The domestic supply, on the other hand, has been furnished from the first by the private company. The corporation trustees have already expended fifty thousand dollars in their work. Five glass factories have been brought in to depend on the supply of gas which the corporation offered, without charge, for five years, or rather at the nominal charge of five dollars per annum for each factory. The names and lines of production of the glass factories are as follows: Canastota Glass Company, window glass, twenty pots; Buckeye Novelty Glass Company, table ware, six pots, and one tank of the same capacity, equals twelve pots; Lythgo Glass Company, table ware, fruit jars, etc., six pots; Crystal Glass Company, table ware, bottles, etc., ten pots; Safe Glass Company, bottles, jars, etc., one tank, equals eight pots; total, window glass, twenty pots; table ware, thirty-six pots. These factories require for their daily supply 1,400,000 cubic feet of gas for the window glass plant, and for the table ware, four plants, 1,800,-

000 feet, or a total supply of 3,200,000 feet per day. To meet this demand, the trustees have drilled in all twelve wells in the territory which they had secured, mainly in the northern sections of Portage township. Nine of these wells are still in the line, but three have completely failed. None of these wells exceeded in daily volume one million feet per day when they were first drilled; their best average would probably not have greatly exceeded five hundred thousand feet. The field did not prove adequate to a demand of this character, and consequently the wells were overdrawn and their rock pressure and volume began to decline to an alarming extent in the winter of 1888 and 1889. The decline has continued without abatement or reduction of rate up to the present time, the last registration of the gauges of the company showing but 100 pounds in the wells.

During the past year, in the vain attempt to meet the heavy demand that had been already established, the wells have been allowed to flow without any back pressure, and consequently they have been invaded by oil and water to a troublesome, or even to a fatal degree. The trustees see no promise in drilling new wells to relieve the situation, for the reason that the later wells, when brought in, show the same exhausted condition of the gas rock as that which the earlier wells show. In other words, the decline of their gas territory affects the entire region which the leases of the company cover. During the last winter the smaller glass works that were nearest the field secured a moderate supply of gas for themselves, but the larger factories that happened to be built to the northward of the town were subject to a constantly increasing shortage of fuel, until at last their fires went out altogether. The trustees have endeavored to induce their neighbors of the private gas company, and also the Northwestern Ohio Gas Company, whose line passes near the corporation boundary, to undertake the supply of these factories in their place; but neither company seems disposed to respond to the call, and the largest glass company is now planning removal to some other location. These works were destroyed by fire in the early part of 1889, but were re-built by a contribution of $25,000, raised by the citizens. They had previously received a considerable donation from the town in the shape of land, in addition to fuel, without charge.

The Bowling Green Natural Gas Company, the private corporation above referred to, has maintained a good supply of gas for domestic fuel through the town during the last two years. The lands of this company interlock, to a considerable extent, with the lands of the municipal corporation, but it has been possible for it to take proper care of its own wells, and accordingly they are in much better condition than those last described. The rock pressure has, however, declined in all of them, so that it nowhere registers above 170 pounds at present. The last of the wells to be drilled, which was completed in the fall of 1889, on comparatively fresh territory, showed an initial pressure of 190 pounds. The gas itself shows the incipient exhaustion of the field. It is less lively than at first, from the constant invasion of oil. The mixers become clogged and its flow is obstructed in ordinary use.

The company has become satisfied that if it would maintain its supply, it must acquire new and more productive territory, for its home sources are practically exhausted. It has, accordingly, bought land and gas rights to the extent of $36,000 in Bloom and Henry townships, to the south of the Portage swamp, already described, and it proposes to extend its lines to this field. The wells that are being drilled there at the present time find a rock pressure of 325 to 330 pounds. If this field, with this pressure, is judiciously treated, it ought to prolong the life of the supply by several years.

Lime burning by natural gas has been carried on in a large way at Bowling Green and at Portage for the last three years, and probably with as much success as at any point in the field. The limestone that makes the eastern boundary of the corporation offers the best of facilities for obtaining the rock. The quality of the rock is high, its composition showing it to be an almost chemically pure dolomite, like most of the Niagara limestone of northern Ohio. All the difficulties experienced in the first attempts to manufacture lime by the use of gas as a fuel have one by one been overbcome. The lime burned has been mainly dependent on the wells of the private company, rather than on the line of the municipal corporation. The products of these quarries and kilns is highly valued by the glass manufacturers of the new field, as well as by those of Pennsylvania and eastern Ohio. For this use the raw stone is ground, in part, and in part the lime itself is ground, while still other manufacturers prefer to use the lime in bulk. The four kilns of this district average in daily production from 75 to 100 barrels each. By anemometer measurements, taken one year ago, it was found that each kiln consumed from 150 to 175 thousand feet of gas in the production of a hundred barrels of lime, or 1,500 to 1,750 cubic feet in burning one barrel of lime. The price charged for the fuel used in burning the lime is three cents per barrel. The cost of fuel, if wood were used, even at the cheap rate of $1.25 per cord, at which it can be furnished in Bowling Green, would be at least twice the price which is paid for the gas. The magnesian lime of Bowling Green has also been brought into requisition for paper factories and pulp works to some extent. Both of these lines of consumption have heretofore been directed entirely to the hotter limes derived from the true carbonates.

THE TRENTON LIMESTONE.   155

In the history of Bowling Green we can see the stages through which all the other towns that have introduced gas, as a fuel, must each in its turn expect to pass. The failure of the supply in Bowling Green has come sooner than was anticipated by any one, but the several stages have, after all, been distinctly marked. In 1887 the rock pressure was 450 pounds; in 1888, 375 to 390 pounds; in 1889, February, 290 pounds; in 1890, May, in the gas company's wells, 170 pounds; in 1890, May, in the gas trustees' wells, 100 pounds. The volume has given out in apparently the same proportion. The remnant of the gas of the field will doubtless be highly valued, and domestic fuel in considerable amount can still be supplied by it, but the larger uses are apparently already at an end.

(6) *Remaining Townships.*—In Middleton and Perrysburg townships small quantities of gas have been found in the Trenton, just enough to lure on the companies drilling the wells to repeated trials. No value has thus far been derived from the supply. Gas is, of course, found in considerable quantity in association with the oil of Montgomery and Freedom townships, but no store has been found separate and distinct from the oil. These occurrences will, therefore, best be treated under a subsequent head.

(7) *The Waterville Gas Field.*—No better point will be found in which to give a brief history of the Waterville gas field than the present. Although it belongs in an adjoining county, all the approaches to the field were made through the northern townships of Wood. Its development was begun by parties representing Maumee interests. An effort was made to establish a glass plant here, and in the search for an adequate supply of fuel wells were drilled in the river valley, at intervals, several miles above the town. They were finally extended to the village limits of Waterville. The corporation of Maumee was at last led, in 1887, to purchase the territory and wells that had already been tested, to lay a pipe line, and to undertake the supply of its population with fuel. Eight wells have been drilled in all, in this subdivision of the field. The gas was brought in to Maumee by five miles of four-inch pipe, opening into one mile of six-inch pipe. When the work was begun the supply was counted ample for the town, but it proved insufficient when less than 500 stoves had been attached to it; and in the course of the first year of its use the supply was found to be overtaxed when 300 stoves were dependent on it. The wells of the corporation were measured in March, 1889, with the following result:

Cobb well, No. 2...	59,227 cubic feet per day.
" " 3...	15,780 " "
" " 4...	46,209 " "
Hutchinson well...	'73,440 " "
Haskins well...	70,560 " "
Ballou well, No 1...	30,672 " "
" " 2...	60,768 " "
Starkweather well...	73,440 " "
Total production...	430,000 " "

These wells found the Trenton at a fairly favorable depth, viz., from 1,125 to 1,150 feet, but the rock was lacking in porosity. The closed pressure of the wells was never reported above 300 pounds. Several of the wells showed a small quantity of oil in the Clinton limestone.

The corporation has since abandoned the vain attempt to supply fuel from this source, and the people have gone back to one of the Northwestern Ohio Company's lines, which passes through the corporation limits. The gas rates established by the home company, while its supply was maintained, was one half of the Toledo rates. The latter are in force under the service of the Northwestern Ohio Company. The entire amount invested by the corporation in the plant must be counted lost.

(C.) GAS WELLS OF AUGLAIZE COUNTY.

Auglaize county is distinguished rather as oil territory than as a source of gas. But one of its townships, viz., St. Mary's, together with small portions of two other townships, viz., Washington and German, has proved fairly productive of gas. From this field the supply of Lima, St. Mary's, Wapakoneta, Minster, New Bremen and several other smaller villages is now drawn. The most productive portions of this district at the present time, are the following sections of St. Mary's township, viz., 10, 11, 12, 13, 14, 15, 22, 23, 24—all of them located in the eastern half of the township. The southwestern quarter of the town is least developed, but it contains a number of excellent wells, and if it had been drilled to the same extent as the east side, at an earlier stage in the history of the field, it would have probably furnished even larger wells than are found in the first named portion. The north line of sections of German township, and the west line of sections of Washington, may be included in the St. Mary's field. The early history of the exploration in this township is quite fully given in Volume VI. At the date of that report it was recognized that resources of great value lay buried beneath the monotonous surface of this township, but the outcome has been much better than any promise that was then foreseen. For the last two years all of the fuel and much of the power employed in manufacturing in the important towns and villages above named, have been derived from twenty-five or thirty wells drilled within the limits of the sections named above, and the supply will undoubtedly be maintained from the same source for several years to come. Brief descriptions will be given of the main developments thus far.

(1) *St. Mary's Village Corporation.*—The municipal authorities of St. Mary's, under legislation provided therefor, have bonded the village for $32,000, and with the proceeds arising from the sale of the bonds they have leased gas territory, laid a pipe line and furnished a supply of fuel to the citizens, as well as free gas to two large manufacturing plants, viz., a chain factory and a strawboard factory. The gas territory which they have secured lies to the south and east of St. Mary's. It consists of 1,100 acres lying in an almost unbroken tract. The annual rentals for the lands do not exceed, as a rule, one dollar per acre. Thus far it has not been found necessary to drill more than a half dozen wells.

The pipe line by which the gas is conveyed from the field to the town is four inches in diameter; within the corporation six-inch pipe is used. A rock pressure of 315 pounds is reported at the present time. The original rock pressure for this level was 360 pounds. The rates at which fuel is supplied are low, viz., one dollar per stove per month. The fuel furnished to the two factories named above is given without any charge whatever. The supply has thus far proved satisfactory in every respect. The Krein & Standish Manufacturing Company manufacture proof tested chain. The works consist of twenty-eight forges, a sixty-horse power boiler, and an annealing oven. The forges, when tested in 1889, were found to be using a total of 450,000 feet per day. The other uses of the establishment would increase the amount to about 600,000 feet per day. The wells have never been drawn upon heavily enough to reduce their back pressure below the point of danger. As long as this state of things can be maintained, the territory is doing as well as it is possible for it to do.

(2) *The Lima Natural Gas Company.*—The greatest draft on the gas of St. Mary's township is made by this company, although the Mercer Gas Company has several good wells connected with its Piqua line in the township. For many interesting and important facts pertaining to the St. Mary's field, the Survey is indebted to Dr. S. A. Baxter, President of the Lima Company. The Lima Company holds gas rights on about 7,000 acres in the township. The following list shows the location of the wells drilled to August, 1889. The wells are arranged in the order of the sections of the land on which they are drilled.

GEOLOGY OF OHIO.

PARTIAL LIST OF WELLS OF THE LIMA NATURAL GAS COMPANY IN ST. MARY'S TOWNSHIP.

Name of landowner.	Section.	Quarter.	Elevation of surface.	Depth of Trenton below tide.
Barrington	11	N. W	887 feet.	304 feet.
Longsworth	13	N. E		
Kirten	14	S. E	905 feet.	215 feet.
Giddens, 1	15	N. E	899 "	204 "
" 2	15	N. E	901 "	216 "
Koop	15	S. E	902 "	
Miller	15	N. W	911 "	216 feet.
Wilkins, C., 1	15	S. W	903 "	177 "
" 2	15	S. W	907 "	182 "
" 3	15	S. W	906 "	
Wilkins, R., 1	15	S. W	914 "	203 feet.
" 2	15	S. W	914 "	205 "

The list fairly represents the field. Neither the largest nor the smallest wells of the district are included in it. The earliest measurements of one or two of these wells rose nearly to seven million feet, and none of them fell below one million feet. The average original volume would probably be about three and a half million feet. Most of them were drilled in 1887. Some of the original list have been overrun with salt water during the last year. All have fallen off notably in volume and rock pressure. From 1888 to 1889, the shrinkage may be represented by figures like the following which are taken from the records of three wells:

October, 1888.................... 4,553,400   July, 1889..................... 3,381,000

October 1888.................... 3,995,000   July 1889..................... 2,771,000

October 1888.................... 3,925,800   July 1889 1,667,100

These figures are probably fairly representative of the facts for the ten months included between the dates named. The shrinkage has proved, in the first of these wells, about 25 per cent. of the original volume, but in the third it rises to 60 per cent.

A very important fact remains to be named. To undergo this shrinkage of pressure and volume it is not necessary that a farm or a quarter section should be directly drawn upon a well drilled upon it and connected with a pipe line. The force of its gas may be abated nearly as rapidly by wells that are separated from it by intervals of a quarter, or even a half mile. A very instructive case is furnished by the Axe well. The early history was given on page 256, Volume VI. It is located in the northwestern quarter of Section 30, and the nearest well to it is the well on the Rump farm, one-half mile to the eastward. This last well is in the Mercer Company's line and was drawn upon very heavily during the winter of 1888-9. The Axe well itself has never been reached by any pipe except by the one-inch line that connects it with the house of the farmer on whose land it is located. One or two fires in this house it has supplied for the last three years. In 1887 its daily volume was found to be 2,357,000 cubic feet. In August, 1889, it had fallen to 1,420,000 cubic feet, a loss of forty per cent. Its rock pressure had fallen, meanwhile, from the first recorded figure, viz., 390 pounds, to 360 pounds; a decline of $7\frac{1}{2}$ per cent., but worst of all, it throws a strong column of salt water with the gas. As soon as it was opened, on the occasion of the measurement last referred to, the cattle that were pasturing near, hurried towards the well, having learned to regard the blowing off of the gas as an opportunity for obtaining their rations of salt. They eagerly licked up the salt that was thrown by the blast of the gas over the surrounding vegetation. This example is a very instructive one. It establishes the exhaustibility of the gas rock beyond the limits that would generally be expected. A half mile of separation is shown to be no barrier against the drainage originating in a well that is worked to its full capacity. A farm of a quarter section, for example, can be robbed of all its gas without a well being drilled upon it. Nothing demonstrates more clearly the fatuity of the policy which multiplies wells to the number of ten or a dozen, or even more, to the hundred acres. There is no part of the Trenton limestone underlying Ohio that can give any respectable duration to wells that are thus crowded.

The explanation of the origin of the rock pressure of the gas of the Trenton limestone, already given, is based upon the facts of this field, as much as upon those of any other portions of the gas territory. In fact the explanation was originated in connection with the study of these particular facts. The Axe well, for example, had a recorded pressure a few months after its completion of 390 pounds. The Nedderman well of the adjoining township, in Mercer county, all the conditions of which are almost identical with those of the Axe well, originally showed a rock pressure of 395 pounds, and it is altogether probable that this figure would have been reached by the Axe well, also, if early enough observations had been made.

From the table of elevations previously given, it will be seen that the well head in the case of the Axe well, is 919 feet above tide, and that the Trenton limestone was struck at 1138 feet, or 219 feet below tide. The gas was found in the limestone from a depth of twelve feet downward, the well being finished at nineteen feet in the Trenton limestone, or 238 feet below tide. That this last named depth is the approximate level of the salt water column is evident from the history that has just been given.

Counting the specific gravity of the salt water 1.1, the weight of a foot of water with a square inch for its section is .476 pounds. The height to which the salt water rises in cases where the Trenton is found possessed of its full porosity in the adjacent region, is 600 feet above tide. The weight of the column, therefore, of salt water which must give to the gas all its energy, will be the product arising from the multiplication of 838, the number representing the depth of the full salt water column (600 feet above tide and 238 feet below) by this last named figure, .476 pounds, the weight of one foot of salt water having a cross section of one square inch. The product is 398 pounds.. The 395 pounds of the Nedderman well and the 390 pounds of the Axe well, especially when taken in connection with many other records in which the agreement is equally close, serve to establish the explanation of rock pressure previously given. These several sets of figures furnish, in fact, a demonstration of the cause of the rock pressure of gas in the Trenton limestone gas fields. Closer appropriations may subsequently be attained as to the average density of the salt water and the average height to which it rises in the rock. Any change in either factor would necessitate a corresponding change in the other, in order to match the figures as now obtained; but it is not probable that the final figures will deviate much from those already given. The Lima company furnishes an excellent supply of fuel to its patrons. All of its work is managed with care and sagacity.

(3) *The Wapakoneta Pipe Line*—The Wapakoneta Natural Gas Company was organized rather late in the development of the field, viz., in 1888. It comprised a number of the leading business men of the village. The company proceeded to lease prospective gas lands in Washington and St. Mary's townships. In the former it secured 165 acres in one tract, in Section 17, and an eighteen-acre tract in Section 18. On each of these tracts it has drilled one well. The first is known as the Shroer well, and the second as the Hudson well. The first was never a large well, but its gas has proved uniformly dry and uniform in flow, and it is highly valued on these accounts. The Hudson well was a larger well to begin with, but it has been overtaxed, and it has lost a large measure of its volume and force. It is also overrun with water to a troublesome extent. It is evidently nearing the end of its usefulness.

In St. Mary's township the company has secured 208 acres in Sections 14, 15 and 22. Three wells have been drilled on these lands, all of which are wells of good volume. They constitute the main reliance of the line. Their average production in July 1890 was about 1,300,000 feet per day.

The pipe line consists of eleven miles of six-inch pipe, expanding into eight-inch pipe within the village limits. The collecting in the field

THE TRENTON LIMESTONE.   161

is done by four-inch pipe. The line consists of good material and is well laid.

The rock pressure at the present time is 248 pounds. It fell as low as 190 pounds last March. A varying pressure, ranging from twenty to eighty pounds, is kept on the line, and these variations affect the low pressure side to some extent. The aim is to keep four ounces of pressure on the distributory system.

There are about 800 stoves supplied, and two flouring mills are also furnished with fuel for power at a rate of $50 per month.

The business of the company is well managed, and if any such plant can be made to pay out this will do so. The trouble lies in the ever-increasing expense in maintaining the supply. The lands of the company are interlocked with those of the Lima company to some extent, and the wells are multiplied unduly along the borders of the small tracts.

The rates of the company are as follows:

DOMESTIC USE.

Heating.		Cooking.			
October 1st to May 1st.		October 1st to May 1st.		May 1st to October 1st.	
Size mixer.	Per month.	Size mixer.	Per month.	Size mixer.	Per month.
No. 7...............	$2 50	No. 7...........	$2 50	No. 7...........	$1 50
No. 5...............	1 75	No. 5...........	1 75	No. 5...........	1 00
No. 3...............	1 75	No. 3...........	1 00	No. 3...........	1 00

The New Bremen Pipe Line.—A company was formed at New Bremen soon after the organization of the Wapakoneta Company, and it has done its work along the same general lines as the latter. It has secured several small tracts in St. Mary's township, has drilled two wells and has maintained a satisfactory supply for the village. Its line is four miles in length and consists of four-inch pipe.

(*J.*)   GAS WELLS OF MERCER COUNTY.

The important gas production of Mercer county is confined at present to three townships, viz., Franklin, Marion and Granville. The gas field of Franklin, which is developed considerably in advance of either of

11   G.

the others, is a bodily extension of the St. Mary's gas field last described, sharing all the peculiar features of the latter. The Trenton limestone lies in it at a depth of about 1,100 feet below the surface, and about 200 to 250 feet below tide. It gives rise to somewhat larger wells than the eastern half of St. Mary's, the maximum figures being attained in the Nedderman well, section 26, southwest quarter. In 1888, this well showed fifty-five pounds open pressure in a three-inch pipe, which stands for a daily production of 9,062,000 cubic feet, which is practically 10,000,000. The original rock pressure of the Nedderman well has already been given in a preceding paragraph, viz., 395 pounds. This is the highest pressure registered in this section of the field. As shown in the discussion above referred to, it is, however, about the normal pressure that the Trenton limestone, under the conditions as to depth which here prevail, should show.

Nearly the whole of Franklin township is counted gas territory, the southwestern sections only being excluded from the boundaries which are recognized at the present time. The main development has been made in sections 20, 21, 22, 23, 24, 25, 26, 27, 28, 29, 30, 33, 34, 35, 36, 1, 2 and 3, in all embracing nearly twenty square miles. Marion township has been tested mainly on its northeastern border, where it unquestionably shows the character of the Franklin township field. There is no present ground for expecting the southern half of the township to repay further exploration.

The Granville township gas field, as far as developed at the present time, consists of about ten square miles in the southeastern quarter of the township, with sections 25, 26 and 27 for the northern boundary of the field.

The character of the gas production of these several centers can best be shown in a brief review of the several pipe lines that are carrying gas away from this field.

(1) *The Celina Pipe Line.*—A private corporation, viz., The Celina Light and Fuel Company, consisting of thirty stockholders, with capital stock of $90,000, of which $50,000 is paid up, is furnishing Celina with fuel for domestic use, and also, to some extent, for manufacturing purposes, The company holds under lease about 500 acres of approved gas land in sections 28 and 30, Franklin township, upon which it has already drilled five wells. The territory is fairly compact, but still several small tracts are included within it, of which other gas companies have obtained control. The Mercer, the Van Wert and the Urbana companies hold the interlocking territory.

The line consists of seven miles of four-inch pipe and two miles of six-inch pipe, the latter being distributed in the town. The rock pressure which the wells showed when first drilled was 380 pounds. Early in 1889, it fell to 350 pounds, in 1890 to 325 pounds, and at the present time, June, 1890, it registers 540 pounds. The pressure sometimes falls below the danger line under the demands made upon the gas.

The locations of the wells are as follows: No. 1, northwest corner of northwest quarter of section 30; Nos. 2, 3, 4 and 5 are all in section 28 and mainly in the southwest quarter. The volumes of the several wells are approximately as follows: No. 1, original volume 1,500,000 cubic feet; a small production of oil came with the first gas and has gained upon the gas so that the well is no longer of great value. No. 2, originally estimated 5,000,000 cubic feet; probably about 2,000,000 feet at the present time. No. 3, by measurement from three-inch pipe, early in 1890, 3,935,000 cubic feet; No. 4, 2,187,500 cubic feet. The latter measurement was taken in the tubing. The domestic use of gas in Celina does not extend to more than about a thousand stoves. In addition, a flouring mill, several boilers in small factories, and two glass furnaces are supplied with fuel from the lines of the company. The glass furnaces consume a good deal more gas than all the rest combined. The ten-pot window glass factory uses about 700,000 feet per day upon the average, as has been determined by a month's careful observation of a pipe line guage. The tank of the second glass factory has not yet settled to regular work and no estimate can be therefore formed of its consumption.

The company already finds it somewhat difficult to keep up the supply, and this difficulty is sure to increase in time to come. The gas is to be furnished to the glass furnaces free for five years, by a contract entered into on the part of the company and common council, but there are some possible complications arising from the terms of the contract. The ten-pot furnace was built on the assurance that it required but about 300,000 cubic feet of gas per day, while the actual amount of this and every other ten-pot furnace in the gas field is more than twice this amount. If the company could have secured any protected area of gas which could be held for its own use, it would undoubtedly have conduced far more to the public advantage to have maintained this supply for domestic use alone than to have burned it as rapidly as it is now doing in these glass furnaces. This most admirable of fuels could have been maintained under such circumstances for a term of a dozen, or possibly a score of years. But, deriving their supply from a field which is reached by ambitious corporations whose lines go out to large centers of population and manufacturing enterprises, the smaller companies have no resource but to take the gas while it is going, and to obtain their share of advantage from it in every way possible. The 500 acres of the company can not long survive the heavy draft which it is now obliged to make upon them. Its territory has already lost at least one-fourth of the original pressure of the gas, and the volume has fallen in like proportion. If the company could even now get free from its contracts with the glass houses, a longer lease of life could be assured for the domestic supply.

Since writing the above paragraph, the Celina Municipal Corporation has purchased from the company named above the entire plant, land, lines and distribution service, and another case of the supply of fuel and light at the public charge is to be recorded in the State. The company received from the corporation two dollars for every dollar invested. The rates for gas remain as fixed by the original company, viz., one dollar per month for a stove—a price far below the real value of the service.

(2) *The Mercer Pipe Line.*—The Mercer Natural Gas Company, in which eastern capital is largely represented, makes by far the largest use of the gas of Mercer county. In fact, it transports more gas than any company in the State, the Northwestern Ohio Company alone being excepted. It derives from Franklin township the bulk of the supply which it is furnishing to the cities and villages to the south of it, including Dayton, Springfield, Piqua, Troy, Sidney, Tippecanoe, Covington, Versailles, and several small villages in addition. It has a few wells in Marion township, which adjoins Franklin on the south, and it also holds a considerable acreage in St. Mary's township, upon which a number of good wells have been drilled, and from which the Company has, at times, drawn very heavily. Its pipe line consists of two main stems, one of which, starting from Section 36, Franklin township, extends to the southward as far as Piqua and Troy. This line is eight inches in diameter through its entire extent; but from a point due west of Sidney, a six-inch pipe is taken off, which delivers gas to that town. The gas for this system is gathered by a six-inch pipe, which traverses a number of land sections in Franklin and in St. Mary's townships. Two miles south of Troy, the Piqua line unites with the other main stem, which consists of a twelve-inch line with about five miles of ten-inch pipe nearest to the wells. It starts from the St. Henry's, or Dwyer wells of Granville township. This is known as the Dayton line. A few miles south of Troy, a ten-inch line goes out from the united stem to Springfield, while the main twelve-inch line continues to Dayton. These lines are all constructed of the best material and are laid in the best manner, and the entire service is kept up to the highest standard of efficiency.

Wells have been drilled for the Company on the following named farms in Franklin township:

THE TRENTON LIMESTONE. 165

PARTIAL LIST OF WELLS OF MERCER NATURAL GAS COMPANY IN FRANKLIN TOWNSHIP.

Name of landowner.	Section.	Quarter.
J. Offenhour	20	S. E.
H. E. Bennett	21	N. E.
I. Brandon	22	N. W.
C. Schmidt	24	S. W.
L. Doenges	25	S. E.
R. Wellman	25	S. W.
L. Strassburg	25	S. W.
R. Long	26	S. E.
W. F. Nedderman	26	S. E.
A. H. Vornholt	26	S. W.
I. Selby	27	S. W.
E. A. McGee	28	S. E.
H. Schwieterman	33	S. W.
W. C. F. Ahlers	35	S. E.
G. Bertke	35	N. W.
D. C. Ahlers	36	N. W.
H. J. Doenges	36	N. W.
J. Temple	36	N. E.
J. F. Dammeyer	36	S. E.
W. Kawell	1	N. W.
C. Roettger	1	N. W.
I. C. Greene	1	S. E.
II. F. Dammeyer	1	N. E.
J. C. Schierholtz	1	S. W.
A. H. Hirschfield	2	N. E.

Of this list, the Nedderman, Schierholtz, Offenhour wells are counted among the strongest, the first one having a volume of very nearly ten million cubic feet per day when first drilled. In 1889, there were probably but two or three wells of the entire list that produced less than one million feet per day, and the average production of the list would probably exceed three million feet per day, and might possibly reach three and a quarter million feet. This is certainly an excellent record. The company holds a very large acreage in an almost continuous and unbroken tract in the eastern half of the township, and especially in what is counted the best gas land. It is thus able to protect its territory, except from the excessive draft of its own lines.

That the territory must feel the draft already established on it goes without saying. It is probable that the reduction of volume in the wells already enumerated for the year ending August, 1889, would not fall below 25 per cent. Such a decline, at least, is found to be the case with the wells of the neighboring district.

The highest original rock pressure observed in Franklin township, as has been already shown, was 395 pounds. Parts of the township still show a summer pressure of 340 pounds. The decline in pressure has been much slower than the decline in volume.

(3) *The Van Wert Pipe Line.*—The Van Wert Natural Gas Company is now drawing a supply of fuel for the town to which it belongs from the Franklin township field. It has leased several hundred acres of land in Sections 28 and 31, and has drilled five wells, all of which show good volume and pressure. These lands interlock with those of the Mercer and Celina companies.

The company did not abandon its own immediate neighborhood until it had been demonstrated that no gas supply was available there. The wells first drilled in the vicinity of Van Wert seemed to have encouraged the company to such an extent that in 1888 it proceeded to pipe the town in advance of securing a supply of gas. When later it began this important part of the work it found itself disappointed on every side. The exploration was kept up until fourteen wells had been drilled in Ridge and Pleasant townships. Several of these were total failures, and the very best that were obtained were inadequate to the supply of 250 stoves in the town. There had now been expended fifty thousand dollars, and there was nothing to show for it. It was in this emergency that lands were leased in Mercer county. Of the first two wells drilled in the new field, the production of one was light, but the second was counted good for six million feet per day. The two were thought to promise an adequate volume, and the company proceeded to lay a pipe line from Franklin township to Van Wert. The line is thirty-one miles long. The first twenty miles of it consists of six-inch pipe; the balance is eight-inch pipe. The gas is gathered in the field by four-inch pipe. The line is laid under water across the Mercer Reservoir, the Board of Public Works giving the company this privilege at an annual rental of $100. The rock pressure, when the wells were drilled in the summer of 1889, was 385 pounds; the reduction during the last year has been but forty pounds, the gauges now showing 345 pounds. The draft upon this section of the field is just beginning, and its prospective duration can be estimated more safely after another year of use. The two glass furnaces of Celina are making the heaviest demand upon it at present.

(4) *The Urbana Pipe Line.*—Urbana has been very unwilling to take "no" for an answer to the question, whether gaseous fuel could be found in the rocks that underlie the town. As is proper, the answer has been sought at the point of the drill, but the importunity of the town has been very costly. In Vol. VI, Geology of Ohio, the records of five tests of the Trenton limestone in this immediate neighborhood are given. In one well the limestone was penetrated to a depth of 380 feet, where a strong flow of salt water was reached. In other wells the effects of heavy shots were invoked, and in fact nothing was omitted in the way of proving the

new horizon. These wells were all failures. No value worth recording was developed in any of them.

In 1889, however, legislative authority was sought and obtained for the submission to the popular vote of a proposition to bond the town for $250,000, the funds to be used in finding and utilizing natural gas. The proposition was voted upon, and a vote of 1,240 votes cast, only twenty-seven of which were recorded in opposition to the issue of the bonds. Five gas trustees, selected from among the leading citizens of Urbana, were appointed by the Governor; and the first work done by this board, presumably in obedience to the popular demand, was to bore another deep well in the neighborhood of the town. In this well, the driller was able to get down 2,100 feet before finding a strong flow of salt water; but the flood found at that depth could not be shut out from the well, and the privilege of using public money in sinking the well more than 800 feet below any geological horizon in which gas has ever been discovered in the hundreds and thousands of wells that have been drilled in the country at large, was denied the town. In Dayton and in Springfield private means had been expended in drilling wells 1,800 feet and 2,100 feet, respectively, below the top of the Trenton limestone, without any result but the discovery of a great many different horizons of salt water.

This last test seemed, however, in some way, to satisfy the people, that it was not worth while to drill longer in their immediate vicinity. There is ground for congratulation on this result being reached at length. The record of this well was like the records of those that had preceded it, and it was entitled to no more respect than had been awarded to them. It settled nothing that had not been settled already.

The next step of the trustees was to visit the northern gas fields and to secure territory there. Locations were sought in Mercer county as the nearest section of good gas land. About 450 acres of land were leased in Marion township, mainly in Section 12, directly south of the great Schierholtz well of the Mercer Company. Of the lands thus leased, 320 acres lie in a compact body. Three wells have been drilled for the company, the aggregate gas production of which, from the tubing, without the use of torpedoes, is reported as ten million feet per day. The gas is entirely dry, neither water nor oil being found associated with it in any of the wells. The rock pressure of the field at the present time is 340 to 345 pounds. The lands of the company lay somewhat outside of previously proved territory and thus make a valuable addition to what was before known as gas land.

The length of the pipe line to connect the field and the town is nearly forty-five miles, and in the distribution within the corporate limits, about seventeen miles of pipe of various sizes will be used. Bids have been invited for the furnishing and laying of the entire system. For the main line separate bids are asked for six-inch pipe for the entire distance, and for twenty-seven miles of six-inch pipe, with the balance of eight-inch pipe. It is not yet certain, however, that the bids for the whole service can be brought within the limits of the $250,000 that are available for this use. If not, the project will necessarily be abandoned, at least for the present. A division of sentiment in the Common Council of the town prevented the construction of the pipe line last year. It is believed that the line could have been laid at that time within the limits of the available funds; but doubts are entertained as to whether this can now be done, on account of the advance in the cost of pipe. (The contracts have been let and the construction is going forward.)

The rates that the trustees propose, if the gas is brought to the town, are the same as those that are in force in the neighboring towns. It seems to be assumed that the business of furnishing gas is certain to be a remunerative one, and that though Urbana pays the same rates for fuel as its neighbors who depend upon private companies, the people of the city will be in some way benefited by the investment of a quarter of a million dollars in the gas plant. This result could be obtained by taking up the bonds of the corporation as they mature from the proceeds of the gas rates. If a surplus should accumulate after all the bonds have been provided for, it could be used in reducing the rate of taxation in the city, and the investment could thus be made to serve the entire population. Another view of the possible advantages to be derived from a city gas line, is that by the introduction of natural gas into a town, manufacturing interests will be stimulated and enlarged, and perhaps new enterprises attracted. By this means the population will be increased, new demands will consequently arise for real estate, and all branches of business will feel the influence of the rising tide of prosperity.

Most of these towns that have made this sort of investment rely altogether on the second line of advantages. They count the public money well expended in promoting the business activity of the town. Of course such business prosperity must affect the population of the town very unequally. There are many who are unable to avail themselves of it, and who find the new prosperity rather a burden and a damage than a source of profit to themselves. The expenses of living and the rates of taxation are increased, and they may be so situated that no corresponding advantage can accrue to themselves. The only advantage would be that they could, perhaps, obtain more for their real estate if they choose to sell it.

As to refunding the money expended in the establishment of a natural gas plant from the proceeds arising from the sale of fuel, there has not even an important beginning been made as yet in any Ohio town. The question in Findlay, for example, to-day, after $350,000 have been expended in this line of service, is how much shall this debt be increased for the present year, whether by borrowing $50,000 more, or by borrowing a $100,000. It is found impossible to maintain the plant and the supply on the entire income. Similar conditions obtain in Bowling Green, in which a vote was recently taken authorizing the council to issue $100,000 additional of natural gas bonds to extend the lines of the company and continue the supply of free gas to the glass factories, in Fostoria, Tiffin, North Baltimore, Maumee, and in fact in almost every city or village of the State in which municipal control of natural gas has been obtained. Not a dollar has yet been paid in any of these towns from the proceeds of the gas on the original indebtedness; and, further, there is not the remotest prospect that a dollar ever will be paid in this way. More than the entire income from the plant is constantly required to maintain and extend it so as to cover an evergrowing deficiency, caused in part by the general reduction of the field, and oftentimes by increased consumption. In the case of towns that supply domestic fuel and light to their people, the situation is somewhat improved, when the gas rates are kept below the intrinsic value of the supply, as is shown by their being below the expenditure previously required for the same service. By means of these low rates, the taxpayer is able to recoup himself to some extent from the increased taxation that he has to meet, and perhaps he can, in this way, be made good for the entire amount of his outlay for the plant. There has come about in this way an undesigned and unconscious application of the principles of nationalism to some of our important civic problems.

In the case, however, of the towns that furnish gas to manufacturers only, the resulting gains are very unequally distributed. The larger individual shares come to the manufacturers who become residents of the town for the sake of the advantages which are offered. The owners of the real estate who secure the location of a factory on or sufficiently near the lands which they hold for sale, often realize large amounts from the advance in price. So, also, tradesmen and mechanics have a chance to derive some advantage from the increase of the business of the town, but there must always be a considerable body of citizens who find their taxes increased without being able to discover any compensation to themselves. It now seems inevitable that the gas bonds of every town will remain to be paid after the final exhaustion of the gas. As long as the much coveted fuel lasts, all the revenues which can be gotten together will be used in protracting the life of the supply.

The strong arguments that can be urged in favor of the municipal ownership of gas-works and water-works can not be safely applied, it appears, to the introduction of natural gas under like municipal control. The reason seems to lie in this: natural gas is in reality a product of mining enterprise, and it is surrounded with all the glamour and uncertainty of other mining enterprises. A speculative element is almost necessarily introduced into the search for it, and it sometimes happens that the most unwisely confident members of a community become its accepted guides in this sort of exploration and development. The best that can be hoped is that after the wonderful advantages of gaseous fuel have been demonstrated to a city by the introduction of natural gas, and the available sources have become exhausted, the people will call to their service their soundest business men and charge them with the duty of adopting some system for filling the exhausted pipes with fuel gas, all the elements and stages in the manufacture of which are thoroughly understood and susceptible of exact determination. The immense saving in the use of crude fuel that would be effected by such a course, and the great advantage in the way of convenience and cleanliness that would accrue from its use, makes such a result very much to be desired. It is certain to come, and the date of its introduction on the large scale will mark one of the great advances of civilization, inferior to but comparable with the application of steam power to manufactures and locomotion, or of electricity to the various services that we are now obtaining from it.

(5) *The Greenville Pipe Line.*—In 1889, permission was obtained from the legislature for the municipal corporation of Greenville to submit to a popular vote a proposition to bond itself for $130,000, the proceeds arising from the sale of the bonds to be applied in procuring a supply of natural gas to be used as fuel and light in the town. The proposition was carried by a large majority, and a board of five trustees was forthwith appointed by the mayor. Political considerations were apparently entirely excluded in the appointment, and the selection was made from among the most prudent and successful business men of the community, including the presidents of three banks. This mode of appointment, so far as can be judged by a single example, seems preferable to appointment by the Governor or election by the people, as removing the positions further from the reach of professional politicians. Certainly, no board appointed by a Governor represents the town to which it belongs as satisfactorily as the present board represents the interests of Greenville. The board organized by making one of its own members superintendent. His administration has been sagacious, energetic and thoroughly economical from every point of view. Greenville furnishes by far the best example of municipal control of a natural gas plant that has been found in the State, and it goes some ways towards redeeming the system from the unfavorable conclusions to which most of the administrations would lead the unprejudiced

student of facts. It is repaying the citizens for the outlay in two ways, viz., by a low rate for fuel and by prompt redemption of the city bonds. The trustees were preceded in their work by a gas company that had leased about twelve hundred acres of land in Granville township, Mercer county, the land lying in Sections 25, 26, 27, 30, 33 and fraction 25. Most of the leases were taken at a rental of one dollar an acre, the leases to be exchanged for two hundred dollars royalty on each well; drilled and used. By experience the trustees have learned that some of the lands that have come in their possession are of little promise, and they are therefore allowing some leases to lapse.

The old company drilled two wells, and the corporation has since added three. The number will be doubled during the present season. Well No. 1 produces dry gas, but the amount is not large. Measured in February, 1888, it was found to yield 417,500 feet per day. Well No. 2, measured at the same time, produced about two million five hundred thousand cubic feet per day. The gas rock yielded also a small amount of oil and salt water with the gas, but this well is still valuable. Well No. 3 was characterized by an immense flow of shale gas. In well No. 4 the lower limestone was barren when first struck. It was drilled fifty feet into the Trenton limestone and then was heavily shot. A fair volume was developed by this treatment, but the presence of salt water requires a back pressure of at least 120 pounds on the well to keep the gas dry. Well No. 5 is estimated to produce two and a half million feet of dry gas. It is, all things considered, the best well of the list. The total capacity of the wells at the present time is estimated at eight million cubic feet.

The original rock pressure of well No. 2 is reported as 412 pounds, the highest record of this part of the field. By the time the last well had been drilled the pressure of the entire district had been reduced to 350 pounds. In May, 1890, it had fallen to 265 pounds. It will probably recover fifteen or twenty pounds beyond this figure during the present summer. A pressure on the line of 180 to 200 pounds is maintained. In the entire length, with present use, the pressure falls but five to fifteen pounds. In gathering the gas four-inch pipe is used. A six-inch wrought iron pipe, laid with lead joints, extends for eleven miles from the wells. At Ansonia an eight-inch line begins of wrought iron and screw joints, which continues to Greenville, a distance of eight miles.

The village of Ansonia is to be supplied from the Greenville line, the municipal corporation of Ansonia laying the distributing pipe in that town, and paying the Greenville company forty per cent. of the Wapakoneta gas rates.. The gas rates in Greenville are as follows : Cook stoves, $1 per month. Heating stoves, $1.50 per month. Gas is also supplied to a tile works and a flouring mill, and to five boilers for power. For such uses the aim is to charge about seventy-five per cent. of the cost of coal. There are 2,000 stoves dependent on the line in Greenville. The gas is distributed in town under six to ten-ounce pressure. The aim is to keep the pressure at six ounces.

(E) GAS WELLS OF OTTAWA COUNTY.

Oak Harbor.—The only gas field of Ottawa county, at present, is the one which was described at considerable length in Volume VI, that, namely, of Oak Harbor. A great deal of drilling has been done at other points within the county since the publication of Volume VI, but there are no results that require chronicling. Nine wells have been drilled in and immediately around Oak Harbor. Six of them were drilled by the Oak Harbor Natural Gas Company, which has expended nearly $16,000 in this work and in piping the town, so as to make the supply available. The three remaining wells were drilled by the Cleveland Syndicate, and are known as the Axworthy wells. The latter have not been utilized to any considerable extent, and two of them are very weak. The average cost of a well at Oak Harbor is somewhat less than $1,500. All of the wells have the same general character. They are cased in the Niagara shale at 400 to 420 feet below the surface. and this depth of casing has proved sufficient to keep them dry until, at least, the Trenton limestone is reached. The Clinton generally yields a small amount of gas. The section is normal throughout, as the records of the wells previously published indicate. In all of them the drilling is continued in the Trenton to a depth of twenty to thirty feet. The gas is found at the very surface of the rock. As the drill descends a few feet further oil is invariably found. But the gas generally is delivered dry until after the wells are torpedoed. The result of shooting the wells is marked. A greatly increased production immediately follows the shot, after which a rapid decline sets in that lasts for about a month, and from that time on the wells show but little change aside from the gradual reduction that characterizes all gas wells that are being drawn upon. The amount of this reduction, in the three years since the wells were drilled, is variously estimated at from ten to twenty-five per cent. From its six wells the Natural Gas Company supplies something less than 175 stoves. A small amount of gas is also used for lighting purposes. The wells have all that they can do to meet even this small demand. Not more than half the town is supplied with this fuel. Whenever the temperature falls to an unusual degree a shortage is even now experienced. The rates are indicated in the accompanying schedule:

THE TRENTON LIMESTONE. 173

From October to May, monthly charges, for cooking stoves.................. $3 90
"   "   "   "   "   " heating   " 6 00
Annual charges for the same time are.. .... 35 00
For furnaces forty or fifty dollars are the annual charges.

(F) GAS WELLS OF SANDUSKY COUNTY.

The main interest of this county in this connection is in oil, rather than in gas, at the present time, and the new oil field will be discussed in the succeeding section. A little gas is, however, used at two points in the county, viz., Gibsonburgh and Lindsey.

(1) *Gibsonburgh.*—In the supplementary chapter of Vol. VI, brief mention was made of the occurrence of gas and oil at both these points. Gibsonburgh is now coming into unexpected importance as an oil center, and its gas is losing force and being overrun with oil to some extent. Still the supply has proved exceedingly serviceable. Two large lime interests have turned the gas to account, and the dwellings of the village all make use of it as fuel.

Zorn and Hornung manufactured 100,000 barrels of lime last year, with gas as fuel, and Smith and Dohn 50,000 barrels. This year both will reach 100,000 barrels. The gas supply is no more than adequate to this production. Each of the firms has drilled one or more wells, and all are turned into a common line that unites all the wells. In the winter, when the domestic use is largest, the kilns are not in operation. The gas is burned somewhat wastefully in the new kilns of Smith and Dohn. A cloud of black smoke escapes from the top of the kilns as when wood is used. This effect is desired by the company, as it gives assurance that no overburning is going on. To secure such a result, the gas is burned undiluted with air. No long life can be expected for the gas under the circumstances. The wells that furnish what gas is now used, all produce more or less oil; and the latter element increases in relative amount. One year ago the rock pressure of the gas was 440 pounds; it does not now rise above 340 pounds. The original rock pressure should have been not less than 515 pounds to the square inch. There are no figures at hand that go back to the opening of the field. The largest production of any of the wells does not probably exceed 500,000 cubic feet per day. Salt water rises to the level of Lake Erie, or perhaps even a few feet above in the wells in the center of the township, as in Sections 17 and 28.

In the same township, however, two much more vigorous gas wells than those found at Gibsonburgh have been recently struck, viz., in Sections 35 and 27, Madison. The first well is known as the McCarty well, and its volume is estimated at 1,500,000 feet of dry gas per day. It belongs to the Ohio Oil Company. It seems to promise a gas supply to the village of Helena, that is but a mile and a half east of the well. The second well was drilled by a company of farmers. Its gas production is reported as quite large for this field.

The Gibsonburgh Gas Company has expended more than $6,000 in providing a supply of gas for the village. The rates are $15 for a cooking stove and $12 for heating stove per annum, or $25 for both. For burning lime three cents per barrel is charged.

(2) *Lindsey.*—The wells drilled in 1888 have been in steady operation since that date, but though the supply for the town is limited to domestic fuel in 200 to 300 stoves, it has been found necessary to re-enforce the original wells by drilling a new one during the last few months. It is located to the west and south of the village, and is reported to yield more gas than all the others combined.

So far as can be now made out the gas supply of Sandusky county is likely to be of small force and comparatively short duration. It will be exhausted in the development of the oil resources of the county which is going on so rapidly. The structure of the field will be considered at more length in the succeeding section.

(*G*) GAS WELLS OF WYANDOT COUNTY.

The results of the early drilling at Carey and Upper Sandusky were duly reported in Vol. VI. The recent facts will here find place.

(1) *Carey.*—Thirteen wells were drilled at this point and in the immediate vicinity before the expectation of finding a home supply of natural gas was abandoned. The city has expended several thousand dollars of public money in this search, but it at length became evident to most that gas must be brought in from outside if the town was to enjoy the advanta of the new fuel. For a year great expectations were placed on the Ridge, a somewhat elevated region that circles around the town to the north and west. Several of the wells drilled to the northwest had shown fairly good promise and the gas had been piped in to the town from them. A company based upon outside capital had meanwhile bought the wells of the corporation and the right to supply the residents with fuel and light. The company had proceeded to pipe the town for the distribution of the gas, but the Ridge wells upon which their first reliance was placed also proved inadequate and treacherous, and the loss of the entire investment seemed imminent. At this juncture one of the stockholders and managers of the company went over into Marion township, Hancock county, adjoining or constituting a part of the Findlay field, and began leasing lands on his own responsibility in a district known to be productive. After securing leases upon several hundred acres of land,

a well was drilled which was found to produce dry gas in large volume. This well and the territory leased were then sublet, with privilege of purchase, to the original Carey company. A pipe line was laid from the new wells to the old mains of the company and Carey was, in 1890, for the first time, put in possession of a full and generous supply of gas.

The company now holds leases on 550 acres in a half dozen separate tracts, the largest of which is 120 acres. These tracts interlock with the Northwestern Ohio (Tiffin) Company's wells, and also with the Kenton Company's wells. Such interlocking is always dangerous to gas property. Four wells have been drilled in all by the Carey interest, the united production of which from the casing, at the date when the wells were first completed, is reported as 26,000,000 cubic feet per day. The rock pressure is reported as having been 380 to 390 pounds, when the wells were completed in 1889, but in one of the Tiffin wells it has fallen as low as 260 pounds, and in the entire district it has fallen to 300 pounds or lower. This exemplifies the source of danger in wells so situated. The temptation of one or the other company will be to run the wells beyond their proper capacity. The pipe line is 14.7 miles in length—six miles consisting of 5⅝-inch pipe (casing), and the balance of 4½-inch pipe. Two and one-half miles from the wells the rock pressure is reduced to ninety pounds, and this pressure is maintained to Carey with but very little diminution. The loss is sometimes but five or six pounds. There are but 600 stoves and a few steam boilers at present on the line in Carey, but the small village of Vanlue, intermediate between Carey and the wells, is also furnished from this line.

One of the Carey wells was drilled within six hundred feet of the famous Adam Roth well, which belongs to the Northwestern Ohio (Tiffin) Company. This well was made to furnish the entire supply for both villages for several weeks, and at no time was its pressure materially decreased thereby. The Roth well, it will be remembered, when first drilled, produced a remarkable volume of gas, the measurement showing more than 15,000,000 cubic feet per day. But the well was soon overrun by salt water, and this result threw discredit on all the surrounding territory. The Carey well found the gas rock eight and a half feet higher than it was in the Roth well, and thus far it has shown no trace of salt water or oil. The uncertainties of gas production are well illustrated by these facts. The most sagacious operators of the new field abandoned the territory around the Roth well because of the record it had made. The reservoir was counted small and consequently short-lived. It must, however, be borne in mind that the draft on the Carey line is thus far very light, and that the conclusion above named has not yet been set aside. Steps are now being taken to secure a wider market for the gas, as will presently be shown. When this use begins a severer test of the life of the wells will be made than has been thus far possible. On general principles, an enduring gas supply can not reasonably be expected from the vicinity of the Roth well for the reason that the salt water lies so near the gas.

One fact in the history of the Ridge wells, referred to above, deserves to be put on record. There were two wells drilled on adjacent farms that may be designated numbers three and four. The interval between them was fully three quarters of a mile. Well No. 3 was almost destitute of gas and had no appreciable value. Well No. 4, on the other hand, showed a fair volume of gas. It was packed with a Hoadley packer just below the casing so that it could get the advantage of the upper veins of gas from the Hudson River shales. From the date of the packing of No. 4, gas began to appear in well No. 3, three quarters of a mile distant. The farm houses near by were at once connected with the well, and for a number of months they enjoyed an ample supply from this source, and the gas was constantly flowing in a strong current from an escape pipe besides. The superintendent of the line, suspecting that the packing of Well No. 4 was in some way the source of the new life of No. 3, determined to lower the packer and set it near the Trenton limestone. The moment that the packer was disturbed the pressure fell away altogether in No. 3 and it has never returned. It thus appears that the gas was transmitted fully three-fourths of a mile through some channel of communication in the Hudson River shales.

In Volume VI, page 206, an anomalous condition of things was reported in the case of well No. 1 of the Ridge series. It showed a good volume of gas and when shut in would very promptly register a pressure of sixty pounds, but beyond this figure it never rose. No explanation of the anomaly was attempted at the time, but in the light of the more recent experience recorded here a possible clew to the interpretation can be found. The gas may have escaped through the rock when the pressure rose beyond the figure named.

The present gas rates at Carey are as follows:

Cooking stove, No. 5, mixer	$2 25	per month.
" " 7, "	3 00	"
Heating stove, No, 3, "	2 50	"
" " 5, "	3 00	"
" " 7, "	4 00	"

A discount of ten per cent. is allowed from all these rates on payments made before the 10th of the month.

(2) *Upper Sandusky.*—By reference to Volume VI it will be seen that several wells were drilled during 1887 by the village corporation in and

adjacent to the village limits. All of them proved unproductive. The county commissioners were next induced to undertake the work of exploration at the instance of many citizens, locating and drilling a well on the infimary farm, four miles northwest of the court-house. This well yielded a light flow of gas, but a spray of oil came with it, especially when the well was allowed to flow unrestricted. The amount of gas was ample, however, for heating and lighting the infirmary buildings and its use has been maintained without interruption for the last two years. The original daily flow of the well was about 75,000 cubic feet of gas.

This partial success encouraged the Upper Sandusky village council to resume work, but an injunction was presently served upon this body to prevent any further expenditure of public money in this way. A private company was then formed that took up the work on the same lines and forthwith proceeded to sink three wells. Drilling was done on the infirmary farm and well No. 1, of the company, was located about a quarter of a mile northeast of the county well already described. It was completed in the fall of 1888. It yielded but little gas at first, but what there was proved dry. A torpedo of eighty quarts increased the flow to about 175,000 cubic feet per day. This was a decided advance on the first well drilled upon the farm. The Trenton limestone was found to carry, at this point, a bed of porous dolomite, essential to production, a feature which was entirely lacking in the village wells so far as could be judged from the drillings.

Well No. 2 was located 2,500 feet northwest of Well No. 1. It was also completed in the latter part of 1888, but it was entirely unproductive. Well No. 3, which was located 1,000 feet northeast of No. 1, turned out to be a respectable gas well, yielding, after being torpedoed with sixty quarts, dry, about one and one-half million feet per day and not a trace of oil or water was found with the gas. This gave great encouragement to the drilling company. Early in 1889, Wells Nos. 4 and 5 were drilled. No. 4 was located 1,500 feet southeast of No. 3. It proved much stronger than the latter. A measure taken February 14, showed the daily volume to be three and a half million feet. Well No. 5, 1,800 feet north of No. 4, was finished in March, 1889. It was at least as good a well as No. 3. The company had now drilled five wells and four of them were productive. The gas was entirely dry and one of the wells showed a volume that would be counted fair in any field. The success with which their search was at last had attended, put a new face on the whole question of a gas supply for Upper Sandusky. A field of considerable apparent promise had been brought to light within three or four miles of its boundaries. Every one was eager to have gas brought into the town, but the company was not

12   G.

able to construct a line and to pipe the town at its own charges. The choice must therefore be made between foreign capital, invited in for this purpose, and municipal purchase and control. The latter proved decidedly the favorite scheme. The necessary legislation was procured and the corporation at once proceeded to bind itself for the purchase of the well, the drilling rights of the old company, and for the necessary outlays in the utilization of the gas. The rights of the old company, together with its wells, brought them somewhat more than $30,000, a sum that repaid the company five or six times its investment. The introduction of gas was at once begun. Meanwhile new wells were drilled by the gas trustees of the village corporation, so as to insure, if possible, a full supply for all purposes. On May 1st, Well No. 6 was completed. It was located 3,000 feet southeast of No. 4; it was practically a failure. At this time the case stood as follows: Six wells had been drilled in the new district, and the total output of the four that were productive was about six and a half million feet of dry gas per day. Several other wells had been drilled in the same neighborhood, one or more of which produced smaller volumes of gas than those already described. The rock pressure of two of the corporation wells, as measured by certain representatives of the gas interests of the Findlay field, was reported by the trustees to the Geological Survey as follows:

Well No. 1.. .... 515 pounds.
"   5.. 525   "

The figures were considered entirely trustworthy. Well No. 7 was then located on the Robert Gibson farm, 1,600 feet south of No. 5, one-half mile due east of Well No. 3, and about the same distance northeast of No. 4. Its location was in a sense central for the territory that had furnished the best wells thus far and large expectations were consequently built upon it.

Meanwhile a line of levels had been run to all of the wells drilled to date and the structure of the new field was brought quite clearly to light. The records of the wells are as follows:

	Elevation at—	Drift.	Casing.	To Trenton limestone.	Trenton below tide.	Depth of well.
Well No. 1.........	805 ft.	43	314	1,268	464	1,308
Well No. 2.........	815 "	78	314	1,308	493	1,386
Well No. 3.........	804 "	30	314	1,262	458	1,294
Well No. 4.........	820 "	44	315	1,269	449	1,298
Well No. 5.........	820 "	52	318	1,288	468	....
Well No. 6.........	827 "	45	318	1,295	468	1,333
Infirmary well.....	807 "	....	....	1,285	478	....

An examination of these figures shows that the surface of the Trenton limestone in the Infirmary well was found 478 feet below tide. Well No. 1 of the county had fourteen feet advantage in this respect; the Trenton limestone, in other words, being that much higher. In Well No. 2, the same stratum was found sixteen feet lower than in the Infirmary well. In No. 3, an advantage of twenty feet was found and in No. 4, an advantage of twenty-four feet, as compared with the first. In Wells Nos. 5 and 6, the surface of the limestone was ten feet higher than in the first. These figures do not furnish us all the essential facts. The depth at which the gas was found must also be taken into consideration. The gas and oil streaks are not altogether uniform, but they generally occur between ten and thirty feet below the surface of the limestone. The depth of the main gas, for example, in Well No. 4, was 478 feet below tide; in the Infirmary well the gas and oil level was about 494 feet below tide. The startling fact was thus revealed that the entire range of the top of the Trenton limestone for the wells that had been drilled was less than thirty feet, and the range of the dry rock was much less than this, not exceeding at the outside twenty feet. It was also shown by the records of other wells that had been drilled upon either side of the productive territory, that there is a rapid descent of the limestone both to the east and to the west. Moreover, the two failures in this group of wells had brought to light another fact of great importance in this connection, viz., an unsteady or unreliable character of the Trenton limestone as to porosity. Nos. 2 and 6, for example, had been found dry. Well No. 2, as is apparent from its depth, would have been a salt water well if it had produced any thing; but its failure was due altogether to the defective character of the rock, the level of the limestone being the same as in No. 5.

The gas trustees of the corporation were at once notified of the unwelcome revelations of the level, and the urgent need of economy at every step, if the field were to furnish any valuable supplies to the town, was set before them. Up to the date of this discovery it had seemed probable that Upper Sandusky might profit more from its gas field than some of the towns that had discovered and utilized the gas at an earlier date. The lessons of experience could be heeded and greater economy observed in the use of the great gift of nature.

It was at this time, September, 1889, that well No. 7 was completed. Its record is as follows: Elevation of well head, 826 feet above tide; drift, fifty-three feet; casing 310 feet; top of Trenton, 1,268 feet; top of Trenton below tide, 442 feet. At sixteen feet in the Trenton a good vein of gas was found, a second vein at seventeen feet, and at thirty-two feet a monstrous and uncontrollable volume was released, making absolutely insignificant any well that had hitherto been found in the field, or even the combined volumes of all the wells that had been previously drilled. It was, undoubtedly, the largest well, or one of two or three of the largest wells that had been drilled up to date in this State. The top of the Trenton limestone was found seven feet higher than in any other well, but the main gas came from 474 feet below tide, or only two feet higher than the gas of No. 4. It thus appeared that the new well, enormous as its volume was, had added but little to the scanty volume of the dry gas rock of the field, and it was manifestly pouring forth into the air the stored resources of the reservoir at a rate that could not be maintained but a little while without exhaustion. The exact figures of its production can not be given. An open pressure in the casing of from ten to eleven pounds was reported, but these figures were afterwards recalled as somewhat in excess of the facts. Such a pressure as this would have shown a flow of eighteen to twenty million cubic feet per day. The production was probably not less than fifteen or sixteen million feet; it may have reached 18,000,000 feet for the first two or three days. This would be a monstrous well in any field. But even these figures failed to satisfy the local "experts," so-called, who kept on figuring until one "insatiate archer" had reached a daily output of 54,500,000 cubic feet, while another kindly drew the line at 47,800,000 cubic feet. It is enough to say that there is no properly authenticated case on record in which even 40,000,-000 cubic feet ever came out of the casing of a gas well in twenty-four hours.

The entire community, and especially the people of Upper Sandusky, were greatly excited over this astonishing display, and large plans for the utilization of the gas were at once formed. But the history of the field from this date proved brief and disappointing. The great flow of well No. 7 was struck on September 6, 1889. The well was tubed and packed with difficulty, four-inch pipe being used; but in the week of its unrestrained flow it was noticed that the production was steadily declining. Public exhibitions were made of it thereafter, however, during the county fair, but on Saturday, the 21st, the gas was accidentally set on fire. It burned for thirty-six hours before the flame could be brought under control. On the 23d the well began to show indications of salt water; on the 24th it threw salt water in a steady stream, though a large volume of gas was still escaping. On the 25th oil was delivered with the salt water and gas, and it was presently made manifest that the tremendous flow of the well had not only exhausted its own portion of the reservoir but that of the entire district as well. For examination of the adjacent wells at once revealed the unwelcome truth that they were being overrun with oil and salt water. No portion of the Upper Sandusky field was any longer, therefore, able to supply dry gas. Various attempts were made by lock-

THE TRENTON LIMESTONE. 181

ing in the wells until several hundred pounds back pressure was obtained, or by separating the water mechanically to improve the condition of the gas. But none of these attempts were more than partially successful. The supply from all the wells has been insufficient during the past winter for 1,500 stoves, and the patience of the consumers has been severely tried by the frequent interruptions resulting from water and oil in the pipes. All the expectations of the town, which during the first half of 1889 seemed to be so reasonable and well founded, were thus brought to naught. The gas trustees, however, continued their explorations within the same general limits. Other companies were also drilling wells around the margins of their territory, but with results even less valuable than those already reported.

All of the drilling above described was done in adjoining sections of Salem and Crane townships. Wells 1, 3, 4, 5, 7 and 8 are in Section 12, Salem township. No 2 is in Section 11. No. 6 is in Section 13. The registers of the remaining wells of the Upper Sandusky corporation is found in the list below:

	Drift.	Top of Trenton.	Total depth.	
Well No. 9........	58	1,291	1,325	Oil and salt water.
" " 10........	55	1,337	1,356	Oil—small amount.
" " 11........	45	1,322	1,351	Oil—35 bbls. per day reported.
" " 12........	44	1,323	1,355	Gas—oil near by.
" " 13........		1,277		Dry.
" " 14........	62	1,336	1,377	Gas in small amount.

In all these wells, so far as productive at all, gas is found at from thirteen to fifteen feet in the Trenton, and oil from four to nine feet below the gas. The prospect of an oil field within the limits above named has awakened even greater excitement than that which was produced by the discovery of the gas. The facts pertaining to this latter phase will be taken up on a succeeding page. The value of the district in this particular will undoubtedly be determined early in the present year.

The corporation has already bonded itself for $95,000 in this interest. Further expenditures will bring up the amount to considerable more than $100,000 of public indebtedness. The village has a valuable plant in the ground, and it is hoped that from the sale of the oil rights of the territory which it controls, a handsome sum may be realized. The Carey Gas Company, it is understood, stands ready to connect its present line with the Upper Sandusky gas line. This could be done by laying six miles of six-inch pipe at a cost of $25,000. The wells of the Carey Company, it

182   GEOLOGY OF OHIO.

will be remembered, are located in Marion township, a part of the Findlay field.

Further explorations will probably be undertaken in the Marseilles district, on the southern border of the county, during the present year. The surface limestone indicates a proper disposition of the Trenton as a reservoir of gas and oil, but in the tests already made the rock was found hard and dry. If a proper quality occurs at any point within the limits indicated by the surface geology, there is reason to expect fair response to the drill. The rock pressure of the Upper Sandusky field has already been given, viz., 515 pounds in well No. 1. The gas was struck in this well at a depth of 478 feet below tide, and as we have subsequently learned, the oil and salt water level was perilously near. Calculation, based on the method of the preceding chapter, would indicate that the pressure should be 513 pounds. This agreement is certainly close enough with the pressure as reported.

(H) . GAS WELLS OF HARDIN COUNTY.

(1) *Kenton.*—In Volume VI, the resolute attempt of Kenton to find an available gas field near at hand was duly reported. Gas was piped from the McElree wells, of Jackson township, to the town and used as far as it would go, but the supply was altogether inadequate. The search was persistently kept up through 1888 by the company until the entire circuit of the town had been made in these tests, so far as fifteen or twenty wells could be made to serve such a purpose. When all of these efforts had proved virtually fruitless, the company began to turn its attention to outside fields. The nearest large production was found in the vicinity of Houckstown, Jackson township, Hancock county. Several wells had been drilled here by Findlay parties and a fair volume of gas had been discovered. The main drawback was the indication of salt water at no great depth below the gas. A well of two to three million feet, however, and drilling rights on several hundred acres of land were purchased by the Kenton Company at this point, and a six-inch pipe line about twenty miles in length was completed to the town. Other wells were also drilled, and for a few months a satisfactory supply was enjoyed at Kenton; but in the winter of 1888 and 1889, it was found necessary to draw upon the wells for all they could produce and they proved unable to bear this treatment, salt water soon appearing in them and in the pipe line. As is uniformly the case, this element, when once it had found entrance, proved aggressive, gaining steadily upon the gas, and the Houckstown field was presently recognized as practically exhausted for large supplies.

THE TRENTON LIMESTONE. 183

The Kenton Company once more extended its lines. Tracts aggregating about 700 acres were leased for gas purposes in Marion township in the neighborhood of the great Thorntree well, eight or nine miles north of the Houckstown field. Three wells have been drilled in this neighborhood and the company is at present able to furnish an abundant supply in Kenton for all purposes. The tracts of the Kenton Company in Marion township interlock, as has been already stated, with the lands of the Northwestern Ohio Natural Gas Company (Tiffin Natural Gas Company), and also with those of the Carey Company already described. These facts seem to indicate a comparatively short life for the field, especially when taken in connection with the disclosure of water and oil, both dangerously near the gas, in both the Thorntree and the Roth wells, which have been previously described. The rock pressure is reported at 315 pounds on August 1st, 1890.

Home capital has undertaken and provided the supply of gas for Kenton, and in this respect the town is in contrast with most of the towns around it that have secured a supply thus far. The common practice has been either to invoke the aid of foreign capital, or to put the burden of the search for and the utilization of gas upon the public treasury. The company has already expended $130,000. Its line is now thirty miles in length. It is a wrought iron, screw joint, six-inch pipe, and is well laid. Kenton furnishes at present a demand represented by 1,000 mixers, two-thirds of which are No. 5. Gas is furnished to the Pulp Works, the City Water Works, the Champion Iron Company and the flouring mills. The price charged these large consumers is designed to equal the cost of coal displaced. Toledo rates are in force except that the discounts below the third mixer are not in force.

(2) *Forest.*—In Volume VI the drilling of one well which proved without value within the village limits of Forest was reported. In the same record it was pointed out that as far as the surface geology could be trusted, more favorable conditions were likely to be found a mile or so to the westward. A gas company consisting of fifteen to twenty members was presently organized and drilling was begun one and one-half miles southwest of the village. Five wells were drilled upon a single farm; four others were distributed through the same neighborhood. The five wells first named all proved to be small producers of dry gas. Their flow was somewhat improved in all cases by the use of a torpedo, but the total production was still very light. All the wells but one were tubed with two-inch pipe. The Trenton limestone was found at about 1,350 feet below the surface, or about 425 feet below tide. The rock pressure, as observed in May, 1889, was about 300 pounds.

184   GEOLOGY OF OHIO.

The wells were measured for the company early in May, 1889, and again in July of the same year. In the first measurement the wells had not been opened for more than a half hour before the gauges were applied. Before the second measurement they had been left open for twenty-four hours. By the first measurement, the combined daily production of the wells was found to range between 400,000 and 500 000 cubic feet. By the second measurement, a production of not more than 150,000 feet was shown. The company piped the gas to the village during the summer of 1889, and its use has been going on from that time forward.

(3) *Ada.*—An early test of the Trenton limestone was made at Ada, as reported in Volume VI. In 1888, a company of nine members was organized to carry on a more thorough search for gas, to be used in the supply of the village. The citizens were also invited to contribute to the test with the guaranty that returns should be made to them, in case of success, at the rate of two dollars for one. The drilling has been distributed over a number of farms, but mainly through a district from two to three miles northwest of the village, in Sections 5, 6, 7, 8 and 9 of Liberty township.

The first well of the new company was drilled on the Lynch farm, near the center of Section 8. The level of the surface was approximately 950 feet above tide; the drift was twelve to fifteen feet thick. The Trenton limestone was struck at 1,354 feet, or about 400 feet below tide, and it was penetrated to a depth of 1,394 feet, when the drilling tools were lost. They were never recovered. The well yielded a little gas, but gave no promise of value. A portable rig was used in drilling this well, and six months were occupied in sinking it.

The second well was drilled on the Tressel farm, about the center of Section 9. It was sunk to a depth of 1,634 feet without a show of gas, oil or water.

The third well gave decidedly more encouragement. It was located in the northeast corner of Section 7, on the farm of James Harshee. The drift beds were sixty feet thick. The elevation of the well head was about 950 feet above tide. The Trenton was found at 1,372 feet below the surface, and the drilling was continued to 1,405 feet. The main gas was found at seven feet below the surface of the limestone. The supply at first was small, but the amount was greatly increased by a heavy shot of 100 quarts of nitro-glycerine. Throughout its entire history the well has produced nothing but dry gas. Its flow was measured in May, 1889, and the well was found to produce, in round numbers, one and one-half million feet per day through the two-inch tubing. The measurement was repeated in April, 1890, and, although several wells had been allowed to blow unrestrained for some weeks in the immediate neighborhood, no falling off

THE TRENTON LIMESTONE. 185

was apparent in the production of this well. The rock pressure as taken at the time of the last measurement, was 318 pounds in one hour's time. It rose to 261 pounds in fifteen minutes. The well is decidedly the most promising that has been drilled by the company thus far.

The fourth well of the company was drilled on the Van Valkenburg farm, in the northwest quarter of Section 5. The drift was here fifty-six feet thick; the casing was set at 470 feet; the Trenton was reached at 1,357 feet, and a good vein of gas was found at seventeen feet in the rock. But when the drill reached 1,390 feet a very strong brine was struck, which is now delivered with the gas. The well was subsequently shot with eighty quarts. Its gas production from the two-inch tubing is a trifle over 1,000,000 feet per day. When the well has been locked in for several days the gas will escape dry, upon opening it, for a half hour or so.

The fifth well was drilled on the Turner farm in the northwest quarter, and near the western boundary of Section 8. The drift was found thirty-nine feet thick. The casing was set at 476 feet. The Trenton was reached at 1,367 feet. At seventeen feet in the rock light gas was reported, and salt water in considerable volume at twenty-two feet. The water rose 300 to 350 feet, and the well was then plugged and abandoned.

The sixth well was drilled near the center of Section 6, on the Shaw farm. The drift beds were fifty-nine feet thick, the casing was set at 498 feet, and the Trenton was reached at 1,380 feet. Oil and salt water were struck twenty-three feet below the surface of the limestone. The elevation of the ground may be counted as approximately the same as that of the Harshee well, a half mile distant. On this basis the following facts come to light: In the Harshee well dry gas was reached at 1,379 feet, or approximately at 430 feet below tide. In the Shaw well oil and salt water were found at 1,403, or approximately 450 feet below tide. The entire amount of dry gas rock, according to this calculation, must be less than twenty feet.

The seventh well was drilled on the Bauman farm, in the southwest corner of Section 5, and but one-third of a mile distant from the successful Harshee well. Its daily production was found to be 1,160,000 cubic feet. Its rock pressure accumulated for one hour is 301 pounds. The gas thus far has proved entirely dry. It reproduces the record of the Harshee well very closely, and the same thing can be said of two wells that have been drilled on the Nichols farm, in the southeast corner of Section 6, by parties from Indiana. The wells are known as the Fulton wells. The united production of these wells, measured in April, 1890, was found to be about 1,000,000 cubic feet per day. The rock pressure in No. 2 rose to 291 pounds in twenty-six minutes. The gas from these two wells and from the Bauman well, previously described, is entirely dry.

The last of the company's wells has now been completed. It will be seen that the company has secured by the drilling of seven wells an available stock of dry gas of 2,600,000 cubic feet per day, derived from two of the wells. Another 1,000,000 feet has been unlocked by the two wells drilled between these, on the Nichols farm, as above reported, but these do not, in reality, add to the resources of the field. The Harshee and Bauman wells would, undoubtedly, draw all the gas from the territory which these outside wells occupy if time enough were given to them. The amount of gas is large enough and its rock pressure is high enough to warrant the piping of the gas to Ada, but the presence of the salt water, as above described, is a fact of evil omen in the field, and it does not seem probable that if the gas rock were drawn upon in an amount large enough to meet the demands of the village of Ada, that it would show much vitality.

The corporation has voted upon the purchase of the wells and the piping of the town. The proposal was defeated. This case deserves special remark, as it is the only instance in this section of the State in which a question of this kind has been voted down. The result indicates a more discriminating population as to the burdens of taxation than most of our towns possess.

It is still undecided whether the gas will be conducted into the town. The productive territory which the Ada company has discovered is, in all probability, continuous with the rather feeble production of gas and oil that was developed several years since in Orange and Union townships, Hancock county, and of which Cannonsburg was the center at that time.

(4) *Dunkirk.*—A second well has been drilled during the last year in this village, and its record is regarded as more encouraging than that of the first. It was located in the center of the village and drilled at the expense of a prominent business man—Thomas Appleman. The drift was but seven feet thick, the casing was set at 410 feet, and the Trenton limestone was found at 1,370 feet, or 420 feet below tide. Gas appeared as soon as the limestone was reached and oil presently followed. The column was lifted above the top of the derrick, and it was estimated that a hundred barrels of oil flowed out before it was brought under control. Territory was at once leased with reference to further tests for oil.

(*I*) GAS WELLS OF SENECA COUNTY.

The present record of this county is substantially confined to two towns, viz., Tiffin and Fostoria.

(1) *Tiffin.*—The drilling that was so energetically carried forward in 1886 and 1887 in Tiffin and its immediate vicinity, in the search for gas and oil, exhausted itself in the opening months of 1888. It became at

last apparent to all that the Trenton limestone underlying Tiffin furnished too shallow a reservoir to give any good promise of supplying the town. At the longest, five weeks of open flow of the wells that yielded at the outset dry gas, brought oil or salt water, or both, into every one; nor was the oil in large enough amount to justify the drilling of wells to obtain it. The Loomis and Nyman wells produced continuously for a year or more from two to three barrels of oil per day. From another well a production of twelve to fifteen barrels per day was reported in 1887, but how long the flow was continued at this rate is not known. These were probably the best records of the field in this particular. The necessities of the town in the way of fuel were provided for at an early date in this history, by the introduction of gas from Hancock county through the pipe lines of the Tiffin Natural Gas Company, a branch of the Northwestern Ohio Company, which represents the interests of the Standard Oil Company in this field. Gas was also furnished for manufacturing purposes by this company, but the rates at which the large consumers were supplied were in reality based on the rates for domestic use, some abatement, of course, being made for the largest consumption. Tiffin could not, of course, compete on these terms with Findlay, Fostoria, Bowling Green, and a number of smaller towns that had found gas near their own borders and that were offering it, if not as free as air to all manufacturers that would locate in them, still at a merely nominal cost, no matter how large the amount required or how wasteful the use might be. The project for a city line to supply gas to manufacturers on as favorable terms as their neighbors were offering began to be agitated. As is usual in such cases the plan found favor with the majority of the voters, and when the question was brought before them for action there was practical unanimity in its adoption. Unusual ingenuity was displayed in finding authority for using public funds for these purposes in existing legislation, but new legislation was subsequently secured. The city gas trustees at once proceeded to lease and purchase gas lands, proved or prospective, to drill wells and to lay a pipe line to the city. Their lands are located in Bloom and Perry townships, Wood county, with a single tract in Cass township. The lands leased in Bloom township are mainly in excellent territory, but they are held in comparatively small tracts, and therefore interlock with the gas lands of other companies, especially with those of the Northwestern Ohio and the Fostoria companies. Two of the purchased tracts, consisting of forty and eighty acres respectively, are situated in the very heart of the best production. The Bloom township lands of the company aggregate 333 acres, on which seven wells are already drilled. The lands leased in Perry township can scarcely be said, in the light of present knowledge, to be gas lands at all.

The city paid $20,000 cash for the gas rights of about 1,200 acres. Nine wells have been drilled on the lands, but most of them are already rejected from the line, because of the oil and water that they produce. The property that the city paid $20.000 for would have been counted dear at the time by any competent judge of the facts at one-tenth part of this amount.

The city pipe line is nineteen miles in length, and consists of fifteen miles of eight-inch pipe, and four miles of six-inch pipe. Besides this there are three miles of four-inch pipe connecting the wells and the line. The character of the supply has already been discussed in the description of the Wood county field. The expenditures of the city, in this interest, already aggregate $250,000, according to the testimony of the trustees. Free gas was promised to the large companies for terms of three to five years, and therefore the income derived from the gas is very small. It is all used in keeping up the supply.

In the establishment of manufactures, on the new basis, Tiffin has been highly successful. There are now thirty or more manufacturing establishments, of various grades, that are dependent on the city lines. This list includes three gla-s factories, viz., the Beatty Glass Works, the Tiffin Glass Works, and the Belgian Glass Works. The Beatty Works manufacture table ware exclusively. Their plant consists of the equivalent of forty-five glass pots, and the establishment is the most complete in this line of manufactures in the country. The Tiffin Glass Works also manufacture table ware, the equipment being based on twelve glass pots. The plant of the Belgian works is an eight-pot factory. Its specialty is colored or Venetian glass, and in this manufacture it is very successful. The total number of glass pots is sixty-five.

The Brewer pottery is a large establishment, built and equipped according to the best knowledge of our time. In it the most successful experience and the highest skill of the eastern potteries are represented. It makes use of about 450,000 cubic feet of gas per day. A brief account of it will be given in a succeeding chapter. Among the remaining industries that rely upon the city gas line there may be named the three brick yards engaged in the manufacture of common brick; a Pulp and Paper Works Company, that uses twenty tons of straw per day, and that makes use of five 120 horse-power boilers; two flouring mills, with a daily united capacity of three hundred barrels; a nail factory, and many other industries. One of the brick yards turns out four million bricks in a season. Draining tile is also manufactured in the same yards. These works pay fifty cents per thousand for the gas used in burning brick. The kilns of one company produce 200,000, and of another, 340,000 A rough estimate, based on approximate measurements, made the amount

THE TRENTON LIMESTONE. 189

of gas used in firing one of the smaller kilns, 1,500,000 cubic feet. At this rate the gas would be bringing to the company six and two-third cents per thousand, which is an ample return as compared with charges for other lines of manufacturing. Fifty cords of wood would be required for doing this work, and on this basis 30,000 feet of gas are equal to one cord of wood. Similar results have been obtained in other calculations. The gas daily used in burning common brick in Tiffin will probably amount to at least one million feet. The brick are sold at $4 per thousand or for even less than this. While this fuel is much cheaper than wood in original cost, this factor is only one among several in the saving that is effected by the use of gas. The quality of the product, for example, is greatly improved, and the total number of marketable brick is increased; and, furthermore, the labor used in burning the brick is much reduced. The Tiffin brick yards do not indicate any excessive waste of gas, but the application of so large an amount of the finest fuel of the world to purposes so rude is utterly inexcusable. In fact no word in the language describes it better than the somewhat opprobrious word—vandalism. As has been abundantly proved, the stocks of this fuel are definitely limited in amount, and the supply can not in any case be maintained for many years. But under the conditions of the introduction of the gas at the public expense these results can not, perhaps, be avoided.

The presence of this cheap supply in the city has naturally aroused uneasiness and discontent on the part of those who are paying the regular rates for fuel that the Northwestern Ohio Company has established in all of the towns that it supplies. The city line has, in fact, displaced the old supply in some of the public buildings, as the court-house and the orphans' home. The question very naturally comes up among the taxpayers why the latter should not altogether be displaced by the production of the wells that have been drilled at the public expense, especially when it is held that the new supply need cost but a fraction of what the people are now obliged to pay. The drilling in of two wells at Bairdstown during the present summer has increased the available supply of the city to such an extent that the project for furnishing fuel to the city, as well as to the manufacturers, seems likely to be pressed. Both of these wells are drilled within the limits of the village corporation. The first one, which was completed in February, is located on an eight-acre tract owned by Emerine & McMurray. The rock pressure on June 10 was found to be 300 pounds strong. Its volume, tested after the well had been opened but twenty minutes, was found to be 3,737,400 cubic feet per day. A considerable reduction might follow its open flow for several hours.

The second well, known as No. 18 of the Tiffin trustees, produced about two million feet per day from the casing before it was torpedoed. A shot of sixty quarts increased the flow to somewhat more than 6,000,000 feet per day. Using the measurement from the center of the tubing (3-inch) the flow is found to be 6,334,500 cubic feet. Averaging the flow, the figures 6,160,000 cubic feet are obtained. The rock pressure is 300 pounds. The Northwestern Ohio Gas Company has drilled a well within 136 feet of the Tiffin well and is apparently duplicating its history. The close proximity of these wells renders the speedy exhaustion of both certain.

(2) *Fostoria.*—Fostoria has made great progress as a manufacturing center by means of the fuel which has been brought in by the city pipe line. The establishment of this plant was duly reported in Volume VI, as was also that of several of the leading factories based upon the gas supply. The city has now expended more than $50,000 in securing territory, in drilling wells and in piping and distributing gas to consumers. All the income of the plant is also used in this way. But little new territory has been acquired within the last two years. The annual rentals on all lands of fair promise as gas territory has been greatly increased during this interval. It now reaches as high as $14 per acre for the best lands, and probably averages $8 or $10. The gas lands of Fostoria are situated mainly in Perry and Washington townships, but a few small tracts are also owned in Bloom township. These lands interlock with those of the Northwestern and Tiffin Gas Companies, and the Toledo City trustees are also leasing lands in the same field.

The company now has nine wells in its line. Two wells have been cut out because of the oil that they produced. In one of them oil was found when the well was first drilled, but the amount increased until the gas could no longer be profitably used. The second of these wells produced dry gas at first, but began to throw oil during the last year. Two new wells have been recently drilled by the company in Section 23, Bloom township, one of them a few rods east and the other a half mile southwest of Eagleville. Both of them proved to be light wells when drilled, but the volume of the second was greatly increased by the effect of a heavy shot. Unfortunately, however, salt water came with the gas. Neither of these wells has been put into the line as yet, but the second will soon be tried. The rock pressure in these wells is said to be good, as the territory is comparatively fresh. As in all other parts of the gas field that are undergoing development, the wells of the city line show a gradual reduction of pressure and of volume. The oil and salt water by which the gas territory is every-where surrounded are steadily advancing, encroaching on the gas levels and taking permanent possession of them One of the best wells, which two years ago had a daily capacity of three and one-half million feet, is now reduced to one and one-half million feet, a loss of 57 per cent. From all of them the oil and water now need to be removed by the process of blowing, two or three times a week, and some which are known to be in the worst condition receive more frequent attention. The rock pressure falls least rapidly in wells that have the largest areas to draw from. For example, well No. 1 of the city line is nearly a mile distant from any other wells and it maintains a better pressure than the rest. It is, however, overrun with water and oil to the extent of four or five barrels per week. The actual figures as to rock pressure are not given by the company. The trustees have no knowledge of the total amount of gas which their wells supply, nor of the quantity used by any one of the several establishments that are depending on their line. The main effort is to keep the pressure in the line to the point demanded by the factories. This task must, of course, be an increasingly difficult one and deficiencies can not be overcome in the future as easily as they have been thus far by drilling new wells, for the reason that the levels of oil and water are rising in the entire territory as the gas is withdrawn from it. The last wells drilled furnish striking testimony on this point.

The principal manufacturing establishments now depending on the Fostoria line are the following, viz.: The Mambourg Glass Works, window glass, ten pots; The Crocker Glass Works, window glass, ten pots; The Fostoria Glass Company, table ware, twelve pots; The Nickel Plate Glass Company, table ware, sixteen pots; The Calcine Glass Works, window glass, one tank—equal by schedule to eighteen pots; The Butler Art Glass Works, established here in 1888, was recently burned and a division of the local interests that had been united in it was called for by the stockholders. 'Out of it two glass companies have been organized, viz., The Butler Glass Company, chimneys and bottles—one tank equal to ten pots, and The Fostoria Lamp and Shade Company, sixteen pots. The total glass production is thus counted as 92 pots.

In addition to the glass factories there are dependent on the line the Cadwallader Milling Company; the Electric Light Works; the Fostoria Buggy Company; the Lloyd Lime Kilns, three in number, and two establishments for the manufacture of common brick and draining tile. The milling company pays $300 a year for its gas; the electric light works are rated at 300 horse power, and the lime kilns pay about $350 per annum. These prices show that the rates for gas are scarcely more than nominal. An annual rate of $20 per pot was fixed for the first glass works, but the later establishments have been called to pay twice this amount. The largest amount paid by any one establishment is $500 per year. Brick have been thus far burned at the rate of fifteen cents per thousand, and tile at eight dollars per kiln.

On the basis of calculation employed in the Findlay field, the gas used in Fostoria in glass manufacture is, at the lowest possible figure, 5,500,000 cubic feet daily. The window glass companies that pay $20 per pot for their annual rate obtain for this sum not less than 21,000,000 feet, and accordingly the rate is something like one mill for 1,000 feet. The charge for the gas daily used in each glass pot is about five cents. The amount of gas used in the Fostoria glass works every day, if sold for domestic use in the surrounding cities that are eager to avail themselves of it and that expect to pay at least ten cents per thousand feet, would, at this lowest rate, command $550. The monthly income would be $16,500, and the annual income $198,000.

The total amount of gas used in Fostoria when all the manufacturing establishments are in operation can not fall below 7,000,000 feet per day. It may greatly exceed this amount.

The Fostoria pipe line consists of six to seven miles of six-inch wrought-iron, screw-joint pipe, extending from the wells to the corporation. Diverging from this point two lines of the same size are carried out that extend completely around the town, united on the opposite side from the point of departure.

A further account of the gas supply will be found in a preceding section describing Perry township, Wood county.

(J) GAS WELLS OF PUTNAM COUNTY.

One other attempt to find and utilize natural gas must be given at this point. The village of Ottawa is at the present time engaged in searching for natural gas, to be used as a public fuel supply. The search is being conducted at the point of the drill by the common council of the village corporation. Authority has been granted by the S ate Legislature to bond the village for $45,000 for this purpose. The proposition was submitted to the people and a well nigh unanimous decision in favor of it was given, the opposition making less than four per cent. of the total vote.

The council has taken leases on several farms lying three or four miles to the southeast of the village, and it has thus far drilled six wells at an outlay of something more than six thousand dollars; the first well of the series, however, being located in obedience to the popular demand nearer to the village limits. This immediate territory had already been tested by three or more wells and no value, whatever, had been found in it. The new well confirmed the unfavorable judgment of this location. Of the remaining wells only two have given any promise of service, viz., Nos. 3 and 5. Both of them are situated in the valley of Riley Creek.

Well No. 3 was drilled in the fall of 1889. When the Trenton was reached at a depth of 1,290 feet, or about 600 feet below tide, a small volume of gas was found in it. The gas was at once turned to account in drilling other wells near by. Its entire volume has been used for that purpose almost uninterruptedly up to the present time, and the well has, naturally, been considerably reduced by this treatment in volume and production. Measured on June 27, 1890, its volume was found to be 110,880 cubic feet per day, and the rock pressure rose to forty pounds in thirty minutes. The supply of gas is insufficient for running the boiler with which the drilling of the new wells is being done. Well No. 4 was drilled deeper into the Trenton than No. 3, and a few feet below the gas horizon oil was reached. These two forms of petroliferous accumulation are perilously close in the entire region when either is found, and thus far there has not been developed enough of either to justify the outlays necessary to obtain it. This well is not counted of any value.

Well No. 5 was but little removed from the list of dry holes until it was shot with forty quarts of nitro-glycerine. By the effect of the torpedo, a light flow of gas was developed. The volume of the well, after being opened for one hour, was found to be 148,300 cubic feet per day; and its rock pressure, under the same conditions, increased as follows:

100 pounds in 5 minutes.
200 pounds in 23 minutes.
250 pounds in 60 minutes.
290 pounds in 15 hours.

The well would undoubtedly have fallen to lower figures in production if it had been left open for a longer time, and its rock pressure would have increased correspondingly slower. No use has been made of this well, but it has probably been affected by the draft on No. 3, which is not more than 1,500 feet distant from it. Several other wells in the same general district are now under contract. In all these cases, the Trenton limestone is found at a depth of about 1,300 feet below the surface, and the sections of the wells are normal in all respects. The two wells producing gas show a small amount of relief in the surface of the Trenton limestone, as compared with the other wells.

If sufficient gas is found to warrant utilization, it is expected to bring it into town by a four-inch pipe line. As there are less than a thousand stoves to be supplied, and as the distance of the wells from the corporation boundary does not exceed four miles, a pipe of this size will undoubtedly answer the purpose, provided volume and pressure prove sufficient.

The territory is not such as would invite the investments of any person acquainted with the general business of drilling wells for oil and gas, and at the same time conversant with the character of the northwestern Ohio production, as thus far developed. In other words, no individual and no private company would think for a moment of doing with their own means what the municipal corporation is now doing. The balance of probabilities against the success of the undertaking is altogether too great to allow those who have only their own money to spend to drill a dozen wells, one after the other, in a region that has been as fully tested as this. The territory presents every appearance of belonging to that large division of northwestern Ohio, in which the Trenton limestone is found slightly petroliferous, but without accumulations of either oil or gas that can be made to repay exploitation.

SECTION II.

OIL PRODUCTION OF THE TRENTON LIMESTONE, 1888 TO 1890.

The Trenton limestone is by far the most important single source of petroleum in the United States at the present time. The oil production of Pennsylvania, New York and West Virginia is derived from not less than six distinct strata of sandstone of very unequal value as oil rocks; and these several strata are distributed through several thousand feet of the Devonian, Sub-carboniferous and Carboniferous series of these respective States. Of these petroleum-bearing rocks the Bradford sand has undoubtedly been the most important, but the period of its greatest production has long passed. It is not necessary to compare the Bradford field of twenty-five years ago with the Trenton limestone of to-day; but it is certain that neither it nor any other of the great sand-rocks of the eastern field is now producing or can be made to produce one-half as much oil as this last found source, which proves to be a magnesian limestone of Lower Silurian age. The oil-producer and the geologist alike find it hard to adjust themselves to these surprising facts.

The discovery of oil in the Trenton limestone was made early in 1885 in the Paper-mill well at Lima. Gas in large amount had been found in the same stratum a few months before at Findlay and Bowling Green, and the discovery of oil was consequently only a question of time. No stratum is known in the geological scale that furnishes gas in large amount which does not, also, in some part of its extent, produce oil as well.

An account of the remarkable development of the new oil fields was given in Volume VI, Geology of Ohio, bringing the history down to the date of issue, viz., to the close of 1887. At this time there were three principal centers of production, viz., the Findlay field, the Lima field, including a continuous development through several townships of Auglaize and Mercer counties, and the North Baltimore field. Oil had also been found at various other points, but in comparatively small quantity. Two or three light wells were being worked at Bradner, and at Tiffin and Gibsonburg a little oil was also produced with the gas, which was being utilized at those points, and which was the main object of the search.

When in 1886, an oil field of considerable dimensions became apparent in northwestern Ohio, the Standard Oil Company appeared upon the stage under the name of the Buckeye Pipe Line, assuming the relation to the new field that it usually bears to oil fields, in purchasing, storing and transporting the oil. It would not have consisted at all with the established policy of this company to allow a field of such importance as this promised to become to be developed outside of its control. It also began about the same time an extensive refinery at Lima. Other companies also undertook the refining of the new oil during 1886 and 1887. One such refinery was established at Findlay, two at Lima, one at Bradner, and a previously existing refinery at Toledo was set to work on Trenton limestone oil.

The price that the Standard Oil Company established for the oil when the field was first opened was forty cents a barrel, Bradford oil at that time ranging between eighty and ninety cents. But it was soon found that oil production in the new territory required very small outlay as compared with production in the eastern fields. Not more than 400 feet of casing was, as a rule, required, and the depth of the wells never exceeded 1,300 feet. Sections in which large production was possible were beginning to be reached. During the latter months of 1886, 10,000 barrels of oil were brought to the surface every day, and the Pipe Line Company was kept busy in tank building. Two thirty thousand-barrel tanks were needed every week to cover the production.

The state of things in the new oil field during the last half of 1887, and the beginning of 1888, can not be better shown than in the following extract from a report made by the author in the summer of 1887, and published in the Eighth Annual Report of the United States Geological Survey:

"PRODUCTION AND PROMISE OF THE FIELD.

"Drilling in the Lima field was begun in the spring of 1885. It was a year, however, before the oil producers entered vigorously upon its development. The wells on the Shade farm, south of the town, made the first significant departure from the day of small things with which the work was begun. All these were flowing wells. The early summer of 1886 marked the beginning of rapid development. The production of single wells increased from sixty and seventy barrels to 100 barrels a day; and presently, in the Hume well, to 250 barrels in a day, and a little later to 700 barrels in the Tunget well. To the southward great wells were presently found. The Ridenour farm, the Hueston, Moore,

Ditzler, Ballard, Lehman, Goodenow and Spear farms all became centers of large and certain production. By October 1 the character of the field had come into clear view as second to none yet found in the United States in volume of production. During September, 1886, thirty-three wells were added to the 128 previously drilled. Of these, one was dry. The total production of the new wells was 2,455 barrels daily, shewing an average of seventy-five barrels to the well. Six of these wells were credited with an aggregate production of 1,300 barrels daily. In November a number of other great wells were brought in, and the Douglas, Crumrine, Boop, Mechling, McLain and other farms were added to the prolific areas. A well drilled during this month on the Alonzo McLain farm, Section 13, Shawnee township, reached a production for its first day of nearly or quite 1,000 barrels. This well is still flowing at the rate of 150 barrels a day. The largest production in the Lima field for a single day is that of a well on the J. W. Ridenour farm, Section 18, Perry township. It put into tanks in the first twenty-four hours, 2,760 barrels of oil. Its rate was 115 barrels per hour.

"Of twenty wells completed in November, one was dry, and nine produced daily 100 barrels each or more. Of twenty-two wells completed in December, one was dry, and eleven wells produced daily 100 barrels each or more. The eleven wells of this group are credited with 2,500 barrels daily.

"On January 1, 1887, according to the published accounts, there were in the Lima field 235 wells, with a daily production of 9,488 barrels. In January, thirty-five wells were added to the list, and in February, thirty-four. Of the latter, sixteen wells were reported as producing from 100 to 250 barrels daily. It is unnecessary to follow the development in detail further.

"On the 1st of May, 1887, there were 444 wells in the Lima field. The number has been increased but slightly since this time on account of the determined effort of the Buckeye Pipe Line Company (the Standard Oil Company) to restrict production. The price of the oil was reduced in the latter part of 1886 from forty cents to thirty-five. Other reductions, each of five cents, have subsequently followed, the latest being made on July 20, when the price fell from twenty to fifteen cents per barrel, at which point it rests at this writing. These successive reductions, the company insists, are justified and rendered necessary on several grounds. Prominent among these is the bringing in of the great wells of the North Baltimore field of Wood county, one of which has reached the amazing production of 5,000 barrels of oil in a single day. This is the highest mark of the Trenton limestone.

"At a conference between the producers of the field and the Buckeye Pipe Line Company in July, 1887, it was agreed that drilling should be suspended for the rest of the year, or at least until some efficient means of reducing stocks should be found, and that the torpedoing of wells should be entirely abandoned. The average production for the total number of wells drilled in the Lima field does not reach a very large figure, because the early wells were mainly drilled on the edge of the field where the oil rock lies near its dead line. In the wells drilled during the last six months nearly 50 per cent. have been of the 100-barrel rate, or even larger. The average for the new wells of several separate months has exceeded seventy-five barrels. The proportion of dry holes has been very small since the laws of the field have been approximately ascertained— probably not exceeding five per cent. The highest daily production of the Lima field proper is not far from 14,000 barrels. It must be borne in mind that this production has been reached under the most adverse circumstances. Drilling has been confined during the last few months to the holders of leases for the main part, and it is being avoided now, in many instances, by the lessors waiving the terms of the lease in this regard.

"THE QUALITIES AND USES OF TRENTON LIMESTONE OIL.

"The Trenton limestone oil is in all respects a typical limestone oil, dark in color, rather low in gravity, and containing a percentage of sulphureted products which though small, make themselves offensive and resist expulsion with great stubbornness.

The extremes of gravity observed in the new fields are thirty-one and forty-two degrees, but the great bulk of the oil is included between thirty-five and forty degrees.

"The initial experiments with Lima oil seemed favorable. The quality of illuminating oil obtained from it was thought to be equal to any, though the percentage was smaller than of Pennsylvania petroleum. The Standard Oil Company undertook the large expenditures necessary in taking care of the oil and afterwards entered upon the work of refining it on an extensive scale. Independent refineries were established with considerable outlay at Lima and Findlay, and more recently at Bradner, and the oil has also been handled at a Toledo refinery in small quantities.

"With all this expenditure and experience we are still unable to make positive and final statements as to the value and capabilities of the oil on account of the diametrically opposite testimony that is given by different parties in the field. The Standard Oil Company has planted in the new field more than $2,000,000, and it now avers, through its representatives that it has made a great mistake, and declares that the numerous, extensive, and very costly experiments conducted by it in seeking to obtain from Lima crude an illuminating oil that will fairly compete with Pennsylvania oil in open market have resulted in complete and utter failure. The company declares that out of 200,000 barrels refined by them no oil that could be successfully used as an illuminant has been obtained. Representatives of the company further declare that the only use that they have been able to find for Lima oil is for fuel, and to its introduction for this purpose they are now directing all their efforts. They have more than 2,000,000 barrels already stored in the field, and the stocks are increasing at the rate of 15,000 to 20,000 barrels a day. This increase has gone forward in spite of the severest attempts at repression in the reduction of the market price of the oil.

"There are, however, other companies in the field engaged in refining Lima oil, and their testimony is not of the same tenor as that already quoted. They declare that they are obtaining satisfactory results in refining Trenton limestone oil. They claim that the deodorization of the oil is practicable, and that the cost of the process is not excessive. One of the companies so engaged reports as the result of its operations, when fresh oil of 40° Baume at 60° Fahr. is treated, 50 per cent. kerosene of 150° fire test, 10 per cent. gasoline, and the same proportions and qualities of lubricating oils that are obtained from Pennsylvania crude. The quality of the illuminating oil is excellent. A larger percentage of loss than in eastern oil is admitted, but it is alleged that the loss is not excessive.

"Laboratory experiments on crude petroleums can not always be trusted to indicate what their behavior will be when treated in a large way for commercial purposes, but the results of a few analyses recently made for the Ohio Geological Survey will be found instructive.

"Professor Lord, chemist of the Ohio survey, adopted the comparative method in his examinations. Crude oil from the Macksburgh field, the character and yield of which are well known, and crude Trenton limestone oil from northwestern Ohio, were subjected to the same treatment with the following results, viz.:

	Macksburgh oil, 41 gravity. Per cent.	Trenton limestone oil, 39 gravity. Per cent.
Naptha	16.	15.
Kerosene, between .73 and .83	38.	33.
Sulphur	.025	.535

"The distillation was arrested before "cracking" had begun. It is known that the Macksburgh oil can be made by the latter process to yield a total of seventy to eighty per cent of distillates. It is probable that the limestone oil would closely follow these figures if treated in the same way.

"The enormous disproportion in sulphur compounds in the two oils can not fail to attract attention. It is not certain, indeed, that all of the sulphur present in the oils is shown in the analyses, owing to possible defects in the method used.

"The refiners of the Trenton limestone oil are certainly able to mask, more or less completely, the offensive sulphur compounds by their several methods of treatment, but they fail in some of the processes, at least, to remove them. This is shown in the following results from the examination of one sample of oil:

Crude Trenton limestone oil, sulphur.. .553
Crude distillate, sulphur......... .... .52
Refined distillate (deodorized) sulphur .... .36

The results of the chemical examination here reported seem to show that the new petroleum has about the same character as the Macksburgh oil, except in its high percentage of sulphur compounds.

"In considering the conflicting testimony to which attention has now been called, we should not lose sight of the fact that very large interests and investments elsewhere are involved in the success or failure of the Lima oil, nor of the further fact that decidedly the greatest oil field of the United States, so far as capacity of production is concerned, is coming into view in the Lima district, to the equal surprise of practical and scientific observers. Its development on the scale that we are now compelled to recognize is no'hing less than revolutionary so far as the present interests of production and refining are concerned. An output of 20,000 barrels a day, as already shown, has been forced upon the Standard Oil Company, which has undertaken the task of purchasing and storing the petroleum of the country. The company has built more than a hundred tanks in the new field, each holding 30,000 to 36,000 barrels, and at the rate which the producers were maintaining in spite of the severe repression by the reduction of the price from forty to fifteen cents a barrel, the company found itself obliged to add to its plant two or three tanks each week. In fact, it became apparent that Trenton limestone oil could be produced, at least from one section of the new field, with a profit, even at fifteen cents a barrel. No fact illustrates more significantly the character and possibilities of this production. To check this marvelous yield it was, at length, found necessary to warn producers in substance that no further provision would be made for new wells during the year 1887. Under this compulsion the drill was finally brought to rest.

"If the price of Lima oil had been maintained at forty cents, there is no question that the field would now be producing 100,000 barrels a day. If the price should be raised to thirty cents, a production of 50,000 barrels a day would be reached inside of sixty days. These estimates are certainly within the limits.

"It is obvious that the exploitation of the new field is premature. The markets of the country can not endure without a total collapse of prices the influx of even 20,000 barrels a day of crude oil from new sources, to say nothing of thrice or five times that much. It thus becomes a question whether the new oil shall be temporarily marked down to a price far below its first cost, its production being thereby greatly restricted, or whether by a general leveling of prices the eastern stocks shall be ruinously depreciated. The older centers could easily be impoverished without enriching the new. With such a field at hand as that which has now been described, in which the expenses of drilling and production are reduced to their lowest terms, crude petroleum is certain to be cheap in any case.

"Taking all the sources of information into account, the following statements seem warranted in regard to the new petroleum:

"(1) Trenton limestone oil is inferior to oils of the Bradford fields, or, in other words, to the best oils of Pennsylvania, on the following grounds, viz., (a) it yields a smaller percentage of illuminating oils, unless cracking is resorted to; (b) it contains a vastly larger proportion of offensive sulphur compounds which must be removed before the oil is ready for market and which resist removal with great stubbornness; (c) it suffers a larger percentage of loss in distillation.

THE TRENTON LIMESTONE. 199

"(2) The best of the illuminating oil produced from it is fully equal to the best oil of any field. It endures comparison with any as to the brightness, the clearness and the duration of its flame, but a good deal of the refined oil that is in the markets from this source can not endure the test; it crusts the wick and clouds the chimney of the lamp in which it is burned.

"(3) Trenton limestone oil can be deodorized with small expense, to this degree at least, that it can enter the market without serious prejudice or disadvantage arising from its odor. Complete deodorization is claimed by most of the firms that are engaged in refining it, but while the possibility of the entire removal of its sulphur compounds is beyond question, this result has not thus far been generally attained.

"(4) The lubricating oils and the other accessory products of refining are of a high degree of excellence.

"(5) The present price of Trenton limestone oil, viz., fifteen cents a barrel, is in no way a measure of its real value as compared with the present price of Pennsylvania oil.

"There is one use of Lima crude oil in regard to the success of which all are agreed, viz., its use as fuel. It is excellently adapted to the convenient and economical production of heat for almost every purpose. It has been applied to simple uses, as to cooking and heating stoves, and also to the production of power in stationary steam-boilers and to locomotives to a small extent; to the heating of gas retorts, to puddling and reheating furnaces, and to various other uses. In all these it has demonstrated its adaptability and great value.

"Various processes for using it safely and conveniently have been devised, and there is probably room for important additions in this field. Four barrels of oil are counted equal to one ton of soft coal. At the present price of crude oil it could scarcely be displaced by natural gas where it is introduced. The crude oil ought to be deodorized before being applied to any of the purposes already named, but this has not yet been done where it is used for fuel, except in an experimental way. There seems to be no doubt that this result can be easily accomplished.

"If all other and higher uses of petroleum are dropped entirely out of the account it is still evident that an enormous stock of fossil power, vastly greater than all that can furnished by the newly discovered natural gas fields of this part of the country, is made available to us in the Trenton limestone oil."

The foregoing statements show the estimation in which Lima oil was held in 1887:

During 1888, a rapidly extending market was found for crude Lima oil. Excellent modes for burning it were brought into use, and an unlimited demand could well enough have been created for it at the price that then prevailed. The Buckeye Pipe Line (Standard Oil Company) constructed an eight-inch line from Lima to Chicago, the length of the line to the city limits being 208 miles. The highest elevation on the line is near the point of beginning and but ten feet higher than the Lima station, and the total fall is about 300 feet, most of which is accomplished in the last seventy-five miles. There was but one pumping station to begin with, and this was at Lima; but a second was soon established at Laketon, which is nearly intermediate between the two extremes. The maximum delivery with a single pumping station and with 750 pounds pressure at Lima, is 10,000 barrels in twenty-four hours. With ordinary pressure of 400 to 500 pounds, the delivery ranges from 6,000 to 8,000 barrels per day.

Under these conditions the embargo was little by little removed from the drill and its vibrations were again resumed, and even multiplied.

It is probable that the Standard Oil Company really entertained a poor opinion of Lima oil during the time above referred to, while the price was being gradually forced down from forty to fifteen cents per barrel. It had attained no better success, apparently, in refining the oil at that time than the smaller companies had achieved; but there is no reason to doubt that, like the smaller companies, it was during all this time getting fair results in its great refinery. The probability is that it was taking the heart of the oil for refining, satisfying itself with a small percentage, and turning over the bulk to the fuel department.

But a change soon appeared in its policy. The independent producers were multiplying and growing strong during 1888. The small refineries were carrying on their work successfully. Some of them were finding distant markets so promising that the Standard Oil Company apparently counted it necessary to begin to hold them in check. The districts which they were occupying were flooded with anonymous circulars, prejudicing, as far as possible, their sales. Up to 1888 the Standard Oil Company had purchased no oil territory. It probably gained some additional knowledge in the course of this year as to the real value of Trenton limestone oil, perhaps through the development of the Frasch process, presently to be named. At any rate, it entered during the year upon a policy which it had not heretofore adopted in any field, that, namely, of purchasing territory and producing oil for itself. The new departure is a very important one, so far as Ohio oil is concerned, and certainly so far as the interests of the company are concerned. It puts this field, which has far greater productive capacity than any other in this country, more entirely into the hands of the great company than any other field has ever been.

It began by absorbing the holdings of the most sagacious or the more fortunate of the independent companies. The Ohio Oil Company was in the front rank of the producers. It held a large acreage in the heart of the Lima and Auglaize county fields. The Standard interest bought out this company bodily, and retained its name for its own use in its new capacity. It bought out the Trenton Rock Oil Company, the bulk of whose lands were in dead territory, but which still held some valuable production. At a later date it bought out the Lima Oil Company, the Sherman Oil Company, and scores of other companies, and individual producers in every section of the field. It turned its attention also to promising districts that were still in the hands of the original landowners. Where oil rights could be obtained, it purchased them in the large way, but it also bought many thousands of acres in fee simple. In acquiring new territory in which possible production is indicated, the company has competed eagerly for possession during the last year, seeming to prefer to deal with the landowners direct than with oil companies after they have become strong. This policy has been of wonderful advantage to the landowners.

All these purchases, let it be remembered, were made on the basis of oil at fifteen cents a barrel, the price to which the product of the Trenton limestone had been forced by the Standard control. It must also be repeated that this price has no relation to the intrinsic value of the oil. According to the rates at which Bradford oil was selling through all this history, Trenton limestone oil was, in reality, worth four or five times what was paid for it. Taking all these facts into the account, it is easy to see that the Standard Oil Company is likely to gather more wealth from Trenton limestone oil than all that it has accumulated in the eastern fields. The Black Swamp of northwestern Ohio will enormously increase the almost fabulous wealth which it has accumulated elsewhere during the last twenty years.

All that was claimed in regard to the oil in 1887, in the passage quoted on a preceding page, has been made good during the last year, and the claims still fall short of the reality. Trenton limestone oil is now yielding as fine a quality of illuminating oil as has ever been produced in the eastern field.

THE REFINING OF TRENTON LIMESTONE OIL.

(a) *Paragon Refinery.*—It is to the year 1889 that the great advances in the recognition of the real value of the new oil must be ascribed, so far at least as the knowledge of the outside world is concerned. Much of the advance is due to the work of a single factor, viz., the Paragon Refining Company of Toledo. This company, compact in numbers and financially strong, thoroughly acquainted with the oil production and the refining interests of the old fields, through the persistent experimentation of one of its members, viz., George H. Van Vleck, of Buffalo, New York, came into possession of a process, worked out by Mr. W. H. Pitt, professor of natural science in the Buffalo High School, by which the sulphurous compounds that so stubbornly inhere in Trenton limestone oil, and that have thus far, though more or less masked by the process of refining, been able to defy expulsion, were at last eliminated so far as all offensive properties are concerned. The essential feature of the Paragon process, which has been covered by a patent, is the removal of the sulphur compounds by means of iron filings, while the oil is in a state of vapor. The process thus agrees closely with one of the best processes for the purification of ordinary coal gas, and like the latter it is thoroughly successful. A sample of oil, taken from the tanks of the Paragon Company, was submitted for chemical examination to Prof. N. W. Lord, the chemist of the Survey. It was carried through a thorough examination for sulphur, side by side with a sample of the best eastern oil that could be obtained in Columbus, and the result showed ,that there was no more sulphur in the Paragon than in the Pennsylvania oil, though originally there was fifteen or twenty times as much.

The new product has naturally been submitted to many practical tests, all of which show it to belong to the very highest grade of illuminating oils. When it passed the critical and not over-friendly inspection of the Oil City Exchange, and no fault could be found with it, all questions as to its quality might safely be counted settled. There is no particular in which it shows any inferiority whatever to the most perfect types of eastern oils and it has certain advantages of its own.

The refinery of the Paragon Company is one of the most complete and best equipped in the country. It occupies seventeen acres of land, well situated with reference to railroads, on the south bank of the Maumee River, three miles below Toledo. At the present time there are in operation four stills of 400 barrels capacity, and four of 500 barrels capacity. In addition there are two steaming tanks of 800 and 1,200 barrels capacity respectively. The company owns tank-cars and controls a considerable amount of oil-producing territory, largely in the Gibsonburg field. Its total holdings are said to be about 5,000 acres. During 1889 the refinery was able to purchase as much oil in the field as it desired, but the consolidation of the producing interests in the hands of the Ohio Oil Company, which has been reported as in rapid progress at the present time, will probably change this in the immediate future.

The Paragon Company makes great claims for Ohio oil as contrasted with Pennsylvania oil, but it does not give the percentage of the former to the public as yet. It affirms that the recovery of the parafine from its oil is greatly facilitated by the process to which it is subjected in the elimination of the sulphur.

As intimated above, the process is owing to the determined purpose of Mr. Van Vleck, the president of the company, to master the treatment of Ohio oil so far as its sulphur is concerned. For this purpose he built, several years ago, on his own ground at Buffalo a miniature refinery and began his work, trying every thing which his knowledge of the oil business could suggest as promising success, and at the same time calling in the chemical assistance already named. For six months he continued his experiments without being able to report progress. At last the substance of the present method was hit upon. After the process was perfected in the experimental way, Mr. Van Vleck put it to a practical test in a small refinery, built by himself at an expense of several thousand dollars. He found the results all that he expected. The present company was then formed and the large works at Toledo were begun. Tested on the large scale, the process is said to work even more satisfactorily than it had worked in either of the trials through which it had been previously followed.

(b) *The Solar Refinery* —The great refinery of the Standard Oil Company is established at Lima. In its equipment nothing has been spared which could contribute to the efficiency of such a plant. It is now running twenty-nine stills of 500 barrels capacity, with which are connected five agitators and acid recovery works. The stills are run six or seven times in a month. The company has introduced within the last year a new process for treating the oil and eliminating the sulphur. It is known as the Frasch process, from the name of the chemist who originated it. It is similar in its desulphurizing agency to the Paragon process, though differing in other respects. It is unquestionably a decided advance on the previous methods of treating the oil in the Solar works. As to how it compares in efficiency with the Paragon process, there has been no opportunity to determine by comparative analyses, but the resulting product is unquestionably of very high grade. The company is now shipping its product under the brand of the Solar Refinery and it has no better illuminating oil. During the last year, pipe lines have been extended from the Ohio field to the great refineries of Cleveland and Oil City, and the company is, without doubt, assured that when consumption permanently overtakes production in the eastern districts, it has the great resources of northwestern Ohio upon which to draw for a long term of years, and with the product of which it will be able to maintain the highest standard of quality to which it has ever yet attained. •It is building near Chicago a refinery of enormous size to which its oil pipe line will be tributary.

(c) *The Eagle Refinery.*—This refinery was established early in the history of the Lima field and has been pursuing the even tenor of its way from that day to the present. Its outfit is comparatively small. It has seven stills of 250 barrels capacity. It holds a process of its own in eliminating the sulphur. This is understood to be some modification of the lead process. The company has made steady improvement during the last two years in treating the oil, improving its quality and at the same time using constantly smaller percentages of the necessary chemicals. It has always furnished a thoroughly marketable and acceptable oil. By its treatment the odor of the oil is almost entirely removed. A little clouding of the chimneys still remains, owing to the percentage of sulphur, which resists elimination. In its practice it obtains from seven to ten per cent. less of water-white oil than Pennsylvania crude is expected to yield. The percentage of benzine is stated to be in excess of twelve. The lubricating oil and the residues are eagerly taken up by those who treat these products. The waste is reported as relatively large.

The company owns its own oil production, at least in part. It has given over the use of oil from the Lima field proper altogether, on account of its low gravity, which, as will be remembered, ranges between thirty-seven and thirty-nine degrees, B. The gravity of the North Baltimore oil is about forty-one and one-half degrees, B., and gives correspondingly better results in distillation. The company has, accordingly, secured a considerable acreage in the North Baltimore field which, when fully drilled, is expected to produce a full supply for the refinery. At present the crude oil is all received by tank cars from the North Baltimore field.

The refinery has done its work thus far on fifteen cent oil. How it will be affected by the new conditions that are being established in the field, remains to be seen.

(d) *The Peerless Refinery.*—This establishment is located at Findlay, and has been in operation with various fortunes during the last four years. During the last year its business is reported as very prosperous. It commands its own oil production, holding about 4,000 acres in the best part of the Findlay field. Its wells and tanks are connected with the refinery by its own pipe lines, so that it commands every advantage in this respect. Findlay oil is not quite equal for refining purposes to North Baltimore and Gibsonburg oil, but no complaint is made of it here. This company, like the one last named, uses some modification of the lead process in its treatment of the sulphur of the oil. Like the last, also, it has made great progress in its work during the last year or two. It is now furnishing, beyond question, an excellent and popular oil, which there is no trouble in maintaining in the markets. The refinery is turning out about 1,500 barrels per month, and it proposes to double its plant forthwith.

(e) *The Bradner Refinery.*—This is a small establishment, built in 1887, but it has been in operation for only a small part of the intervening time. It was located at Bradner with the expectation that it could obtain in the immediate vicinity a supply of oil of the best grade; but the wells first drilled proved small or failures, and for several years the location has worked greatly against the success of the refinery. Though removed but a few miles from the North Baltimore field, a car loaded at the wells of this district would be obliged to traverse the lines of three railroads before reaching the refinery. But recently fortune has proved more kind. An important oil field has been developed within two or three miles of the refinery, and the owners of the latter have secured a large amount of the best territory in the new district. The mode of treating the oil in this refinery, when in operation, was quite similar to that in force in the two last named; but not having been constantly engaged, as the latter have been, in the work of distillation, it has probably failed to keep pace with them in their improvements. The business of producing oil for the general markets has proved more attractive to the company of late than the work of refining it. If, however, the company should resume its proper office it would be free from many of the disadvantages that have attended its work hitherto.

From this brief review it can be seen that the work of refining Trenton limestone oil has certainly been mastered by two companies, and that refined oil, of as high quality as has ever been produced in the country, can now be supplied in the largest amount from this great field. It has been also shown that several other companies have attained fair success in their work under the conditions that have heretofore prevailed in the field. It has thus become certain that Trenton limestone oil is henceforth to be valued as a basis for refining and not for any inferior uses. The very fact that it is available for the higher uses forbids its being turned to these commoner applications. All the oil suitable for refining in the country will be needed before many decades go by.

OTHER USES OF TRENTON LIMESTONE OIL.

Reference has been made in the preceding section to the low estimate of value that was at first placed upon the new petroleum, especially by the Standard Oil Company. This company felt obliged to take care of the product of the Trenton rock because it was oil; but for the first two years of its occupancy of the field, it failed to realize the value of what it reluctantly found itself obliged to handle in the execution of its well-known purpose to control the oil interests of the country. During this time the main use for which it could recommend Lima oil was for fuel. As soon as the proper means were contrived for handling and burning the oil conveniently its natural excellence asserted itself, and all who used it were only anxious to be assured that a supply would be maintained at the rates at which it was first offered.

It was found equally available for the production of power, the manufacture of fuel gas by the new processes, and the various uses of fuel in connection with iron-working and other like industries. Wherever it was introduced it became at once exceedingly popular. The manufacturers of the northwest sent representatives to the Ohio field to make sure, if possible, by the purchase of productive territory, of maintaining their supply, and all along the Atlantic seaboard the appreciation was equally emphatic. This state of things made a brisk market during 1889 for fifteen-cent oil; and wherever the production of the rock was generous, drilling went forward with considerable activity. Many companies were growing fairly strong by the sagacious handling of their own product in meeting these new demands. Several of the more enterprising were buying oil at a slight advance above the price which the Standard Company had fixed in 1887. One company kept a standing offer of two and a half cents more per barrel than the Standard Company would pay, but up to the present summer it has never needed to change its rates.

But Trenton limestone oil is altogether too precious a form of stored power to be applied to these common uses, and the fact was discovered none too soon.

These common uses have been brought about by the insignificant figures to which the Standard Oil Company had crowded down the price of the oil, and by the missionary work done by this company during 1887, in teaching the people of the country what an admirable fuel Trenton limestone oil is. The company long ago discovered its mistake. The pipe line that it had built to Chicago, ostensibly, and probably at the outset in reality, for the conveying of fuel oil was now made to terminate in a gigantic refinery, one of the largest in the United States, and the original pipe line is being duplicated. It did not renew its contracts for fuel oil when they expired, but the independent producers stood ready to take them up, and even to greatly extend this sort of use. But as the oil began to be refined on the large scale the refineries themselves needed the markets which had been secured for the crude oil for the benzine that they themselves were producing. The crude oil could be sold on the seaboard and in the northwest at about three cents a gallon, so long as the initial price was kept at fifteen cents a barrel; and while this state of things was maintained benzine could not be sold for the same uses at five cents a gallon, the price which the refineries needed to obtain for it.

The remedy for these conditions was to be found either in marking up the price of Trenton limestone oil, or in buying out the independent producers, or in both lines of action. The independent companies, under the new conditions above described, were already paying several cents per barrel more than the Standard Company, and were obtaining a growing share of the outside production. Prominent among these companies were the Lima Oil Company, the Shawnee Oil Company, the Sun Oil Company, the Peerless Refinery Company, etc.

The first advance was made by the Standard Oil Company on March 6, 1890. It was then officially announced that from that date the Buckeye Pipe Line Company would pay twenty cents per barrel for Lima oil. This was two and a half cents in advance of the price which several of the independent companies were at the time paying, but the latter instantly raised their offers above twenty cents. Three times in the course of the week, beginning with March 6, advances were made by the Pipe Line Company, leaving the price at the end of the week twenty-three cents. On March 19, it was raised to twenty five cents by the company. Each advance was promptly met by the independent producers. On April 8, the Standard price was raised to twenty-seven and one-half cents; on April 15, to thirty-two and one-half cents; and on May 6, to thirty-seven and one-half cents, where it rests at the present time, the independent producers paying meanwhile forty cents for the oil, an advance of 266 per cent. in sixty days.

Side by side with this exciting competition, the absorption of the more active companies has been going forward. The Lima Oil Company was one of the first to receive the price at which it held its property and business. The terms of the sale were private, but it is fair to suppose that the sale was not effected on a basis of fifteen cent oil. The demands of several other strong companies, it is said, have been so far reached by the Standard too late, the advancing rate of oil carrying a constantly increased valuation. Of all these other companies we may say, "They a little longer wait, but how little none can know." There is no reason to doubt that the great corporation will ultimately secure full control of the entire field. In fact it has, at the present, but very little more to do to reach this result. It already owns either the oil rights or the fee of by far the most important portion of every subdivision of the field. The independent companies that are at work beside it are not in the field as representatives of any high views of public policy for which they would be willing to make all needful sacrifices; they are in the field to make money, and whenever they find that the Standard Oil Company will pay them more for their property than they can reasonably expect to make out of it themselves, they will sell. In addition to all this, the pipe lines, the tankage, and the refining interests of the company would put the field virtually under its control, even if it did not own a large preponderance of the production. The stocks of oil that the company holds give it another overwhelming advantage as against the independent producer. There are now in the tanks of the company in northwestern Ohio more than 14,000,000 barrels of oil, paid for at fifteen cents, but by a stroke of the pen converted into thirty-seven and one-half-cent oil, and in reality worth even twice this figure. The company added more than three and a half million dollars to its credit by simply writing a new figure for the price of the oil, and it could just as easily double this amount in the same way. With such a leverage in the hands of a company that is commonly reputed to know no scruple in its treatment of competitors, it seems impossible for individuals or companies to permanently hold their place in the Ohio field; they exist but by sufferance.

At no previous time in the history of the field has there been any thing like the excitement that sprang up under the advance of prices that has been described in the preceding paragraph. When the price reached thirty cents, a basis was at last afforded on which new territory could be explored, and the driller has turned to this work with great energy. All territory that could be counted as giving any promise, either from its history or its situation, has been covered by the operator's leases, and scores of wells are now bringing in their reports from new districts and will continue to do so through the coming season.

Gas is relegated to decidedly the second place by the new movement. Even in centers like Findlay it has already become "a back number" and its rapid decline is noted without undue excitement, the speculative element that has been connected with it in the past being now absorbed in the fortunes of the oil field. "The king is dead; long live the king," is the motto for the occasion.

The new movement has put into circulation a large volume of money which is being widely distributed through a half dozen counties in northwestern Ohio. Few leases are now taken in territory of any real promise without a bonus ranging from one to ten, or even fifteen dollars per acre. It is safe to say that the farming community of these counties have paid their taxes during the last month easier than they ever paid them before. It must also be added that through the same agencies the districts that are being explored and developed in the new interests have been turned for the time being into mining camps. An unwholesome and restless excitement prevades whole communities, making the gains of ordinary industry seem insignificant, and giving rise to widespread speculation and extravagance. It is not in all respects an advantage for a farming district to be turned into an oil field.

GEOLOGICAL FACTORS IN THE OIL PRODUCTION OF THE TRENTON LIMESTONE.

(a) *The Oil Sand.*—The oil sand of the new horizon, as is known to all who have made themselves intelligent in regard to the subject, is a magnesian or dolomitic limestone. It sometimes constitutes the very surface of the Trenton limestone, being struck by the drill as soon as the latter has passed through the Utica shale; but it is more frequently, or even generally covered by a hard cap, one to ten feet in thickness. This cap is a true calcareous rock. It is quite likely from its situation to be brought up from the well by the explosion of torpedoes, and we consequently have many opportunities of learning its character. It is often very pure, ranging between 93 and 97 per cent. carbonate of lime. It is generally highly fossiliferous, carrying the common fossils of the formation. Wherever it occurs as a pure limestone, it may be suggested that the process of dolomitization did not have time to transform it before the interruption in the conditions of the sea occurred that is represented in the formation of the Utica shale. We know that the dolomite is in all cases a secondary formation, the limestone from which it results being dissolved, atom by atom, and replaced in part by the new material.

The oil sand lies, as has been said, directly below the hard cap, when the latter is present. It consists of one or two, or sometimes even more beds of porous dolomite, interstratified with the ordinary limestone of the Trenton type. The main or upper bed varies greatly in thickness. It seldom, if ever, exceeds fifteen feet, and a thickness of three to ten feet would cover most of its occurrences. This sand does not, therefore, generally exist more than twenty to twenty-five feet below the top of the Trenton. The second bed is often found, and especially in the most productive portions of the field, separated from the first by an interval of fifteen to twenty feet. The second sand has all the characteristics of the first and is even more productive than the first in many cases. Nearly all the extraordinary flows of oil that are reported are derived from the lower stratum. The second oil streak especially characterizes the Wood county field.

(b). *Presence of Salt Water.*—The salt water occupies a very different place in the new oil field from what it holds in the eastern fields. In the latter its appearance is generally a sign that all is lost; in the former it is no longer regarded with suspicion or disfavor. It is thought that the oil rock is kept in better condition when it produces with the oil four or five barrels of salt water in a day. Such a production would be preferred by many operators to a well producing oil alone. Even where wells produce twenty, thirty or fifty barrels of salt water in a day, they may still be highly valued as sources of oil. The salt water gains in many cases but slowly. In present practice in the Lima field, wells are universally drilled to a depth of fifty feet in the Trenton limestone, and this depth is generally sufficient to release more or less salt water. The difference in the eastern and the western fields in these respects is obviously connected with the differences of structure by which they are characterized. The Pennsylvania field is marked in most instances by the presence of more distinct anticlinals or arches than appear in Ohio. In the latter the terrace structure prevails, and broad tracts of apparently level oil rock are revealed by the drill. On the margins of these terraces, the water column is often aggressive, but in the interior it works its way forward but slowly. It is this factor which protects the oil rock from being overflowed. The same structure protects the gas fields of Bloom township, Wood county, and also of Franklin town-

14   G.

ship, Mercer county, for example, from as speedy reduction as Findlay and Stuartsville have shown.

Just outside the oil boundaries, at a little lower level in the limestone, a flood of salt water unmixed with oil, lies which rises nearly to the surface when it is struck, and which pumps are as powerless to exhaust as they would be if connected with the sea itself. But the driller always knows wells of this character as soon as they are struck. They are in no sense oil wells at the present time or prospectively. Abundant observations show that the salt water, when it rises most freely, attains a height of about 600 feet above tide.

(c) *Acreage demanded by Oil Wells.*—Opinions vary considerably as to the proper acreage to be assigned to an oil well, among those who have the most experience in the field. It is probable that different sections of the field would require somewhat different answers in this respect, but no judicious operator would locate wells so that any one would have less than ten acres tributary to it. Most hold that in territory where they are not obliged to guard against rival interests, economy would be consulted by giving to each well at least twenty acres, and some place the limit as high as fifty acres. In the best sections of the field a well will undoubtedly draw oil from a much larger area even than the last named, if time enough is given to it. There are a few cases in which the oil rock lies more unsteady than usual, where a part of the production might be missed, unless wells were drilled closer together than any of the limits assigned would require. The most of the answers would name ten to twenty acres as the proper territory to go with a well.

(d) *Production of Oil to the Acre.*—As to the total production to be realized to the acre, it is too early in the history of the field to give results. Only estimates are available, and here also the estimates vary considerably. No estimate obtained has placed the total production of what is called good territory at less than 2,000 barrels to the acre. Many judicious estimates name 2,500 barrels to the acre, and some operators are confident that the best territory will range between 4,000 and 5,000 barrels to the acre. There is no doubt that the last named figures will be attained in the vicinity of the greater wells.

(e) *Capacity of Single Wells.*—As to the production of single wells, it is still too early to report. The Slaughterbeck well No. 3, of Henry township, Wood county, had produced a total of 200,000 barrels one year ago, and it was still a good well. The Alonzo McClain well of Shawnee township had reached a total of 160,000 barrels a year ago and was still a good well. Probably a score of wells have passed the 100,000 barrel mark without losing their vitality. One operator reports an average production of

THE TRENTON LIMESTONE. 211

30,000 barrels to thirty-five wells, all of which were still in fairly vigorous production.

Probably no single well has produced 10,000 barrels in a day, but several have started off at this rate. There are three or four wells that have put into the tanks at least 5,000 barrels per day.

(f) *Life of the Oil Wells.*—As to the life of the wells of the Trenton limestone, we know that three years does not exhaust them when proper care of them is taken. There are numerous instances of wells yielding twenty to fifty barrels to the pump at the end of the third year, and a few of them produce nearly as much even, spontaneously, when they have attained this same term of years.

(g) *Number of Oil Wells in the Trenton Limestone Fields.*—In August, 1889, there were about 1,200 wells producing oil from the new horizon. The number has been largely increased during the last three months. The state of things in the several districts is shown in the appended report of the Buckeye Pipe Line Company for June, 1890. This report betokens great activity in all of the established districts:

	Wells Completed.	Drilling.	Rigs up.
Lima District	29	36	50
Findlay	29	31	29
North Baltimore	58	59	68
St. Mary's	21	15	26
Gibsonburg	28	40	63
Upper Sandusky	...	3	3
Spencerville	...	4	...
Totals	165	188	239

Wells abandoned in June—Lima district, 1; North Baltimore district, 1; Gibsonburg district, 3; total, 5. Dry holes completed in June—Lima district, 1; Findlay district, 1; North Baltimore district, 2; St. Mary's district, 2; Gibsonburg district, 5 total, 11.

There are now more than 600 tanks in the different portions of the field. The tanks average at least 30,000 barrels.

DEVELOPMENT OF THE SEVERAL FIELDS.

A brief account will now be given of the new features in the oil production of the Trenton limestone during the last two years, and particularly of the new fields that have been developed since the date of the preceding report. For the facts pertaining to the early history of the main fields, the reader is referred to Volume VI, Geology of Ohio. They will not be treated in this report, except as they may be incidentally mentioned.

The divisions of the oil field will be considered in their geographical relations, rather than in the order of their importance, and the review will begin with the westernmost counties. Oil is now produced from the Trenton limestone in Mercer, Van Wert, Auglaize, Allen, Hancock, Wyandot, Seneca, Sandusky and Wood counties.

(A) OIL WELLS OF MERCER COUNTY.

The Reservoir Oil Field.—Two townships of this county, viz., Franklin and Granville, have been famous centers of gas production for the last four years, but the discovery of oil in quantity large enough to be taken account of belongs mainly to the last year. Oil has been found in paying quantity in Jefferson township, directly north of the reservoir, and the productive rock also extends into Center township. Exploration is going forward in all the northern and western townships of the county.

The chief factor in the extensive work which is being done in Jefferson and Center townships is a well drilled upon the farm of Mrs. McMann during 1890. It started with 400 barrels per day, and for a number of weeks kept up to a 300-barrel rate. There are a half dozen wells finished in Jefferson township that indicate a fairly remunerative production, so long as oil does not fall below the present price. This territory is pretty thoroughly covered with leases. There is no longer room for the impecunious operator. Leases can not be obtained without a bonus of at least one dollar an acre, and the rate is generally higher near the centers where production has been proved. South of the reservoir is a great gas field; immediately north of it, as is now seen, an oil field of some promise is coming into view. Speculators are now looking at the 16,000 acres of the reservoir, covered with a depth of ten or twelve feet of water, with longing eyes. This district is certain to contain both forms of petroliferous wealth. If the State were prepared to lease the lands handsome returns could, no doubt, be secured. The control of the lands is shared by two boards at the present time, viz., by the Board of Public Works and by the Canal Commission. It is understood that there is no present disposition to lease the lands for these purposes. If they are held back for a year or two the gas that underlies the reservoir will be mainly withdrawn to fill the pipe lines of the companies who are so eagerly competing for this buried fuel in Franklin township.

The oil production of Mercer county, at the present time, as will be seen by this review, is of scanty proportions, but its promise is counted fair.

(B) OIL WELLS OF AUGLAIZE COUNTY.

This county is one of the five principal oil-producing counties of the State at the present time. Its development was well under way at the date of the publication of the last geological report, and since that time

THE TRENTON LIMESTONE.

it has been steadily progressing. The boundaries of production remain about as they were indicated on the map of 1887, though an occasional section has been added to the southern boundary in one or two townships. Oil and gas are limited thus far to the eight northwestern townships. The rock fails to the south and east in production apparently for want of porosity. The present features can be described under two headings, viz., the St. Mary's field, including St. Mary's and Washington townships, and the Buckland field, including Moulton and Noble townships.

(1) *The St. Mary's Field.*—The oil production of St. Mary's is somewhat irregular in its distribution. The township is rather to be counted gas territory than oil territory, but in spots throughout its northern half, and increasingly toward the northern border, oil is found instead of gas. The latter conditions are also found in Noble township along the common boundary. These districts mark the westernmost limits of oil in important quantity. It would seem as if the Ohio oil field of Auglaize, Mercer and Allen counties is the corresponding term to the great gas field of Indiana. The latter in reality extends into Ohio in the Mercer county field. The bodily connection between the two has not yet been discovered, but there is little reason to doubt that such connection exists in the shape of continuous beds of porous rock.

(2) *The Buckland Oil Field.*—Under this designation, an account will be given of one of the leading centers of production from the new horizon. The field will be made to include Moulton and Noble townships. On its northern and eastern boundary it is directly connected with the Lima and Cridersville fields, from which, in any case, it must be separated, if at all, by an arbitrary line. All the boundaries of this part of the oil field, in fact, are recognized as arbitrary. Careful study may reveal natural boundaries in salt water troughs that will give rise to a number of minor subdivisions.

The surface of Moulton township is very flat, ranging mainly between 840 and 870 feet above tide. The bedded rock is covered by a series of drift deposits that generally range between 100 and 350 feet in thickness. The deeply buried Trenton limestone that underlies this monotonous surface is found by the drill to exist in the shape of a terrace that has scarcely more relief than the drift-covered surface above described. There is, however, no correspondence between the elevations and depressions of the one and the elevations and depressions of the other. The upper surface of this limestone, as revealed by the work of the driller, has a range of only thirty or forty feet throughout the township. The highest portions of it are about 310 feet below tide, and the lowest troughs are less than 350 feet below tide. There are entire square miles in which the surface of the Trenton limestone will not vary in elevation more than four or five feet. If revealed at the surface under the same conditions that prevail under ground, the limestone would constitute a swampy plain, from which the water would find it difficult to escape; or, if partially overflowed with water, two or three long troughs would be found filled to a depth of ten to twenty feet, after the fashion of the Mercer Reservoir to-day, while much the larger portion of the surface would appear as broad and irregular ridges. These ridges constitute the oil field, while the depressions which would form the shallow lakes above represented would be found buried in salt water. One of these salt water troughs has been found by the drill to cross the township in the vicinity of Glynnwood. Another passes just south of Buckland, and still a third, on the eastern border of the town. A section taken by the Survey across the township in a southeast direction, beginning near Buckland, gives the following results:

	Trenton below tide.	Results of drilling.
Bowlby well, No. 1	310 feet	400 barrels of oil, with large amount of gas.
Johnston well	323 "	Oil and salt water, the latter preponderating.
Dixon well	342 "	Salt water only.
Doering well	320 "	130 barrels oil per day.
Harshberger well	314 "	200 " "
H. T. McConnell, No. 1	323 "	50 " " salt water in excess.
" No. 2	336 "	Salt water only.
Crow well	333 "	" "
Sheffer well	310 "	80 barrels oil per day.
Sharp well, No. 2	321 "	Good oil well.
Bowsher well, No. 2	333 "	Salt water only.

These figures are significant and will repay study. They show how absolutely the relief of the Trenton limestone dominates its production. The salt water wells found along the line of the section show the following levels of surface of the Trenton, viz.: 342, 336, 333 and 333 feet below tide. Of two other wells that report salt water in excess in connection with the oil, both find the Trenton at 323 feet below tide. In the oil wells proper, the limestone was found at the following levels, viz.: 310, 320, 314, 310 and 321 feet below tide. Three productive ridges of the Trenton were crossed in the line of the section, indicated respectively by the Bowlby well, Trenton, 310; the Harshberger well, Trenton, 314, and the Sheffer well, Trenton, 310. These elevated tracts can not be called anticlinals in any strict use of this term. The Trenton limestone in these oil fields lies like a carpet on a floor before it is nailed to its place; there are many and irregular, albeit small, ridges and furrows crossing its surface in varying directions.

Among the more productive districts of Moulton township may be named Sections 15 and 16. These sections can be safely estimated as good for at least 2,500 barrels to the acre. In other words, a well with twenty acres area tributary to it will furnish 50,000 barrels of oil. This is believed to be a moderate estimate. Sections 11, 12, 13 and 14 are occupied in part by the salt water troughs above described. The southern tier of sections of Logan township are the only sections from which important production has been so far obtained. In the salt water territory the water rises to 1,000 or 1,100 feet in the wells, or to a maximum elevation of about 600 feet above tide.

(3) *The Cridersville Field.*—Under this head a brief account will be given of Duchouquet township. As remarked above, it is directly continuous with the Lima field, and is separated only for convenience in description. The boundary lines remain about the same as in the report of 1887-8, except that on the southeastern border a little productive territory must be added. The northwestern sections, and particularly Sections 32, 33, 34, 3, 4, 5, 6, 7 and 8, have yielded as good wells, all things considered, as are to be found in the western oil counties. Section 7 has proved very prolific. The oil sand reaches a maximum thickness of twelve feet, an average thickness of eight to ten feet. It is, generally, covered by the hard, non-productive cap, previously described, five to ten feet in thickness. Salt water is expected in all wells at a depth of seventeen to thirty feet, and is welcomed by the driller, unless the quantity is excessive. Four to five barrels a day are counted as a decided advantage in oil production. The water column does not prove to be aggressive. Salt water may lie upon the oil in this field for three months without seriously affecting the production of a well, while in Pennsylvania the value of a well would be probably destroyed by the salt water lying upon it a single week. The Shawnee Oil Company holds a very important production in this township, ranking next, at the present time, to the Ohio Oil Company (Standard Oil Company). The Shawnee Oil Company owns not only its oil territory, but has its own system of pipe lines, tanks and tank cars as well. It finds abundant market for all that it can produce as far east as the Atlantic seaboard. Its oil is sold for fuel purposes exclusively.

(*C*) OIL WELLS OF ALLEN COUNTY.

This county still holds a very prominent place in the oil production of the Trenton limestone. For the first two years of the new production it was decidedly in the lead, but with all the rest of the field it has been overshadowed by the wonderful developments in Wood county during the last two years. There is practically but one subdivision of the field.

Shawnee, Perry, Bath and Ottawa townships are not separated in their oil production by salt water troughs, and they can, accordingly, all be rated under one head.

(1) *The Lima Oil Field.*—The oil production of the townships named above constitutes this field. The first two townships contain most of the real value. Their production agrees, in all respects, with that of Duchouquet and Moulton townships, described in the last section, except that as their wells have been drilled longer, the territory has suffered a somewhat greater reduction in vitality than that. This is shown by the fact that new wells come in smaller than they would have done two years ago in the same territory, and they decrease more rapidly after being drilled. This is simply saying that the Lima oil field behaves like all other oil fields.

The best portions of this county for oil production are probably Sections 7, 8, 9, 16, 17, 18, 19, 20, Perry, and the southeastern sections of Shawnee township. Much of this territory promises to far exceed 2,500 barrels to the acre. A well on the Alonzo McClain farm, which started with 1,000 barrels per day, had produced 160,000 barrels of oil in the summer of 1889 and was still a good well. A well on the Ridenour farm, which started with 1,300 barrels per day, had passed the 100,000-barrel limit a year and a half ago, and was still flowing from twenty to thirty barrels per day. It is believed that a considerable number of wells can be found that have reached a total of 100,000 barrels. Wherever such wells are found, the total production to the acre must rise to 4,000, or even 5,000 barrels. This is a splendid showing for any oil territory. Thirty-five wells, the production of which had been followed by the operator who drilled them and owned them, had reached an average of 30,000 barrels each before they were sold by him. Their total production was probably not more than half delivered at the time of the sale.

Some of the most experienced operators declare that in territory like this, provided they could fully control it, they would set wells 1,500 feet apart. They believe that they would obtain all the oil by this system and with the least possible outlay. This would give more than fifty acres to a well. No judicious operator advocates setting wells nearer than 750 feet, and this would give to each well about thirteen acres.

Lima has been made the center of the interests of the Standard Oil Company for this part of the new field. It has profited very greatly by the outlays made here. The Solar Refinery, which has already been briefly described, has grown to very large proportions. The pumping station o f the Chicago pipe line is also located here. These two interests require great concentration of tankage. The 30,000-barrel tanks of the company cover farm after farm as closely as they can be safely set. The rising price of oil, together with the growing disregard of the presence of salt water has led to a renewal of drilling to the east and southeast of Lima; and some wells, condemned three years ago because while producing some oil they also produced salt water, are thought to warrant further outlay at the present time. The tests that are now being carried on will determine whether any considerable additions are to be made to the field along those lines. Present appearances do not seem to favor such additions.

(2) *The Spencerville Oil Field.*—A considerable amount of drilling has been going forward during the last two years in Spencer and adjoining townships of Allen county, and in Jennings township, Van Wert county, which joins the former on the west. This territory must be called an oil field by courtesy only, at the present time, as it has not yet been proved to deserve the name.

The principal part of this work has been done in this area by the Geyser Oil Company, which takes its name from the owner of a farm in section 12, Spencer township, on which one of its first wells was drilled. The company has taken up about 35,000 acres of land, a large part of it in the western portions of Allen and Van Wert counties. During the latter part of its leasing, it was obliged to meet sharp competition from the Ohio Oil Company. It has drilled thirty-four wells, seven of which are unproductive. A few of these wells produce dry gas, and this product has been utilized in the supply of Spencerville and of Delphos. The drilling in this region was begun by a company representing the interests of the last named town, the object of their search being gas for the general use. This company drilled eight wells in Section 12, Spencer, and Section 8, Marion townships, and found enough gas to warrant them, as they supposed, in the building of a pipe line three or four miles in length to Delphos. But the supply, when tested, proved entirely inadequate for even 400 stoves.

The Geyser Company took up the work where this company left it, by drilling another well in Section 12, Spencer township. The result was not very different from that already attained by the Delphos Company, a small quantity of gas being found in the rock; but in addition a small flow of oil was also secured. The company located its next well two and a half miles southwest, on the Nicholas Kill farm, Section 22, Spencer. The Trenton limestone was found here at a depth of 1,167 feet. It was drilled ato for fifty-one feet, and the well is reported as giving promise of being an excellent one. Storage for the oil has been but recently provided, and therefore no full tests of the wells have been possible. A 38,000-barrel tank is now completed and nothing apparently stands in the way of determining what the field as thus far drilled is worth.

In Section 28, Jennings, a light gas well was found; in the same Section, nearly a mile distant, a well estimated at two million feet of dry gas was obtained. This well was drilled but twenty-five feet into the Trenton. Oil would undoubtedly have been reached by sinking the well a little deeper. The gas was conveyed to Spencerville by a two-inch line from this well, and from Spencerville by a three inch line to Section 12, to which point the six-inch line of Delphos had already been laid with which it was there connected. Gas enough was now secured for both villages, at least temporarily. The original rock pressure of the gas is reported at 440 pounds.

In Section 16, Jennings township, the Nicholas Miller well is located. The oil rock was found in it at 1,163 feet. This well gives the best promise of any drilled in the township thus far. In Section 10, one and a half miles northeast of this last well, the Trenton limestone has fallen sixty feet. This descent would stand for a salt water trough had not the rock been dry. Other wells have been drilled in the two townships as follows: In Sections 8, 16, 19, 21, 28, of Jennings township, and in Sections 11, 12, 14, 18, 23, 26 and 27 of Spencer. The Geyser Oil Company is composed of as sagacious and successful operators as there are in the field. It is said to have already expended $150,000 in its work so far. We should expect that its confidence, as evinced by this large expenditure, would have a solid foundation. The grounds of this confidence are not, perhaps, fully apparent as yet, but from what is reported from the wells already drilled it is probable that the field at best will be a spotted and irregular one, dry holes, gas wells and oil wells alternating through the whole territory.

(D) OIL WELLS OF HANCOCK COUNTY.

(1) *The Findlay Field.*—The Findlay oil pool maintains nearly the same boundaries that it showed two years ago, being almost entirely confined to Findlay and Liberty townships, except in one particular, which will be hereafter named. To the westward and southward no extension has been reported, the salt water holding undivided possession of the porous Trenton limestone in that direction. The dead line of the field is still the line of 500 feet below tide. In the rarest instances has any oil been derived from a lower level. The lines have opened, however, on the northward, so as to embrace all the sections of Liberty township. They have not been found thus far to include any territory of value in Portage township. The field has lost in great part, its relative importance, by reason of the development in Wood county to the northward.

During the last three years the field has receded in vitality necessarily, because it has been undergoing steady development during all this period. Some of its best lands have already yielded 3,000 barrels to the acre, with the promise of a large addition before they are finally abandoned. The Ohio Oil Company has secured control of by far the largest portion of the production, and has covered several farms with its extensive system of tanks. The Peerless Oil Company, perhaps, comes next in production at the present time. It holds about 4,000 acres under lease, in what is counted the best territory of the township.

The geology of the Findlay oil field was treated at considerable length in Volume VI, and nothing remains to be added from more recent work.

As will be remembered, the level of the oil rock was originally between 400 and 500 feet below tide throughout the Findlay field. The extension of oil production, in what was originally dry gas territory, which is now in progress in the township, is a matter of unusual scientific interest. It completes the demonstration of the identity of the gas rock, the oil rock and the salt water rock of the Trenton limestone, and of their complete continuity. It compels even the most undiscriminating observer to recognize the fact that the gas is driven forward in its reservoir by a sheet of oil, accompanied with salt water, that slowly rises to take the place of the gas as the latter is withdrawn. The facts are most significantly shown in the heart of the Findlay township gas field. Wells are now being drilled expressly for oil in what was unquestioned gas territory, and the apprehension exists that the comfort of the town will be materially interfered with if drilling is allowed to go forward in this interest in the districts that are more or less occupied as residence quarters. As to the total production of the replaced rock there are no data for determining the facts at present, but it would scarcely be expected to equal the production of those portions of the limestone which received their stocks during the vast periods in which the contents of the porous stratum were slowly differentiated under the influence of gravity. In other words, a great oil field is not to be looked for in an exhausted gas field. The largest production that has been noted in such a case is that of the Adams well, which was drilled in the early history of the field, and which yielded dry gas for six or eight months. After the oil had taken the main possession of the rock it produced from fifteen to twenty-five barrels per day for three or four months.

(2) *The Stuartsville Oil Field.*—Allen township has, during the present year, aroused as great an excitement in regard to oil as its great gas wells had previously done. A well that was drilled in the spring of 1890, by McConica & Co., in the northwest corner of Section 36, led the way. It was drilled with the confident expectation that it would produce dry gas as the nearest localities tested had all done. But it found the Trenton about 450 feet below tide, which showed it to be within original oil territory. This well produced within the first two days 1,965 barrels of oil.

The unrestrained flow was, however, too much for it and it began forthwith to produce salt water with the oil. It was then locked back to a production of about 600 barrels a day, which it maintained for some time. Great excitement followed this unexpected record, and there were at least twenty derricks erected in Sections 25 and 36 by May 1. As many operators as could find standing-room had hurried to the scene. None of the wells subsequently drilled have quite equaled in production the first, though the list embraces many excellent wells for any field. The surface elevation of this district is about 810 to 825 feet above tide. The Trenton limestone is commonly struck in it between 1,212 and 1,260 feet. This shows that the upper surface of the limestone ranges from 400 to 450 feet below tide. A part of it is thus seen to have been originally gas territory which has been overrun with oil by the rise of the latter into the portion of the stratum which the great gas wells have drained. A small part of the territory was originally oil rock.

(3) *Marion and Cass Townships.*—An oil field can not be predicated of these townships as yet, but some of the gas wells, including the famous Thorntree well, show oil in such an amount that if they were allowed to flow without restraint it is fair to infer that they would speedily be converted into oil wells of moderate capacity. Whether oil or salt water lies nearest to the clusters of wells that have been drilled by the several companies represented here, has not been made apparent in all cases as yet. There seems no reason, however, to expect any important oil field in these two townships.

(*E*) OIL PRODUCTION OF WYANDOT COUNTY.

The determined search for a home supply of natural gas, which was made first by Carey and afterward by Upper Sandusky, though failing in its direct object, has led to the discovery of oil in several townships of the county in quantity large enough to command the interest of the oil producer, especially since the advance in price previously recorded. Many of the Carey wells found a little oil associated with the gas that they were searching for, but it was finally demonstrated in a very expensive way that there was not enough of either at this location to justify its exploitation. It was thought in the early stages of the work that the Trenton limestone descended below the salt water level of the field immediately beyond its occurrence at Carey, but it has since been learned that a broad terrace of the limestone extends to the southward and southeastward of Carey, occupying in part the following named towns: Crawford, Salem and Crane. The lower limestone is not characterized, as is shown by the drill, by an even surface, but many minor folds and troughs traverse it without any order that has yet been learned.

No further advance was made in the vicinity of Carey after its early experience until the present year, and even then the new drilling which has opened up a possible oil field, advanced from the southward. The experience of Upper Sandusky in the search for a natural gas supply in its own neighborhood has already been narrated. The elation over its one extraordinary gas well was great, but short-lived. When, two weeks after it was struck, it began throwing salt water in quantity, together with a little oil, signifying that the reservoir of dry gas had already been emptied, all the earlier gas wells of the neighborhood began to throw oil also. The gas field was, in fact, turning into an oil field, but no important production was yet realized in any of its wells. Among the new wells, however, that the trustees forthwith drilled in adjoining territory, one or two that were finished early in 1889 gave somewhat more promise in this direction. The Swable well, located in the northeast quarter of Section 12, Salem township, was in no sense a gas well at any stage, but when allowed to flow, it was thought to be good for twenty to thirty barrels of oil per day. The surface of the Trenton limestone was reached in this well at 1,322 feet, or about fifty feet below the highest gas level of the immediate neighborhood. The Gibson well No. 2, located in Section 7, same township, and the Russman well, in Section 14, northwest quarter, were also counted oil wells. The former showed a descent of the surface of the Trenton limestone of at least seventy feet within 2,000 feet of horizontal measurement.

These discoveries occurred just as the price of Lima oil was beginning to be advanced and while the possibilities in regard to the enhancement of price seemed very great. The promise of a new field came to the oil producers opportunely at this juncture, and they competed with great spirit for the possession of Crane and Salem townships, to which the production thus far was mainly confined. One of the great prizes was thought to be the acreage of the Upper Sandusky municipal corporation, leased primarily for gas, but with a clause covering oil production also. One company is said to have offered $50,000 for the oil rights of the corporation, but this offer was presently withdrawn. Other companies offered heavy royalty. The Ohio Oil Company took a leading part in the acquisition of territory. Numerous other companies, and also individual producers, spent money very freely in getting control of the land. Many tens of thousands of dollars were distributed among the landowners of these townships during the spring of 1890. A dozen wells were started at once, though not altogether confined to Salem and Crane townships, and at the present time the results of these tests are beginning to be available. They are not encouraging in the townships named. There has nothing been brought to light better than the Swable well already noticed, and that was of doubtful value.

Among the wells begun about this time, however, was one located near Crawford Station, northeast quarter Section 23, in Crane township, on one of the Carey farms, by the Ohio Oil Company, that has brought in a much more encouraging record. The well yields a considerable amount of gas with its oil, but the quantity of the latter is estimated at 75 to 100 barrels per day. This result has renewed and extended the interest in this township, but it will require a number of wells to confirm the claim that it marks the beginning of a new oil field of any importance. The tests are already going forward, and during the present summer the character of the oil promise of Wyandot county will be definitely determined. The promise does not seem at the present time to be very brilliant.

(F) OIL PRODUCTION OF SENECA COUNTY.

In the first wells drilled in this county, as in fact in all the early drilling of northern Ohio, the object of the search was gas, not oil. To miss the former was failure, and small compensation was found in a light production of oil that was occasionally met. It resulted, therefore, that little account was taken of the numerous cases of this sort that presented themselves throughout the counties in which the bulk of the drilling was being done. No proper tests were made of such wells. During the last three years, however, there has been a slowly rising appreciation of oil in the field, as compared with gas, and during the last year it has taken decidedly the first place in economic importance, and no such neglect of oil indications would occur in any field under the present conditions. We shall soon learn whether the small oil wells named above can be made to expand into a regular and valuable production.

The statements above made explain why four years after oil was first discovered in Tiffin we are still unable to say whether or not there is any value in the production. The Loomis and Nyman well continued to produce four to five barrels of oil per day as long as it was allowed to remain open. So, also, in well No. 2 of the corporation series, oil rose within 150 feet of the surface at the time of drilling. The well has been shut in during the interval, but it is opened three or four times a year and a production of 150 to 175 barrels of oil has been secured from it for each of the last three years.

The drilling done near Tiffin shows marked flexures and irregularities of the lower rocks, but thus far all the portions of the Trenton that have possessed the proper relief for oil or gas accumulation have appeared to exist in small and insulated areas. Every gas well, for example, has been overrun by oil or water within six weeks of the date of its completion.

Companies are still being formed in Tiffin, and the leasing of territory is even yet going forward. Under the present interest it will certainly happen that the value of the new wells will be at once tested and determined. There is no production in sight of real value in Seneca county.

(G) OIL PRODUCTION OF SANDUSKY COUNTY.

Under this head we reach a really important section of the history of Trenton limestone oil. Sandusky county ranks next to the four counties already named as the main centers of oil production, viz., Auglaize, Allen, Hancock and Wood. Its history is an interesting one from every point of view. The first fact to be noted is that two low anticlinal ridges are shown by the geological map to traverse the county in a north and south direction. The structure may, perhaps, be better described by saying that a relatively broad syncline extends from the south line of Jackson and Ballville townships in a northerly direction, bearing a trifle to the westward, to the lake shore, a distance of about twenty-five miles, and taking in all or part of twelve townships in Sandusky and Ottawa counties. The average breadth of the syncline is about six miles. The surface of the county being exceedingly uniform, the age of the limestone that makes the surface determines the elevation or depression of the series. When, for example, the Niagara limestone constitutes the surface, the presence of a low arch or anticline is assured; and by the same token an area of Lower Helderberg limestone stands for a depression or trough in the series.

On either side of this syncline oil and gas production have been obtained; on the west side at Gibsonburg, Helena and Lindsey, and on the eastern uplift at Oak Harbor. The latter has already been described under another head. Its production is not important in any sense and never has been. The western area, however, holds a very different place. Madison township is becoming a large and increasingly important source of oil, and with it a few sections of Washington must be counted. Jackson township and Woodville township also make contributions of some prospective value. A single oil well has been drilled in Scott township also.

The Gibsonburg and Helena Oil Field.

The discovery of oil and gas in this district goes back to 1887. The main object of the early search was here, as elsewhere, natural gas. At Gibsonburg the long-established lime-burning interest led the way. Gas-burned lime was beginning to come into threatening competition with wood-burned lime. A supply of gas was found here, as shown on a preceding page, but its value was thought to be greatly reduced by a small quantity of oil that was produced with the gas. Up to this time, while oil in small quantity was found at many points in this vicinity, the production had been insignificant, and this fact, taken in connection with the insignificant price for oil that then prevailed, made its occurrence in the gas wells a serious drawback. At Gibsonburg, however, the oil that appeared with the gas was utilized from the first. It was also noted that the oil was of the Wood county type rather than of the Findlay and Lima type. Its gravity was not below 41° B., and it was counted less impregnated with sulphur than the Lima oil. These points especially recommended it to the refining interests that were now in the field, and during 1888 and 1889 a good deal of leasing of prospective oil territory was going on in the vicinity of Gibsonburg. By the early summer of 1889 fifteen wells had been drilled in Madison and Washington townships, and one of these wells, viz., the Shoemaker, No. 2, was credited with a production of 400 barrels per day for its initial flow. In a month after its completion, however, the salt water overtook the oil. Others that were finished about the same time were found good for varying quantities of oil, reported as ranging from fifteen to seventy barrels per day. These results awakened great activity among the rival oil companies, and high prices were paid during the last year, and during the first half of 1889. The Ohio Oil Company took a leading part in this development, paying as high as $25 an acre *bonus* for some territory counted unusually promising, and $8 and $10 per acre for considerable territory besides, while royalties ranged all the way from a fifth to an eighth. Other companies were, of course, obliged to meet these figures. The Paragon Refining Company has had an interest in the field from the beginning, and has acquired a large acreage and production. The Sun Oil Company also holds a large territory here, and has drilled a considerable number of wells. Naturally, with the advance in the price of oil, the excitement has been intensified, and at the present time nearly all of the ten townships named, and a great deal of territory besides, has been covered by the several oil companies and by individual operators who are established in the field.

The general conditions of oil production in these townships are about as follows: The surface of the country ranges in elevation between 625 and 675 feet above tide. The Trenton is found in productive wells at a depth of 1,200 to 1,250 feet, or from 575 to 625 feet below tide. The depth of the casing does not exceed 400 feet in any oil well. Where more than 400 feet of casing is required the Trenton, if porous, is found full of salt water. Salt water rose in the field, in very many examples, to a maximum of 600 or 625 feet above tide. The separation of gas and oil territory is of course marked by differences of elevation in the Trenton limestone, just as in the fields previously described. Every foot of elevation is brought into the account in this separation. The oil wells have a good degree of vitality, some of them flowing for more than a year without interruption. When salt water is struck in connection with the oil, pumping is necessary from the start. The boundary of productive territory is in many cases quite sharp and well defined, but such boundaries can be found only by the drill. There are no well-marked structural lines traversing the field so far as present developments indicate, unless such a line shall be found in a salt water trough that traverses the following named sections of Madison township, viz., 28, 21 and 17. This trough bears, as far as it can be followed, a little to the west of north. The Trenton limestone is found here at about 1,280 feet in depth, and the casing of the wells is 425 feet or more. Two or three dry gas wells can be connected by a line parallel to the salt water trough referred to above. This is the only feature that can be claimed as recognizable in the way of structure in Madison township, and this is far from being positively established.

The best production of the township has been realized thus far in Sections 10, 11, 12, 22, 23, 24, 25, 26, 35 and 36; or, in other words, on the eastern half of the township. A dozen wells belonging to a single company, half of which have been drilled in the last year, have averaged during the present summer fifteen barrels. Many wells begin with forty to fifty barrels, but in a week they fall away to about half that production, and this latter rate they maintain thereafter for some time. The production to the acre can not be safely estimated as yet. It does not promise to be large.

The Ohio Oil Company, on the 1st of May, 1890, had drilled thirty wells in the Gibsonburg district. At the same date there were about twenty wells belonging to other parties in the same field; of this number, eleven belong to the Paragon interests. The numbers have been greatly increased and probably doubled during the present season. The Helena field, so-called, is strictly continuous with the Gibsonburg field. Much of the work at the former point is concentrated in Section 31, Washington, but adjacent sections in Jackson are also occupied by the driller. The village lot has come into requisition here and the derricks of rival companies confront each other at intervals of 50 or 100 feet. Such a collocation illustrates, not the strength of the oil rock but the weakness of human nature. In only rare instances will any of these crowded wells repay the driller in the oil that they produce. He must count himself paid by the rendering of his neighbor's investment worthless, seeing that he has lost his own.

Drilling in this general neighborhood has been done in Woodville township on Sections 1, 4, 5, 11, 12 and 28. A well in Section 4 has produced fifty barrels a day without the use of the torpedo. In Scott township, east half of Section 4, a twenty-five-barrel well has been drilled, while barren rock was found in Section 1. Section sixteen has also been tested by a single well.

So far as known no other prominent indications of gas or oil have been reported from Sandusky, but it is evident that at least three or four of the townships last named are now making, and likely to continue to make valuable contributions to our oil supply.

CHAPTER IV.

THE CLINTON LIMESTONE AS A SOURCE OF OIL AND GAS.

This is the first chapter ever written in the whole range of geological literature under the title given above, or under any heading indicating the line of facts represented in the title. It has been the singular fortune of Ohio Geology to make known to the world, during the last five years, two entirely new and most unexpected sources of petroleum and of the gas derived from it on the large scale, viz., the Trenton limestone and the Clinton limestone. As shown in the preceding chapter, the former is the largest single source of petroleum now known in the geological scale of the continent. A large part of Volume VI was devoted to an account of this great discovery. The Clinton limestone has acquired most of its importance in this connection within the last three years, or since the date of the last previous publication of the Survey, and consequently the present is the first opportunity afforded for a distinct presentation of this new history.

It is not intended to convey the impression in the above remarks that petroleum and gas have never been reported from the Clinton formation before. There are numerous instances in which mention has been made of such occurrence, but no one has heretofore considered the facts of importance and significance enough to deserve a distinct treatment. But the time has now come for describing as fully as possible the conditions under which the Clinton formation proves to be petroliferous on such a scale as to become economically valuable.

PREVIOUS MENTION OF PETROLEUM IN THE CLINTON FORMATION.

An early notice of the Clinton limestone, as a source of oil, is found in Dr. John Locke's account of the Clinton limestone, in the Second Annual Report of the First Geological Survey, 1838, page 225. In describing that part of the cliff limestone which has since been separated from the combined series and identified as the Clinton limestone, he says:

"On striking with a hammer to detach a specimen, I distinctly perceived the odor of bitumen, petroleum, or rock oil. I have since learned that petroleum has been collected from cavities in the rock by the quart."

Another of these previous references is contained in the report on the geology of Preble county, Geology of Ohio, Vol. III, page 407, 1878:

"In close connection with this last named fact, viz., that the formation is made up of organic remains, it is to be added that petroleum abounds through many of the exposures in the county.

"When the excitement caused by the discoveries on Oil Creek was at its height, the show of oil along the outcrops of this formation did not fail to attract attention and rights to explore and develop the territory were bought up through several counties of Ohio and Indiana. Companies were formed and wells were sunk at several points in southwestern Ohio. The deepest of these wells was at Eaton, where the boring was carried 1,170 feet below the surface. There was, however, no geological promise in these undertakings. The Clinton limestone, it is true is rich in petroleum in many localities, but its thickness does not exceed a dozen feet and there have been no disturbances in its stratification by means of which reservoirs for the oil have been prepared. When the Clinton limestone was passed in the boring, the long series of the Cincinnati shales and limestones were met with and the 1,170 feet above named were not enough to exhaust the limestone series of the State. . . . The samples of rock saved from different depths in boring were turned over to the Geological Survey by the persons who had them in charge, together with the records of the company. These latter show alternations of hope and disappointment, dependent partly on the geological series traversed. The boring was begun in the Niagara, and when the Clinton was reached, the show of petroleum was sufficient to kindle a blaze of excitement. The telegraph was used to announce to distant stockholders the success of the enterprise and the work of boring was temporarily arrested until a tank could be provided 'so that there might not be a sinful waste of the oil.'"

Again, in the Preliminary Report on petroleum and natural gas, Geology of Ohio, 1886, the following statement appears with regard to the Clinton series of the State:

"It is distinctly petroliferous, oil oozing out at numberless points along its line of outcrops, and giving rise to surface indications that led twenty-five years ago to the expenditure of considerable amounts of money in futile attempts to secure paying wells at this horizon."

Again, in Volume VI, page 12, Geology of Ohio, 1888, the following statement was found to be warranted, viz.: "The limestone contains a notable quantity of indigenous petroleum throughout most of its outcrops, but no very valuable accumulations of oil or gas have been found in it thus far. It is the source of the low pressure gas of Fremont (upper vein), and also of the gas at Lancaster, from 1,962 feet below the surface, and at Newark from 2,100 (2,400) feet below the surface. * * * In a single instance in Wood county it is proving itself an oil rock. A well near Trombley, drilled to this horizon, has been flowing twenty to thirty barrels of oil for a number of months, the oil being referable to this horizon."

These statements mark a good deal of progress in regard to this formation. It was by this time found to be a gas rock and oil rock under cover. Many references occur in regard to this series in the body of the volume, and much interesting information can be found as to the petroliferous production of the Clinton group in Ohio.

It thus appears that ever since geology has been cultivated in Ohio, the Clinton limestone has been known to be petroliferous; that in 1885 it was found to be a gas rock at Fremont, though of small force; that in 1886 it was found to be an oil rock in Wood county, supporting a production of twenty to thirty barrels per day for several months from a single well; and that in 1887 high pressure gas had been discovered in it at Lancaster and Newark. The beginning of the present importance of the Clinton limestone as a source of gas and oil came into view in connection with these last named facts.

COMPOSITION OF THE CLINTON SERIES.

This widely extended series of rock formations takes its name from Clinton, Oneida county, New York, where, in connection with other strata, it includes several valuable deposits of a unique and most characteristic iron ore, known variously as the "fossil ore," the "dye-stone ore," the "flax seed ore" and the Clinton ore, in the different localities where it occurs. This ore is a red hematite, of fair grade. The peculiarity of its occurrence is that it abounds in marine organic remains, well and often beautifully preserved. The red oxide of iron is prejudicial to marine life, and wherever it abounds fossils are generally wanting. The replacement of fossils by this mineral is exceptional to a high degree. No good explanation can be given of the chemical facts involved in this peculiarity of the Clinton ore.

But this well marked ore is only one out of several kinds of rocks that belong in the Clinton series. In Western New York, where the series has a considerable development, it is a truly protean formation. Beds of limestone, sandstone and shale alternate with the iron ore already described in its outcrops. In southwestern Ohio, as first separated from the Cliff limestone and described in the Geological Report of 1869, it is simply a limestone, well marked by its composition, its lithological character, its fossils and its stratigraphical relations. It is not necessary to describe these characteristics here.

During the last five years we have had unexampled opportunities, through the wide-spread drilling that has been going forward, of studying the composition and character of the several elements of our scale as they exist under cover and far away from their outcrops. It has been possible to follow the Clinton formation in particular, with great certainty, by means of the definite characteristics by which it is distinguished. It is enough to say at this point that, as it is followed eastward under cover into central Ohio, the unity of the formation, as shown in its outcrop, is lost, and it is transformed from a solid sheet of limestone into an alternating series of limestone, shale and iron ore, with which some thin beds of sandstone are also associated; and it has been expanded from a maximum of fifty feet in outcrop to two or three times this measure in the district named. In a word, the Clinton limestone formation of central Ohio is taking on the characteristics of the formation in New York.

THE GAS ROCK OF THE CLINTON FORMATION.

The sandstone above noted, so far as the sparingly obtained samples show, is of very sharp and well-characterized grains, like the Hillsborough and Sylvania sandstones that are found in other limestone horizons. To this interpolated and intermingled sandstone is now ascribed the very important office of storing the gas and oil of the new field in central Ohio. It is the limestone itself that is petroliferous in the outcrops of the formation and under the shallower cover of northern Ohio, and it was from drillings identical in composition with the Clinton limestone of these outcrops that the gas rock of Lancaster was first recognized. It was more than a year after the first wells were drilled before any correction was made of the earlier statements with regard to it. In Volume VI a short account is given of the drilling of a number of wells in the Lancaster field in which the limestone is described as the gas rock. These statements, it will be understood, were based upon the best information attainable at the time. According to some later reports, however, the Lancaster gas rock is a bed of sharp sand, ranging from zero to twenty feet in thickness, which is found buried in the formation. It may be asked why the statements in regard to so important a point in this connection are so indefinite even at this time? The answer is to be partially found in the difficulty of getting accurate results from the point of the drill at a depth of 2,000 feet or more, and with the well filled with salt water, as it often is when the gas rock is reached. A part of the confusion must also result from careless observation on the part of those engaged in the work of drilling. It is doubtless true that there is some sharp sand in the gas rock of all the wells, but whether the entire mass of the gas rock is sandstone has not been demonstrated. Some good observers deny this and insist that the account already current is entirely correct.

It may be urged that under these circumstances it would be a misnomer to speak of the Clinton limestone as a source of gas and oil, if it is a Clinton sandstone that is the real source. To this it may be answered that alike in southern Ohio and in northern Ohio, as in the Fremont and the Wood county fields, it is the limestone itself that is petroliferous. No sandstone has ever been reported there. The limestone is also the characteristic element in the deep wells of central Ohio, in any case, whether reenforced by a variable bed of sand or not.

HISTORY OF THE DISCOVERY AND UTILIZATION OF CLINTON GAS.

The early stages in the discovery and utilization of high pressure gas from the new source at Lancaster and Newark are given in Volume VI, and do not need to be repeated in detail here. It is enough to say that the people of both these towns, in 1886 and 1887, essayed to reach the Trenton limestone, and that at a depth of about 2,000 to 2,400 feet—but still at least 1,000 feet above the goal for which they had set out—they found included in the Clinton series a horizon of high-pressure gas. In both towns the gas of the first wells was feeble, a fact partly due to the conditions under which the drilling had gone forward, a heavy column of salt water resisting the ascent of the gas in the wells, but in both cases encouragement was found for further drilling. Lancaster led the way, and during 1888 new wells were drilled, some of which reached a daily production of 800,000 cubic feet. The town was piped and the gas was brought into general use. The supply ran short in Lancaster in the winter of 1888 and 1889, however, but the scarcity was soon relieved by the discovery, early in 1889, of a gas well that would be counted great in any field. Other wells of like character followed and the town entered upon a period of great speculative excitement, in which large manufacturing enterprises were brought into it.

Newark, in like manner, soon found better wells than the first. A large number of wells has been drilled, the town has been partially piped, and a considerable part of the people are now enjoying the advantages of gaseous fuel.

Meanwhile, a gas line or gas belt had been brought into view through this experience. Newark is northeast of Lancaster, and this time-honored direction was seized upon as the line of fortune. A Columbus company took up the work of testing the intermediate territory and attained a great success from the start. Their wells are located near Thurston, on the Toledo & Ohio Central Railway, about thirty miles distant from Columbus.

232   GEOLOGY OF OHIO.

Gas was introduced into Columbus in January, 1890, and is coming into extensive use. These are the main features in the history, but a more detailed account will be given of the several advances here named under the different sections that are to follow.

GEOLOGICAL SECTION OF THE CLINTON GAS WELLS.

All of the wells that have proved successful in finding gas in the Clinton limestone have been begun in territory where the Waverly group (Sub-carboniferous), constitutes the surface rocks. At Lancaster, for example, the Berea grit lies about 400 feet below the surface of the valley, the interval being occupied by either the drift or the Cuyahoga shales. At Newark the stratum in question is found at a depth of about 550 feet below the valley level. At Thurston its position is intermediate between these two figures, or about 500 feet below. At Lancaster the condensed section is about as follows:

Drift and Waverly group, approximate	500 feet.
Bedford and Ohio shale	650 "
Limestone, Devonian and Upper Silurian	700 to 800 feet.
Niagara shale	50 to 80 "
Clinton series	75 to 125 "

The Newark section is about the same as the Lancaster section, except that the Bedford and Ohio shales show a thickness of eight or nine hundred feet against the 650 feet in the former section. In the Thurston sections the drift, as a rule, ranges from 150 to 350 feet. The Cuyahoga shale with sandstone courses intercalated, taken with the drift, makes up 500 to 550 feet. The great shale series has a combined thickness of 700 to 800 feet. The limestones aggregate as above 700 feet. The Niagara shale is about eighty feet thick, and the Clinton shows a total thickness of 75 to 100 feet. It includes always one and sometimes two red bands.

GEOLOGICAL STRUCTURE OF THE NEW FIELD.

Upon this point there are not facts enough in hand on which to base a theory. There is, of course, every reason to believe that some form of relief, probably that produced by anticlinal structure, lies at the bottom of this gas accumulation. The northeasterly trend of the gas field is in harmony with all the earlier structural features of southern and eastern Ohio. The Cincinnati Axis has this direction, marking, as has been suggested, the earliest folds of the Appalachian system, but going back for its date to the end of Lower Silurian time. The low anticlinals of southeastern Ohio belong unmistakably to the same system as those of western Pennsylvania, and all of them are referable to that great series of movements to which the eastern border of the continent is due. The general date of these movements we know. They took place at the end of Carboniferous time. It is possible that the structure to which the accumulation of the Lancaster gas is owing belongs in date between the two systems of movements already noted, viz., the disturbance at the close of Lower Silurian, and that which took place at the end of Carboniferous time. It is further possible that this particular movement has been completely masked by the subsequent history of the region. Upon an early fold the beds of later date may have been deposited unconformably, leaving no trace of the fold to show through to the surface. This view has been suggested in substance by Mr. John G. Deshler, President of the Central Ohio Natural Gas Company, who has taken a leading part in the development of the new gas field. He draws his conclusion from the facts that he has found in regard to the thickness of the Ohio shales that overlie the great limestone series. The shales, as before remarked, are about 650 feet at Lancaster, but they expand rapidly to the eastward. In the experience of the Columbus Company, the gas has thus far been confined to areas where the thickness of the shale does not exceed 700 to 800 feet. If this be the explanation of the geological structure involved, it is obvious that the discovery of such a field must always be altogether due to accident, as was the case in this instance. The surface could furnish no clue whatever. Such a theory gives some encouragement to the hope that in the random drilling going forward in this and other portions of the State other gas or oil fields may be struck upon arches that give no sign of their existence or at least that can show themselves in no other way than by responding to the drill when reached by it.

In Volume VI the suggestion was made that a low arch is shown passing near Lancaster, the suggestion being based upon the position which the Berea grit holds at that point. This appearance of an arch may be illusory, the apparent uplift being due possibly, to the fact that all our strata rise to the westward, and that this point in the section is a little further west than that with which it is connected. No other facts bearing upon the existence of such an arch have been accumulated by subsequent observations.

There is nothing to awaken any doubt that the gas of the new horizon is held under salt water pressure and driven by the same, as has been demonstrated for the gas of the Trenton horizon. Whether a deposit of oil lies between the water and the gas, as a general rule, has not been made manifest. Oil has been struck in small quantity in two wells at Lancaster and in larger quantity in one well at Thurston. The presence of salt water in the gas rock, if it had been found there, would be masked to some extent by the presence of a salt water horizon in the overlying Niagara.

That it has been already found in several instances, there is no room to doubt.

A brief account will now be given of the three prominent centers of production of Clinton gas.

(1) THE LANCASTER GAS FIELD.

Within the compass of about four square miles, with Lancaster as a center, twelve or more wells have now been drilled, eight of which are owned by the municipal corporation, and four by private parties. The corporation will add two more wells during the present season, and private parties are likely to increase the number still further. Beyond the limits specified above, other wells are now going down in the immediate neighborhood of the town.

The municipal corporation has raised $75,000 by the sale of bonds issued for this purpose, and has invested this amount, together with the entire proceeds arising from the gas plant thus far in drilling wells and piping the town. The corporation bought three or four wells of the company that discovered and developed the gas, but none of these wells reached a capacity of more than 800,000 feet, while the smallest production was less than 100,000 feet per day. One well of this number became impaired by the caving of the shale at an early date. During the early winter of 1888 and 1889, the gas supply ran very low throughout the town, and much discouragement was felt as to its being maintained in a large enough way to justify the outlay which the city had been led to make, but just at this time, after six of the moderate sized wells already described had been completed, and which had seemed to show definitely the character of the field, a well was drilled in the center of the town that entirely changed the situation and gave altogether a new aspect to Clinton limestone gas. This well was put down by Theodore Mithoff, Esq., on a city lot that he owned, for the supply of power to his machine shop. As already stated, he had no reason to expect a well of different character from the rest of the series that had been already completed. The well was drilled without casing out the salt water which is uniformly found near the bottom of the Niagara limestone, and consequently there was in it a heavy column of the brine during the later stages of drilling. The gas rock was reached on Sunday, February 17, 1889, at a depth of 1,948 feet, which showed a marked elevation of the surface of the rock, as compared with the level in the surrounding wells of the Clinton limestone; this well was peculiar also in this respect, that the Clinton contained no red rock in its uppermost beds. There was instead twenty to twenty-five feet of a very hard stratum in its place. When this hard stratum had been passed, the average amount of gas for the Lancaster wells was promptly found, but for some reasons the owner insisted on the drill being kept still at work. A hard shell was found below the first gas vein, and when this was penetrated it was obvious that a much larger volume was sent out than had been obtained from any previous well in the field. The productive rock had now been penetrated to a depth of fifteen feet, and the open flow of the gas showed a pressure of one and a half pounds in the center of the casing. This stands for a volume of about seven and one-third million feet per day. The salt water that entered above the gas was thrown out with the gas in a storm of spray. On a succeeding day the drill was got down six or eight feet deeper still, and by this time a really great gas well was opened in the Clinton limestone. The open pressure rose, according to the observations of Prof. G. W. Welch, to three and seven-eighths pounds, which stands for 12,000,000 feet per day. The well was finally tubed with three-inch pipe and was packed, and its daily volume was thus brought down to something less than 7,000,000 feet per day, its open pressure in the three-inch pipe being eighteen pounds.

The proposition for increasing the bonded indebtedness of the town for obtaining a gas supply was pending at this time. If the vote had been taken on Saturday, before this well was drilled in, it would probably have been defeated, but after the discovery of such a supply the proposition carried triumphantly. The flow of the gas was turned, by special arrangement of the owner, into the scantily filled lines of the city service, and for the first time a full and vigorous supply was enjoyed by the town. The well, as has been stated, was never cased and its condition has always been unsatisfactory, more or less salt water being thrown with the gas. The water is accounted for by the imperfect packing of the well. Probably enough gas has been sold from this well to the city line to pay the cost of drilling, and fuel has been constantly supplied for the machine-shops, above referred to, since its completion. The well, in its best days, would attain a pressure of 650 pounds in three-quarters of a minute.

The municipal corporation drilled the next well (well No. 6). It was located on the county fair grounds and was completed in the summer of 1889. Its record was not marked by any unusual features, but in volume it nearly equaled the Mithoff well. Its initial flow was estimated at 10,000,000 feet per day. The next well drilled by the city (well No. 7), to the north of the fair grounds, proved entirely unproductive. The rock was hard and close. The effect of a torpedo might well be tried in such a case.

One other well, No. 9, drilled by the city during the past year, has also proved unproductive, but well No. 8, located one-half mile east of the fair grounds, yielded six to eight million feet from the casing when first completed. These two fine wells make the reliance of the city.

The strange folly that seems bound up in the heart of a municipal corporation when it obtains a good supply of gas, that it must find some one that can use the fuel up in the largest way and most rapidly to whom to give it, without money and without price, broke out also in Lancaster. An ill-omened arch, bearing the illuminated inscription, "Free gas to manufacturers," spans the main street of the town at the railroad crossing. A ten-pot window glass works was the first factory to be brought in under the new offer. Under the most economical management a ten-pot furnace will consume 700,000 cubic feet of gas per day. The municipal corporation agreed to furnish all the fuel required, without limitation and without charge. The company was organized and managed by a number of glass blowers from the eastern field; on the co-operative plan the capital was drawn from Lancaster, the city giving it free gas and the citizens furnishing besides five and one-half acres of land and $14,000 in cash, the amount required to put up the works. The last item was regarded as a loan.

The cost of the plant was, in fact, $19,000, and the company started in without proper working capital. It was in operation from October, 1889, to April, 1890. Its output was sold at 10 per cent. below the regular rates. In April, 1890, the establishment passed into the hands of a receiver, by whom it was sold in June for $15,000. The furnace used Massillon and Toledo sand and Kelley's Island ground limestone. The failure is held to have resulted from a lack of proper business management.

The Teil de Granmont Optical and Plate Glass Company was organized in the summer of 1889, with a capital stock of $100,000. The citizens of Lancaster took $40,000 in stock, liable to a 60 per cent. assessment, the returns from which were to be guaranteed as 30 per cent. on the investment. A building site was also furnished free. The plant has never been put into operation. The company assigned in April and the sheriff sold the plant for $8,000, the cost of which was not less than $20,000 It is expected to convert this also into a window glass factory.

A rolling mill, built by eastern capital in large part, is also getting ready for operation. To it is assigned, for its fuel supply, another of the large wells of Lancaster, viz., the well that is known as "The Judge." Several other factories have been brought in, including an auger works and a buggy seat factory.

A vigorous movement was begun in real estate a year ago, but the failure of the manufacturing enterprises established here, as noted above, has checked the speculative spirit for the present. The town feels, however, the effect of the great discovery, and if the gas supply shows even a moderate vitality it must reap, in various ways, large advantage from its surprising fortune.

Fuel is supplied in the city at the following rates, viz.: Cook stoves using a No. 5 mixer, $1.00 per month, or $12.00 per year; heating stoves using a No. 5 mixer, $1.00 per month, or $7.00 per year. Whether any funds are ever saved from the gas receipts to pay the gas bonds as they fall due or not, the people are already receiving their pay in the reduction of fuel bills, let alone the advantages that they enjoy in the use of the most perfect form of fuel.

A good measure of economy in the use of the gas has been maintained on the whole. Comparatively little has been consumed in vain display. The most striking exception occurred in the fall of 1889, soon after the fair grounds well was brought in. Four-inch pipe was laid entirely around the half mile race track, opening into frequent standpipes. By this means the track was lighted up at night as never race track was lighted before, and the trials of speed went forward under this wanton illumination. The idea was novel and the scene unique and brilliant, but the waste was barbaric all the same.

The rock pressure of the field now stands at about 450 pounds. It has been reported as high as 700 pounds in single wells and probably attained a higher figure in some. During the last year it has gradually fallen to the figure which it now shows. The drain on the field has been on the whole very light. If two glass furnaces and a rolling mill get under full headway this fall, the first real test of the supply will be made.

The city has little or no land leased outside of the corporation. The county infirmary farm which lies two miles to the northeast of the town is held for the use of the corporation, and the county commissioners are now engaged in sinking a well on this tract. But almost every thing else in a northeast direction, and for two or three miles in breadth between Lancaster and Newark, has been secured by the Columbus company. The city must soon feel the need of more territory if its use of gas for manufacturing purposes is much extended, or even if it is continued upon the scale on which it is now established. Additions may be made to productive territory in unexpected quarters, of course, which may effect the needful relief.

(2) THE NEWARK GAS FIELD.

The earlier history of the search for natural gas at Newark has been duly chronicled in Volume VI. The Everett Glass Works are established and in operation in the town. The competition arising from the use of natural gas in this manufacture, both in Pennsylvania and in northwestern Ohio, was being constantly more keenly felt by the proprietor, and he counted it to his interest to leave no stone unthe search for gas, upon which he entered. The record of this determined pursuit is given in Volume VI. At 2,240 feet a strong flow of heavy brine was struck, which rose 1,700 feet in the well. We now know the horizon at which this salt water appeared. It is the bottom of the Niagara limestone, or the dividing line between the limestone and the shale. At 2,385 feet a small volume of gas was found between two beds of red rock, which helped to determine the horizon. The well, however, was in bad condition and soon became valueless, and the most that was obtained from it was the assurance that the Lancaster gas rock was to be found also in Newark. A new well was forthwith projected, removed two miles from well No. 1, and guided by a knowledge of what was to be expected, much more rapid and satisfactory progress was made in the drilling. The lower salt water was duly cased out with four-and-a-quarter-inch casing, and the gas rock was reached in good condition. A fair flow of dry gas, probably 300,000 feet per day, rewarded the driller. It was piped at once to the glass works and put into use there as far as it would go. The supply was not sufficient, however, to meet all the requirements of the works. Other wells were drilled forthwith with similar results, and finally a supply largely in excess of the demands of the glass works was secured. The largest production of any one well would probably reach a million feet per day. In 1889 Mr. Everett counted the supply and the promise of the field good enough to warrant the piping of the town with reference to furnishing gaseous fuel for domestic use. There has been laid within the corporation limits up to the present date something like twenty miles of pipe of varying sizes, and the central portion of the town has been already mainly reached. The glass works, an eight-pot bottle furnace, has also been dependent on the line for the larger part of its fuel, but during the last winter there was not enough for both uses. Mr Everett and the interests represented by him have secured the gas rights of something like 12,000 acres of land, extending towards Lancaster for a distance of five or six miles, and also extending beyond Newark to the northeast. Six wells have been drilled south of the town, two of which are entirely unproductive. Three wells have been drilled north of the town, including the first which was lost through ignorance of the conditions of the field, and a fourth is now nearing the gas rock. One well north, and one south of the town rank about alike, each reaching a production of about one million feet per day. The wells connected with the pipe line are thought to average about 500,000 cubic feet per day.

The rock pressure of the wells was originally 800 pounds per square inch. This high pressure gives a great advantage to the field. It is counted desirable to constantly maintain a back pressure on the wells of at least 300 pounds, but under the exigencies of the demand this pressure has often been withdrawn, but never without endangering the wells. Salt water appears promptly and unmistakably in one or two of them under such conditions. The rock pressure and the volume of the wells are both undoubtedly declining, but just how rapidly is not known. The main object of the line is to furnish gas for domestic use. The furnishing of power is not attempted at the present, and it may result that the glass works, for which the search was originally begun, will be suspended in the interest of adding to the public supply. It can be counted that the furnace above named will consume somewhat more than a half million feet per day. The rates for gas in the town are the same as the Dayton and Piqua rates.

PRICE OF GAS FOR FUEL AND HEATING PURPOSES IN NEWARK.

For Cooking, from November 1st to May 1st.

	Monthly Charges.	Dis.	If paid in advance before the 10th. Charges.
No. 7 Mixer	$2 78	28 cts.	$2 50
No. 5 Mixer	2 22	22 cts.	2 00

From May 1st to November 1st.

No. 7 Mixer	$1 66	16 cts.	$1 50
No. 5 "	1 39	14 "	1 25

For Large Cooking Range from November 1st to May 1st.

No. 9 Mixer	$3 33	33 cts.	$3 00

From May 1st to November 1st.

No. 9 Mixer	$2 22	22 cts.	$2 00

For Laundry when Gas is Furnished for Cook-stove also.

No. 7 Mixer	$1 11	11 cts.	$1 00
No. 5 "	83	08 "	75

For Heating, No. 7 Mixer.

1st Mixer	$5 00	50 cts.	$4 50
2d "	4 44	44 "	4 00
3d "	3 89	39 "	3 50
4th "	3 33	33 "	3 00
5th "	2 78	28 "	2 50
6th "	2 22	22 "	2 00

Annual Charges.

1st Mixer	$30 00	$3 00	$27 00
2d "	26 64	2 64	24 00
3d "	23 34	2 34	21 00
4th "	19 98	1 98	18 00
5th "	16 68	1 68	15 00
6th "	13 32	1 32	12 00

No. 5 Mixer.

	Monthly Charges.	Discount.	If paid in advance before the 10th. Charges.
1st Mixer	$3 89	39 cts.	$3 50
2d "	3 33	33 "	3 00
3d "	2 78	28 "	2 50
4th "	2 22	22 "	2 00
5th "	1 66	16 "	1 50
6th "	1 39	14 "	1 25

Annual Charges.

1st Mixer	$23 34	$2 34	$21 00
2d "	19 98	1 98	18 00
3d "	16 68	1 68	15 00
4th "	13 32	1 32	12 00
5th "	9 96	96	9 00
6th "	8 34	84	7 50

Furnaces, Monthly Charges.

A Mixer, 21 in f. p.	$6 95	$ 70	$6 25
B " 24 "	8 66	86	7 80
C " 26 "	9 44	94	8 50
D " 28 "	10 00	1 00	9 00
E " 30 "	11 66	1 16	10 50
F " 35 "	13 89	1 39	12 50

Furnaces, Annual Contracts.

A Mixer, 21 in f. p.	$41 70	$4 20	$37 50
B " 24 "	51 96	5 16	46 80
C " 26 "	56 64	5 64	51 00
D " 28 "	60 00	6 00	54 00
" 30 "	69 96	6 96	63 00
F " 35 "	83 34	8 34	75 00

No. 3 Mixer (for Heating Small Rooms and for Special Purposes).

Monthly—1st Mixer	$2 22	22 cts.	$2 00
Monthly—2d Mixer	1 66	16 cts.	1 50

(3) THE THURSTON FIELD.

The production of the district now to be considered is by far the largest and most important that has thus far been derived from the new gas rock. It comprises parts of four townships, viz., Pleasant and Walnut townships of Fairfield county, and Union and Licking townships of Licking county. The most of the developments thus far are confined to Walnut township, in which a dozen or more wells have been already drilled. The discovery of the field is due, more than to any other one person, to Mr. J. O. Johnston, Superintendent of the Central Ohio Natural Gas Company, an operator of experience in the eastern field and also practically acquainted with the new oil field of northern Ohio. He had been engaged in the work of exploration that is now going forward in Newark and Lancaster. It was a natural thing for him to connect these two points on the map, following the analogy furnished by many of the famous fields of Pennsylvania, in which the axes of the anticlinals can be traced for miles in an unbroken direction, swerving neither to the right nor to the left. The direction in this case was easily determined by the wells drilled at the points named above. It was a line bearing north, twenty degrees east, a line that is held in honor in many Pennsylvania fields. A company was soon formed in Columbus in which abundant capital, energy and business sagacity were happily joined. After a fair acreage had been secured a trial well was drilled near Thurston. The well was drilled deep enough into the Clinton limestone to render it certain that gas was to be found in this field also, but the work was suspended at this point and the leasing of land to protect the discovery already made was continued along the line indicated. As a final result, a belt two to three miles wide, extending from the corporate limits of Lancaster on the south to within four or five miles of Newark has been secured. For the larger part of the distance the territory is held by the company in almost unbroken and continuous possession, so far as the gas rights of the land are concerned. Along the northern boundary of its leases the lands of the Newark Company interlock to some extent, but two wells drilled by the latter company on the line, as was thought, and six miles distant from Newark, have proved unproductive.

After securing and proving the territory, the next step was to obtain the right to supply Columbus with natural gas. A liberal franchise was granted by the city council, and during 1889 eastern capital was enlisted in the enterprise, and the construction of the pipe line was begun. The line is a ten-inch pipe of the best quality and construction. It has a length of thirty miles from the field to the city limits. The entire plant of the company, both in the field and in the city, has been kept up to the highest standard of excellence and efficiency from the first. No expense has been spared in obtaining the best possible results. The line was completed in December and gas was introduced in this city early in January of the present year. A distressing accident that occurred a few weeks after the gas was introduced, through a leakage from an uncaulked joint into the gravel trenches and thence into the cellars of buildings contiguous to the line, put back the introduction to a considerable extent for the winter. But all the closely built portions of the city are now being reached by the lines of the company, and the coming winter will doubtless find at least 45,000 people enjoying the advantages of the supply. Gas is furnished for power in considerable amount by the company. It has also felt called upon to furnish fuel to the Hayden Rolling Mill, to the Hallwood Paving Block Works, and to a half dozen other factories; several of these are large consumers, not less than a million and a half feet per day being required by the rolling mill. These coarse industries ought not to have the advantage of this superfine fuel, even though they pay for it at the current rates. If they can afford to pay as much for it as is charged for the gas used in domestic supply, then a high enough price is not charged for the latter service. If such works require gaseous fuel, they should make it for themselves. Some consolation can be found in the fact that these industries, by their enormous consumption of the natural supply, will all the sooner inaugurate the coming era of artificial fuel gas.

The original pressure in the Thurston field was about 700 pounds. The volumes of the larger wells have reached seven or eight million feet per day. A few dry holes have been found. When such a case occurs, either here or in the Newark field, the cause is plainly found in the irregular and interrupted stratification of the Clinton formation. Beds of shale alternate with the limestones, and the sharp sandstone which serves as a receptacle of the gas is wanting in the section. The porosity of the series is effectually interfered with by the intercalation of the shales.

The rates for gas in force at Columbus are the Toledo rates, the schedule of the latter city being adopted without change. Gas is furnished by meter to small consumers at ten cents per thousand. The company aims to charge its largest consumers eight cents per thousand feet.

SUMMARY.

The most surprising chapter in the Geology of Ohio is herewith completed. Though following the discovery of the immensely valuable accumulations of gas and oil in the Trenton limestone, there was scarcely a better preparation from this experience for the history that has now been traced than there would have been without it, and there is far less of rational explanation of the facts of gas production in the new field than was obtained at the outset in the Findlay field. A structure necessarily favorable to the accumulation of gas and oil was brought to view in Findlay as soon as the development fairly began; but at the end of three years there is nothing known of the new field at all comparable in significance with the great structural features brought to light in northwestern Ohio. This difference is due in good part to the difference in the expense of drilling in the two fields. In the Findlay district $800 or $1,000 makes ample provision for a well, and consequently wells are multiplied on every side. In the Clinton a well costs from $4,000 to $5,000, and the number of tests is consequently small. It is much to be hoped that the dominating facts of structure, for assuredly such there are, will be brought to light during the extensive exploration that is now going forward. These facts can not fail to enrich geological science if they are discovered and made known.

DEEP WELLS DRILLED AT OTHER PLACES IN SEARCH OF CLINTON GAS.

The success that the drill had achieved in the districts named above, has awakened or renewed the courage of many communities in their search for natural gas, and during the last year several wells were drilled or deepened to an unusual depth that would not have been thought of except for the success of Lancaster and Newark.

Amanda.—One of these deep wells was drilled in the village of Amanda, eight miles southwest of Lancaster. It was begun by the Amanda Natural Gas Company in October, 1887, a contract having been made that it should be carried to a depth of 2,000 feet. The work went forward very slowly. A little gas was discovered in the Ohio shale at 480 feet, and another small volume in the Clinton at 1,680 feet, but the latter horizon was not reached until August, 1888. Salt water was struck at 1,000 feet in the Lower Helderberg limestone, but it was not cased off until the Niagara shale had been reached at a depth of 1,635 feet. Regular casing was put in to this depth and afterwards four and a quarter casing was set 408 feet below this point. The Clinton limestone being found without value it was then decided to sink the well to the Trenton limestone. A new company was organized and the work resumed in 1889, but after spending a good deal of money the tools were left at the bottom of the well at 2,785 feet, at least 100 feet above the upper surface of the Trenton limestone. The section was carefully reported to the survey from time to time by W. J. Dum, Esq, all the lower part of the record being verified by samples of the rock drillings. The record reduced is as follows:

```
Drift................................................................................     57 feet.
Cuyahoga shale and Waverly black shale.........................     93  "
Berea grit.......  ............  ......................................................     10  "
Bedford and Ohio shales .................................................    775  "
Devonian and Upper Silurian limestones...........  .............    550  "
Niagara shale......  ............................................................    175  "
Clinton limestone ...............................................................     45  "
Medina shale.........  ......................................................    145  "
Hudson River and Utica shales ........................  ............. 1,042  "
```

The figures in the last line do not exhaust the series. The well was dry when the tools were lost.

Mt. Vernon.—A good deal of drilling has been done first and last in Mt. Vernon and in its immediate vicinity. It might have been safely concluded that there was not a great deal more to be learned in regard to its underground geology. It did not seem so, however, to its ambitious business men, and legislative authority was procured, allowing the municipal corporation to expend $10,000 of public money in making more thorough tests of the possibilities of the town in the way of gaseous fuel. To this course they were led in large part by the experience of Lancaster and Newark, and by an erroneous geological inference which they had drawn for themselves from this experience. Lancaster found the gas rock at 2,000 feet below the surface; Thurston at 2,200 feet, and Newark at 2,400 feet below. The erroneous inference referred to was, that since Mt. Vernon is situated as far north of Newark as Newark is north of Lancaster, the Clinton limestone ought to be correspondingly deeper at Mt. Vernon than at Newark. A well was drilled at Mt. Vernon in 1887 to a depth of 2,000 feet. As no value was found in this well, the gas trustees held that the Clinton limestone had not been reached in it. This, however, was a mistake. The place of the Clinton is about 2,200 feet below the surface, and it had been passed through in the well in question several hundred feet before the drill was stopped.

The gas trustees determined to include the Trenton limestone also in their search, if the Clinton failed them, and contracts were drawn for the drilling of two wells 3,500 feet deep, with the privilege of stopping the work at 1,500 feet, or any point below. The record of the first well, which was completed in the fall of 1889, is as follows:

Drift	224 feet.
Cuyahoga shale and Berea shale	173 "
Berea grit, carrying salt water	38 "
Bedford and Ohio shales	705 "
Corniferous limestone and Upper Silurian limestone	895 "
Niagara shale	90 "
Clinton reached at	2,125 "
Red rock	18 "
Shale and sand	20 "
Red rock	50 "
Hard sand	15 "
Medina shale, beginning at	2,275 "
Hudson River shale, beginning at	2,475 "
Well finished, probably in Utica shale, at	3,200 "

Salt water was struck at 1,725; a still stronger vein at 1,765 feet, the water rising to within 100 feet of the surface. The horizon which produced it was the Lower Helderberg limestone. The well was cased with four-anda-quarter-inch pipe to 1,972 feet, and was kept dry thereafter to 3,200 feet. Nothing of value was found in the lower portion of the column, but at a depth of about 900 feet a considerable flow of gas was observed. It was cased out in the progress of drilling, but when nothing else was realized from the well the casing was drawn to the point noted (891 feet), and what gas was found there was turned to account. In December, 1889, the volume was measured and was found to be 78,000 feet per day. It gained a pressure of 145 pounds in one hour, and 185 pounds in one and a half hours. It was utilized by being conveyed to the boilers of the water-works pumping station, near which the well was drilled. The gas has been considerably reduced since that time. The second well was drilled to the Clinton limestone only. Nothing of value has been reported from it.

Mansfield.—A well was begun at Mansfield early in the excitement in regard to the Trenton limestone, with the expectation of finding this rock within easy striking distance. But as its horizon seemed to recede before the drill, one company after another became discouraged and laid down the work of attempting to find it. Encouragement to make the final trial was undoubtedly derived from the success of Lancaster and Newark. When at last the Trenton limestone was reached, Mansfield had one of the deepest wells of the State. Its record, in brief, is as follows:

Sandstone, Logan group .... 140 feet.
Cuyahoga shale......... .... 400 "
Berea shale........ .... 40 "
Berea grit.. 15 "
Bedford and Ohio shales.. 640 "
Devonian and Upper Silurian limestones .... 945 "
Medina, Hudson River and Utica shales .... 1,314 "

Trenton struck at 3,550 feet; well completed at 3,594 feet. The $5\frac{5}{8}$-inch casing extends to 561 feet, and 4¼-inch casing to 2,200 feet. The well was necessarily an expensive one, the last rate for drilling being $5.00 a foot. Three different contractors were employed. The company was reorganized several times during the progress of the work. The Clinton was well marked in the descent, but was found to be without value. The Trenton limestone was hard, dry and unproductive.

Coshocton.—A company was formed at Coshocton to drill to the Clinton limestone, after it had been proved to be petroliferous by the experience related in the present chapter. No different section was expected from that found at the points mentioned. The company took advantage of a boring begun in 1886, the record of which is contained in Volume VI, page 368. The new work was begun at 1,280 feet below the surface. In this well the Berea grit was struck at about 860 feet. The great shale series underlying it was found 1,600 feet thick. The Devonian limestone was struck at 2,513 feet. The only important fact developed by this drilling, so far as known, is that the Lower Helderberg series expands in this part of the State into a series of gypsiferous shales of considerable thickness. The courage of the company gave out when a depth of 3,100 feet had been reached. The last drillings were in the shales above reported. The Clinton limestone, to which the drilling was all directed, still lay undisturbed in its original security, several hundred feet below the bottom of the well. It could not have been found without a descent of at least 150 feet lower than the drill had reached. The most probable figure for its depth would be 3,300 to 3,400 feet.

Dresden.—A well was also sunk at Dresden in 1889 that would not have been undertaken but for the success of Newark. The last record of this well was obtained from a reported depth of 2,525 feet. The drill showed that the gypsiferous shales of the Water lime (Lower-Helderberg) series, noted in the preceding paragraph, had been reached at this point.

Plain City.—During 1889, two deep wells were drilled at Plain City, the encouragement to undertake which was borrowed from the successful wells drilled at Lancaster.

The record of these wells is as follows:

	No. 1.	No. 2.
Drift	120 feet.	128 feet.
Casing set	521 "	535 "
Red rock, Medina 540 to	600 "	
Trenton limestone		1,721 feet.
Finished	1,530 feet.	2,000 "

In the first well the cable broke at 1,530 feet and the tools were never recovered from the well. There was, of course, no geological promise at at any time in drilling in this locality. The region had been tested on all sides, and a monotonous record of failures in all the horizons of gas and oil now known had been obtained. The only point of interest developed in the drilling was a noble flow of rock water from a depth of 350 feet. The volume of the stream is undoubtedly large enough to supply the entire village, and a favorable showing as to the quality of the water would be expected from the results of chemical analysis. The Lancaster horizon was reached in the Plain City well at about 500 feet, but the limits of depth, as fixed by the company, seem to have been determined by the fact that the Lancaster gas was found at about 2,000 feet in depth.

Somerset.—Another deep well, the courage to undertake which must have been borrowed from the success of Lancaster and Newark, was drilled in Somerset, Perry county, during the latter part of 1889. The record of this well, as furnished by Professor Patrick Henry, Superintendent of Schools, is as follows:

THE CLINTON LIMESTONE.

Drift...	44 feet.	
Limestone (Lower Mercer?)..............................	5 "	
Shale and sandstone (Conglomerate Coal Measures, Logan-Cuyahoga, etc.).......................................	927 "	
White sand (Berea grit)....................................	30 "	(Strong salt water.)
Red rock (Bedford shale)...................................	30 "	(Cased here.)
Shales, blue and black (Ohio).............................	1,056 "	
Limestone (Devonian and Upper Silurian)............	708 "	
Total...	2,850 "	

Salt water was struck at 2,665 feet in so strong a flow that it could not be shut off. It rises to within 400 feet of the surface, or to about 800 feet above tide level. It is derived from the Lower Helderberg series. Drilling was kept up under this heavy column of water for several hundred feet, but the progress was slow and discouragement finally overtook the company before the Clinton goal was reached. The drill must have reached to within 300 feet of the new gas rock when it was arrested.

CHAPTER V.

REMAINING SOURCES OF OIL AND GAS IN OHIO.

In the present chapter a brief review will be attempted of the most important facts that have been accumulated in the last two years as to the production of petroleum and gas from the remaining rocks of the Ohio scale. The several strata that yield these products will be taken up in the geological order (ascending) in which they occur. The two horizons that have been already treated belong, as will be remembered, to the lower portions of our column.

(I) THE OHIO SHALE.

This great stratum must not be omitted in this review, but the character of its production has long been known, and but little of special value has been added to our knowledge of it during the interval named above. It continues to furnish low-pressure gas in moderate amount for household use, especially along the shore of Lake Erie, from Huron River to the Pennsylvania line. New wells have been added by the score throughout this region, but all the facts of production remain about as they were. The gas reported in a previous chapter, from a depth of 900 feet, at Mt. Vernon, is derived from the Ohio shale. The pressure which it accumulates when the well is shut in, viz., 185 pounds, is exceptional for the gas of this formation, and would seem to indicate a water pressure in the shale as its source. The shale is generally composed of impervious beds, but it sometimes happens that some of the beds are hard and slaty in structure, and are broken by frequent joints to such an extent as to become practically porous. The Ohio shale formation in Kentucky, for example, possesses this character. It yields gas in considerable quantity, and it also contains below and behind the gas, salt water in large amount. The gas is, in this case, really held under a salt water pressure, as in ordinary reservoir rocks, but as the wells are comparatively shallow, their depth not exceeding 400 feet, their pressure does not rise above 120 pounds to the square inch. In the case of the Mt. Vernon well, the presence of a water column may also be inferred.

Shale gas of lower pressure is found to be the most persistent. Such gas is certainly not driven by a water column. The moment that water pressure is brought into the account, a limit to the life of the well becomes apparent. All the shale gas wells that serve as the stock examples of unfailing and perpetual supply to those who know very little about natural gas and yet feel called upon to speak and write upon the subject, are of very small volume and feeble pressure. The famous Fredonia wells of western New York are of this character. A little oil is also occasionally found in the shale series. The largest quantity noted of late comes from just outside the State limits. At Erie, Pennsylvania, a lubricating oil of fine quality (28° B. at 66° F.) is afforded in quantity large enough to be offered in the local markets.

But in the large way the great formation remains what it was—a widespread source of feeble gas wells, which apparently do not depend upon the structural arrangements of the strata, and which are not driven by the pressure of a water column.

(II) THE BEREA GRIT.

This famous stratum has been tested during the last two years very largely throughout southeastern Ohio, or, more strictly speaking, the tests that were going forward two years ago have been continued and multiplied since that date.

The unbroken continuity of this stratum throughout the portion of the State above named was demonstrated in Volume VI. It was there traced as far as the Ohio River in a series of sections that he who runs could read. It approached our southern boundary always as an oil rock or a gas rock, sometimes of great value, as, for example, when found under the designation of the Macksburg sand. It has since been followed, by fresh developments, into West Virginia and Pennsylvania, and by the same order and stratigraphical relations that it holds in all Ohio sections it has been identified in these States, first as the Murrysville sand, the great gas rock of the Pennsylvania scale, and second, as the Gantz sand, the prolific oil and gas rock of Washington and Greene counties, and of West Virginia as well. Prof. I. C. White, who is easily our highest authority on the order of the series in the upper Ohio Valley, counts this determination well established at last. If accepted, it does a great deal towards clearing up the geology of the oil fields, and is a very important step in unifying the somewhat discordant columns of Ohio and Pennsylvania.

There is but one oil field yet established in the Berea grit, and that is the Macksburg field, which was already waning fast when Volume VI was published. It still maintains a small production, but all of its present importance is due to some of the oil rocks of the Coal Measures that are found in the same section overlying the Berea grit. Many attempts to work out new oil fields in this stratum have been made, and some attempts are still going forward. Generally this attempt has been conjoined with a search for gas. Both lines of facts can be best treated, therefore, under a single head.

(1) THE CADIZ OIL FIELD.

A large amount of drilling has been done in the central townships of Harrison county during the last three years. There has been just enough encouragement in the wells that have been completed to keep up the interest in the work. The series traversed by the drill is regular; the oil rock is in its place, and in the adjacent districts it is, or it has been, the basis of important production. The structure that is known to be indispensable to large accumulation has been demonstrated to be present, and last of all, oil and gas have both been found in almost every well that has been drilled—the oil of a quality to command a premium in the markets—and in a few cases but little short of paying quantity, and the gas in volume that suggests, if it does not warrant, utilization. The operators in the field have been men of experience, and they have counted the facts as developed consistent with the possibility of important production close at hand, and they have been loth to relinquish the search, though well after well, up to a dozen or a score in number, has fallen short of the demands from the stand-point of business success.

The history of the work that is going forward here is as follows: In 1888 a company was formed in Cadiz to test the territory for gas, the Artificial Gas Company taking an important interest in the search. Two or three wells were drilled within the compass of a few miles from the court-house, each well being located by individual caprice, or at least without any well-considered plan of operations as a basis. The successive failures, therefore, proved nothing whatever as to the territory taken as a whole, except that these wells were not included within any limits of production. The series, as remarked above, was found regular. The Berea grit, which was the objective point in all the wells, generally contained salt water, but it carried also a showing of oil or gas.

It occurred at last to the company that if geology could throw any light on these problems its aid should be sought. It had long been known that an anticlinal axis of more or less force traverses the rock series of Harrison county near Cadiz, but in the work thus far undertaken no reference had been paid to it. The axis was found easy to define. One or two lines of east and west sections run by the engineer's level, the great Pittsburgh coal seam being used as the geological base, sufficed to establish the fact that a well-marked up-lift, reversing or at least interrupting the normal southeasterly dip of the strata, passes through Cadiz and Green townships, the center of the arch lying about a mile east of the court-house. This arch, it may be remarked, can be traced for a long distance. It is recognizable at Quaker City, though in very feeble force, thirty miles to the southwest, and it is highly probable that it is the same axis upon which the Macksburg field depends. To the northward there is a slight fold recognizable at New Salisbury on Yellow Creek, which is probably a continuation of the Cadiz arch. On the basis of the structure thus made known, it was easy to see that the records of failure thus far were just what should have been expected, the location of the wells not only giving them no advantage from the geological structure but positively condemning the territory on which they were located.

A new series of wells was forthwith projected, and all the facts developed in them, have borne out the geological inferences as to this structure. The oil rock was found at a noticeably higher geographical level, and it was no longer overrun with salt water. If it yielded but a small quantity of oil or gas, in any case, this fact could be accounted for by the physical condition of the oil rock when found. Sometimes it proved too thin, and sometimes it was too fine grained and muddy for large storage. The geologist, of course, undertakes to furnish no testimony as to this line of facts. His labor ends when he shows that a relief suitable and indispensable to petroliferous accumulation is to be found in a field at a given locality. The quality of the rock, on the other hand, can be determined only by the drill.

About a dozen wells have now been completed under the new dispensation. The bulk of them are situated in the contiguous Sections, 28, Green township; 27, Short Creek township, and 33 and 35, Cadiz township. Nine wells have been drilled here, all of which would be included in a circle described with a radius of one-half or three-quarters of a mile. In addition, three or four wells have been distributed through the same townships so as to indicate, in part, the character of a larger area. The best results have been obtained in the first group of wells. The geological section of the wells is in all respects normal. They are all likely to begin not far from the horizon of the Pittsburgh coal, either a little above or a little below it. This seam is a universal element in the geological scale of the county, except where eroded in the deeper valleys. The red clays of the barren measures are passed through in their order, and the Crinoidal limestone generally makes its mark in every record. The only other noteworthy element is a coal seam that the drillers agree in counting from five to six feet in thickness, that is found at a depth of 500 to 550 feet. There is reason to believe that this buried seam is the Upper Freeport or Cambridge coal, though the interval is somewhat longer than would be expected. This seam has been struck in wells at least six miles distant from each other in an east and west line, and has been recorded in most of the drillings. Its occurrence is a matter of great importance in the resources of the county, though practical account will not be made of it for several generations yet. But it is worthy of distinct record that such a seam exists here under the conditions named. A seam of the same thickness and at the same approximate depth, and doubtless identical with this one, is reported from Quaker City, in the edge of Guernsey county. Samples of the coal brought up from the Quaker City boring were submitted to chemical analyses, and they proved the coal to be of excellent quality. It may therefore be set down as one of the most valuable results of the drilling that is going forward, that an extensive field of the Cambridge coal, with its normal thickness of five to six feet, extends through eastern Guernsey, presumably through western Belmont and through central Harrison county, at a depth of about 500 feet below the Pittsburgh coal. The same seam, if this be the Upper Freeport, crops out to the north of Harrison county and is there known as the Dell Roy or Sherrodsville coal.

When the Coal Measures and the Conglomerate Coal Measures are passed by the drill, the great Waverly conglomerate or Logan group is reached by it. This stratum is now known in Pennsylvania and West Virginia as the "Big Indian" sand rock. Under this stratum is the well-marked Cuyahoga shale, darkening in its lower portion into the equally distinct Berea shale that is here found thirty feet thick, under which, at a depth below the surface varying from 1,325 to 1,400 feet (the depth depending upon the accidents of the surface) is found that wonderfully steady and widely extended stratum, the Berea grit, the possible contents of which constitute the object toward which all this outlay is directed.

The wells are cased with regular casing to a depth of 400 feet, and smaller casing extends to about 1,050 feet, resting just within the limits of the Cuyahoga shale.

The Holliday well, located in the southwest corner of Section 28, Green township, gives as good promise as any of the wells have given. When first drilled the oil rose in it 400 feet in a single night. An attempt was afterwards made to torpedo the oil rock, but the shell exploded prematurely in the casing and allowed the wtaer from the Logan sandstone to find its way downward. This difficulty has not been entirely remedied, but the well is now flowing about five barrels of oil per day. The gravity of the oil is 47° B. It is sold at a premium of fifty cents. A part of the oil of the field is even lighter in gravity than this, reaching 51° B., but another part is considerably heavier, falling as low as 41° B. The Boden well in Section 26, Short Creek township, and the Morgan well, Section 33, Cadiz township, both give fair promise as oil wells The pay-streak in the latter is reported to be fifteen feet thick, but the sand is fine and muddy. The well was producing, when last reported, from two to three barrels per day

Of the gas wells the Mitchell well, near the center of Section 33, Cadiz, and the Fryer well, southeast quarter of northeast quarter Section 35, Cadiz township, have given the best promise until recently. Within the last few weeks a well has been drilled on the Walter Craig farm that shows much greater value, as a gas well, than any that has preceded it. It is located near the middle of Section 28, Green township. It is estimated by good judges to yield 1,000,000 feet per day. The town will forthwith be piped for the introduction of gas as fuel, and a good deal more drilling will be carried forward, though the inferior character of the sand is acknowledged by all.

How shall the character of the Cadiz field be summed up? It is obvious that it has not fulfilled the expectations of the experienced operators that have been testing it. Money has been freely spent upon it, but so far, it has been like water poured upon the ground, the principal exception being found in the Craig well last named. If a tract has been discovered that will furnish gas to the village of Cadiz for a few years, this will redeem the entire district from the charge of barrenness and failure. It goes hard to give up so good promise as the field has shown without some adequate return.

The following companies have been at work within the general limits of the territory above described, viz.: The Cadiz Oil & Gas Company, The Berea Grit Oil Company, The Standard Oil Company, Joseph Post, Clark & McCormick, F. E. Boden, Galbraith & Watson, Brainard & Company.

A deep well recently drilled one and a half miles northeast of Flushing, in Belmont county, gives the following record. It was begun at the level of the Meigs Creek coal. The Pittsburgh seam was struck at ninety-seven feet, sixty feet of limestone being passed through in the interval. At 595 feet a coal seam, seven feet thick is reported, another seam, four to five feet thick, is reported at 700 feet, and still a third seam, three to four feet thick, at 815. Salt water was struck at 900 feet. The great Waverly or Logan sandstone fills the interval between 1,015 and 1,250 feet with unbroken salt water rock. The Berea grit was reached at 1,635 feet. The uppermost fifteen feet are soft and dark, followed by thirty feet of soft white sand. The salt water rose in the well 700 feet in eight hours. The occurrence of the coal seams is the feature of interest in this record. The Upper Freeport seam, previously referred to, is shown here in full value. The next seam below is probably one of the Kittanning coals.

(2) THE BARNESVILLE GAS FIELD.

The search that Barnesville has carried on in the underlying rocks during the last two years has had but a single object, viz., a supply of gas for the use of its citizens and for the glass factory which is established here. The beginning of this investigation was made by the village corporation at the public expense. Authority was obtained from the Legislature to expend $5,000 in this way. The trial well was located within or near the corporation limits and was drilled to a depth of 2,700 feet. The Berea grit was struck at a depth of about 1,600 'eet, and a little oil and considerable salt water were found in it., This work was done in 1888. Not discouraged by the failure a company of citizens was then formed to continue the search. Two more wells were sunk, but only to the Berea grit, but they made no great improvement on the record of well No. 1, but a little encouragement was found in each in the small production of oil and in the other evidences of continuity and porosity of the Berea grit. It was then decided to call in geological advice as to the location of further trial wells. Mr. F. W. Minshall, of Marietta, made an examination of the territory for the company and found a feeble axis to the northwest of the village. The first well drilled under the new guidance made an agreeable change in the record that had been thus far maintained. A considerable flow of gas was secured. The volume was reported at 750,000 cubic feet per day, and the rock pressure proved to be 640 pounds, and although a little oil and salt water were produced with the gas, it was evident that there was far more to encourage in the new location than had been found in the previous wells. A second well was therefore located 1,600 feet to the northeast of No. 1, which yielded dry gas of the same rock pressure, and of approximately the same volume as No. 1. Both of them are located on the Parker farm, and they are distant about one mile from the corporation line. They were drilled during the summer of 1889.

Measured for the company in June, 1890, the volume of well No. 1 was found to be approximately 300,000 feet per day. The salt water and oil have been gaining upon the gas apparently in the interval since it was drilled. Well No. 2 was in better condition. Its gas is dry and its daily volume is 500,000 feet. The company has leased 1,800 acres of land thought to be most favorably situated with reference to gas production, and has also secured the right to pipe the town for fuel supply. The amount of gas already found would be of great service if brought to the village and applied to domestic use, but it would not meet the demand of a glass factory if the whole of it were to be applied to this purpose. If a few more wells as good as the last were drilled, it would give an apparently safe basis for the domestic supply of the town for a few years at least.

A few wells have been drilled in other portions of Belmont county during the last two years, and favorable accounts are current as to the gas production of some of them, but authentic data have not been secured in regard to them for the present report.

(3) THE CAMBRIDGE GAS FIELD.

The persistent and costly search for gas on the line of the Cambridge arch, that was recorded in Volume VI, has been carried on still further since the date of the publication of the report named above. A half dozen wells carefully located with reference to the arch, by the aid of geological and engineering work, were drilled during 1888, in Liberty township to the east of Kimbolton, where a well reported on page 381 of Volume VI had been already drilled, the promise of which had been considerably better than that of any previous trial in this vicinity. Four wells were drilled here about 500 feet apart, on an east and west line designed to cover the top of the arch. The outcome justified to a considerable extent the geological prevision. Gas was found in all of them and in two of them in considerable volume; but no measurement of the wells were made, or at least none were made public. The wells showed a good rock pressure. At this stage eastern capital was brought in, the representatives of which had no previous acquaintance with the business of oil and gas production. The company formed is known as the Southeastern Ohio Gas and Fuel Company, and under this there are several subordinate companies. The investors supposed themselves in possession of a stock of gas ample for the domestic supply of Cambridge, distant about ten miles from the wells, and also sufficient for the largest manufacturing plant that could be established here, as, for example, a large rolling mill. The plans of the new company contemplated also the supply of Zanesville at an early day from the same field. A ten-inch line, five or six miles in length, was laid to serve as a common stem from the wells for both cities, and from it a similar line was carried into Cambridge. The gas was brought to the town in 1888, permission to pipe the town having been previously secured, but the franchise did not give the company exclusive right in these respects. A few hundred stoves were taken on, but the supply proved very irregular and unsatisfactory. Various explanations of the failure were offered. The real cause was undoubtedly an insufficient amount of gas.

The wells were measured for the first time for the company in September, 1889, and their condition was found unpromising. Wells Nos. 1 and 3 together yielded about one and a quarter million cubic feet of gas per day at the well heads, but both were badly overrun with salt water. Well No. 2 produced about 70,000 feet per day and it was a wet well also. Wells Nos. 4 and 5 were found too feeble to be measured even by the anemometer. The larger wells had been neglected for some time previous to the measurement and this condition was afterwards considerably improved by proper care, but their real character appears in the statements made above. The results of these measurements were a great surprise and disappointment to the eastern investors, but in order to keep the plant from becoming an entire failure, other wells are to be drilled in the hope of obtaining a larger supply. The company holds an extensive acreage under lease which it does not cost great outlay to maintain. Its investments have exceeded $100,000. The rates in force at Cambridge are the following:

```
Cooking stoves, per annum........................................................ $15 00
First grate,         "    "   ..................................................... 10 00
Second grate,        "    "   .....................................................  8 00
Additional grates,   "    "   .....................................................  6 00
Heating stoves       "    "   ..................................................... 16 00
Additional heating stoves, per annum.........................................  5 00
For large rooms, 500 feet floor space........................................ 16 00
For each additional 100 feet ......................................................  1 00
```

A home company was also formed in 1888 in Cambridge to supply fuel to the town. It secured its territory within a mile or two of the corporation. It has drilled a half dozen wells, has laid a four-inch line from the wells to the town, and has laid its distributing service through a portion of the corporate limits. Its wells are none of them large, though some of them are understood to have attained a production of several hundred thousand feet a day. Salt water is yielded with the gas in all the wells, but it does not prove immediately fatal to their production. This peculiarity of the Berea grit gas was noticed in the account given in Volume VI of the Neff wells, page 339. The salt water, if promptly removed from the wells, does not shut off the gas. In some fields, on the other hand, it comes with an overpowering force and takes exclusive occupation of the rock for all time to come. The company does not connect any larger number of stoves with its lines than it can fully supply. Between the two companies, Cambridge is enjoying the inexpressible convenience that comes from the use of natural gas as domestic fuel.

As to the prospects of the Cambridge field, the comments in Volume VI upon its character can be repeated with renewed emphasis in the light of all subsequent history. The arch, where it has been struck, is too flat to give proper relief for the separation of gas and oil from water. A few additional feet of elevation at any point would change this record, and it is by no means impossible that some happier location will at last be struck.

(4) THE OHIO VALLEY.

While there has been a great deal of activity in this district, there is but little substantial progress to be reported. Exploration has been going on uninterruptedly in one or another portion of Washington, Noble, Belmont, and Jefferson counties during the last two years. On the south side of the river, some valuable oil territory has been brought to light, and this discovery makes the driller more than ever certain that the region above named will somewhere be found to afford new oil fields that will repay the search for them.

The most important facts that can be stated in this connection are the following, derived from a recent number of the *American Manufacturer*. The facts do not pertain to the productiveness of the oil rock, but rather to a new method of distributing the profits arising from an oil field when one is discovered. It is greatly to be regretted that the method was not invented many years ago, for it would certainly have resulted in a vastly more equitable and healthful distribution of the enormous profits that have accrued from oil production. It is hereby most cordially commended to the farmers and land owners of the state. For the origination of the method we are indebted, it is said, to the Farmers' Alliance.

It appears that a representative of one of the Wheeling oil companies lately found reason to believe that the Eureka field extended across the Ohio river, in a direction in which no tests had been made. The company decided to lease some land within the lines as indicated. The first farmer to whom they applied expressed his willingness to lease his farm of 200 acres. "A lease was accordingly made out by the company in the ordinary form, allowing the land owner his eighth royalty, and agreeing to put a well down in a certain time. When the lease was brought back for the farmer to sign, he flatly refused. When asked why, he drew on them a lease of his own, printed and filled out with the company's name, and ready for the signatures. It provided for the leasing of the farm in tracts of fifty acres each, and gave the farmer control of ten acres of each fifty. It further provided that the ten acres might be drilled into by the farm owner, or any one to whom he might lease that portion of the tract, at any time either before or after the holders of the lease on the other part of the tract had commenced development. This was a surprise for the representatives of the oil company, they having been accustomed to the land owner taking almost any thing offered. The farmer's proviso gave him the power to hold a share of the production of his land from the company, and in such shape that, no matter where the leasers might strike oil, he would have at least ten acres in the immediate vicinity, which he could drill upon himself, or re-lease, or sell at the price which the leasers' development might place upon it. The lease was not signed at once, but the leasers found that all the farmers in the township had leases of the same style, and that the land could not be secured on any other terms."

CHAPTER VI.

THE UTILIZATION OF NATURAL GAS IN OHIO.

In the preceding chapters it has been shown that a few favored districts of the State have obtained large supplies of natural gas during the last few years, and the uses which the people of these districts are making of the new source of heat have been incidentally mentioned in many varying connections. The latter subject is, however, so important that it seems to deserve a more distinct and detailed treatment than it has thus far received. The present chapter will accordingly be devoted to a description of the various uses to which natural gas is now applied in Ohio, and such data as have been accumulated as to the amounts of gas consumed in the several applications will here find place.

USES OF NATURAL GAS.

For the sake of convenience the uses of gas in Ohio will be considered under the following main heads and subdivisions:

I. Domestic fuel. { (1) Cooking stoves, ranges, etc.
{ (2) Heating stoves, furnaces, grates, etc.

II. Fuel for manufacturers. { (1) Power.
{ (2) Fuel proper. { (a) Glass manufacture—window, bottle, table ware.
{ (b) Iron working, rolling mills, nail works, wire mills, etc.
{ (c) Clay working, potteries, brick, pressed brick, common brick, tile manufacturing.
{ (d) Lime burning.

I. *Domestic Fuel.*—This is by far the most important use of natural gas, if measured on the scale of general service. It contributes to the comfort and convenience of a much greater number of people in this than in any other line of use. The service that it renders it is hard to exaggerate. It effects an immense saving in the never-ending labors of house-keeping. To the communities that have found access to it, it has not only rendered great practical service already, but it has given to them a lesson that is of even greater value than this practical service. It has demonstrated the advantage of gaseous fuel and has inclined all who have become acquainted with these advantages so strongly to its use that they will never willingly go back to the grosser forms of stored heat. Whatever brings the world forward towards this result is rendering a most important service.

Considerable outlays are required before the gas can be made available as fuel to the people of a city or village. Not only must gas territory be secured and wells be drilled, but a pipe line must convey the gas from the wells to the city, and when the latter is reached a costly net-work of pipes of various sizes must be laid to provide for its proper distribution. When the gas fields are a score or more miles distant from the point where the gas is to be used, and where a considerable supply has to be provided, the cost of the pipe line rises to large figures. The pipe for such service must be eight, ten or twelve inches in diameter, and the cost, therefore, runs up to many thousands of dollars per mile.

As a consequence it is as a rule only large aggregations of capital that undertake this work. Capitalists look on the supply of gas to towns as they do on other modes of gaining mineral wealth. There is a considerable element of risk involved, but when successful the returns may be extraordinarily large. The companies that have taken hold of this work throughout the country are for the most part those who have gained their wealth by successful operations in oil, and they consequently bring to the business the training that comes from the largest attainable practical knowledge in regard to it.

But before the supply of the city can be undertaken, the right to furnish a supply, including the privilege of using the streets and alleys for the purpose, must be obtained from the people through the municipal authorities. This gives to the City Council an opportunity to fix the rates that are to be charged for gas, or at least to fix the maximum rates that may be charged. Under the circumstances, it is eminently proper that this right should be exercised, for, as a rule, competition in the supply is impossible, and it would be wholly unwarrantable to leave so large public interests as these at the mercy of corporations organized solely with reference to large returns for their investments. If, for example, a town, after enjoying the luxury of gaseous fuel, should be required to make choice between going back to coal and paying twice the price of coal for gas, all who could possibly afford it would choose the latter alternative. But it is evident that even if the same price is paid for gas that the coal which it displaces would cost, the business of furnishing it becomes, under favorable circumstances, enormously profitable. The consideration of questions of this character by the people and their representatives in the municipal governments, especially in localities where the supply of gas is found close at hand, naturally led to projects of furnishing fuel to such

UTILIZATION OF GAS. 261

towns through the agency of the municipal government. Findlay led the way in this direction. The history of the steps by which the result was finally accomplished is given at some length in Volume VI. Bowling Green, Fostoria, Upper Sandusky, North Baltimore, Greenville, Lancaster, Tiffin, Toledo, Ottawa, and a number of smaller towns have followed along the same general line, although not in all cases undertaking to supply domestic fuel to the towns. The chief interest of many, and the exclusive interest of some, in fact, has been to furnish fuel to manufacturers, and the work in this connection will be treated under a separate head. Where household fuel has been included, the rates have been in all cases made moderate, averaging not more than twelve to fifteen dollars per year for a single fire.

Entering without experience on this line of work, however, and even selected for it sometimes on account of their sanguine views and hopeful theories as to the nature of the gas supply, the municipal corporations or gas boards have had a great deal to learn. Frequently, by the time that a member has acquired better knowledge of the work that he has in hand, he is displaced either for what the board may have done or failed to do in this connection, and a new man takes his place, and gains in like manner his practical education at the public expense. The faults to be expected in such an administration have been realized in most of the municipal gas plants. These faults are failure to secure adequate territory, improper construction of the lines, irregular and defective supply, and, worse than all, great wastefulness of fuel. The discovery of a store of fuel and power of this character was so surprising and unexpected that it is no wonder that to those who were so favored, it seemed for awhile that it had "come to stay," to use the current phrase in regard to gas. And then, too, such wanton waste was in progress on every side that any nice regard for economy seemed as foolish as it was futile.

This state of things is passing away in the older centers, and the warnings that the supply of this precious stock of heat and power is limited are so plain that no one can any longer fail to recognize them. The system by which gas has been introduced as fuel into Ohio towns by both public and private corporations, has unfortunately had some vicious features, in some respects, from the beginning. The consumer is charged not for the amount of gas he uses, but in a general way for the amount that he is able to use by the service with which the company supplies him. The gas meters in use at the beginning of this experience were not adapted to the natural supply, and their expense stood in the way of their adoption at first. Charges were therefore based by the companies upon the size of the burners which they supplied to individual consumers These burners are technically known as mixers. The openings by which the gas escapes are measured in given fractions of an inch. The mixers in common use are known as numbers 3, 5 and 7. The diameter of the aperture in number 3 is three thirty-seconds; in number 5, four thirty-seconds; and in number 7, five thirty-seconds of an inch. The amount of gas that passes through these mixers depends upon the pressure which is maintained upon it. Under a pressure of four ounces, according to an experimental test made by a careful observer, by means of a gas meter, a number 3 mixer passes thirty-two feet, and a number 5 mixer, forty-eight feet per hour. These figures are not exactly in the proportions to be expected from the relative sizes of the pipes; there should be a greater disparity between them. According to another experiment, under a nine-ounce pressure, a number 3 mixer consumes forty-eight feet per hour, and a number 5 mixer, eighty-five feet per hour. The latter measurements are properly proportioned to each other, in any case.

The range of pressure in natural gas lines is often considerable. Most lines aim to secure a pressure of four ounces for domestic service. None would willingly exceed eight ounces for this use, but through defective management ten and even twelve ounces are sometimes reached in the distributing pipes.

(1) In the mixer, which is in by far the largest use, viz., No. 5, it is certain that at least fifty feet per hour will be consumed under any of the pressures likely to be found in the lines. Counting fifteen hours a day as the probable limit for the largest use, viz., in cook stoves, in the winter months, it is seen that at least 750 feet must be taken as necessary for the demands of each stove. At this rate a cook stove will use in one month 22,500 feet. At four and a half cents per 1,000 feet this amount would cost $1.01. At nine cents per 1,000 feet it would cost $2.02. The figures given, viz, $1.00 to $2.00 per month, practically cover the entire range of the prices at present charged for the gas applied to domestic use in its most important application, viz., the cook stove. And thus it appears that such fuel is paid for in the State at rates ranging from four and a half to nine cents per month for the largest possible supply. The actual supply must be considerably less than this, and by this means the price realized from the gas is greater than that given. The amount named above can not be far from being the equivalent of a ton of coal, and the price of gas can be accordingly estimated on this basis. The rates for summer use are in most of the cities and towns reduced below the figures given above.

(2) For heating stoves it is not as easy to make calculation on the price realized for the gas, because of the fact that when more than a single grate or heater is employed, discounts, varying in amount, are allowed according to the number. There are also differences in price for the different

seasons of the year. Some companies make no charge for five months of the year for heating purposes, and others reduce the rate of the winter months by giving an annual rate that is half the maximum for the particular mixer employed. The latter is the usage of the great companies.

For the gas used in heating it is probable that a considerably higher rate is realized than for that used in cook stoves. If this is true, it is as it should be, for the advantage of the lower rates comes to those least able to pay for gas as a luxury.

This whole system of disposing of gas has already been characterized as a vicious one. The objection to it lies in this fact, viz., that the consumer is under no adequate motive to economy. He is in danger of even making himself uncomfortable by overheating his house in the endeavor to get the worth of his money. The current complaints as to the extraordinary heating power of natural gas have their root in this system. If illuminating gas were supplied at a certain price for a jet of specified size, as natural gas is supplied at a certain price for a mixer, every city would forthwith take on a brilliancy at night never known before. There would be continuous illumination such as we now see only on festal occasions. There is no more need of warping and racking a house through the effect of extreme heat by natural gas than by any other fuel. But the fact of its steadiness is made to contribute easily to this result. It can be maintained, day in and day out, without abatement, and it is this fact that mainly leads to overheating. There is, however, a common defect in its introduction into dwellings that helps to bring about the same result. Flues are unduly constricted when gas is brought in, and the heated products of combustion occur to a very unhealthful amount in the room.

The whole system of burning gas is, however, in a very crude state. A small fraction of the heat produced by the combustion is at present made available for our use. By means of the best appliances now known the consumption of gas could be reduced to less than one-half, and perhaps to less than one-third of what is now used, without trenching upon the required amount of heat. It is along these lines that the principal encouragement to the introduction of manufactured fuel gas is to be derived.

The remedy for the evil complained of, viz., extravagance in the use of the gas, can be effectively reached by the introduction of meters. Meters have now been constructed for this specific purpose, and they certainly ought to be introduced forthwith into all cities and villages, unless the very small villages situated directly in the gas fields shall be exempt. When a proper price is placed on the gas, and when each consumer is obliged to pay for what he uses, an adequate motive to economy will for the first time be brought into operation. It is to the common interest of the gas companies and the consumers that these results shall be attained as soon as possible.

In the two preceding chapters the rates prevailing in the towns now supplied with gas have been given.

II. Fuel for Manufacturers.

(1) *Power.*—For use in the boilers of steam engines natural gas finds one of its large and important applications. It is applied to the generation of power for a large variety of manufactures, for pumping the water required in a city supply, and for conversion into the light derived from electric illumination. In each and all of these uses it is simply the perfect type of fuel, to the attainment of which the civilized world, especially in its great cities, is sure to come. The economies brought into operation by its introduction are numerous, and among them may be named the reduction of labor in maintaining the fire and in the removal of ashes and clinkers, and especially in the greater durability of the boilers and engines through the steady supply of heat. To the cities in which gas is used for power, one of the desirable results also is found in the happy exemption that they enjoy from the smoke and soot that coal so used produces.

Amount Consumed.—As to the important question "What amount of gas is required for an engine of given horse-power?" no general answer, unfortunately, can be given. Such an answer can not be given even in terms of coal, for the reason that there is no uniformity in the consumption. Two boilers rated at the same horse-power and doing the same work, may require amounts of coal differing from each other by a considerable percentage. The fuel consumption is affected by many factors which need not be enumerated here. This entire subject is, so for as the general practice is concerned, in a very unscientific and unsatisfactory condition. Coal has been so cheap throughout the world that manufacturers have knowingly tolerated its wasteful use rather than take the trouble which the correction of such waste would involve. The subject is, however, commanding much larger consideration at the present time than it has heretofore had and great advances and improvements are in sight. The efficiency of fuel probably reaches its highest point in the engines of ocean-going steamships.

In determining the amounts of gas used in steam boilers and other applications, we have heretofore labored under the great disadvantage of lacking any simple means of measuring these amounts. Meters adapted to such work have not been at hand until very recently at least, and for large consumption they are held at high prices. The recent invention of a pipe line gauge by Prof. S. W. Robinson, of the Department of Mechanical Engineering, Ohio State University, has changed all this, and it is now entirely feasible to determine the amount passing through a supply pipe of any size and under any pressure, by simply tapping the pipe and introducing the gauge. A full account of this instrument and of the method of using it, together with a table showing the results derived from it, is given in the succeeding chapter. Professor Robinson's previous work in this direction, in devising an easy means of determining the volume of great wells, was a most important contribution to the natural gas interests of the country. It was the first, and is the only system made public, by which any thing better than guesses can be given as to the capacity of gas wells. Its foundation on the mathematical and physical side is secure, and its validity has never been questioned by any competent authority. The sapient critics who complain that the tables contain such numbers as 1,578,150 cubic feet for the production of a well, and shrewdly inquire how anybody can be sure as to the 150 feet in the last three places, are not included under the head named in the preceding sentence as competent authority. They would find the same trouble with all sorts of tables which grow out of established formulas, and their objections it belongs to the district school-teacher to overcome. But the present contribution to the natural gas interests of the country is far more important than the first, because more directly connected with practical interests. It puts it into the power of the company or municipal corporation to apportion its charges intelligently and justly among its consumers, large and small, and this power no natural gas company has heretofore enjoyed. When such a company undertakes the supply of a manufacturing concern requiring large amounts of gas, the effort is made to learn the amount of coal that has heretofore been used by the factory. The true answer to this question it is not always easy to obtain. But supposing the gas company learns the exact amount of coal required to do the work of the factory, can it proceed from this basis to fix a proper price for the gas which displaces it ? The municipal regulation often comes in to aid in settling the question, by an ordinance forbidding the company to charge more than three-fourths of the price of the coal displaced; but without this decision from the outside, can the company translate the tons of coal into terms of gas measurement so as to do justice to all interests ? It can not. No man knows what number of cubic feet of gas are equivalent to a ton of coal for a specified purpose and used in some particular way. It may be asked, with surprise, whether we do not know the equivalent of a ton of Pittsburgh coal, for example, in Trenton limestone gas. We know the theoretical but not the practical equivalent. The figures deduced from such measurements as have been made, range from 14,000 to 30,000 cubic feet as the equivalent. For many purposes 25,000 feet will be found nearly an equivalent, and this is probably the best general figure that can be assumed. In a pumping station in Ohio, a careful measurement showed that 25,066 feet were required to do the work of one ton of coal. In other cases 28,000 cubic feet have been found to be the approximate equivalent, and, as before observed, the equivalent falls as low in some cases as 14,000 cubic feet.

Justice to all interests requires, of course, that all consumers should pay for the gas which they respectively use at the same rate, some allowance being made, as is proper, for the decreased expense of distribution to large consumers. A price per thousand feet should be given on which all could count. But to establish rates on such a basis measurements must be practicable; or, in other words, a meter or a gauge must be employed. The meter is not forthcoming, at least in practicable shape and within practicable limits of cost. A gauge is, however, at our hands. It is simple in construction, inexpensive, and applicable to every purpose. In cases where the use of the pipe line is constant, one observation answers for a day or a month. Where the use varies, observations must be made for its several stages. It has been in hand too short a time to afford a large series of facts as to the amounts of gas used under steam boilers; but such facts as have been obtained show an extremely wide range, even in the same general line of work. These discordant records serve to set in clear light the careless and unscientific way in which fuel is commonly used for the generation of power. Under the most approved method of consumption it is stated, on good authority, that a 20-horse-power boiler can be run on 1,000 feet of Trenton limestone gas per hour. Results corresponding to this in efficiency are very rare. The results of the measurement of gas used in three flouring mills are at hand. In the first, the number of feet of gas required per barrel is given as a little less than 1,000 (960). In a second mill the rate was found to be 1,640 feet to the barrel. In a third, the rate was found to be 2,500 feet to the barrel. In the first mill the best system of combustion was in force. The rate of several of the gas companies to flouring mills is four cents per barrel.

A boiler rated at 70-horse-power was found to be using 4,920 feet per hour. Another of about the same rating was found to be using 4,620 per hour. A third set of boilers, rated at 120-horse-power, was using 11,370 feet per hour. By some companies about fifty feet per hour are counted to 1-horse-power. By others about eighty feet are counted to 1-horse-power. Six pounds of coal are thought to be equal to the same power. Facts like these show that the precious stock of volatile fuel, that we have lately acquired, is being wantonly reduced by a very wasteful system of use, in which two or three feet are taken to do the work of one.

The strawboard works of the several towns in which they are supplied with gaseous fuel are very large consumers.

(2) *Fuel Proper.*—Under this head by far the largest consumption of natural gas in the country is to be found. A part of this use is allowable, at least with qualifications and under protest; a large part is wholly indefensible. It is little less than vandalism to turn this superfine fuel, in amounts aggregating many millions of feet every day, to the commonest uses of fuel; as, for example, the burning of common brick or draining tile, or in calcining common limestone, or to be consumed in an iron mill. For such use no adequate justification exists. Neither cupidity nor stupidity should be allowed to work out these evil results. If the State were wise enough and were armed with proper power, it would surely forbid such an abuse of its priceless resources.

GLASS MANUFACTURE.

Among the industries to which natural gas is applied on the large scale as fuel, there is one to which its adaptation is so happy, and in which it brings about such valuable and important results, that if any such consumption is to be tolerated at all, it should be in this case. This industry is glass manufacture. A fuel that can be applied in steady force and in unvarying amount, that is possessed of enormous heating power, in the combustion of which neither smoke nor ashes ever appear, and the introduction of which releases a considerable body of the least desirable labor employed in the factory, is easily recognized as the ideal of the glass-maker; and as soon as it was possible to make use of it any where in this way, such a use became almost a necessity to the entire interest. For fuel of this character, the manufacture could well afford to have paid a considerable advance on the price of the coal which it displaces. In fact, if he paid only the price of the coal displaced, he would receive a notable advantage from its introduction—an advantage that would seriously threaten his competitors. But what shall be said of the conditions of the manufacture when it is remembered that this new fuel was supplied at first for much less than the displaced coal would cost, and that shortly afterwards, on the discovery of the new gas fields of Ohio and Indiana, not only was it offered absolutely free, or at a merely nominal price for a term of years, but that large benefactions in the shape of lands, buildings, and sometimes cash subscriptions, awaited any manufacturer who would remove his plant to the Western fields or build a new plant there.

It is easy to see that these new conditions must have been revolutionary in their effect upon the business at large. There are now more than 700 glass pots in parts of Ohio and Indiana where four years ago not a factory had ever been thought of. A full half of the table ware and pressed glassware of the country is now manufactured in the new gas fields.

Among these interests are included the largest single plate glass works of the United States, which commands the product of seventy glass pots, and also one establishment which sends out as fine cut-glass as this country has ever produced.

The glass manufacture of the country ought not to have been subjected to such hard terms as those described above. Before natural gas was applied to this use, this interest was in a sound and healthful state. As such industries always tend to do, it had established a number of centers of production. The prominent ones for the Mississippi Valley were in western Pennsylvania, in eastern Ohio, and in West Virginia. Those of Pittsburgh were among the first to obtain the new fuel, and they maintain it still, though on a tenure that is growing more precarious every year. The supply for the other districts named has been interrupted and unsatisfactory at the best, and has finally given out altogether, or at least has been reduced to such small proportions that it can no longer be depended upon. It is from these last districts that the main draft has been made in the building up of this industry in the new fields. Many of the old factories are struggling to maintain themselves until the storm of free gas shall pass by. Some have been transferred bodily to the new fields; but in many cases the younger members of the firms, and sometimes the glass-workers themselves have taken part in the foundation of the newly established factories. In part of the instances, the municipal corporations of the towns that have found access to the gas, and in other cases, private companies from the gas districts have made the offer of free gas, which the eastern manufacturers have found it impossible to resist. In Ohio, municipal corporations have led the way; in Indiana, private companies, whose interests were based on real estate which a glass factory would bring into market, have taken the lead. The results of these solicitations have been already stated in general terms, i. e., in the establishment of 700 new glass pots in these gas fields.

Neither towns nor companies knew what they were offering when they lavished free fuel upon the glass makers. They had come into possession of a surprising fortune in this fuel that flowed forth from the earth from what seemed to be inexhaustible fountains. To persuade manufacturers to avail themselves of this wonderful supply would be doing a double service. It would build up the towns, adding value to every interest, and it would make the manufacturers themselves rich. As has been shown in a preceding chapter, Findlay alone has secured the building of more than 200 glass pots, distributed through a dozen factories. Since these were first brought into operation they have made, by themselves, a very severe draft upon the gas resources of the town, and it is

UTILIZATION OF GAS. 269

plain to all that the supply which they require can not be indefinitely maintained.

It is vain to point out a more excellent way that might have been pursued—but suppose, for a moment, instead of this demoralizing offer of free gas and the accompanying grants and benefactions, the glass manufacturers had been assured that they could secure fuel in the new gas fields at the price of coal, the gas to be supplied by measure, as coal is paid for by weight. While Findlay would not have gained half the number of factories, she could have assured this half a far longer lease of life with all the incidental advantages of such a continuance, and this policy would have wrought much less hardship and loss in the old glass manufacture, and possibly less in the end to the new companies. Such speculations are vain. The facts, including especially the human nature involved, being what they are, it was necessary that what has happened should happen. Still, we must be allowed for a moment to deplore the short-sighted and foolish policy that has resulted in such an extravagant and wasteful use of these new resources.

How much gas does a glass factory consume in a day? Up to the present time no answer to this question has been made public. It is probable that the great gas companies have reached some approximation, based either on actual measurement by meter, or on some translation of the coal used in the furnace into cubic feet of gas. But whatever figures have been reached have been counted private property and have not been turned over to the general service. Certainly not a glass company nor a gas company in Ohio, up to three months ago, had any definite opinion, not to say knowledge, on the subject. The only exceptions to this statement that have been met are the following, viz.: A report obtained from one person, that a ten-pot glass works required for the melting alone, the gas being consumed in the most economical way, 288,000 cubic feet per day; and, secondly, an estimate made by a glass company in its negotiations with a village council, that a ten-pot window glass factory would not exceed 300,000 feet per day in its use. The amount of coal used could, of course, be easily determined. Forty bushels per day is, by a current figure, counted a sufficient supply for each pot of a window glass works, and twenty-eight bushels for each pot of a flint glass works. In this calculation Pittsburgh coal is taken as the standard.

Furthermore, no distinction is made by the gas companies, as a rule, between window glass and table ware factories. A glass pot is counted a glass pot, whatever its capacity or use. The Robinson pipe line gauge has put an end to this state of ignorance and indifference as to gas consumption in connection with this manufacture. It has now been applied to thirteen of the principal glass factories of northwestern Ohio, and while the results are in some respects surprising, and especially because of the large amount of gas that they show is being used, they are entirely consistent with each other. Besides the complete tests already named, tests of partial use have been made in many other instances, the figures derived from which agree with those of the complete tests. The tests were made on factories of different numbers of pots, with supply pipes of different diameters and under different pressures. It is obvious, therefore, that the glass pot is the only unit of measure that can be adopted in this report.

Furthermore, the tests were made alike on window glass and flint glass or table ware houses, including also bottle works and chimney works as well. The manufacturers, as indicated in a preceding paragraph, are well aware of a considerable difference in the fuel consumed by window glass houses and flint glass houses, but the gas companies, as a rule, make the same charge for both. The window glass houses, however, use about forty per cent. more gas than the flint glass works. The same difference, it will be observed, obtains in the use of coal. Some of these tests were repeated several times; in a single case, the entire consumption of a factory was observed and averaged for thirty days. All the fuel use of the establishment, it will be observed, is included under this head, such as flattening ovens, glory holes, layers, pot arches, and steam power. While these tests were being made, the figures obtained from the tables were given out to the manufacturers and gas companies interested, *subject to revision*. Further work done during the publication of the present volume has introduced an important correction which is now applied for the first time. The results given in the following tables are considerably less than the figures to which partial currency has been given in the way indicated above. The earlier figures have also been used in the preceding portions of this report and particularly on pages 121, 152, 188 and 192. All of these must be reduced by about 12 per cent. to agree with the facts as shown by Professor Robinson's latest investigations. The tables used are entirely reliable, but corrections must be applied for the several elements involved in the measurements.

A window glass works divides the day into three stages of unequal length, viz., melting, blowing and blocked furnace. Each of these stages has to be separately tested, and calculations must be made for its duration. The bottle glass works agree in the main with the window glass factories, while the lamp and chimney works come under the same head as the flint glass factories. Five window glass and bottle works were gauged through the several stages of their daily run, with the following results:

UTILIZATION OF GAS. 271

1. 58,800 cubic feet per pot for twenty-four hours.
2. 60,000   "   "   "   "
3. 61,200   "   "   "   "
4. 61,360   "   "   "   "
5. 60,270   "   "   "   " (Bottle works.)

The figures given in No. 4 show the average of a thirty days' run of a ten-pot window glass factory. This last result is, of course, the most valuable. The close agreement in these measurements will not escape notice. The facts that the number of pots in the list of glass furnaces measured ranges from eight to eighteen, that the supply pipes varied in size, being respectively four, five and six inches in diameter, and that the pressure in the lines ranges from sixteen to sixty ounces, render it clear that the gauge in use in all these determinations must be able to fasten with accuracy upon the essential elements. It may, therefore, be counted established that every window glass pot in the new glass centers of northern Ohio is using 60,000 cubic feet in twenty-four hours, its proportion of the general service of the works being counted in. This is far in excess of the estimates based on the use of coal. As already observed, forty bushels of coal per pot are held to be enough to run a window glass works twenty-four hours. From this it might be expected, according to one of the most commonly accepted scale of equivalents, that 40,000 feet of gas would suffice for a day's run per pot. But whether from lavish use or from other causes, about fifty per cent. additional is actually used. There can, however, be but little doubt that if the glass manufacturers were required to pay five or six cents per thousand feet by meter or gauge, a large economy would at once be effected.

Coming to the flint glass manufacture, we find the following results, the tests being made on factories in which the number of pots ranged from eight to forty-five:

1. { 31,230 cubic feet per pot for twenty-four hours.
   { 39,270   "   "   "   "
2.   37,430   "   "   "   "
3.   38,470   "   "   "   "
4.   40,530   "   "   "   "
5.   41,230   "   "   "   "
6.   41,370   "   "   "   "
7. { 44,450   "   "   "   "
   { 49,875   "   "   "   "
8.   50,100   "   "   "   "

The disparity in these results will attract attention at once. In explanation it can be said that some works were being run to their full capacity when the tests were made, while others were not. Two separate measures are given for each of two factories. These measurements were taken on different days, or on different parts of the same day, and perhaps show the range of consumption.

The figures go to show that the flint glass works in the Ohio field use 35,000 to 45,000 cubic feet of gas per day, the use covering glory holes, layers, pot-arches and boiler power, as before noted. It will not be far amiss to count the amount used 40,000 feet per pot for twenty-four hours.

According to the measurements given above, a window glass pot consumes 60,000 cubic feet of gas in a day, 1,800,000 feet in a month, and 18,000,000 feet in a working year (ten months). A flint glass pot, on the other hand, consumes 40,000 feet in a day, 1,200,000 feet in a month, and 12,000,000 feet in a year (ten months). At the rate of one cent per thousand feet of gas, every window glass pot should pay $18 per month, and a flint glass pot, $12 per month. The highest rate charged by the municipal gas plants of Ohio is $20 *per annum*. In other words, these corporations receive $20 for 18,000,000 feet of gas, if a window glass pot is paid for. This is at the rate of one mill for a thousand feet of gas. The price of Pittsburgh coal, translated into these figures would be somewhere between two and five cents per ton. Fostoria is now advancing its rates from $20 a pot *per annum* to $40. When the advance is made she will be receiving two mills for each thousand feet of gas used in the window glass works in the place, and three mills for the gas used in the flint glass factories. The Toledo glass factories pay the highest rate established in Ohio, viz., $30 per pot *per month*. This rate gives about one and three-fourths cents for the gas used in window glass. The flint glass works use the gas with economy, and thus pay a higher rate for what they use. The Pittsburgh rate is $60 per pot per month. This establishes a rate of three and one-half and five cents respectively for window and flint glass houses, supposing Pittsburgh gas to be used as lavishly as that of the new fields. Raising the price of gas does not lead to economy in its use unless meters are introduced at the same time. It is the vicious system of selling it by the mixer, or the glass pot, or by lump contracts generally, that is responsible for the monstrous waste that is in progress.

The number of glass pots in northwestern Ohio can be approximately counted at the present time as 500. The reason why the exact number can not be given is that several tanks are to be taken into account, and their equivalent in pots is not absolutely fixed. Of the entire number, about 164 belong to window glass works, and 320 are devoted to table ware and lamps and chimneys. On the basis named above the window glass pots require 9,840,000 cubic feet of gas daily, and the flint glass pots require 12,800,000 feet daily. The total daily consumption is thus seen to be 22,640,000, and the annual consumption (300 days) would be expressed by the figures 6,720,000,000 feet, an amount sufficient to meet the entire fuel demands of a population of 100,000 people for a year.

The glass manufacture of northwestern Ohio at the present time is giving profitable employment to a large number of people. A considerable part of the labor employed is skilled laber and commands large wages. The advantages derived from the use of this large amount of gas that is shown in the above calculations, are distributed widely through the communities in which the work is going forward. While much the largest use of gas as fuel is to be charged to the account of glass making, there is certainly more to be said in favor of it, than for any other of the industries that make these large demands. So valuable has it become to the towns that have doubled or trebled their population within five years because of it, that every effort should be made to economize and thus lengthen the supply. It would be a serious calamity to northern Ohio if its infant industries should be transplanted to other fields because of the premature exhaustion of its gas supply.

IRON AND CLAY WORKING.

The group of industries to which we now come are to be regarded with much less favor in their relations to natural gas than the glass manufacture already described. There is, in fact, very little to be said in behalf of supplying iron and clay-working industries with the new fuel, beyond the incontrovertible fact that it is wonderfully convenient for the manufacturers and laborers, and the additional fact that the manufacturers are often willing to pay the current prices for it. But the amounts of gas used in these lines of manufacture are so large, and the work to which they apply it is for the most part so coarse and common, that it is contrary to the public interest to allow them to use it at any price. Its introduction into iron manufacture is decidedly the worst mistake that has been made in its application thus far. It is true that this was the first kind of manufacturing enterprise to which it was applied, but a year or two of its exhaustive demands ought to have been enough to satisfy any candid observer that there is not enough of it and that it is too good for work of this grade. Its application to iron and clay working, and especially the former, in any community simply means the cutting in two of the duration of the supply, or perhaps even a greater reduction than this. No field has been found as yet, and none will be found, that can endure the draft of a well-expanded iron manufacture for a half dozen years. The Murryville district is perhaps the most prolific gas territory yet discovered by the drill. Its resources have proved truly astonishing, but six years have been sufficient to bring it to the verge of exhaustion. The rock pressure has fallen to less than 25 per cent. of what it originally was, and it is only by means of pipe lines of a size unheard of before, and in some cases of gas pumps located upon the lines, that the remnants of the gas of this great field are now reaching the market.

Iron Mills.—It is fortunate for the Ohio field that iron industries are more complicated, and are moved with less facility than glass manufactures. While the latter have been established in strong force in the new gas fields, comparatively few iron mills have been here built up. A large rolling mill in Toledo that was in operation before gas was discovered in northern Ohio, was unfortunately taken on its lines by the Northwestern Ohio Gas Company at an early date. At this time the company apparently did not appreciate the drain which this enormous and steady use would make upon its resources. It is probable that the mill has used nearly one-half of the gas brought to the city limits by one of its main lines. The difference in service between this half and the other half, which is distributed through the households of the city and used in the production of steam power and small manufactures there, is immense. In the one case, a few less laborers would be employed by the burning of natural gas, a result not in itself especially desirable; and, secondly, those that are employed would find their work considerably lightened, a worthy result if not bought at too great cost; and, in the third place, the owners would obtain the advantage of the finest fuel of the world far below its cost. In this last result, there is no service that should specially recommend it. The iron mill was here before gas was known, and it will remain when gas is gone.

On the other hand, when applied to household use, the same amount of gas would lighten the labors, and add greatly to the comfort of many thousands of people.

Findlay has two rolling mills, a wire nail works and some smaller iron working industries dependent upon its gas lines. The first important manufacturing plant brought into the town after gas was discovered here was the Briggs works. It has had from the first practically free gas. It has expanded with the growth of the town until the tool works with which it began is but a small part of the present plant. To this original enterprise there has been added, from time to time, a twenty-inch mill, a ten-inch mill and a chain works. The Wetherell mill was built four years ago, but it has not been in steady operation. During the present season it has been running with moderate force.

Measurements of the amount of gas consumed by the first named of these establishments have been made and repeated. The amount is necessarily large. There are sixteen puddling furnaces in connection with the 20-inch mill, also one heating furnace and a battery of boilers. At one test fourteen furnaces were found running; at another test but ten. At the first rate 216,300 feet were being used each hour. At the second rate 168,000 feet were being used each hour. Counting twenty hours as the average daily duty of the mill, and the last named rate as certainly within the average consumption, this branch of the works is seen to be using at least 3,360,000 cubic feet of gas per day. The remainder of the work as determined by a single measurement, will add to this consumption 599,200 feet for ten hours' duty, making the total consumption, at the lowest figure that can be accepted, 3,960,000 cubic feet per day. The average will undoubtedly be more likely to exceed 4,000,000 feet than to fall below this figure. For this amount of fuel, the company has paid the city something like $200 *per annum.*

The consumption of the Wetherell mill was found to be, by a single set of measurements, about 962,500 feet per day. The amount of gas used in these two mills would supply 125 table-ware glass pots. It is obvious that the latter use would furnish employment to a much larger number of laborers of various grades than the iron mills do, and would therefore be considerably more advantageous to the town. Such considerations do not appear to have entered the minds of the gas trustees. They have given gas to those who asked it and from those who would borrow it they have never turned away. If their purpose had been to get rid of the wonderful fuel as soon as possible, they would not have needed to pursue a very different policy from that which they have followed.

Clay Working.—There is one branch of clay working, that, viz., of the manufacture of pressed brick of high grade, that has a right to natural gas in its manufacturing business, based on the value of its product. Findlay and North Baltimore are both manufacturing brick of a class that commands in the markets $20 per thousand. The gas used in burning them has a respectable field for its operations, since the product can well sustain a proper price for the gas. Natural gas is also employed in Columbus in the manufacture of the Hallwood Paving Block, a brick of high grade, and for the gas employed a fair price is paid. Its adaptation to this line of work is simply admirable.

There is another use of gas, however, in the same general line that is wholly indefensible, and that ought in every case to be instantly arrested. In Findlay, Fostoria, Tiffin and North Baltimore gas is being used in the large way for burning the commonest of bricks for the commonest of uses. There are in Findlay three brick yards dependent upon the city lines, and two large establishments that are making brick by the use of gas from their own wells. Their aggregate production reaches many million brick each year. The products of these yards are sold at prices not exceeding $4 per thousand. The charges for the gas used by the companies so far have had no relation to the fuel consumed. They are as follows: For brick burned in open kilns, twenty-five cents per thousand and for brick burned in closed kilns, twenty cents per thousand.

Fostoria has three brick yards and a draining-tile works actively engaged in the manufacture of the ordinary products. The capacity of one of the brick yards is 2,000,000 brick per year. The city has heretofore charged these companies for the gas used in burning, fifteen cents per thousand, and for the gas used in the tile furnaces, $8 per kiln. The rate is thought to be about the same as fifty cents per ton for coal.

Tiffin has three brick yards of large capacity depending upon the city lines. One of them turned out 4,000,000 brick last year. In addition, one yard carried seven draining-tile kilns. For the gas used, the manufacturers have paid fifty cents per thousand for marketable brick. The price of the latter at no time exceeds $4. The seven tile kilns named above pay $50 monthly.

The fluctuating use of gas in brick manufacture renders gauge measurements unsatisfactory unless many observations are made. A series of determinations by the anemometer, which of course are subject to the same objections as a gauge, taken in 1889, indicates that a single yard was using at least 250,000 feet of gas per day; and, further, that to burn a thousand brick, about 7,500 cubic feet of gas were required, no account being made of the gas used in the steam power employed in the preparation of the material. During the season in which the works are driven to their full capacity, not less than 1,000,000 feet of gas per day has been called into requisition for this unworthy application in Tiffin alone. Comparison with the wood displaced in the brick yards seems to indicate that for this particular use, 30,000 feet of gas are the equivalent of one ton of hard wood. In the Pittsburgh district, the price of gas for burning brick is at the present time $1.30 per thousand in the summer, and $1.75 in the winter, and the kilns must in every case be enclosed.

Lime Burning.—This is another of the uses of gas that is wholly unjustifiable and which should no longer be tolerated. Bowling Green led in this manufacture in Ohio. Fostoria followed early, as also did Findlay, Fremont and Gibsonburg. More recently Sandusky and Columbus have applied gas to the same poor use.

For this lavish and unworthy use of the new found fuel, the municipal corporations of the several towns that have obtained access to the gas fields are chiefly responsible. Much of the disastrous drain upon the fields which they have caused is due to their ignorance of the nature of the gas supply. But even when they have become better instructed than they were at first, they have found themselves unable to resist the demands of the brick manufacturers and the lime burners and the iron workers, who bore a part of the public burden of introducing gas into the

UTILIZATION OF GAS. 277

town and who have no other way of drawing advantage from their portion of the expenditure than by turning the gas to the uses here complained of. But in yielding to these demands, they have given to these coarse industries an amount of this priceless fuel vastly in excess of any legitimate claims that they could urge; and in so doing they have inflicted irreparable injury upon the great body of the tax-payers, whose main common interest is in the maintenance of the supply of fuel for household use as long as possible. These corporations have given away this limited and measured store almost without money and without price. The manufacturing interests of Findlay, it is estimated, consume 80 per cent. of the gas brought into the town. They pay less than one-tenth of the entire revenue of the field. A brick maker turns out from his kilns 4,000,000 brick in a season, for example, and consumes in burning them thirty or forty million feet of gas. He obtains the gas for a fifth or a tenth of what the equivalent wood or coal would cost him. But what advantage is it to the bulk of the population that the brick maker has got his fuel for little or nothing? He has shortened the total enjoyment of gaseous fuel by months in so doing, but beyond a small reduction in the price of brick for those who chance to be making use of it, he, has brought no corresponding return whatever to the community.

What adequate return, for example, has been made, or could be made to the people of Findlay, taken as a whole, by an iron mill which has depleted the common store of fuel to the amount of at least 5,000,000,000 cubic feet during the last four years? What justice is there in giving away this vast amount of stored power, equal in volume to 200,000 tons of Pittsburgh coal, to one manufacturer? The tax payers of the town are already paying a heavy burden in keeping up their gas supply, and when the supply shall have failed, it seems probable that they will still have a half million dollars of debt to meet, incurred solely on the account of supplying free gas to manufacturers.

The great gas companies have not sinned in this way. They have understood the nature and value of the gas supply from the beginning, and their constant aim and purpose has been to convert the gas into gold. In this they must have been successful to a high degree. The business can scarcely be other than extraordinarily lucrative when a great city is reached by a pipe line that draws its gas from prolific territory. But while intent on making money, their policy has tended to the common good in this respect, that they have been disposed to save the gas mainly for household use. This is the use that at once serves the community best and pays the gas companies best.

Why can not the municipal gas boards learn from the experience that has accumulated in this field? For the wasteful policy that they have thus far maintained they are not altogether to blame, for there has been up to this time no known mode for determining in an inexpensive way the actual consumption of gas in the various industries that they have undertaken to supply. Happily this problem has now been solved, and every gas board can learn by a small amount of trouble how much gas it is bringing into the town by its lines, and also the several principal uses to which it is devoted. What remains for these boards is to make these measurements and then place a proper price upon the gas that they are introducing, and, furthermore, to establish as far as their obligations will allow uniform rates for all consumers. Above all they need to disown and repudiate, as far as they are able, the unfortunate and demoralizing policy of supplying free gas to manufacturers. It is best for the manufacturers, it is best for the several industries which they represent, and it is best for the towns, that all shall pay their own bills.

SUMMARY.

Some of the conclusions to which the facts and discussions herewith presented would lead us may be summarized as follows:

(1) Natural gas finds its highest and most valuable use as domestic fuel. It is here that it does the greatest good to the greatest number. In all our dealings with it, this fact should be kept constantly in view. To maintain it for the longest period for this service is our highest interest in relation to it.

(2) If there is any use for which gas should be sold below the price of the fuel which it supplants, it is its use in cooking stoves. The less fortunate members of the communities should be the favored ones in this regard. For the gas used in heating there is no occasion to mark the price below the cost of coal; neither is there any justifiable demand for a discount on gas bills increasing according to the number of fires supplied. If a sliding scale is introduced it might, perhaps, better be made to slide the other way, charging consumption beyond the average at a higher rate.

(3) An advance in price on the part of all municipal corporations for all the uses that they undertake to supply, is their proper policy. The price at which they have furnished it hitherto leads to undervaluing and wasting the gas. The supply will do the towns more good by serving them longer, if they are required to pay a higher price for the gas.

(4) All gas should be sold by measured volume. Meters and gauges ought to be introduced every-where. No adequate motive to economy can be brought to bear on many consumers until they are obliged to pay at a proper rate for what they use.

(5) Next to domestic use, the use of gas in the production of steam power is to be counted the most suitable application of it. Comparatively small amounts of it are required for this purpose, and great convenience and economy result therefrom. The most skillful use of it will find a rate of fifty feet to 1-horse-power sufficient, but a use of more than eighty feet to 1-horse-power should not be allowed, even if the user is willing to pay for it.

(6) Of the various manufacturing uses in which the gas is applied as fuel proper, glass-making has probably the best rights. It contributes larger returns to the community in the shape of wages than other like industries. While its introduction into northern Ohio has been greatly overdone, and while much of it has been accomplished by the exercise of a mistaken policy, it should be maintained as long as possible. To this end economy should be every-where enforced. The window glass works might, perhaps, be required to introduce coal into their furnaces for melting, at an early day, reserving gas for the stages of blowing and flattening.

(7) From certain uses to which gas is now largely applied it should be at once entirely withdrawn. It is a great wrong to the community to allow it to be used in burning common building brick and in calcining limestone. These processes consume large quantities of gas and make no returns except to their owners. For these uses wood and coal are good enough.

The industry that consumes gas in by far the largest amount is iron working. It is a grievous mistake on the part of any community or company to allow a rolling-mill access to its gas field. An ordinary mill uses as much gas every day as several thousands of families would consume, and the returns to the common good by such an application are small compared with any other ways of using the gas. Even though a rolling-mill stands ready to pay as much per thousand feet as the small consumers pay it ought not to be supplied. If it is willing to do this it shows that there is not enough charged for the gas. It may be to the interest of the gas company to get its money back rapidly, it is true, but the community has interests, if not rights as well, that should not be overlooked in relation to this supply. The State interferes when an oil well is left without being plugged, or when a gas well is allowed to blow into the air without use. Why? Because these precious stocks of mobile power are fitted to do good to great numbers of the people and no man has a right to take any action by which they shall be needlessly wasted. A like reason could, perhaps, be found for forbidding entirely the use of gas for the rough work that has been named above.

(8) If economy is every-where insisted on and practiced, the last days of natural gas in Ohio may be its best days. If, on the other hand,

the wasteful policy that is now so largely in force should be maintained, there is sure to be, and at no very distant day, great disappointment and reaction in the communities that have obtained it and that have been stimulated by its acquisition to what may prove an unhealthful activity.

(9) Natural gas is merely a transient phase of the stored power of the earth. It is folly to talk of its taking anything like a permanent place in the work of the world. The claim that it can do so springs only from enthusiasm or sciolism. There is, in reality, but little of it, and this little is found in but very limited regions and can not last long whenever its utilization is undertaken by the eager and masterful activities of our day.

(10) Natural gas has a very important work to do. It should prepare the world for something much better than itself. It is giving an object lesson to great communities as to the advantage of gaseous fuel, and it can hardly be that this lesson will be given in vain. The exemption from the soot and dust inseparable from the burning of bituminous coal in our cities and the positive addition that gaseous fuel makes to the comfort and convenience of the entire community when used. as domestic fuel and as a source of steam power, are results in themselves too valuable to be abandoned when these small and treacherous stocks of buried power are exhausted. The conversion of the coal now burned in a large city into gas before being used would result in an immense economy in fuel, besides affording the incidental advantages alluded to above, and this economy of stored power is an object to which the civilized world will soon be obliged to address itself in good earnest.

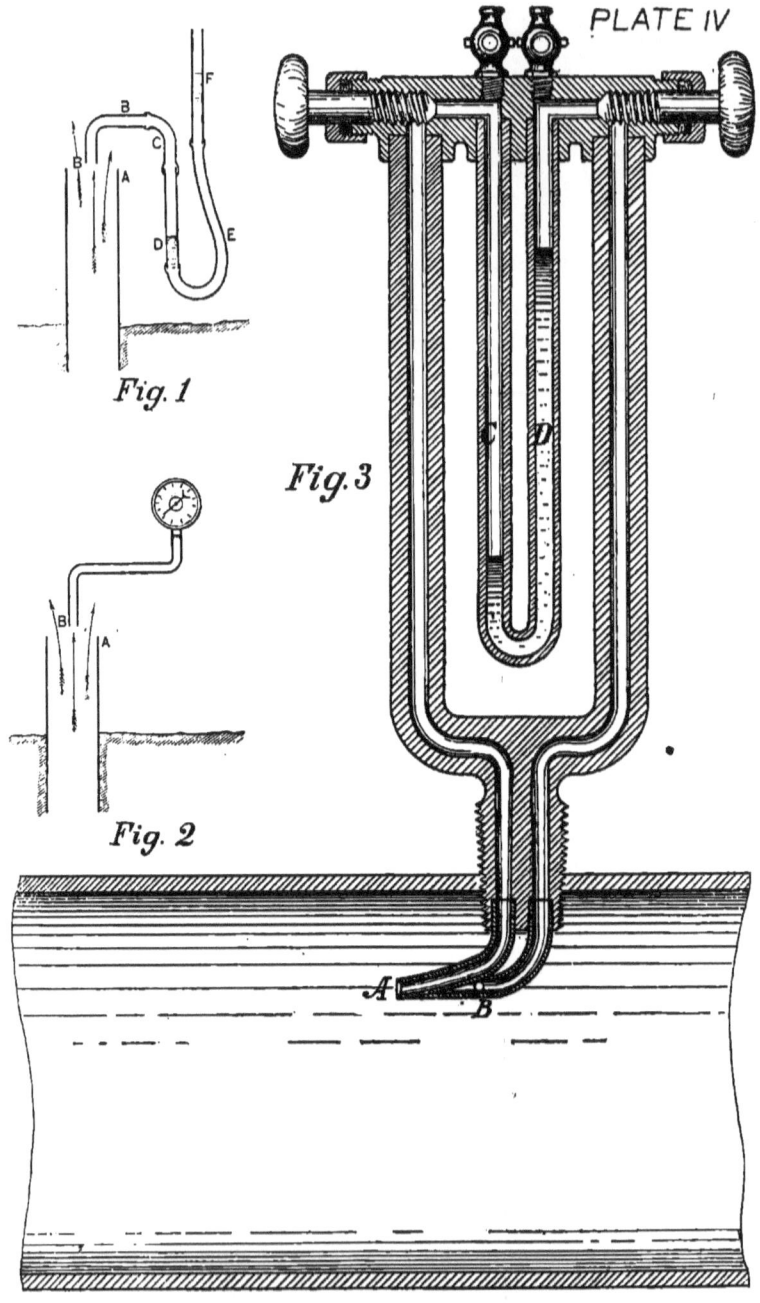

CHAPTER VII.

THE MEASUREMENT OF NATURAL GAS,

INCLUDING GAS WELLS, PIPE LINES, SERVICE PIPES, ETC.

BY S. W. ROBINSON, C. E.

PROFESSOR OF MECHANICAL ENGINEERING, OHIO STATE UNIVERSITY.

The object of the present chapter is to set forth a new method of determining the production of gas wells and the amount of gas carried by pipe lines. It will involve a description of the instrument employed, a discussion of the principles involved and a presentation in the most convenient form for practical use, of the rules and tables by which the system is applied.

I. THE PITOT TUBE GAUGE.

This instrument is called the *Pitot Tube Gauge* from its inventor, Pitot, and is equally remarkable for its simplicity and accuracy of results. It is applicable only for measurement while the fluid measured is in motion, as for gas, air, water, flowing in pipes, orifices, rivers, wind currents, etc.; in short, all cases of fluid streams, and the principle is that the instrument gives the velocity of the current at the point of its application which velocity, multiplied by the sectional area of the stream, gives the volume of flow.

This is a perfect instrument, if we may call one perfect when its practical results agree with the theoretical ones, while at the same time the instrument itself may be either fine or rude in construction.

Elaborate experiments have been made to determine the co-efficient of reduction or multiplying factor by which to reduce the measured velocities to the actual ones, and always for water, air or gas with the result, 1. for multiplier. On this point see *Van Nostrand's Eng. Mag.*, Vol. XXXV "*Measurement of Gas Wells;*" Vol. VI, Ohio Geological Report; and *Morin's*

Hydraulique, p. 136. Several careful comparisons of measurement of this instrument with the Westinghouse Meter and with pipe line measurements have shown results varying within a small per cent.

FORMS OF THE INSTRUMENT.

1st. *Stream with free exit.* Figures. 1 and 2, Plate 4, are given to illustrate the simplest forms of the instrument as used at the gas well mouth, or at the exit mouth of any pipe, or in fact any discharge orifice such as an opening in the side of a tank from which the flow is free into air.

In Fig. 1, B is a tube which for convenience is bent to an angle so that its mouth end B can readily be placed as required, square in the stream of gas flowing from A. A piece of rubber tubing C connects B with a glass tube D. The opposite end of D is connected with rubber tubing E to a second glass tube F. All this tubing is open free throughout.

In using this instrument charge it with water or mercury, and hold it as shown, so that the difference of level (D F = h) can be read off. This value of h in inches is to be found in the first column of the tables when mercury charges the instrument or in the second column for water.

Fig. 2 is intended for the case where the pressure produced by the impact of the stream against the open end B is too great to be conveniently measured by water or mercury, the pressure being here measured by a pressure gauge. The size of mouth B is immaterial. In some cases the pressure in Fig. 2 has been observed as high as fifty pounds per square inch.

2d. *Stream enclosed.* In Fig. 3, Plate 4, is given the form of tip and of instrument to be used in such cases as measuring the velocity of flow at any point in a pipe line where the pressure of the flowing gas is above or even below that of the air.

This instrument has been used in pipes where the pressure was above 100 pounds per square inch without inconvenience, or detraction from accuracy of results.

In this form, Fig. 3, the tip A B is seen to have two openings, the Pitot tube mouth proper, A, the same as in Figures 1 or 2, and besides this, the lateral opening at B in the smooth uniform side of the tip. In ordinary cases of pipe lines, B may be at some distance from A, even in a separate piece of tube. But for convenience of application to pipe lines the double tip is made so that it may be screwed air-tight into a single ⅜-inch-pipe size hole. The end A B is then bent into an L of 90°, so that A may be made to face up stream to catch the current, while for B the gas moves past without increasing or diminishing the pressure in B as due to motion of gas, while yet the standing or static pressure is

THE MEASUREMENT OF NATURAL GAS. 283

transmitted into B. Thus the pressure exerted at A, when the instrument is in use on a pipe line, is equal the static pressure in the pipe plus the pressure due to impact, or to velocity of current, while at B the static pressure only is exerted. The static pressure is that which we measure by a pressure gauge placed on the pipe line. It is apparent from Fig. 3 that the pressure at A is transmitted to C, and that at B to D.

Now, to complete the instrument, a gauge in the form of a U tube of glass containing water or mercury may be placed at C D. Then the C side of the water or mercury in the U will stand lowest, and the difference of level will be the head due to velocity. This head for inches of mercury is to be found in the first column of the tables, for water in the second column, and for alcohol in the third. It will be rare if ever a higher pressure than ten inches of mercury will be observed on any pipe line or service pipe, so that it is not necessary to provide high pressure gauges for C and D.

The pressure observed in Figs. 1 and 2, or that at C, Fig. 3, in excess of that at D, is produced by the swift moving gas driving against the mouth B and being there brought to a stop. By the theory of the instrument the gas compressed into the tube B would, by being permitted to flow out again against the same surrounding pressure, attain the same velocity as that in the stream from which it was brought to rest. Not only is this realized perfectly by experiment for the pressures, but the like holds relative to temperatures

In the case of gas wells the forms of instrument, shown in Figs. 1 and 2, Plate 4, are employed, and the pressure observed is sometimes called the "open pressure."

In case of pipe lines, service pipes, etc., Fig. 3 is employed.

APPLICATION TO GAS WELLS.

VOLUME OF FLOW AT A WELL MOUTH OR AT AN ORIFICE.

This is the simple case where the static pressure of the jet or stream is that of the atmosphere, at the point of observation with the Pitot Tube Gauge, since, for this, the mouth B of the tube should be placed at the plane of the orifice A; at which point the internal pressure of the flowing gas will be that of the air into which the gas flows. The simple form of the apparatus is then all that is required, as shown in Figs. 1 and 2, consisting of a single mouth-opening, at the end of a pipe, presented square with the jet, and connected air tight with the pressure gauge or manometer. The size of the openings A and B Figs. 1, 2 or 3, is immaterial provided they are not so large as to offer obstruction to the current, and yet not so small as to become clogged by particles flowing in the current.

Then the formula giving the cubic feet of gas per day of twenty-four hours of uniform flow (See Ohio Geological Report, Vol. VI, p. 560–580) is

$$V = 1462250 d^2 \left\{ \left(\frac{p. + 14.6}{14.6} \right)^{0.29} - 1 \right\} \quad (1)$$

Where $d =$ diameter of well mouth or of orifice in inches, and $p =$ the gauge pressure in pounds per square inch.

In using the formula, correct for temperature according to foot note to Table I, also for density sometimes considerable.

From this formula Table I was made out, pressure gauge values being found in third column.

When the water gauge is employed take, in formula (1.),

$$p = \frac{h'}{27.5}$$

In this case $h' =$ inches by water gauge, and is to be found in second column of Table I.

When the mercury gauge is employed giving h inches of mercury take, in the formula,

$$p = \frac{h''}{2.03}$$

Here $h'' =$ the inches of mercury, and is to be found in first column of table.

These formulas may be used when the experiment gives data that lie outside of Table I.

VELOCITY OF FLOW.

To find the velocity of the gas in feet per second divide the quantity discharged *per second* by the area of the orifice in square feet. To find the quantity per second divide the quantity per day by 86400.

PRECAUTION TO BE OBSERVED.

In applying the instrument, Figs. 1 or 2, to gas wells, the mouth B may be held a little down into A, in case the latter is a pipe without fittings. But sometimes a T, or a reducer, etc., perhaps including a valve, may be on the end of A. In such case the end B should be placed at several points in the open end of A, and the mean of observed results taken For instance, suppose a T be placed with its outlet horizontal, but plugged. The cavity in the fitting under the plug will cause serious eddyings and the pressure taken at any one point can not be relied upon. But with normal flow the tip should be held at about the first fourth of the diameter, and if at the center multiply by .97 to account for the so called velocity curve which for orifices is flatter than for pipes.

THE MEASUREMENT OF NATURAL GAS. 285

It would be improper in this case to insert B to such depth into A as to go below the fitting, because the fitting will modify static pressure by reason of its resistance to flow. A larger pipe than A below the fitting would have a less mean velocity than A, and yet give a higher pressure reading, except the double tip, Fig. 3, be used, which may, in fact, always be employed where the difference of pressure in C D is not too great to be measured by that gauge.

When the exit mouth is not fair, a piece of pipe three or four feet long may be screwed on, and B, Figs. 1 and 2 applied at its end, where the conditions of the stream will now be practically normal. Or if more convenient the instrument, Fig. 3, may be placed on the main pipe leading up from the gas well by tapping into that pipe in the usual way.

SERVICE CAPACITY OF GAS WELLS.

When gas flows from a gas well into free air, through a wide open mouth, the discharge will be in excess of that, as it usually flows in service into a pipe line under a back pressure of 200 or 300 pounds.

To determine the *service capacity* or am)unt of gas that would be given off under working conditions of being closed in and discharging gas into a pipe line, an outlet into free air should be made from the well by a branch pipe and valve. Then open this valve and also cut off the pipe line for the moment of experiment and train this branch pipe valve till the pressure of the well is up again to the working pressure of the well when in service, though now flowing into free air. Now apply the Pitot gauge as in Figs. 1 or 2, and make the measurement. The branch pipe in this experiment should be several feet in length to prevent abnormal eddyings, etc., and the same pipe would do for measuring the flow of well at all pressures. Or perhaps a more convenient way to measure the service flow of the well would be to put the complete gauge instrument, Fig. 3, upon the pipe leading from the well to the main pipe line. This pipe might be tapped for receiving the instrument, Fig. 3, at any time, or indeed such instrument might remain there permanently.

Wherever the instrument, Fig. 3, is applied, the pipe on the *upstream* side of the instrument should be free of fittings, bends, etc., for a distance of some fifteen or twenty diameters of pipe to insure normal conditions of flow at the tips A B.

In attempting to use Table I it often happens that the data come between values given in the table when *interpolation* must be resorted to, for accurate results.

GEOLOGY OF OHIO.

TABLE I.—CUBIC FEET OF GAS DISCHARGED BY GAS-WELL PER DAY.

Cubic Feet of Gas Reckoned at 32° F., Discharged by Well per Day of 24 Hours of Continuous Uniform Flow, by Pitot Tube Measurement; the Specific Gravity of the Gas being here taken at 0.6,* (Air = 1.); and the Temperature of the Flowing Gas at Well-mouth being taken at 32° F.

Cubic Feet per Day Reckoned at 32° F., given by this Table may be Regarded as a Quantity of Gas in a Gas Holder at the Temperature of 32° F., for the "Temperature of Storage." For 50° Temperature of Storage, and for other Temperature of Flowing Gas, Correct the Cubic Feet of Gas Obtained from this Table by Aid of Note at Bottom of Table.

Observed pressure by mercury gauge.	Observed pressure by water gauge, as in fig. 1.	Observed pressure by pressure-gauge, as in fig. 2.	1 inch.	1½ inches.	2 inches.	2½ inches.	3 inches.	3½ inches.	4 inches.	4½ inches.	5 inches.	5½ inches.	6 inches.
	Inches.	Lbs per sq. in											
	.1	.0036	12,390	27,860	49,556	77,440	111,516	151,780	198,220	250,890	309,750	393,000	446,040
	.2	.0073	17,560	39,510	70,260	109,740	158,040	215,110	281,040	355,290	439,000	555,9,0	632,160
	.3	.0109	21,480	48,530	85,940	134,250	193,3,0	263,130	343,760	431,970	537,000	679,630	773,260
	.5	.0182	27,720	62,570	110,840	173,250	249,480	329,570	443,520	561,330	693,000	877,000	997,9,10
	.7	.1251	32,820	73,840	131,269	205,100	285,3-9	402,910	525,650	664,610	820,400	1,038,400	1,18,520
	1.0	.0364	39,210	88,281	156,830	243,100	35.2,880	489,450	637,310	794,030	940,400	1,240,700	1,411,600
	1.5	.0545	48,030	108,070	192,120	300,260	432,270	588,400	764,840	972,660	1,200,840	1,511,900	1,729,100
	.22	.0727	55,340	124,520	221,360	345,900	498,960	677,950	885,410	1,120,660	1,383,600	1,751,000	1,982,200
	3.0	.109	67,910	152,810	271,680	421,500	611,100	832,730	1,096,510	1,375,200	1,698,000	2,148,840	2,444,860
	4.0	.145	78,410	176,420	313,660	490,310	705,650	960,660	1,254,650	1,587,800	1,960,400	2,464,800	2,822,800
	5.0	.182	87,610	197,260	350,670	548,4,0	789,030	1,074,880	1,402,670	1,775,316	2,193,6,0	2,738,800	3,156,100
	7.0	.254	103,540	232,480	414,440	646,9,0	931,040	1,267,8,0	1,666,040	2,085,900	2,557,600	3,274,800	3,7,36,000
	10.0	.3636	124,000	276,750	492,000	768,850	1,107,400	1,506,7,0	1,986,800	2,430,800	3,075,500	3,890,800	4,428,400
	13.73	.50	146,220	328,990	564,880	913,840	1,316,000	1,791,200	2,339,500	2,740,900	3,655,500	4,626,500	5,464,200
	20.62	.75	173,350	394,540	701,460	1,196,0,-,0	1,528,150	2,144,160	2,795,600	3,550,800	4,384,400	5,548,400	5,312,600
	27.5	1.00	201,800	454,010	867,260	1,261,200	1,816,050	2,471,900	3,298,500	4,096,100	5,044,600	6,384,600	7,264,300
	41.25	1.5	247,840	557,620	991,370	1,549,000	2,231,010	3,03,600	3,965,000	5,019,000	6,196,000	7,842,000	8,922,000
	55.0	2.0	285,120	641,540	1,140,50	1,782,800	2,566,200	3,453,000	4,162,00	5,774,000	7,12,000	8,921,000	10,265,000
	68.75	2.5	316,500	712,131	1,266,100	1,978,000	2,848,500	3,877,000	5,164,000	6,469,000	7,913,000	10,014,000	11,391,000
	82.50	3.0	341,350	774,280	1,377,400	2,152,600	3,099,100	4,218,000	5,510,000	6,972,000	8,619,000	10,685,000	12,387,000
	96.25	3.5	370,000	832,500	1,480,000	2,313,000	3,330,000	4,532,500	5,920,000	7,493,000	9,254,000	11,207,000	13,320,000

Diameter of orifice, or of well-mouth where observed as in figs. 1 or 2; in inches.

THE MEASUREMENT OF NATURAL GAS.

TABLE I—Concluded.

Diameter of orifice, or of well-mouth where observed as in figs. 1 or 2: in inches.

Observed pressure by mercury gauge.	Observed pressure by water gauge, as in fig. 1.	Observed pressure by pressure-gauge, as in fig. 2. Lbs. per sq. in.	1 inch.	1½ inches.	2 inches.	2½ inches.	3 inches.	3½ inches.	4 inches.	4½ inches.	5 inches.	5⅝ inches.	6 inches.
8.13		4.0	393,000	884,250	1,572,000	2,456,000	3,537,000	4,814,200	6,288,000	7,954,000	9,825,000	12,435,000	14,148,000
8.15		4.5	415,270	934,350	1,661,100	2,596,000	3,737,400	5,087,000	6,644,000	8,409,000	10,382,000	13,139,100	14,350,000
10.17		5.0	436,260	981,450	1,741,840	2,716,000	3,925,900	5,343,000	6,979,000	8,833,000	10,915,000	13,602,000	15,703,000
11.18		5.5	456,260	1,026,500	1,831,800	2,551,200	4,105,500	5,580,000	7,259,000	9,228,100	11,405,000	14,435,100	16,423,000
12.20		6.0	473,750	1,065,900	1,893,010	2,961,000	4,264,000	5,893,000	7,580,000	9,593,000	11,844,000	14,990,000	17,055,000
13.21		6.5	499,840	1,102,100	1,938,400	3,062,000	4,409,000	6,081,000	7,837,000	9,919,000	12,248,000	15,499,000	17,634,000
14.24		7.0	568,930	1,136,300	2,023,700	3,182,000	4,553,300	6,194,000	8,091,000	10,245,000	12,648,000	16,008,000	18,213,000
15.25		7.5	522,010	1,174,500	2,088,000	3,263,000	4,698,000	6,395,000	8,353,100	10,571,000	13,050,000	16,517,000	18,792,000
16.26		8.0	538,500	1,211,600	2,134,100	3,366,000	4,846,000	6,597,000	8,616,000	10,905,000	13,462,000	17,038,000	19,386,000
18.30		9.0	565,970	1,273,200	2,261,000	3,537,100	5,093,000	6,932,000	9,054,100	11,459,100	14,147,000	17,905,000	20,371,000
19.33		10.0	589,270	1,325,900	2,357,100	3,683,000	5,308,000	7,219,000	9,425,000	11,883,000	14,372,000	18,645,000	21,214,000
21.39		11.0	618,340	1,425,600	2,543,300	3,958,000	5,700,000	7,758,000	10,133,000	12,825,000	16,883,000	20,040,000	22,900,000
23.46		12.0	675,040	1,515,800	2,700,000	4,219,000	6,073,800	8,269,000	10,901,000	13,669,000	16,475,000	21,357,000	24,300,000
28.46		14.0	713,550	1,605,900	2,851,500	4,459,700	6,422,000	8,741,000	11,415,000	14,449,000	17,819,000	22,577,000	25,680,000
30.60		16.0	748,650	1,684,500	2,994,600	4,679,000	6,728,000	9,161,000	11,978,000	15,160,000	18,716,000	23,697,000	26,951,000
32.53		18.0	779,350	1,753,900	3,117,400	4,871,000	7,014,000	9,546,000	12,475,000	15,780,000	19,484,000	24,659,000	28,094,000
40.66		20.0	815,150	1,901,600	3,381,000	5,282,000	7,646,000	10,353,000	13,522,000	17,114,000	21,129,000	26,741,000	30,425,000
50.81		25.0	902,180	2,029,590	3,609,000	5,639,000	8,120,000	11,054,000	14,435,000	18,269,000	22,455,000	28,694,000	32,474,000
61.00		30.0	954,820	2,143,300	3,819,000	5,964,000	8,593,000	11,697,000	15,277,000	19,335,0 0	23,670,000	30,211,000	31,373,000
71.16		35.0	998,680	2,247,000	3,995,000	6,242,000	8,986,000	12,234,000	15,979,000	20,223,000	24,967,000	31,599,000	35,952,000
		40.0	1,036,740	2,322,600	4,147,000	6,479,000	9,330,000	12,700,000	16,6 7,000	20,800,000	25,918,000	32,802,000	37,321,000
		45.0	1,072,000	2,412,000	4,285,000	6,700,000	9,648,000	13,132,000	17,152,000	21,708,000	26,400,000	33,919,000	38,592,000
		50.0	1,106,480	2,495,000	4,428,000	6.9 8,000	9,96 ,000	13,589,000	17,710,000	22,454,000	27,672,000	35,024,000	39,849,000
		60.0	1,337,600	2,559,600	4,550,000	7,110,000	10,228,000	13,935,000	18,101,000	23,036,000	28,440,000	36,000,000	40,353,000

For temperature of flowing gas where observed of 30°, 40°, 50°, 60° F., add 4½, 3½, 2½, 1½ respectively.

*To change the result by this to that for any other specific gravity of gas than 0.6 multiply by $\sqrt{\dfrac{0.6}{\text{Sp. gr. gas}}}$

Should 99% alcohol be used in gauge, multiply the readings by 0.8 to reduce to water value.

Examples illustrating use of Table I:

1st example. The Karg well, Findlay, Ohio:
Observed gauge pressure = 15. lbs. by Pitot tube.
Temperature flowing gas = 32° Fahr.
Temperature storage = 50° Fahr.
Diameter of exit mouth = 4 inches.

By Table I, V. day = 11,107,500 (interpolating) for a temperature of storage at 32°. Correction for temperature of storage at 50° is 3 66 per cent., = 406,534, which added, gives V. day = 11,514,034 cubic feet per day.

2d example. The Briggs well, Findlay, O.:
Observed gauge pressure = 6.5 ℔s. by Pitot tube.
Temperature flowing gas = 32° Fahr.
Temperature storage = 50° Fahr.
Diameter of exit mouth = $2\frac{1}{4}$ inches.

By Table I, V. day = 2,510,700 cubic feet found by interpolating between 1,959,400 for a 2-inch mouth, and 3,062,000 for a $2\frac{1}{2}$-inch mouth. The correction multiplier is 3.66 per cent. by foot note. The correction is then 91,891 cubic feet, and the corrected value V. day = 2,602,591 cubic feet per day.

3d example. The Jones well, Findlay, O.:
Observed gauge pressure = 3.79 inches by water gauge.
Temperature flowing gas = 32° Fahr.
Temperature storage = 50° Fahr.
Diameter of exit mouth = $3\frac{3}{4}$ inches.

By Table I, V. day = 871,658 cubic feet, found by interpolating under d = 3 inches, between observed pressures of 3 and 4 inches; also, by interpolating likewise under d = $3\frac{1}{2}$ inches, and then interpolating between the quantities thus obtained for the diameter $3\frac{3}{4}$ inches. Then the multiplier is 3.66 per cent., giving a correction + 31,903, and the final results for a storage temperature of 50°, of V. day = 903,561 cubic feet per day.

APPLICATION TO PIPE LINES.

The recent rapidly increasing demand for natural gas at points comparatively remote from the gas well districts has led to the piping of gas to such great distances as to render a knowledge of the capacity of long pipes for conducting gas a necessity.

It has been stated that the quantities of gas transferred in these long pipes considerably exceeds the amount determined by the ordinary formulas for calculating gas-flow in pipes. This is probably owing to the fact recently determined by trial that the co-efficient of friction of the gas under the conditions of flow of high pressures and comparatively low velocities, is much lower than is usually allowed, indeed for some observed values less than half that value.

This one fact makes it very desirable that some reliable and convenient method of measurement be brought forward where the friction consideration be eliminated. A meter of sufficient capacity to measure a main pipe line would be very expensive, besides being expensive to apply.

Measuring Pipe Lines with the Pitot Tube Gauge.

In this gauge we find the above mentioned desired qualities in the highest degree, such as small cost, ease of application, and accuracy of results. The instrument is furnished ready for attaching to a pipe line by drilling and tapping a $\frac{3}{8}$-inch pipe size hole in the line, and applicable to a horizontal or vertical pipe. This gauge is shown in Fig. 3, Plate 4, as applied to a pipe line, A B being the double mouth tip, and C D being the 10-inch U tube gauge for water, alcohol or mercury.

By the theory of this instrument we have the velocity of flow

$$v = \sqrt{2 g H} \qquad (2)$$

Where g is the acceleration of gravity $= 32.2$ and H the head, in feet, due the velocity. As high as four inches of mercury and 500 feet velocity have been observed in a by-pass with a fall of pressure in the pipe of about half a pound per foot length of pipe. Probably a higher value of head will rarely be observed, so that a 10 inch gauge is ample for all practical cases.

In the above formula H is in terms of the gas flowing. If $h=$the observed head in the water gauge in inches, the velocity of gas in the pipe will be

$$v = 84.6 \sqrt{h \frac{15}{p + 15}} \qquad (3)$$

Where p is the gauge pressure of the gas flowing in the pipe pounds per square inch.

The cubic feet of gas per hour flowing in the pipe will be

$$V \text{ per hour} = 1690 d^2 \sqrt{h \left(1 + \frac{p}{15}\right)} \qquad (4)$$

Where d = inside diameter of pipe in inches and h = inches of water and in which the temperature of flowing gas is taken at 40° F., and that of storage at 50°.

By aid of this formula Table II was calculated.

When mercury is used in the U gauge, look in the first column of the table for h; for water, the second column; and for alcohol in the third.

At the top of the table four lines are given in which to find the observed static pressure of gas in the pipe—the top line if the pressure gauge be mercury; the second if it be water; the third if the pressure is given in ounces and in the fourth if in pounds.

The table gives the cubic feet per hour for a one-inch pipe. For another size of pipe use the multiplier from the supplemental table at the right to change the cubic feet for the one inch pipe to that for the actual size.

Precautions in Use of Instrument.

In selecting a place on the pipe line at which to apply the instrument it is important that the pipe be uniform and continuous for some ten or fifteen diameters up stream from the instrument, also at, and for a few diameters below it, in order to secure normal conditions of flow.

For instance an elbow causes serious eddyings, and a greater velocity at one side of the pipe than the other and the tip of the instrument located in either side will not give fair results.

A T fitting, even if it be plugged, when near the tip, on upstream side will vitiate the indications. Irregularities of conduit on the downstream side of tip is of far less importance than if on the upstream side, and may be allowed to come much nearer the tip.

When locating the instrument in a short portion of pipe, of say fifteen diameters between fittings, it should be placed much nearest the down-stream end to secure the best conditions above named.

Great care should be taken to see that the connections through the instrument are free of obstructions, and perfectly free from leaks at the joints where the instrument is connected up. In most cases the instrument may be tested for this on the spot after connected up, and before applied to the pipe; by turning the cocks tight near top of instrument, and placing the tip ends A and then B in the mouth in succession and drawing by suction. It is very important that all joints be perfectly air-tight. One indication of free action of instrument is the pulsations of the column. The stream of any fluid in a pipe is accompanied with more or less of whirling motion, the mouth of tip being thus more fairly struck at one instant of flow than another, causing a momentary rise of column and vise versa.

THE MEASUREMENT OF NATURAL GAS.

The indications of the U tube should be averaged for the instant of observation by noting an intermediate value among the pulsations. Several such values may be read off and the mean of all taken for the correct result.

In cases where the flow of gas is not uniform which is most apt to be the case in service pipes and branches about a city, the gas supplied for the day should be determined by repeated readings, taken every hour, or perhaps oftener according to accuracy sought.

TABLE II.

For the Pitot Tube Gauge, giving Cubic Feet of Gas per Hour of Uniform Pressure and Specific Gravity, 0.6.* the Temperature of

Pitot tube mercury gauge read'g inches	Pitot tube water gauge read'g in. hes	Pitot tube alcohol gauge read'g inch.*	0. 0. 0. 0.	.63 8.6 .5 0.31	1.26 17.2 10. 0.625	1.91 26. 15. 0.94	2.57 35. 20. 1.25	3.82 52. 30. 1.875	5.07 69. 40. 2.5	7.65 104. 60. 3.75	10.11 138. 80. 5	20.22 275 160. 10	30.87 413. 240. 15
....	.02	.025	239.	242.	244.	247.	249.	254	259.	268.	276	309.	339.
....	.04	.05	323.	342.	345.	349.	353.	359.	366.	379.	391.	437	479.
....	.06	.075	411.	419.	423.	428.	432.	440.	448.	461.	479.	5.5.	5*6.
....	.08	.10	479	484.	488	493.	498.	518.	517.	533.	553.	618.	677.
....	.10	.125	535.	541.	546.	552.	557.	569.	578.	598.	618	691.	7.7.
....	.15	.187	655	662.	669	676.	610.	695.	708.	734.	757	846.	927.
....	.20	.25	757.	765	772.	780.	787.	802.	818.	846.	874.	977	1,070.
....	.25	.312	846.	855.	863.	872.	880.	897.	9 4	946.	977.	1,088	1 197.
....	.30	.375	927	936.	946.	955.	9-3.	9-3.	1,001	1,036.	1,070.	1,17.	1,310.
....	.40	.50	1,070.	1,081	1,092	1,103.	1,114.	1,136.	1,156.	1,201.	1,235.	1,382.	1,518.
....	.51	.625	1,196.	1,209.	1,223.	1,233	1,242.	1 269.	1,292.	1,338	1,381.	1,545	1,692.
....	.60	.75	1,311.	1,324.	1,338.	1,351.	1,364.	1,390.	1,461.	1,468.	1,518.	1,692.	1,854.
....	.80	1.00	1,513.	1,530.	1,546.	1,560.	1,575.	1,605.	1,635.	1,692.	1,747.	1,954.	2,140.
....	1.0	1.25	1,692.	1,710.	1,727.	1,744.	1,761.	1,795.	1,828	1,892.	1,954	2,188.	2,393.
....	1.2	1.50	1,858	1,871.	1,895.	1,911	1,930	1,966.	2,102.	2,076.	2,146.	2,398.	2,621.
.10	1.4	1.75	2,042	2,025	2,123.	2,064.	2,094.	2,128.	2,162.	2,240.	2,312.	2,585	2,831.
.12	1.6	2.00	2,140.	2,164.	2,116.	2,160.	2,228.	2,270.	2,312	2,393	2,47.	2,763.	3,027.
.15	1.8	2.25	2,270	2,291.	2,314.	2,340.	2,368.	2,408.	2,454	2,538.	2,621.	2,931.	3,210.
.15	2.0	2.5	2,383.	2,400.	2,456.	2,466.	2,490.	2,538.	2,585.	2,676.	2,763.	3,189.	3,384.
.18	2.5	3.12	2,656.	2,702.	2,740.	2,778.	2,784.	1,837.	2,840.	2,970.	3,109	3,845.	3,785.
.22	3.0	3.75	2,931	2,968.	3,000.	3,021.	3,050.	3,118.	3,166.	3,277	3,384	3,784.	4,144.
.20	4.0	5.0	3,384	3,409.	3,450.	3,487.	3,522	3,589.	3,655.	3,798.	3,907.	4,369.	4,786.
.37	5.0	6.25	3,784	3,822.	3,867	3,904.	3,932.	4,186.	4,187.	4,260	4,360.	4,895.	5,361.
.44	6.0	7.5	4,145.	4,185.	4,237.	4,272.	4,313.	4,396.	4,477.	4,663.	4,786	5,351.	5,761.
.59	8.0	10.0	4,786.	4,838.	4,886.	4,938.	4,918	5,076.	5,69.	5,351.	5,56.	6,179.	6,796.
.74	10.0	12.5	5,357.	5,407.	5,46.	5,520.	5,569.	5,677.	5,780.	5,980.	6,178.	6,808.	7,567.
.88	12	15.	5,861.	5,917.	5,980.	6,042	6,100.	6,216.	6,331.	6,565.	6,768.	7,167.	8,289.
1.10	15.	18.75	6,558.	6,634	6,710.	6,753.	6,910.	6,890.	7,059.	7,027	7,567.	8,461.	9,268.
1.47	20.	25.	7,567.	7,610.	7,753.	7,799.	7,878.	8,174	8,400.	8,737.	9,777.	10,700.
1.84	25.	31.25	8,461.	8,544.	8,661.	8,721.	8,802.	8,972.	9,138.	9,466.	10,9.5.	11,970.
2.21	30.	37.5	9,268.	9,354.	9,488.	9,553.	9,645	9,829	10,010.	10,305.	11,905.	13,105.
2.91	40.	50.0	10,700.	10,815.	10,940.	11,030	1,440.	11,850	12,010.	12,5 0.	13,5 0.	15,120.
3.68	50.	62.5	1,965,	12,690.	12,230.	12,330.	12,450.	12,690.	12,950	13,360.	13,814.	15,450.	16,9.0.
4.42	60	75	12,708.	13,233.	13,400.	13,510.	13,640.	13,900.	14,160	14,680	15 139.	16,9.0.	18 535.
5.15	70.	87 5	14,160	14,30 0	14,500.	14,500.	14,73	15,010.	15,290.	15 803.	16 350.	18,2 0.	20 U.0.
5.89	80.	100.	15,130.	15 300.	15,450.	15,600.	13 750	16,560.	16 3.0.	16,9.0.	17,472.	19,840.	21,465.
6.62	90.	112 5	16,50.	16,220.	16,405.	16,545.	16 705	17,020.	17,340.	17 980.	18,535	20,725.	22,700.
7.36	100.	125.	16,920.	17 100	17,270.	17,440.	17 610.	17,940.	18,290.	18,920.	19 537.	21,840.	23,830.
8.10	110.	137.5	17,750.	17,920.	18,410.	18,290	18,470.	18,820.	19,170.	19 860.	20 490.	22,910.	25,100.

*To change the result by this table to that for any other specific gravity than 0.6 multiply by

$$\sqrt{\frac{1.6}{\text{sp. gr. gas.}}}$$

TABLE II.

Flow through a one-inch Pipe Line, the Measured Volume being as at Air Storage being 50° F., and of Flowing Gas 40° F.

40.44 550. 320. 20	50.55 688. 400. 25	60.63 825. 480. 30	560. 35	640 40	800. 50	960. 60	1,120. 70	1,280. 80	1,600. 100	— Inches of column by mercury gauge. — Inches of column by water gauge. — ounces. — pounds. } Gauge pressure of gas flow'g in the pipe line.
863.	302.	415.	437.	458	498.	535	569.	602.	663.	*For any pipe.*
517.	551.	586.	614.	648.	704.	756.	806	852.	947.	
633.	680.	718.	757.	791.	863.	927.	947.	1,063.	1,148.	Multipliers for pipes larger than one inch.
711.	782.	829.	874.	916.	996	1,070.	1,189	1,204	1,325.	
819	871	927.	977	1,025	1,111.	1,196.	1,271.	1,347.	1,482	Multiply cubic feet for one inch pipe by value in this table opposite right size of pipe.
1,031	1,070.	1,135.	1,196.	1,255.	1,361.	1,466.	1,561.	1,619	1,814.	
1,156	1,236.	1,311.	1,381.	1,419	1,576.	1,692.	1,802.	1,901.	2,076.	
1,292	1,382.	1,465	1,544.	1,620.	1,761.	1,892.	2,013.	2,129.	2,343.	
1,491	1,514.	1,605.	1,692.	1,775.	1,923.	2,072.	2,208.	2,332.	2,566.	
1,615.	1,714.	1,851.	1,951.	2,049.	2,224.	2,393.	2,548.	2,693.	2,963.	
1,824.	1,954	2,072	2,184.	2,291.	2,491.	2,675.	2,848	3,011.	3,313.	
2,002.	2,140.	2,270	2,393.	2,510.	2,728.	2,930.	3,120	3,298.	3,630.	
2,312.	2,471.	2,621.	2,763.	2,898.	3,150.	3,381.	3,602.	3,808.	4,191.	
2,585	2,763.	2,931.	3,089.	3,240.	3,522.	3,782	4,028.	4,258.	4,686.	
2,831.	3,027.	3,210.	3,384.	3,549.	3,859.	4,141	4,412.	4,664	5,133.	
3,059.	3,269	3,468.	3,609.	3,831	4,168.	4,476.	4,768.	5,036.	5,541.	
3,261.	3,495	3,707.	3,904.	4,100.	4,455.	4,784.	5,096.	5,384.	5,926	
3,433	3,707.	3,932.	4,144.	4,348.	4,721.	5,076.	5,404.	5,700.	6,286.	
3,658.	3,908	4,141	4,348.	4,584.	4,984	5,352.	5,696.	6,020.	6,626.	
4,087.	4,368.	4,646.	4,884.	4,721.	5,568.	5,980.	6,368	6,732.	7,408.	
4,177.	4,784.	5,184.	5,352.	5,612.	6,100.	6,552.	6,976.	7,376.	8,115.	
5,169	5,524.	5,860.	6,178.	6,480.	7,011	7,563.	8,054.	8,516.	9,370.	
5,779.	6,176.	6,552	6,908.	7,244.	7,875	8,460	9,004.	9,520.	10,171.	
6,331.	6,768	7,180.	7,564.	7,936.	8,628.	9,268.	9,864.	10,428	11,477.	
7,910	7,816.	8,248.	8,716.	9,164.	9,961	10,700.	11,392	12,041.	13,252.	
8,173.	8,734.	9,258.	9,768.	10,248	11,136.	11,961.	12,740.	13,468.	14,816.	
8,953	9,571.	10,158.	10,701.	11,226.	12,201.	13,108	13,953	14,750.	16,240.	
10,010	10,671.	11,567	11,968	12,580.	13,644.	14,652.	14,510.	16,490	18,145.	
11,580.	12,350.	13,107.	13,813.	14,491.	15,751.	16,920.	18,015	19,042	20,951.	
12,910	13,815.	14,641.	15,415.	16,200.	17,611.	18,919.	20,140.	21,291.	23,427.	
14,160.	15,135.	16,058	16,921.	17,750.	19,292.	20,721.	22,061.	23,325.	25,661.	
16,350.	17,477.	18,544.	19,537.	20,492	22,275.	23,930	25,475.	26,930.	29,630.	
18,280.	19,537	20,730	21,811.	22,910	24,905.	26,751.	28,483.	31,110.	33,131.	
20,030	21,403.	22,704.	23,928.	25,098.	27,285.	29,305	31,20[illegible].	32,980.	36,300.	
21,615	23,116.	24,516.	25,845.	27,109.	29,468.	31,654.	33,700.	35,623.	39,200.	
23,120.	24,711.	26,211.	27,630.	28,980.	31,502.	33,840	36,024.	38,082.	41,910.	
21,520.	26,111.	27,807.	29,305.	30,735.	33,413	35,891.	38,211.	40,393.	41,150.	
25,930.	27,629	29,308.	31,890.	32,442.	35,221.	37,871	41,290.	43,580.	45,840.	
27,110	28,970.	30,635.	32,402.	33,980.	36,910.	39,670.	42,243.	44,670.	49,140.	

Diam'r.	Multiplier.
Inches.	
1	1.0
1¼	1.562
1½	2.25—2¼
2	4.
2½	6.25—6¼
3	9.
3½	12.25—12¼
4	16.
4½	20.25—20¼
5	25.
5½	30.25—30¼
5⅝	31.64
6	36.
6½	42.25—42¼
7	49.
8	64.
10	100.
12	144.
16	256.
18	324.
20	400.

ABSOLUTE MEASUREMENT TEST OF THE PITOT TUBE GAUGE AS APPLIED
IN MEASURING GASES.

To strengthen and confirm confidence in the Pitot tube gauge for accuracy as applied to gas measurements further than already done by citing its accuracy in streams of water and its agreement with theory in development of pressure due to impact against its tip mouth, some absolute quantitative experiments were recently made in connection with a *gas meter prover*, where a known volume of air was forced through a pipe in a measured interval of time, the same being carefully measured with the Pitot tube gauge, the results of which are given in the following:

TABLE OF COMPARATIVE VOLUMES OF AIR SIMULTANEOUSLY MEASURED BY THE GAS METER PROVER AND THE PITOT TUBE GAUGE.

	Diameter of pipe— inches.	Volume by gauge.	Volume by prover.
12 experiments, October 4, 1890.	1.25	173.	161.
	.865	148.	150.
	.865	182.	185.
	1 73	263.	240.
9 experiments, October 11, 1890.	1.23	201.	200.
	.86	190.	188.
Means...........................		192.8	187.3

Difference, less than 3%.

The Pitot tube mouth was here placed in the center of the pipe, where the current is most rapid, but the figures were corrected for this, as well as for temperature of air and all known causes of error. The final difference of three per cent is believed to be within the errors of observation and might be plus or minus, as indeed the individual comparisons are, indicating that the instrument is practically exact for measurement of gases as well as liquids.

Practical Field Test of Pitot Tube Gauge with Standard Meters.

In the course of practical field work with the Pitot tube gauge, it has been applied to pipes which, at the same time, were conducting gas as measured with the *Westinghouse natural gas meter*, the latter being read and noted each time. Comparative results thus obtained are given in the following:

THE MEASUREMENT OF NATURAL GAS. 295

TABLE OF SIMULTANEOUS MEASUREMENTS BY THE WESTINGHOUSE NATURAL GAS METER AND BY THE PITOT TUBE GAUGE.

Diameter of pipe line—inches.	Gauge pressure in pipe.	Cubic feet hour by meter.	Cubic feet hour by gauge.
6	13.6 ounces.	11,970	12.005
3	10.4 "	4,430	4,025
6	9.2 "	14,933	15,843
6	9.2 "	14,933	15,336
6	7 pounds.	28,900	29.702
6	7 "	32,032	29,460
6	7 "	33,000	34,590
6	19.2 ounces.	20,930	20,611
6	19.2 "	19,063	19,175
6	19.2 "	17,990	17,733
3	8.8 "	4.307	3.924
6	7.0 "	12,720	13 325
6	13.3 "	12,310	12,797
Means		17,500	17,578

It was not always practicable to make the readings absolutely simultaneous, though they were usually separated by less than one minute. In this way the differences between gauge and meter might fluctuate somewhat as indeed they do.

The density of the natural gas where the above figures were obtained was 0.66, and the values obtained from the tables for the Pitot gauge observations were corrected as per foot note to the table, also for the velocity curve as explained below, so that the Pitot tube gauge column of figures is to be regarded as fully corrected.

The meter results were low before correcting for pressures, the values for seven pounds being decidedly low, the correction being nearly 50 per cent. This fact indicates that the Westinghouse meter measures volumes at whatever density the gas passes the meter, so that where the gas is subsequently expanded to the true storage value, that storage result is too low. Hence, in using this meter, a pressure gauge should be an adjunct and be read for the purpose of determining a correction. With these facts in view, the above results of observation are in essential agreement either instrument proving the other satisfactory for accuracy.

CORRECTION FOR VELOCITY CURVE.

In using the Pitot tube gauge the tip A, figure 3, plate 4, should, to avoid correction of the result for the so-called "velocity curve" of the flowing stream, be placed at from one-fifth to one-sixth of the depth or diameter of the pipe, because of the varying velocity of the flowing gas in the diameter of pipe, it being greatest at the center of pipe and about two-thirds this at the side. The mean velocity in the whole pipe at a given cross section is only about 0 85 that at the center, 0 87 that at a third the diameter, 0.92 that at a fourth the diameter, 0.96 that at a fifth the diameter.

To avoid using the above correction multipliers several tips of various lengths may be carried in the instrument kit when, for particular cases, the proper length to employ may be selected, it being the one whose penetration into the line pipe is, as above stated, about one-fifth to one sixth the depth of diameter. But more reliable results are probably obtained by placing the tip at the center of the pipe and applying the correction 0.85.

This correction is to be understood as due to varying velocity in the pipe diameter and not to an incorrect result for velocity by the Pitot gauge, as that is still found to be truly the theoretical velocity for the position occupied by the tip.

In using the instrument alcohol is found to be the best liquid to work free in the glass tubes of the gauge C D, as water acts at times as if the interior of the tube were greasy. Proof alcohol of about 98 per cent. has a specific gravity of 0 8, and the gauge reading for alcohol may be reduced to those for water by multiplying the reading by 0 8 though a column for alcohol is given in Table II.

In using the instrument it is essential that the connection between the tip A B and gauge C D be absolutely air-tight, especially when the openings A and B are small, but with this precaution the gauge C D may be at a considerable distance from the point of application of A B to the pipe line, as for instance in an office fifty feet or more away, and all permanently installed for convenient reading at any moment.

In case of a permanent location the tip B may be separated from A by one or two feet to simplify the construction of the parts.

Examples from actual measurements taken to illustrate application of Pitot Tube Gauge to measurement of pipe lines:

Example 1. Pipe   10-inch main.
            Pressure   24 inches water.
            Flow   0.10 inches water by Pitot Gauge.

Table II, V. hour = 550 6 for 1 inch pipe.
    "   55,060 for 10-inch pipe.

Example 2. Pipe   2 inch by pass.
            Pressure   4 pounds.
            Flow   3.8 inches mercury.

Table II, V. hour = 12 255 for 1-inch pipe.
                    49,020 for 2 inch pipe.

THE MEASUREMENT OF NATURAL GAS. 297

Example 3. Pipe   8-inch main pipe line.
            Pressure 101 pounds.
            Flow   0 24 inches water.
Table II, V. hour = 151,000 for 8-inch main.

Correcting this for the "velocity curve" requires for this case a multiplier of about 0.93, making the value 140,000.

Same case by pipe line measurement, 142,000, by Table III, for which the pressure was 112 pounds at eleven miles from where the above 101 pounds was taken.

Example 4. Pipe   1¼-inch service pipe.
            Pressure 5 ounces.
            Flow   0 19 inches water.
Table II, V. hour, 1,172 for 1¼-inch pipe.
Same by Westinghouse meter, 1,170.

II. BY THE PRINCIPLES OF FLOW IN PIPES.

For measurement of gas actually flowing in an existing pipe line the Pitot Tube Gauge can not be surpassed for simplicity, convenience and accuracy. But as the instrument can not be applied to an imaginary pipe line, such as a proposed line from a gas field to a city, where the capacity of the pipe line must be up to a certain figure, the Pitot gauge will not apply, and here we find an important service for pipe line formulas and tables.

Thus to establish the dimensions of a pipe line for conveying a given quantity of gas per hour and other puposes, the following formulas and tables are given.

The coefficient of friction of the gas against the inside of pipe is here an important factor, its value as determined for natural gas being variable, as well as for other fluids, and closely represented by the expression (see *Ohio Geology Report*, Vol. VI, p. 582),

$$f = 0.00053 \, v^{\frac{3}{4}} \qquad (5)$$

The flow in long pipes, like natural gas pipe lines, will be approximately isothermal; that is, though the gas will expand as it flows along, and become cooled by such expansion, unless protected by non-conductors, yet in an iron pipe, buried in earth, the pipe can readily impart heat to warm the gas as it cools. The work done by the expansion of the gas will aid in overcoming the resistance to flow, as well as the difference of pressure in the pipe at opposite ends. A formula, taking account of all the components producing motion, as well as all the resistances to flow in a pipe for this case, is

$$\frac{v^2}{2g} = \frac{d\ p_2}{8fl\ \delta_2}\left\{\left(\frac{p_1}{p_2}\right)^2 - 1\right\} \tag{6}$$

where v = mean velocity at "down-stream" end of pipe, feet per second.
  g = acceleration of gravity = 32.2 feet.
  d = diameter of pipe, in feet, inside.
  f = coefficient of friction = $.00053\ v^{\frac{3}{4}}$
  l = length of pipe in feet.
  δ_2 = weight per cubic ft. of flowing gas at down-stream end of pipe.
  p_1 = absolute pressure at upper end of pipe considered, pounds per square foot.
  p_2 = like pressure at down-stream end of pipe.

By introducing the value of the constants, and expressing the pipe length l in miles, and the diameter d in inches, factoring and reducing we obtain the cubic feet per hour of uniform flow

$$V\text{ hour} = 760.\left(\frac{p_1-p_2}{p_2\ l}\right)^{\frac{4}{11}}\left(\frac{p_1+p_2}{2\ p_2}\right)^{\frac{4}{11}} d^{\frac{11}{11}} \tag{7}$$

where the correction for temperature was taken at

$$\left(\frac{1}{0.9}\right)^{\frac{4}{11}}$$

The term

$$\left(\frac{p_1+p_2}{2\ p_2}\right)^{\frac{4}{11}} \tag{8}$$

is nearly 1 for quite a range in p_1 to p_2 and it is taken as 1 in calculating the quantities in Table III. But in cases of considerable fall in pressure of the flowing gas as it moves from the upstream end to the lower, it is necessary to include the effect due to the term (8).

This is best done in case of tabular computations by making a table of multipliers from (8) itself. These are given in Table IV. Hence, when a value is taken from Table III it is to be multiplied by the proper value from Table IV, when the latter multiplier has considerable value in excess of 1.

In the tables the pressures are given as *gauge pressures*, that is, the pressure as observed from an ordinary pressure gauge pounds per square inch, and *apparent* pressures, not absolute.

THE MEASUREMENT OF NATURAL GAS. 299

As a rule to guide in the determination of cubic feet of flow of a pipe line—
1st. Find the cubic feet from Table III.
2d. Correct for temperature by aid of foot note to Table III.
3d. Find the proper multiplier from Table IV and apply.
4th. Find proper multiplier from Table V and apply.

The last result is the cubic feet per hour of uniform flow at storage temperature and at atmospheric or storage pressure.

To *determine* a pipe line when the length and the cubic feet per hour are made known also the initial and terminal pressures, find the value in the first column of Table III, and look along to where the cubic feet per hour is found. The diameter at top of this column is the diameter sought for the pipe line. The cubic feet per hour given, however, should be divided by value in Table V before looking in Table III.

Thus suppose a pipe of forty miles length, gauge pressure at upper end 200 pounds, and at lower end forty pounds, and the cubic feet per hour capacity to be 200,000, storage value, or 53,470 at the forty pound pressure at lower end of pipe. Then the value for the first column of table is

$$\frac{200 - 40}{54.6 \times 40} = .073$$

This figure is nearly midway between .068 and .077 of the first column of Table III. Looking along we find the value 53470, under nine inches diameter by proper interpolating. Hence, the required diameter of the pipe line in this case, of the same size throughout, is nine inches.

If the pressures be 100 pounds at the down-stream end instead of forty pounds, as above, we find the first column value of Table III to be .022, and the storage volume of 200,000 cubic feet at 100 pounds pressure is 25,480, and the diameter of pipe line in this case is eight inches.

That is, with the given initial gauge pressure of 200 pounds per square inch, the 8-inch pipe line forty miles long will deliver the same storage value of gas, if the terminal pressure be 100 pounds, as would the 9-inch pipe line, of the same length, with a terminal pressure of forty pounds.

TABLE III. FOR PIPE LINE FLOW.

CUBIC FEET OF GAS CONVEYED BY A PIPE LINE, PER HOUR, OF UNIFORM FLOW; FOR A TEMPERATURE OF FLOWING GAS OF 50° FAHR., AND SPECIFIC GRAVITY OF 0.6.* FOR OTHER TEMPERATURES OF FLOWING GAS CORRECT BY AID OF FOOT NOTE TO TABLE, AND ALSO CORRECT BY TABLE IV. THE VOLUME THUS OBTAINED IS AT THE OBSERVED PRESSURE IN THE PIPE AT THE "DOWN-STREAM" END, AND MUST BE EXPANDED BY AID OF TABLE V TO OBTAIN THE STORAGE VOLUME AT ATMOSPHERIC PRESSURE.

THE FIRST COLUMN GIVES $\dfrac{\text{"FALL PER MILE."}}{14.6 + \text{LOWER GAUGE PRESSURE}}$ WHICH MEANS THE AVERAGE FALL OF PRESSURE IN THE PIPE PER MILE; DIVIDED BY 14.6, PLUS THE GAUGE PRES-URE (APPARENT PRESSURE), AT DOWN STREAM END OF PIPE. THUS, IF THE PRESSURE OF THE GAS IN THE PIPE DIMINISHES THREE POUNDS PER MILE, AND IF THE GAUGE PRESSURE IN THE PIPE AT THE DOWN-STREAM END IS 45.4 POUNDS PER SQUARE-INCH, THEN THE VALUE TO LOOK FOR IN THE FIRST COLUMN OF TABLE IS $\dfrac{3}{14.6 + 45.4} = .05$.

Inside diameter of pipe line; in inches.

Fall per mile, $\div$ 14.6 + lower gauge pressure.	2-in.	4-in.	6-in.	8-in.	10-in.	12-in.	14-in.	16-in.	18-in.	20-in.	24-in.	30-in.
0.005	548	2,819	7,351	14,510	24,388	37,834	54,323	74,680	98,650	126,550	194,720	329,960
0.006	585	3,013	7,856	15,207	26,578	40,434	58,063	79,810	105,430	135,250	208,100	352,640
0.007	619	3,187	8,330	16,444	27,800	42,770	61,420	84,440	111,530	143,070	220,140	373,040
0.008	650	3,316	8,726	17,220	29,190	44,900	64,490	88,640	117,100	150,230	231,130	391,670
0.009	676	3,450	9,070	17,900	30,342	46,690	67,040	92,145	121,730	156,160	240,280	407,180
0.010	705	3,630	9,470	18,630	31,660	48,720	69,970	96,170	127,040	162,970	250,760	424,910
0.014	818	4,212	10,980	21,680	36,780	56,510	81,150	111,560	147,360	189,030	290,860	492,890
0.019	909	4,680	12,240	21,030	40,830	62,800	90,185	123,900	163,760	210,060	323,230	547,740
0.024	987	5,098	13,240	26,150	44,107	68,174	97,896	134,550	177,760	228,020	350,970	594,570
0.029	1,056	5,433	14,170	27,960	47,390	72,920	104,700	143,910	190,120	243,880	375,240	635,900
0.033	1,117	5,750	15,000	29,630	50,160	77,180	110,840	152,350	201,260	258,170	397,240	673,160
0.038	1,175	6,040	15,760	31,100	52,740	81,100	116,480	160,070	211,450	271,250	417,380	707,220
0.043	1,227	6,310	16,460	32,540	55,050	84,720	121,660	167,230	220,910	283,380	436,040	738,900
0.048	1,275	6,565	17,110	33,800	57,760	88,110	126,520	173,910	229,740	294,710	453,470	768,430
0.058	1,364	7,020	18,310	36,150	61,300	94,270	135,450	185,720	245,920	305,490	485,360	822,840

THE MEASUREMENT OF NATURAL GAS.

0.068	1,447	7,447	19,410	38,320	64,940	99,930	143,500	197,240	250,560	334,240	514,300	871,520
0.077	1,520	7,831	20,420	40,300	69,900	105,100	150,880	207,420	274,000	351,500	540,840	916,400
0.087	1,590	8,190	21,350	42,140	71,410	109,870	157,740	216,870	286,500	367,510	565,430	958,270
0.096	1,620	8,520	22,020	43,860	74,330	114,360	164,220	225,730	298,220	382,550	588,60	997,460
0.116	1,775	9,137	23,830	47,030	79,690	122,630	176,090	242,040	319,740	410,160	631,110	1,069,500
0.136	1,884	9,697	25,280	49,910	84,570	130,140	186,880	256,870	339,330	435,290	663,790	1,135,000
0.155	1,955	10,210	26,630	52,572	89,080	137,080	196,840	270,570	357,420	458,540	705,490	1,195,500
0.174	2,077	10,690	27,880	55,030	93,220	143,480	206,050	283,220	374,140	479,950	729,520	1,251,430
0.194	2,166	11,150	29,065	57,370	97,220	149,600	214,800	295,300	390,100	500,300	769,960	1,304,500
0.213	2,250	11,550	30,200	59,629	101,400	155,500	223,200	306,940	405,900	521,000	800,100	1,355,000
0.233	2,330	12,040	31,262	61,700	104,560	160,890	231,600	317,640	419,500	538,200	828,070	1,403,300
0.252	2,404	12,370	32,290	63,680	107,910	166,050	238,450	327,760	432,940	555,410	854,600	1,448,000
0.272	2,480	12,770	33,280	65,680	111,340	171,200	246,000	346,900	446,350	572,940	881,560	1,493,600
0.291	2,550	13,140	34,250	67,600	114,600	176,340	253,100	317,900	459,660	589,540	907,240	1,537,300
0.320	2,587	13,310	34,730	68,540	116,100	178,731	257,200	352,700	466,100	597,600	919,700	1,558,400
0.350	2,672	13,750	35,870	70,790	119,900	184,544	265,000	364,300	481,360	617,310	949,800	1,609,440
0.380	2,752	14,160	36,940	72,900	123,500	190,050	273,550	375,200	495,700	635,700	978,240	1,657,500
0.410	2,829	14,560	37,80	74,940	125,968	195,389	281,200	385,670	509,600	653,540	1,005,500	1,704,000
0.440	2,903	14,940	38,970	76,100	130,310	200,493	288,600	395,890	522,500	670,600	1,032,100	1,748,500
0.470	3,006	15,470	40,345	79,612	134,905	207,363	298,750	409,770	541,360	694,200	1,068,250	1,810,000
0.530	3,108	15,890	41,720	82,320	139,540	214,634	305,900	423,700	559,800	717,840	1,104,500	1,871,500
0.560	3,168	16,310	42,540	83,930	142,500	218,826	314,950	432,000	570,700	731,900	1,136,500	1,908,400
0.600	3,251	16,735	43,650	86,120	145,915	244,550	323,200	443,200	585,600	751,000	1,155,840	1,958,000
0.760	3,439	17,494	46,170	91,110	154,347	237,550	341,900	478,500	619,500	794,400	1,222,500	2,071,500
0.800	3,608	18,570	48,470	95,570	161,918	249,200	358,600	491,900	649,900	833,300	1,282,500	2,173,000
0.900	3,767	19,390	50,580	99,80	169,082	260,200	354,500	513,600	678,640	870,200	1,329,340	2,269,000
1.000	3,912	20,140	52,520	103,600	175,559	270,250	388,500	533,400	704,700	903,700	1,390,600	2,356,500

For temperature of flowing gas of 28°, 31°, 47°, 60°, 70° F., add 3½, 2½, 1½, —1½, —2½ respectively.

*To change the result by this table to that for any other specific gravity of gas than 0.6 multiply by $\sqrt[4]{\frac{.6}{\text{sp. gr. gas}}}$

TABLE IV.

MULTIPLIERS FOR CORRECTING QUANTITIES TAKEN FROM TABLE III, FOR CASES WHERE THE FALL OF PRESSURE OF GAS FLOWING FROM UPPER END TO LOWER END IN A PIPE LINE IS CONSIDERABLE.

Gauge pressure at upper end.	Gauge pressure at lower end of pipe, or terminal pressure.								
	5	10	20	40	60	80	100	150	200	300
20	1.125	1.037	1.							
30	1.197	1.132	1.050							
40	1.261	1.190	1.097	1.						
60	1.367	1.295	1.190	1.060	1.					
80	1.475	1.380	1.260	1.121	1.049	1.				
100		1.460	1.326	1.175	1.090	1.035	1.			
150		1.632	1.468	1.288	1.187	1.110	1.070	1.		
200		1.780	1.590	1.390	1.270	1.190	1.137	1.057	1.	
300		2.018	1.801	1.557	1.417	1.324	1.258	1.147	1.080	1.
400			1.980	1.710	1.540	1.440	1.360	1.235	1.153	1.060
500			2.122	1.823	1.643	1.531	1.445	1.303	1.214	1.105

By comparing these two diameters it appears that the 100 pound terminal pressure is better than the forty, giving diameters of pipe of eight and nine inches respectively. But at a terminal pressure of 200 pounds there could be no flow, and hence there seems to be some one terminal pressure for each constant initial pressure that will give a maximum flow, as expressed in terms of cubic feet at storage pressure.

By a mathematical invesigation a maximum flow for a given pipe is found to exist when

$$p_2 = p_1 \; .5222.$$

for absolute pressures, and

$$p_2^1 = p_1^1 \; .5222 - 7. \text{ nearly, for gauge pressures.} \quad (9)$$

It is a singular fact that the conditions for maximum flow are independent of both length and diameter of pipe line.

This fact of a maximum flow is an important one, and is shown in the following set of figures for a pipe line thirteen miles long, six inches in diameter, with an initial pressure of 97.4 pounds per square inch:

THE MEASUREMENT OF NATURAL GAS.

Then for a terminal pressure of 0 lbs. the flow = 76,000. cubic feet, storage value.
" " 10 " 82,900. "
" " 20 " 88 000. "
" " 30 " 92,000. "
" " 50 " 93,000. "
" " 60 " 91,000. "
" " 70 " 85,000. "
" " 80 " 76,500. "
" " 82 " 73,800. "
" " 90 " 62,000. "

The maximum value, 93,000, occurs at about half the initial pressure as by the formula (9.)

TABLE V.

MULTIPLIERS CHANGING THE VOLUME OF GAS FROM THAT AT THE OBSERVED PRESSURE AT THE "DOWN-STREAM" END OF PIPE, AS GIVEN BY TABLES III AND IV, TO THAT AT ATMOSPHERIC PRESSURE AS THOUGH STORED IN A GAS-HOLDER. THUS, IF THE OBSERVED PRESSURE IS 30 POUNDS, TABLES III AND IV GIVE ONLY ABOUT ONE-THIRD THE ATMOSPHERIC VOLUME.

Observed pressure by gauge at down-stream end.	Multiplier to give volume, at atmospheric pressure.	Observed pressure by gauge at down-stream end.	Multiplier to give volume at atmospheric pressure.	Observed pressure by gauge at down-stream end.	Multiplier to give volume at atmospheric pressure.	Observed pressure by gauge at down-stream end.	Multiplier to give volume at atmospheric pressure.
2	1.137	30	3.055	70	5.795	180	13.330
4	1.274	32	3.192	75	6.137	190	14.015
6	1.411	34	3.329	80	6.480	200	14.700
8	1.548	36	3.466	85	6.822	220	16.070
10	1.685	38	3.603	90	7.165	240	17.440
12	1.822	40	3.740	95	7.507	260	18.810
14	1.959	42	3.877	100	7.850	280	20.180
16	2.096	44	4.014	110	8.535	300	21.550
18	2.233	46	4.151	120	9.220	320	22.920
20	2.370	48	4.288	130	9.905	340	24.290
22	2.507	50	4.425	140	10.590	360	25.660
24	2.644	55	4.767	150	11.275	400	28.400
26	2.781	60	5.110	160	11 960	450	31.825
28	2.918	65	5.452	170	12.645	500	35.250

In Table VI are given the terminal and initial pressures for the maximum of flow through pipe lines. For a 13 4 initial pressure the maximum occurs for the outlet to be into free air. For a fifty-pound initial pressure the maximum flow occurs for a terminal pressure of 19.11 pounds, etc.

TABLE VI.

RELATION OF THE INITIAL GAUGE PRESSURE TO THE TERMINAL GAUGE PRESSURE FOR THE MAXIMUM FLOW, STORAGE VALUE, OF GAS IN A PIPE LINE.

Initial gauge pressure.	Terminal gauge pressure.	Initial gauge pressure.	Terminal gauge pressure.	Initial gauge pressure.	Terminal gauge pressure.	Initial gauge pressure.	Terminal gauge pressure.
13.4	0	45	16.50	100	45.22	210	102.65
16	1.36	50	19.11	110	50.44	220	107.88
18	2.40	55	21.72	120	55.67	230	113.10
20	3.44	60	24.33	130	60.89	240	118.32
22	4.49	65	26.94	140	66.11	250	123.55
24	5.53	70	29.55	150	71.33	260	128.77
26	6.57	75	32.16	160	76.55	270	133.99
28	7.62	80	34.77	170	81.77	280	139.21
30	8.67	85	37.38	180	86.99	290	144.43
35	11.28	90	40.00	190	92.21	300	149.66
40	13.89	95	42.60	200	97.43	310	154.88

Example 1. A pipe line ten miles long, four-inch pipe, initial pressure 200 pounds, terminal 97.4 pounds for a maximum flow. Then

$$\frac{\text{Fall per mile.}}{14\ 6 + \text{lower gauge pressure.}} = \frac{200 - 97.4}{(14.6 + 97\ 4)\ 10} = \frac{102\ 6}{1120} = .092.$$

Looking in first column of Table III, opposite .092, and under four-inch pipe we find (interpolating) 8,360 cubic feet per hour.

If the temperature of flowing gas were 44°, that of storage being 50° F., the correction for temperature would be about 1¼ per cent. which correction applied to 8 360 would give 8,464.

The correction multiplier from Table IV is practically 1.137, which, in round numbers, is 1⅛. Hence, 8,464 × 1⅛ = 9,673 cubic feet per hour.

THE MEASUREMENT OF NATURAL GAS. 305

This volume is still at 97.4 pounds per gauge pressure, and will expand to atmospheric pressure on putting it in a storage gas-holder where it may be regarded as at the storage pressure.

To correct for this expansion to storage pressure, use multiplier from Table V, viz, 7.68, and we get $9,673 \times 7.68 = 74,289$ cubic feet per hour as the maximum flow of the pipe, or the greatest possible amount of gas either in weight, or in cubic feet of gas at storage pressure it is possible to get through the ten miles of four-inch pipe with the stated initial pressure of 200 pounds whatever the terminal pressure.

Suppose this pipe be extended by a six-inch pipe thirteen miles long, making a pipe line of ten miles of four-inch, and thirteen miles of six-inch pipe, twenty-three miles in all, then the initial pressure for the thirteen mile part will be 97.4 pounds.

This thirteen-mile portion will convey more gas, under maximum flow than the ten-mile portion will supply to it, and hence the maximum flow of the system occurs when the ten-mile portion is working at its maximum. This requires the thirteen-mile portion to be working under a terminal pressure such that it will convey the 74,289 cubic feet per hour. This is found to be at nearly eighty-two pounds by gauge. If the thirteen-mile portion were a little longer there would be two terminal pressures that would give this 74.289 cubic feet per hour, either of which could be adopted for the maximum service of the whole line.

In designing pipe lines as of various sizes and lengths of pipe, the first lengths should be of the smaller size, because of the high initial pressure and very considerable fall available in that portion; and then for highest economy in cost of line the several sizes should be arranged so that when one portion is working under maximum conditions, all are.

Example 2. Pipe line forty-two miles, six inch diameter, initial pressure 200 pounds, terminal 97.4 pounds for maximum flow. Cubic feet per hour, storage value, $= 112,360$. If the terminal pressure be thirty-five pounds instead of 97.4 the cubic feet flow $= 100,820$.

Example 3. Pipe line forty-two miles by eight-inch pipe, maximum flow for 97.4 terminal pressure $= 223,790$ cubic feet per hour. For thirty-five pounds terminal pressure the flow $= 198,900$ cubic feet, storage conditions, the initial pressure being the same 200 pounds.

20 G.

CHAPTER VIII.

THE WOOD COUNTY OIL FIELD.

By an unfortunate oversight, the section pertaining to the Wood county oil field which should have found place on page 226 *et. seq.*, was overlooked until after the succeeding chapter had been begun. The section is accordingly raised to the rank of a chapter, but the matter is to be considered as strictly supplemental to Chapter III. All the facts pertaining to the field at large and the character of the oil produced by it which are given in the last named chapter (pages 194 to 211), are to be kept in mind in reading the account which here finds place.

The Wood county oil field is the heart of the production of Trenton limestone oil. The total amount of this oil brought to the surface in the northwestern Ohio fields during October, 1890, has exceeded 50,000 barrels per day. Some estimates place the amount as high as 60,000 barrels. Of this oil, Wood county has produced more than half. Its production is held by some to have exceeded 35,000 barrels during October. The amount of drilling induced by the advance in the price of oil from 15 to 37½ cents, described on page 207, has culminated during the months of September and October in the following remarkable record, taken from the columns of the Toledo Commercial of November 1:

Wood County Oil Wells.

	Completed Wells.	Production.	Dry.	Wells Drilling.	Rigs Building.
September	129	8,208 bbls.	9	116	127
October	147	11,165 "	7	114	125

During the same time, the remaining fields of Trenton limestone oil made the following record:

	Completed Wells.	Production.	Dry.	Wells Drilling.	Rigs Building.
September	178	8,101 bbls.	24	122	83
October	172	6,261 "	25	180	69

THE WOOD COUNTY OIL FIELD.   307

This is the highest mark yet reached in Trenton limestone production. The price of the oil has receded to 30 cents within the past few weeks, and this fact will doubtless check the drill from this time forward to some extent.

Centers of Production

The chief oil production of Wood county is derived from the following townships, viz: Henry, Bloom, Liberty, Portage and Montgomery. Plain has recently been added to the list. Perry adds a little to the general stock, and Freedom and Middleton also belong within the limits of the present production. Henry, Liberty, Portage and Montgomery are the most important townships in this connection, but Bloom township is rapidly rising in value as oil territory.

Structure of the Oil Fields.

The most productive oil district of the county, and of the State as well, is that known as the Wood County Oil Pool. It occupies the eastern portions of Henry and Liberty and makes some small excursions into Portage and Bloom. It is represented under the name given above on the map that accompanies this report. The boundary of production as laid down on the map of 1888 has been changed in a few particulars and notably by an extension to the westward in the vicinity of North Baltimore. It is also being extended to the northward into Plain township. Since the map was engraved, section 34 in the last named township has been added to the productive district on the strength of the records of two wells which are reported as good for 25 and 60 barrels, respectively.

A new pool of great promise is now coming to light to the eastward of the main pool, encroaching to some extent on what was considered, and with the best of reason a year or two ago, as dry gas territory. The new pool as its boundaries now appear takes its rise in section 6, Bloom township, and extends from there due north through sections 31, 20, 19, 18 and 7 of Portage township. The productive belt appears to be less than a mile in width and about six miles long in a north and south line. The characteristic of the southern portion of the new pool is the presence of dry gas in large amount when the rock is first reached. The wells are large gas wells when struck, but in a few days they are converted into strong oil wells, yielding 100 to 600 barrels per day.

The north and south trend of all the prominent structural features of this portion of the county has been insisted upon in all the geological reports that have been published since the discovery of gas and oil in the county. This feature is now recognized by the intelligent oil-producers of the field as a settled fact and account is taken of it in all new development. No one can find rational grounds on which to maintain the existence of a northeast line of structure in the Wood county oil field. A slight deflection of the axis to the westward shows in the two main pools already named.

In Montgomery township, the lines enclosing the chief production have not been made equally apparent, but there is a strong probability that the axis of the new field will be found as in the other cases, to bear to the northward.

As so often shown in previous reports upon these new fields the structure of each productive tract is most closely related to its behavior. Whether a well shall yield oil or gas is wholly a matter of the level at which the limestone is found in it by the drill. Each subdivision of the fields had originally its own dead line, as the level at which the salt water is found can be styled. The withdrawal of the gas on the large scale has allowed the oil and the water that occupied the porous rock at lower geographical levels to ascend to the levels which the gas at first held. This movement has gone forward on a large scale and the oil field is constantly extending itself inland with reference to the dry gas rock. The drillers are recognizing this movement and are obtaining large and valuable wells in what was unmistakably gas land in the beginning of the development. It goes without saying that the gas fields are correspondingly reduced in area and force.

The driller has found his interest in getting the entire oil production of the rock, which is insured by his going down to the salt water. The best practice now in the Wood county wells is to drill until salt water is at least touched. There are wells that are pumping five to ten barrels of water to one of oil, but when the latter rises to fifty barrels or more, even this large amount of dead work can be undertaken. The separation of the water from the oil becomes, however, an added burden to the producer. The use of the torpedo increases the salt water, but it is the universal practice to "shoot" the smaller wells, despite the increase of water. The production of the oil is often multiplied ten fold by the explosion.

SUBDIVISIONS OF THE FIELD.

The North Baltimore Field.

In Henry township, oil in large quantities is found in the eighteen easternmost sections, with the exception of sections 25 and 36, and in addition in sections 21, 28 and 33. Comparatively little of section 15 is counted good territory, in the light of what is at present known, but the remaining sections are counted first-class oil lands, without qualification.

THE WOOD COUNTY OIL FIELD. 309

The development that was in such active progress in 1888 has gone forward with but slight check since that date and during the last summer, at a greatly accelerated rate. The driller could thrive in Henry township with oil at 15 cents per barrel, provided that his product could be marketed as soon as it reached the surface, but when oil was advanced to 37½ cents, with a brisk demand for all that was produced, it was only the fact that the best lands were already held by interests that preferred to keep the oil tanked in the ground rather than to see it brought to the surface, that prevented even the present great production from being multiplied several fold. The Ohio Oil Company which owns the bulk of the producing territory has drilled to guard its lines and leases principally, and not with a desire to increase the production of oil.

The only unexpected additions to the territory are found in sections 26, 27, 28, 33, 34 and 35. A well drilled early in 1889 in the village corporation of North Baltimore began the excitement by starting out with a production of not less than 400 barrels per day. Here was a field in which the local talent of the country could disport itself. Village lots were easy to secure and in the course of a few months more than fifty derricks were in sight within the corporate limits. Drilling was at last forbidden by the common council. Few, if any, of this group of wells have paid for themselves, but the movement thus originated led directly to the discovery of one of the most prolific districts in the township that, namely, of sections 27 and 28.

The salt water boundary passes through section 28, but its eastern half has given rise to a noble cluster of wells. The oil rock lies at nearly 1,200 feet below the surface or about 450 feet below tide. The oil itself is found at a depth of not more than thirty feet in the limestone or at about 480 feet below tide. The wells require a little more than 400 feet of casing. An interesting example illustrating the structure and condition of the oil rock was brought to light in the drilling of the two wells, viz: the Chase well, No. 1, drilled by C. S. Wade and a well located on a small lot adjoining the Chase farm line. The stake for the latter well was driven fifty feet from the boundary of the Wade tract. This was counted rather close for good neighborhood and a new location was forthwith made, 100 feet within the farm boundary, leaving 150 feet between the wells. A race ensued with the oil rock as the goal. The second well won the race and started out at a 2,000 barrel rate. For nineteen consecutive days it averaged 1,400 barrels. But the time of the Wade well was to come. It found a great flow at twenty-nine feet in the Trenton, and the production of the other well was forthwith entirely arrested. But this did not last long; the second well regained its production and the flow of the Wade well ceased altogether. The latter was then drilled seven feet deeper and shot heavily. It started with great vigor, the second well becoming for a short time quiescent. Two more alternations of fortune followed, the one well suspending its functions while the other was in operation, until at last No. 1 settled down to 400 barrels daily while No. 2 produced about 300 barrels daily.

The great wells of 1888 are now being pumped in almost all cases and their production has fallen off to little if any more than 25 per cent. of their initial production. The largest production known in the field is that of a well drilled by the Palmer Oil Company in section 31, Portage township. It has already put into the line 250,000 barrels of oil and is still flowing regularly at the rate of 150 barrels per day.

The conditions under which the oil is found in Henry township are seen in the following well records that fully represent the field, except in production. In this respect the record is more favorable than the average.

In sections 2 and 3, on the Lawrence Cable farm, the records of wells 1 and 2 are as follows:

	No. 1.	No. 2.
Casing set at	368	381
Top of Trenton	1167	1169
Oil at	1190	1190–1195
Finished at	1195	1211
Production first day	400 bbls.	150 bbls.

In section 10, on the Jacob Neier farm, the records of wells Nos. 1, 2 and 3 are as follows:

	No. 1.	No. 2.	No. 3.
Soil and clay	5	8	
Casing set at	376	366	368
Trenton struck at	1167	1163	1164
Gas found at	1200	1190	1187
Oil " "	1207	1200	1204
Finished at	1207	1203	1219
Production first day	125 bbls.	700 bbls.	200 bbls.

In section 11, on William Hamman's farm, the record of wells 1, 2, 3 and 4 are given below:

THE WOOD COUNTY OIL FIELD.

	No. 1.	No. 2.	No. 3.	No. 4.
Casing set at............................	380	365	375	376
Trenton struck at.....................	1156	1150	1170	1168
Gas struck at...........................			1200	{1200 to
Oil " "		1185	1207	{1207
Finished at..............................	1196	1210	1207	1218

On section 13, the famous Slaughterbeck wells afford the following partial records:
Trenton struck at 1142, 1145, 1148, 1144, 1140, 1140, 1141, 1140.

The marvelous steadiness of the Trenton limestone in this field is brought into clear light by these records. It proves to be a terrace more nearly level than any sheet of rock that we can find at the surface, the drift covering of this region being excepted. The surface of this district is exceedingly flat and monotonous.

The records of wells from the other townships of the field agree in all important respects with those already given. A few will be added at this point.

In section 25, Liberty, on the J. M. Weiland farm, wells Nos. 1, 2, 3 and 4 furnish the following records:

	No. 1.	No. 2.	No. 3.	No.
Casing set at............................	365	365	360	350
Trenton struck at.....................	1160	1162	1153	1145
Oil " "	1180	1201	1183	1160–70
Finished at..............................	1198	1303	1188	1179
Production first day...................	75 bbls. (After torpedo.)	700 bbls. (Salt water with oil.)	800 bbls.	800 bbls.

In section 18, Bloom, on the James Madden farm, the following records are found:

	No. 1.	No. 2.	No. 3.	No. 4.
Casing set at............................	347	350	350	350
Trenton struck at.....................	1146	1147	1143	1135
Oil " "	1175	1167	1168	
Finished at..............................	1197	1201	1198	1201

On the western edge of the field the Trenton is found 1,200 feet and more below the surface. Whenever it is struck at 1,225 feet or lower, the territory is condemned. There is not a single important exception known in this field to the deduction of 1886 that salt water reigns supreme in the Trenton limestone when its surface is 500 feet or more below tide.

The Freeport Oil Field.

A very important addition to the oil production of the county has been made in Montgomery township during the last year. During the present season, indeed, this district has been one of the main centers of interest and speculative excitement of the county. In the discovery of the field, the Bradner Oil Company, under the leadership of E. A. Edwards, appears to have taken the lead. Several small wells were drilled at Bradner by this interest at an early period in the development of Trenton limestone oil. To most who knew the record, they seemed to give but little promise, but Mr. Edwards and the company construed the facts otherwise and extended their leases to the westward without any special theory as to the location of an oil belt. A well drilled late in 1889 in section 3, Montgomery township, on the Fralick farm, may be counted as fixing the initial date of what is now known as the Freeport field. This well yielded at least fifty barrels of oil per day. The Bradner Company's leases had been made in many cases on a cash royalty of four cents per barrel, but the drilling of this successful well brought an army of oil-producers into the field and prices were forthwith run up to $20 and $25 per acre, bonus, with royalty of one-fifth, one-sixth, one eighth, etc.

Up to May 1, 1890, twelve more wells had been drilled in sections 2, 3, 4, 9, 10, 11 and 15, all of which proved productive and valuable. The best of them showed a daily production of 150 barrels for the first day, but such wells soon fell to sixty and seventy barrels which they maintained with fair steadiness. All the wells are shot with eighty quarts and the pump is applied to all from the beginning. Most of them are considerably improved by the effects of the torpedo.

The Trenton limestone is struck at a depth of 1,185 to 1,200 feet, the elevation of the surface being about 700 feet above tide. The oil is found at 15 to 20 or even 30 feet in the Trenton limestone, or at a depth of 500 feet and over below sea level, the dead-line of this division being lower by 50 to 75 feet than that of the western section already described. Comparatively little gas is found in the limestone and the salt water column has not been reported as especially aggressive thus far.

During the last few months while the price of oil was held at the figures which were reached in the advance of the early part of the year

THE WOOD COUNTY OIL FIELD 313

the drillers had proved their way to the village of Freeport or Prairie Depot. The usual result that follows the inclusion within an oil field of a village with its numerous subdivisions of land has followed here. The corporate limits bristle with derricks most of which may be regarded as monuments of the greed on the one side and the spite on the other that have located them within 50 or 100 feet of each other. These derricks do not stand for either fair play or good sense. Few and probably none of these village wells can repay the expenditures that have been made upon them.

The importance of the Freeport field can be seen in this fact, that of the 147 new wells completed in October in Wood county, almost exactly one-half (72) are to be credited to Montgomery township. Of the new oil production of the county, of 11,000 barrels for October, nearly 4,000 barrels are assigned to this township. Its inferiority to the North Baltimore field is also shown in these same figures. The largest we ls are reported with a production of 200 barrels, and 20 out of the 72 new wells are reported as having a production of 100 barrels or more.

The oil of the Freeport field is of the best grade that is yielded by the Trenton limestone, its gravity being 42° B. and its sulphurous compounds being less stubborn or at least less offensive than those that are found in the oil of the older sections of the field, as Findlay and Lima. The boundaries of the productive district are not yet made apparent, but a salt water trough, with but little doubt, marks its northwestern limit.

The village of Rising Sun, included within Montgomery township, has bonded itself during the year to the extent of $6,000, the money raised by the sale of the bonds to be spent in prospecting for oil or gas. The Paragon company drilled a well for the corporation on a forty-five acre tract leased by the latter. The Trenton was found hard, dry and totally unproductive at a depth of 1,218 feet. Drilling was continued for at least 100 feet below its upper beds without any valuable result.

The entire summary of the results of drilling to the Trenton limestone in northern Ohio in October will be given at this point. Extracts from it have been used on a preceding page. The list was prepared and published by the Toledo Commercial of November 1. It has the marks and it has the reputation of being a reliable account of the great work of developing the new oil horizon that is now in progress.

Summary of Completed Wells.

	September.			October.		
	Completed.	Production. (bbls.)	Dry.	Completed.	Production.	Dry.
Wood	129	8,208	9	147	11,165	7
Hancock	75	4,320	6	66	2,255	11
Allen	25	903	3	19	583	...
Auglaize	50	2,123	7	48	2,385	5
Sandusky	23	660	6	29	993	3
Miscellaneous	5	95	2	10	45	6
Totals	307	16,309	33	319	17,426	32

Increase of finished wells .... 12.
Increase of new production .... 1,117.
Average of September wells... 53¼.
Average of October wells.. 54¾.

Wells Drilling.

	September.			October.		
	Drilling.	Rig.	Total.	Drilling.	Rig.	Total.
Wood	116	127	243	114	125	239
Hancock	58	33	91	89	16	105
Allen	13	....	13	15	6	21
Auglaize	24	12	36	47	16	63
Sandusky	18	28	46	22	27	49
Miscellaneous	9	10	19	7	4	11
Totals	238	210	448	294	194	488

Increase drilling wells 56
Decrease rigs 16

Total increase.. 40

The Decline in Price of Ohio Oil.

During the last month the price of Trenton limestone oil has been reduced by the Buckeye Pipe Line Company, by three successive cuts, from 37½ cents to 30 cents per barrel, at which point it rests at this writing. A good deal of uneasiness is felt among the land owners and the independent producers as to the purposes of the great corporation in making the reductions named above. If the Buckeye Pipe Line Company decides to go further in this direction, there is none to stay its hand or say to it, *what doest thou?* To this complexion, the great oil field of Ohio has come already. As has been previously remarked, the petroleum markets of the country are in no sense free markets in which intrinsic values rule. The price of Ohio oil for example is absolutely controlled by one gigantic corporation.

While deprecating this result, it is still hard to see what useful purpose is secured by bringing to the surface 50,000 barrels of oil every day, to be exposed to loss by evaporation and leakage and to danger by fire, when not more than half the whole amount is taken up by the markets of the country. An unlimited demand for fuel oil could be speedily established which would leave no surplus from the present or even a far larger production, provided the producer could guarantee rates for a reasonable term in advance, but this is precisely what he can not do. It is not an unmitigated disadvantage that he can not, for it would inflict a serious loss upon the country at large to have this great body of oil that can maintain for many years to come the high standard of illuminating oils which our people have been trained to demand, turned over to manufacturers and made to replace the usual grades of cheap bituminous coals in the commonest and rudest of their applications.

INDEX.

A

	PAGE
Ada gas field	184
Adams county fault	53
Akron arch	52
Allen county oil wells	215
Lima oil field	216
Spencerville field	217
Allen township wells	123
characteristics of field	126
decline of pressure	128
list of wells	124
number of wells	123
rock pressure and behavior	127
Anderson's statement of Mendeljeff's theory	62
Anticline	51, 53
Asphalt—	
in Dayton limestone	80
of Central America	81
of Trinidad	80
use among the ancients	57
Auglaize county—	
gas wells of	156
character	160
Lima Natural Gas Company	157
New Bremen pipe line	161
gas rates	161
ıy's village corporation	157
Wapakoneta pipe line	160
wells	158
oil wells of	212
Buckland field	213
Cridersville field	215
St. Mary's field	213

B

Baku oil field	71
Barnesville gas field	254
Barren Coal Measures, Lower	44
oil rocks of	44
Bedford shale	34
character	34
fossils	35

	PAGE
Berea grit	35
a source of oil and gas	249
character	36
importance	35
origin of name	36
thickness and area	35
Berea shale	37
boundaries	37
character	37
source of oil	37
Berthelot's theory of origin gas and oil	61
"Big Indian" sand rock	252
Bitumens—	
chemical composition	56
distribution	58
early history	57
later history	59
Blue Lick water	13
Bowlders	9
Bowling Green Natural Gas Co	137
lands and rock pressure	153
Bradner Refinery	204
Bradford oil sand	194
Brewer Pottery Company	188
Briggs Iron Works	121
consumption of gas	121
Buena Vista stone	38

C

Cadiz anticline	50
Cadiz oil field	250
character	251
records of wells	253
Calciferous period	13
Cambridge arch	51
Cambridge gas field	255
Carboniferous system of Ohio, relation to gas and oil	43
Carey gas field	174
Carey oil field	221
Cass township gas field	131
rock pressure	131
Cass township oil field	220

INDEX.

	PAGE
Celina pipe line	162
location of wells	163
purchase of	164
Cincinnati anticline or axis	30, 46
direction	47
extent	47-49
Cincinnati group	15
thickness	15
Clay burning	275
Findlay and North Baltimore	275
price of gas in brick making	276
Cleveland shale	29
fossils	32
thickness	30
Cliff limestone	27
Clinton limestone as source of oil and gas	227
previous mention	227
date of tests	229
character	17, 18
composition	18, 229
deep wells, to reach Clinton	243
Amanda	243
Coshocton	245
Dresden	246
Mansfield	245
Mt. Vernon	244
Plain City	246
Somerset	246
discovery and use of gas	231
gas fields of	234
Lancaster	234
Newark	237
Thurston	240
gas rock of	230
geological section of wells	232
geological structure of field	232
iron ore	17
outcrop	18
source of gas	17, 80
source of oil	17
summary	242
Coal Measures, Lower	44
Columbus Gas Company	231
Conglomerate group—	
order	44
thickness	44
Corniferous limestone	24-26
bitumens	79
Cow run anticline	51
Cuyahoga shale	37-39
characteristics of	38
fossils	39

D

	PAGE
Drake well	9
Dunkirk field	186

E

Eagle refinery	203
Everett Glass Works	237

F

Faults in Ohio	54
Findlay break	109
continuation of	23
Findlay gas field. (See also under Trenton limestone)—	
depth of dead line	107
discovery	105
failure of	115
gas production	112
iron works of	120
rates	121
rock pressure	116, 117
summary of facts	122
total gas consumption	123
utilization of gas	119
works using gas	121
Findlay oil field	218
Findlay monocline	48, 54, 67
structure of	91
Forest gas field	183
Fostoria gas field	138, 190
amount of gas used	191
wells	190, 191
Fredericktown axis	50
Freeport oil field	312

G

Gas fields—	
Barnesville	254
Cambridge	255
Findlay	105
Gibsonburg	108
Indiana	109
Lancaster	234
Marysville	273
Mercer county	161
Stuartsville	128
Thurston	231
Waterville	155
Wood county	133
Gas measurement (chapter)	281
Pitot tube gauge	281
examples	288
tables	292, 293
tables illustrating use	286, 287

Gasts measuremen —
Principle of flow in pipes 297
formula 298
rule for determination... 299
table for pipe line flow.. 300,
[301
Gas, natural and oil (see also petroleum)—
Chemical theories 61
Anderson's statement......... 62
Berthelot 61
Mendeljeff............. 61
Geological theories.................... 71
duration of supply........... 84
Hunt's Dr. T. S. theory 77
Newberry's theory 72
Peckham's theory............. 75
quantity of gas supply...... 86
summary of..................... 85
importance 60
modes of accumulation.............. 87
cover.. 88
reservoir 87
porous rock..................... 88
structure 89
anticlinal theory.............. 90
illustrated in Ohio 91
relation to relief............... 92
origin...................................... 60
rock pressure 92
calculated and observed pressure 98, 102
back pressure...................... 104
causes of 94
discussion of theories 95
law of 102
inference from law........... 103
records of 100, 102
White, I. C., theory 96
Gas rates—schedule of—
Cambridge............................... 256
Carey 176
Columbus 242
Findlay 121
Gibsonburg 174
Greenville 171
Lancaster................................ 237
Lima 198
Newark 239
Oak Harbor field.................... 173
Wapakoneta............................ 161
Toledo 144
Urbana 168

Gas utilization of, in Ohio (chapter).. 259
conclusion 280
summary 278
uses—
domestic fuel 259
meters...................................... 263
mixers 262
prices 262
for manufacturers 264
amount consumed 264
equivalent of, in coal........... 265
fuel proper 267
iron and clay working 273
clay working 275
iron mills 274
glass manufacture................ 267
amount consumed per day..269-271
consumption total...... 212
number of glass pots............ 272
lime burning 276
Gauge pressures........ 298
Geological scale of Ohio—
divisions 10–11
thickness 11
Geological structure of Ohio—
character of the ancient seas 45
character of the surface............... 46
eastern Ohio........................49–51
dip 49
fundamental facts 9
marine formations......... 10
northeastern Ohio 51
dip 52
depth of Berea.................... 52
order of deposits 10
stratified deposits...... 9
Geological Survey, First—
date............................ 1
officers 2
reports 2
Geological Survey, Second—
character of reports 3
date.. 3
distribution of reports..............4, 5
officers 3
publications 3
Geological Survey, Third—
advantages of plan................ 6
date................ 5
law 6
objects 7
organization............................... 5
relation to agriculture................. 7
relation to water supply............. 7

INDEX.

Geyser Oil Company..................217, 218
Gibsonburg Gas Company.................. 174
Gibsonburg oil field.......................... 223
Glacial drift.................................. 45
Glass manufacture—
   use of gas in........................267-273
   locations of furnaces,119,144,153,163,
                        [188, 191
   number of pots........................ 272
Greenville pipe line........................ 170
   rates.................................. 171
   rock pressure.......................... 171
   wells.................................. 171
Guelph limestone 19
   character.............................. 19
   thickness.............................. 19
Gypsum beds................................ 21

H

Hamilton shale.............................. 26
   character..........................26, 27
   locality................................ 26
Hardin county gas wells.................... 182
   Ada.................................... 184
      wells of..........................184, 185
      rock pressure........................ 185
   Dunkirk 186
   Forest 183
   Kenton............................182, 183
Hancock county—
   gas production........................ 112
      Allen township 123
      Cass township.................... 131
      Findlay......................105-123
      Marion........................... 131
      Washington 132
   oil wells of—
      Findlay field...................... 218
      Marion and Cass townships... 220
      Stuartsville 219
Helderberg, Lower, limestone............. 21
   bitumens of........................... 79
   carbonaceous matter of............... 22
   description 22
   revealed by drill...................... 23
   thickness.............................. 22
Helderberg, Upper, limestone.........24 - 26
   exposure at Columbus................. 26
   composition........................... 25
   divisions 25
   thickness.............................. 25
Herrick, Prof. C. L.........34, 35, 39, 40, 42

Hillsboro sandstone........................ 20
   characteristics 20
   thickness.............................. 20
Höfer, Hans, Prof.......................... 71
Hudson River group........................ 15
   area................................... 16
   character of........................... 15
   discussion as to name.................. 15
   shales................................. 16
Hunt's theory of origin gas and oil..... 76
   advantages of.......................... 83
   bituminous decomposition............. 77
   essential points....................... 82
   examination of........................ 78
   oil and gas in limestones............. 106
Huron shale................................ 28
Hydraulic Press Brick Works 122

I

Iron mills using gas....................... 274
   Findlay 274
   Toledo 144

J

Johnston, J. O., discovery Thurston
   field 241

K

Kenton Gas Company....................... 183

L

Lancaster gas field..............231, 232, 234
   date of drilling....................... 234
   rates for fuel......................... 237
   rock pressure 237
   utilization............................ 236
   wells of............................... 235
Leidy, Joseph, Prof 68
Lesley, J. P., Prof., theory of rock
   pressure 95
Lima gas field............................. 105
   depth of dead line.................... 107
   structure.............................. 111
Lima Natural Gas Company............... 157
   wells of 158
Lima oil field............................. 216
   amount 198
   character of........................... 196
   Chicago pipe line..................... 199
   date of drilling...................... 195
   prices of oil 198, 314
   production 195
   purchase by Standard Oil Co....... 200
   use of oil as fuel..................... 199
   wells................................. 196

INDEX.

	PAGE
Lime burning with gas	276
Limestone, Subcarboniferous identified by Andrews	43
characteristics	43
localities	43
Lindsey gas field	174
Locke, John, Dr., mention of oil in Clinton	227
Logan group	39–42
best development	40
characteristics	40
conglomerate	39
connection with gas and oil	42
separation by Prof. Andrews	40
thickness	40–42

M

Macksburgh anticline	51
associated with gas	51
associated with oil	197
analysis of crude oil	197
Manitoulin island	106
Marion township	131
wells of	132
Medina shale	16
color	17
thickness	16
Mendeljeff's theory of origin gas and oil	61
Anderson's statement of	62
character of	70
conflict with geology	69
examination of	67
process of formation	65
relation of oil fields to mountains	63
Mercer county gas wells	161
Celina pipe line	162
purchase of	164
Greenville pipe line	170
Mercer pipe line	164
wells of	165
pressure	162
Urbana pipe line	166
Van Wert pipe line	166
Mercer county oil wells	212
reservoir oil field	212
Mercer pipe line	164
wells of	165
Meters for natural gas	263–278
Monclova sandstone	24

N

Newark gas field	231, 237
rates	239

	PAGE
Newark rock pressure	238
wells	238
Newberry, J. S., Prof., theory of origin gas and oil	72
Niagara group	18–21
area	18
bitumens of	79
character of limestone	19
shale	19
thickness	18
North Baltimore gas field	140
North Baltimore oil field	305
Northeast lines	110, 111, 307
Northwestern Ohio Natural Gas Co.	141
towns supplied	142

O

Oak Harbor Natural Gas Company	172
rates	173
Ohio Oil Company, 219, 221, 222, 224,	225
Ohio Valley oil field	257
Oil (see petroleum).	
Oil Creek, Pennsylvania	58
Drake well	59
first important well	59
Oil fields—	
Buckland	213
Cadiz	250
Cridersville	215
Findlay	218
Freeport	312
Gibsonburg and Helena	223
Lima	216
Macksburg	250
Ohio Valley	257
Reservoir, Mercer county	212
Spencerville	217
St. Mary's	213
Stuartsville	219
Wood county	306
Oil production of Trenton limestone. (See Trenton limestone).	
Oil sand	208
of Pennsylvania	30
Oil wells, number in Trenton limestone	211
acreage demanded	210
Olentangy shale	26
Olive shales	41
Ottawa county—	
gas wells	172
Oak Harbor field	172
rates	173
oil field	192, 913

INDEX.

P

	PAGE
Paragon refinery	201
capacity of	202
Peckham's theory—	
origin of gas and oil	75
examination of	76
Peerless refinery	204
Petroleum and natural gas—	
date of great development	59
early history of	57, 109
later history	59
origin	60
origin and accumulation (chapter)	55
vegetable origin	71
Pipe lines—	
Buckeye	195, 199
Carey	168
Celina	162
Columbus	241
Greenville	170
Mercer	164
New Bremen	161
Northwestern Ohio	141
Toledo	144
Urbana	166
Van Wert	166
Wapakoneta	160
rates at Toledo	145
Pipe lines, measurements of	297
examples	304, 305
formula for	298
rule for determination	299
table for pipe flow	300, 301
Pitot tube gauge	281
application to gas wells	283
examples	288
service capacity of gas wells	285
velocity of flow	284
volume of flow at well mouth	283
application to pipe lines	288
absolute measurements	294
tables	294, 295
correction for velocity curve	295
examples	296
measurement of pipe lines	289
precaution to be observed	290
tables for	292, 293
forms of	282
stream with free exit	282
stream enclosed	282
references	281
Point Pleasant quarries	12
analysis of limestone	12
Prairie Depot oil field	314

	PAGE
Putnam county gas wells	192
Ottawa	192
wells of	193

R

Refineries—	
Bradner	204
Eagle	203
Paragon	201
Peerless	204
Solar	203
Refining of Trenton limestone oil	201
Robinson, S. W., Prof.—	
invention pipe line gauge	265
on measurement of gas	281–305
Rock pressure of gas (see gas, natural).	

S

Salina group	20
gypsum beds	21
in New York series	21
Salt water—	
cause of ascent	97
dead line to oil and gas	107
height of column	97
pressure of, in oil field	209
quantity	96
specific gravity	100
Sandusky county—	
gas wells	173
Gibsonburgh	173
Lindsey	174
supply of gas	174
use in lime kilns	173
oil wells	223
Gibsonb'rgh and Helena fields	223
number of wells	225
Seneca county—	
gas wells	186
Fostoria	190
Tiffin	186
pipe line	188
rock pressure	189
utilization of	188, 189
wells	189, 190
oil wells	222
Shale, Ohio, or black—	
character of	27
fossils of	31–33
Newberry's classification	28
oil and gas of	78, 248
boundary of	32
Solar refinery	203, 216

21* G.

INDEX.

Standard Oil Company.................. 195
   advances in price of oil......... 206
   reductions in price................. 310
   in Cadiz oil field...................... 253
   price of oil established by...195–310
   Solar refinery, of..................... 203
St. Mary's village corporation—
   gas line................................... 157
Structure, relation to gas and oil (see natural gas).
Stuartsville gas field................... 128
Stuartsville oil field.................... 219
Sylvania sandstone....................... 23
   locality............................23, 25
   thickness................................ 24

T

Tables—
   cubic feet gas discharged.......286–287
   for absolute measurement........... 294
   for pipe line flow...............300, 301
   for Pitot tube gauge............292, 293
   test for Pitot tube gauge.......294, 295
Thurston gas field...................231, 240
   Columbus pipe line.................. 241
   discovery of gas...................... 241
   pressure................................ 242
   rates at Columbus................... 242
Tiffin Natural Gas Company.......... 187
   wells of..........................189, 190
Tiffin wells............................... 138
Toledo pipe line......................... 144
   legal proceedings involved....149, 150
   rates.............................145, 147
   report of trustees..................... 149
Trenton Falls............................. 12
   character of limestone............... 107
Trenton limestone—
   composition........................13, 106
   cover of................................ 14
   dip of................................... 12
   extent of............................... 11
   gas production (1888–1890)......... 112
      Auglaize county................. 156
      Hancock county................. 112
         Allen township.............. 123
         Cass township............... 131
      Findlay (see Findlay field.)
         change of policy............ 120
         discovery of gas........105, 112
         depth of dead line.......... 107
         failure of gas................. 113
         gas production.............. 112
         growth of city............... 113

Trenton Limestone—
   utilization of gas.................... 119
   waste of gas.....................113, 120
   Marion township..................... 131
   Washington township............... 132
   Hardin county........................ 182
   Mercer county....................... 161
   Ottawa county....................... 172
   Putnam county...................... 192
   Sandusky county..................... 173
   Seneca county........................ 186
   Wood county......................... 133
      Bloom township................ 133
      Henry township................ 140
      Perry township................ 138
   Wyandot county..................... 174
   guides in drilling.................... 111
   oil production of (1888–1890)...... 194
      chemical analysis.............. 197
      conclusions................198, 199
      development of the fields..... 211
      Allen county................... 215
      Auglaize county................ 212
      Hancock county................ 218
      Mercer county................. 212
      Sandusky county............... 223
      Wood county................... 306
      Wyandot county................ 220
   Geological factors................... 208
      acreage of oil wells............ 210
      capacity of single wells........ 210
      life of oil wells................. 211
      number of wells................ 211
      oil sand......................... 208
      presence of salt water......... 209
      prices of oil.................... 196
         [199, 206, 314
      production of oil to acre....... 210
      used as fuel..................... 206
   qualities and uses of oil............ 196
      chemical analysis.............. 197
      conclusions...............198, 199
   refineries—
      Bradner......................... 204
      Eagle............................ 203
      Paragon......................... 201
      Peerless......................... 204
      Solar............................ 203
   refining of Trenton oil.............. 201
   origin of name....................... 12
   place in scale........................ 13
   as reservoir........................... 106
   source of gas and oil............80, 105
   thickness.............................. 14
   thickness in Kentucky................

INDEX. 323

	PAGE
Trenton Limestone—	
topography	108
underground distribution	47
Tymochtee slate	23

U

Utica shale	14
Upper Sandusky field	176
production	180
records	178, 181
wells	177
Urbana pipe line	166
rates	168

V

Van Vleck, George...H	202
Van Wert pipe line	166

W

Wall, G. P., on Trinidad asphalt	80
Wapakoneta pipe line	160
gas rates of	161
Waterlime group	21–24
Waverly group	33, 42
boundaries	34
origin of name	33
Wells, deep—	
Amanda	243
Axe	158
Ballard	114
Bloomdale	136
Carey	175
Carnahan	127
Coshocton	245
Dewey	125
Dresden	246
Eaton	228
Findlay	125
Flushing	253
Gibson	221
Heck	118
Holliday	252
Hume	105
Hutson	125
Jones	114
Kagy	123
Karg	105, 114

	PAGE
Wells, deep—	
Lancaster	235
Loomis	187
Mansfield	245
McCarty	173
Melott	125
Mt. Vernon	244
Newark	238
Pioneer	116
Plain City	246
Roth well	131, 175
Somerset	246
Swable	221
Thorntree	131
Tippecanoe	117
Ware	126
Well records—	
Amanda	243
Coshocton	245
Flushing	254
Lancaster	232
Mansfield	245
Mt. Vernon	244
Plain City	246
Somerset	246
White, I. C., Prof.—	
anticlinal theory of	90
on Berea grit as source of oil and gas	249
theory of rock pressure	96
Winchell, N H.	26
Wood county gas wells	133
Bloom township	133–137
Center and Plain townships	152
Henry township	140, 141
Perry township	138, 139
Portage and Liberty	151
Remaining townships	155
Waterville gas field	155, 156
Wood county oil wells	306
Wyandot county—	
gas wells	174
Carey field	174–176
Upper Sandusky	176–178
records of	178–181
oil wells	220